RESPONSIBLE PARENTHOOD

RESPONSIBLE
The Child's Psyche Through

GILBERT W. KLIMAN, M.D.

HOLT, RINEHART AND

PARENTHOOD
the Six-Year Pregnancy

and ALBERT ROSENFELD

College of the Ouachitas

WINSTON   NEW YORK

Published by Holt, Rinehart and Winston, 383 Madison Avenue, New York, New York 10017.

Published simultaneously in Canada by Holt, Rinehart and Winston of Canada, Limited.

Library of Congress Cataloging in Publication Data
Kliman, Gilbert W.
  Responsible parenthood.
  Bibliography: p.
  Includes index.
  1. Parenting. 2. Child development.
3. Socialization.   I. Rosenfeld, Albert, joint
author. II. Title.
HQ755.8.K57   649'.1   79-3437
ISBN 0-03-040951-9

First Edition

Designer: Nancy Dale Muldoon
Printed in the United States of America
10 9 8 7 6 5 4 3 2 1

Grateful acknowledgment is made to the following authors and publishers for permission to quote from their original publications:

F.C. Fraser, "Genetic Counseling," *Hospital Practice*, Vol. 6, No. 1, H.P. Publishing Co., Inc., New York, N.Y.
V.A. McKusick, R. Claiborne, eds., *Medical Genetics,* H.P. Publishing Co., Inc., New York, N.Y. 1973.
William Kessen, ed., *Childhood in China,* Yale University Press, New Haven, Ct., 1975.
Marshall H. Klaus and John H. Kennell, *Maternal-Infant Bonding,* C.V. Mosby Company, St. Louis, Mo., 1976.
Bruno Bettelheim, *The Uses of Enchantment: The Meaning and Importance of Fairy Tales*, Alfred A. Knopf, Inc., New York, N.Y. 1976.

Contents

Preface

THIS book—which will deal mainly with the first six years of life, especially as they shape the child's emotional future—has gone through a "six-year pregnancy" of its own. For at least that long we have been thinking and talking about it: reading, researching, observing, attending meetings and seminars, writing, arguing, rewriting—trying to sort out and express what it is that we might be able to tell people for sure about responsible parenthood in a chaotic and confusing time for our society. During this period of the book's gestation, we have been startled again and again by the remarkable, and remarkably rapid, changes that have taken place in our public context even as we labored to bring forth our progeny.

At the outset we were hearing expressions of overwhelming concern about overpopulation. Too many children were coming too fast into the world, a world beset by widespread pollution and diminishing resources. Yet a "pronatalist" attitude still predominated. Many people were procreating through inadvertence. Others were doing so with almost the same mindlessness simply because having babies was the thing to do. As a rule such parents never stopped to examine their qualifications to be parents, or their motivation for wanting children—or even whether they really wanted them. Every adult who had the opportunity to marry would of course get married. Every married couple would of course want to have children, unless there was some physiological reason why they could not. Motherhood was still the major career a normal woman was expected to follow.

To be sure, "antinatalist" forces such as the Zero Population Growth movement were already zealously at work, but we could not have believed how well, and how quickly, they would succeed. The Pill and the sexual revolution had long since arrived, but we could not have foreseen the speed and consequences of legalized abortion.

In record time, the birthrate in this country began plummeting. Fewer and fewer married women were getting pregnant, though more and more unmarried teenagers were doing so. It was no longer a rarity for couples to declare openly their decision to go childless, and young people in increasing numbers were questioning the necessity or wisdom of getting married at all. As the various women's movements gained ground, motherhood as a central career—the choice formerly most honored—was increasingly disdained.

Where we had originally been impelled to assure our readers that *not* having children was a perfectly acceptable and honorable alternative (even the preferred choice in some cases), this alternative soon became *so* accepted and so honored that we began to feel the urge to point up the joys and rewards of parenthood. Quite suddenly again, however, with the same bewildering unpredictability, we are being warned by a number of experts that a new baby boom is already upon us.

Obviously, we as a people cannot, either individually or collectively, allow ourselves to be stampeded into a radical revision of our parental philosophy with each changing fashion. Whatever the external social circumstances at any given time, we know that we have not been doing very well by our children, and that we can and therefore should do better. We know too that what is lacking is any deep sense of procreative responsibility, any urgent commitment to our children, not only as children, but as the emotionally mature adults we hope they will become.

It would be fatuous as well as fraudulent for us to pretend that we, or anyone, can write an explicit set of rules that determine parental qualification or disqualification. We have no idea what a perfect parent—or, for that matter, a perfect child—would be like. We do, however, know quite a bit about human *imperfections* and how they might be alleviated, circumvented, or prevented. And we know a good deal about parental liabilities. We know this partly through the study of other people's studies; but mostly we know it through long years of intimate daily observation of hundreds of troubled children and their families at the Center for Preventive Psychiatry in

White Plains, New York. There is no amount of parental or societal guidance we might offer that could guarantee an emotionally untroubled child as the outcome. We would feel much more confident in writing any number of prescriptions guaranteed to produce the opposite—emotionally disturbed children, destined to become ineffective and unhappy adults (though some might turn out to be high achievers).

Of what use is such negative knowledge? Well, if biomedical scientists can identify an infectious bacterium or virus, they can hope to develop an effective drug or vaccine against it—even if they can't give you an effective prescription for, or even a good definition of, health itself. If the mechanisms of a given metabolic disorder or a deteriorative process can be discovered, then work can begin toward a therapy or prevention. Similarly, when we understand the dynamics of childhood emotional troubles, and the circumstances that trigger them, we are well on our way to the possibility of therapy and prevention.

The authors started out with the relatively narrow intention of suggesting how some emotional troubles might be prevented or alleviated by more knowledgeable parenting. Such an intention, however, requires some manner of answer to the question: What are the qualifications for effective parenthood? And no sooner is the question asked and seriously pondered than one understands that, though parenthood is an individual responsibility, carried out for the most part in individual households, it does not operate in isolation. Its success depends more than we often recognize on the complicated psychosocial environment in which parents must function. Thus the book became emphatically addressed not only to parents and would-be parents, but also to nonparents. Those men and women who decide against personal parenthood still play parental or grandparental roles of a sort, usually inadvertently, in the lives of other people's children. Their behavior and attitude toward those children often have an impact—direct or indirect, profound or subtle—on the emotional welfare of those children; and the results have far-ranging effects on everyone, parent or not. It makes a real difference to you whether my child turns out to be, say, a dedicated teacher or a narcotics peddler. If my child is retarded or delinquent, you—without having any vote in the matter—help foot the bill or could be one of his or her victims. All children are everyone's children, or should be; and all adults, in addition to being the specific rearers of their own biological offspring (or those they choose to adopt), are in a real sense surrogate parents for all children.

As a matter of fact, we believe that human individuals, male and female alike, have been biologically programmed for parenthood (and we will develop this point). We suspect, moreover, that those who opt for nonparenthood do so at some emotional risk to themselves (Erik Erikson, for one, believes that we complete our own mature identities through raising our children)—unless they express their built-in nurturant tendencies through some other facet of their lives. And what better way than through a keen generalized interest in children at large? We need a massive new consciousness-raising on behalf of our children and their emotional future. We in America pride ourselves on being a child-centered and family-oriented society; why have we let nations like China and the Soviet Union put us to shame in this respect? We, as a social group, ought to be one big extended family. Ought to be? We already are. But we do need to acknowledge the fact, and turn ourselves into a *good* big extended family, a family whose adults will take joy in every child's triumphs and be distressed at every child's troubles.

The first men and women started out in caves, expending most of their energy on mere survival, understanding little or nothing about how babies were conceived and born, rearing their young largely through instincts and simple grunts of communication. Today, for the first time in human history, the majority of people in the industrialized Western world have reached a point where major energies no longer have to be devoted to mere survival, and where people not only understand the biology of procreation, but can control the number of children they have—and when. This double blessing now frees us to develop a new loving-caring, parent-child-community relationship so advanced in its nature as to constitute, when it is achieved, a marvelous leap in human evolution.

PART ONE

The Question of Parenthood

Do you think, mister, with all that settlement around you that you're freer than me to make your fate? Do you click your tongue at my story? Well, I wish I knew yours. Your father's doing is in you, like his father's was in him, and we can never start new, we take on all the burden. . . .

—E. L. Doctorow
WELCOME TO HARD TIMES

Give me other mothers and I will give you another world.

—Saint Augustine

1

par-ent \ 'par-ant \ n.:
a trustee of the future

It is only in the minds of adults that childhood is a paradise, a time of innocence and serene joy. The memory of a Golden Age is a delusion for, ironically, none of us remembers this time at all. At best we carry with us a few dusty memories, a handful of blurred and distorted pictures which often cannot even tell us why they should be remembered. This first period of childhood ... is submerged like a buried city, and when we come back to these times with our children we are strangers and we cannot easily find our way.

—Selma H. Fraiberg
THE MAGIC YEARS

Each individual human being on this planet is largely the creature of her earliest experiences.* Once we have attained adulthood, each of us likes to think of herself as the manipu-

---

*In this era of consciousness raising, almost everyone who writes about children apologizes for having to use the masculine term when referring to any child, whether female or male. The usual alternative has been an awkward "he or she" or even "he or she (as the case may be)." Lee Salk and Carl Rogers have tried the device of employing he/his and she/her in alternate chapters; others have used "he/she," "him/her," and "his/her"; or even combinations such as "s/he" or "him/er." But these devices seem unsatisfactory and a little confusing—and they can only be read, not said. Until someone invents an acceptably euphonious new word as a neuter-gendered substitute, most authors will accept being saddled with common English usage: the masculine term to denote either one or the other—or to represent both.

In the absence of an ideal solution, and as a corrective exercise to compensate for the general overuse of masculine terminology in our language, we will, for example, use "she" here in Part One to mean any child, male or female. In Part Two, however, through which we talk about the mother-infant dyad, we will retain the masculine designation in order to avoid the confusion that might arise from using the same pronoun for both mother and child. In Part Three, the genders of our pronouns will vary.

lator of her own fate, the molder of her own personality, the chooser of her own character traits and ethical standards. (An individual in disadvantaged or deprived circumstances may of course believe the opposite: that she has no control whatsoever over the conditions of her own life.) And it is true enough that a normal adult, given reasonable opportunity and ample motivation, can still hope to remake herself in a new image of her own devising, can still hope to arrive at the human values she prefers through a process of analysis and reason. But only up to a point.

Our capacity to govern our destinies is limited, to a much greater degree than we are ever conscious of, by patterns laid down long before we were in a position to be consulted. In fact, every individual's emotional future is profoundly influenced by events that take place even before birth.

What were your parents' attitudes toward having children? Did they really want you? Why? Did one parent wish for a boy and the other a girl? Were they disappointed? How healthy were they physically and how stable emotionally? How sound was your genetic inheritance, how ideal the environmental conditions in your mother's womb, how unsettling the obstetrical circumstances of your birth? On all these prenatal contingencies and a myriad more did the person that is you begin to be formed.

Your education began in earliest infancy—in the loving looks and touches that you got or failed to get, in the way you were held and fed and diapered, in the quantity and quality of the sensations that impinged upon your wide-open nervous system.

In your preschool years, the years you have the least recollection of, the years when you were most at the mercy of other people and circumstances utterly outside your control, in those years the limits of what you might become were irrevocably set down. You were, in a word, robbed of a portion of your birthright. But don't feel discriminated against: The same is true of every child on earth. There has yet to be a woman or a man in all of human history—queen or peasant, genius or moron, sophisticate or primitive—whose prenativity and upbringing allowed a full measure of freedom to develop into what the given individual might, at birth, have become.

If you were lucky in your parents (though luck in other areas of your life is also required), then you probably turned out all right. If you were unlucky, then however widely recognized you may be as a "success" in your chosen career, you may carry with you a burden of unresolved emotional troubles. If you do have such troubles, it is important that you recognize them in order to help your children be luckier with *their* parents.

No one ever asked your mother and father if they were qualified to be parents. Such a question would surely have been deemed an impertinence. If you already have children, chances are no one asked if *you* were qualified to be a parent.

Most of us who are already parents believe that we made a conscious, reasoned decision in the matter. That is probably an unwarranted conceit. We are largely the products of our genetics, our nurture, and our culture, and we often act under the influence of powerful forces we are only dimly aware of. The situation is almost universal, so there is no point or profit in wallowing in guilt over whatever mistakes we may have made. (We are aware that an ever-present danger in a book such as this is that guilt feelings will be raised to a high pitch in parents already overburdened with guilt. *Some* guilt in honest acknowledgment of one's shortcomings and mistakes, and a firm resolution to do better, is perhaps healthy and to be recommended. But in general the last thing we wish to do here is to rev up anyone's guilt-making machinery.) In most cases, we could not necessarily have known that our mistakes *were* mistakes. We simply did the best we could—for our time, for our culture.

The parents of each culture, in each period of history, usually do the best they can, by their lights. The specific patterns of child rearing vary considerably from time to time, and from place to place. Parents in Western societies today, for instance, consider that their babies have relative freedom of movement and receive plenty of attention. And they surely do, compared to the snugly swaddled infants of, say, Eastern Europe described by Ruth Benedict. On the other hand, our babies lead restricted and neglected lives compared to those of the "primitive" Yequana Indians of the Venezuelan jungle, which Jean Liedloff has written about so eloquently in *The Continuum Concept.* These infants spend the first year of their lives in constant contact with their mothers—or, occasionally, other adults.

They are carried along to work, taken on outings and expeditions, slept with, played with—nearly always in arms or in skin-to-skin touch—and they are soon free to crawl about virtually without supervision, and apparently in complete safety.

Children in diverse cultures come by their life training in various ways. In the traditional Chinese family, responsibility for the child's socialization is exclusively in the hands of mothers and grandmothers. Among the Ashanti of Ghana, children acquire equally little social indoctrination from their fathers, but for different reasons: the child lives in the mother's house—not with the father, however, but with the mother's brother, who is the dominant male in the household and thus the personal authority figure. In many cultures, parents believe that children have to be frightened into being obedient under threat of punishment by supernatural figures; this has been as true of Hopis in the New World (who have employed fearful oversized Katchina masks) as of Western societies of the Old World (who used God and the demons of Christendom). Yet we, today, in the West, deplore such practices as harmful. (Such phrases as "we in the West" must be used with caution. In the United States alone there exist, side by side and contemporaneously, any number of cultures and subcultures; not all are ethnic—some are self-selected communities that establish their own social systems, including family structures and child-rearing practices.)

The catalog of cultural differences compiled by anthropologists is almost too vast to deal with. In all this diversity, are there any universal patterns, principles, and practices? In the late 1940s, the distinguished anthropologist George P. Murdock made an exhaustive analysis of 250 societies. He found that there was always a nuclear family of some sort to hold parents and children together and that the family had four principal functions: sexual, economic, reproductive, and educational. But Murdock's universals have been challenged by later anthropologists; and Melford E. Spiro, after a careful study of Israeli kibbutzim, declared that the kibbutz family did not fit Murdock's definition of a family at all—unless one viewed the entire kibbutz as the child's extended family.

Not only do the details of child rearing vary with time, place, and culture. Even the prevailing views of what childhood is, what a family is, what the relationship of parent to offspring *ought* to be, are far from fixed. In *Centuries of Childhood*, the French cultural historian Philippe Ariès tells us that in the Middle Ages there was no real concept of childhood as we now think of it. A child was weaned late, sometimes not until the age of six or seven, and then simply became part of the adult world—working, coping, and surviving (with luck) as best she could. The years leading up to weaning were simply a growing-up-to-adulthood, and no one seemed to pay much attention to the details. Childhood education was unheard of. Artists depicted children simply as smaller adults, with adult features, adult dress, adult-proportioned bodies. Even infants, in medieval paintings, possessed the musculature of adults. Nor was there even an adequate language to describe childhood. For a long stretch in France, for instance, from the twelfth to the seventeenth or eighteenth centuries, there did gradually evolve a series of diminutives that referred to little children at younger and younger ages. But, according to Ariès, "there would still remain a gap where a word was needed to denote a child in its first months of life; this gap would not be filled until the nineteenth century, when the French would borrow from the English the word 'baby.'"

During these same centuries, childhood mortality was so high that no records were kept, and certainly no portraits were made, of children who died early. And parents, says Ariès, were loath to become too attached to beings who might not be around very long. For a stretch of time the Basques buried dead children without baptism with apparent casualness, somewhere on or near the family premises. "The child that had died too soon," Ariès surmises, "was buried almost anywhere, much as we today bury a domestic pet, a cat or a dog." And of course there have been cultures, Oriental and Occidental, ancient and modern, that have practiced every variety of infanticide, infant exposure, and abandonment.

So childhood, in Western Europe at least, had to be "discovered" or "invented," according to Ariès. Even so, though child rearing was little celebrated in art, song, or story, the details of how children were brought up *had* to be important in shaping those individuals as adults. And, as Barbara Tuchman agrees in *A Distant Mirror,* her stirring chronicle of the fourteenth century, the resulting immaturity of the adult population helped shape the somewhat bizarre nature of that age.

In fact, it may be that historians, by paying virtually no attention to child-rearing practices through the ages, have deprived themselves of critical insights into the factors that influenced the flow of events. What happened in the cradles of nations may have been more important than what happened on the battlefields. This is the major argument of a new school of historians specializing in the "psychohistory of childhood." Their leader, psychoanalyst-historian Lloyd deMause, has in fact developed a "psychogenic theory of history," which holds that "the central force for change in history is neither technology nor economics, but the 'psychogenic' changes in personality occurring because of successive generations of parent-child interactions."

A colleague of deMause's, historian Glenn Davis, has made a study of the evolution of American child-rearing practices from 1840 to 1965. He was able to trace four major patterns of child rearing that gave way to one another over this period; by studying these patterns as they applied to the upbringing of people like Theodore Roosevelt, Woodrow Wilson, Franklin D. Roosevelt, and Lyndon B. Johnson, he was convinced that he could account in large part for the rise of Progressivism, the New Deal, the Great Society, and the Youth Revolt of the 1960s. All this sounds overly glib in a one-paragraph summation—and so it may be; but the psychohistory-of-childhood movement, employing remarkable scholarship in hitherto unexamined areas of history, is destined to offer us profound insights into how we arrived at where we are.

A favorite word among psychohistorians of childhood is *evolution*. They believe that Freudianism has floundered for lack of an evolutionary concept. Most of us tend to regard child-rearing practices as sometimes faddish and arbitrary, fluctuating from one extreme to the other, often without a discernible pattern. But the psychohistorians see a definite and favorable evolution of parenthood from earliest times to the present day. The farther back one goes in history, says deMause, the worse children were treated. We today decry the abuse of children in our midst. But, by current standards, virtually *all* children in ancient societies were abused. Physical beating and sexual molestation of children was virtually universal in many ancient cultures, including those of Greece and Rome, and cruelties have, through the ages, been visited upon helpless children, even infants, for trivial reasons, for amusement, or in order to "harden" them.

DeMause sees a steadily improving evolution of parent-child relations.* Parents from antiquity to the fourth century AD practiced what he calls the *infanticidal mode*, where the killing of unwanted children was widely accepted and even approved. From the fourth to the thirteenth centuries, as children were declared to possess souls, the *abandonment mode* prevailed. Children were farmed out to wet nurses, to monasteries or nunneries, to foster families; they would not live with their parents for years at a time—even during those first critical years—and, by the age of seven, they were often sent to other homes as servants or hostages, or they suffered severe abandonment and neglect at home. Child beating and sexual molestation continued but on a diminished scale.

The fourteenth to seventeenth centuries featured the *ambivalent mode*, when children were finally permitted to share the parents' emotional lives—though this took the form of molding the child into whatever shape the parents desired. The eighteenth century brought the *intrusive mode*, where parent-child intimacy meant total control of the child's mind and body, thoughts and feelings, desires and satisfactions; but toilet training took the place of regular enemas, and while the child might still be beaten as punishment, she was not regularly whipped simply because she was there; moreover, pediatrics came into the picture and child mortality declined simply because parents began to take better care of their children. Parental practice from the nineteenth to the mid-twentieth centuries is characterized as the *socialization mode* where the child is guided in the proper directions, taught to be moral, to conform, to fit into society; psychological innovators from Freud to Skinner fit into this mode; and, for the first time, the father begins to take some official interest in child rearing.

---

*For further views on this subject, see Kliman's introduction to Alex Arzoumanian's *Love and Mankind's Future*.

Finally, since the mid-twentieth century, we have been in the *helping mode*, which deMause regards as clearly the most advanced. Here it is assumed that "the child knows better than the parent what it needs at each stage of its life, and fully involves both parents in the child's life as they work to empathize with and fulfill its expanding and particular needs. There is no attempt at all to discipline or form 'habits.' Children are neither struck nor scolded, and are apologized to if yelled at under stress. The helping mode involves an enormous amount of time, energy, and discussion on the part of both parents, especially in the first six years, for helping a young child reach its daily goals means continually responding to it, playing with it, tolerating its regressions, being its servant rather than the other way around, interpreting its emotional conflicts, and providing the objects specific to his evolving interests." DeMause admits that "few parents have yet consistently attempted this kind of child care," but claims that "it results in a child who is gentle, sincere, never depressed, never imitative or group-oriented, strong-willed, and unintimidated by authority."

Without necessarily accepting every detail of deMause's theory, or his "helping mode" recommendations (most parents simply cannot devote the enormous quantities of time and energy implied), it is clear that there *has* been a positive evolution of parenthood, and that the "leap in evolution" that we earlier suggested could be made in our generation already has a running start.

In any event, now that some predictive knowledge is emerging, along with rapidly altering social circumstances, there is no reason why those who have not yet become parents cannot begin to make better decisions than we who have thus far been responsible for populating the world.

The generations now alive on earth have an unprecedented opportunity and a new freedom of choice about the kind of children they can bring into being. But with this heady challenge comes the inevitable burden of responsibility that accompanies all new opportunities and freedoms.

Belatedly we have begun to realize that the physical earth is endangered by environmental pollution. But we have yet to understand that humankind is threatened by a spreading psychic blight that disorganizes and unbalances the *social ecology* in critical ways. We used to applaud the enterprise of an industrialist who built a factory with a dozen smokestacks, and were indifferent to a tanker captain who spilled his unwanted cargo at sea. But now we are beginning to demand that the factory owner and the tanker skipper take thought *before* they act, because we all suffer the consequences. Similarly, may the time not have come for us to do what we can to cut down on our biological smokestacks and psychic oil spills? Can we continue to let parenthood be such an unlimitedly free enterprise?

Before anyone can drive a car or peddle peanuts on the sidewalk, he must acquire a license. There is hardly a job, no matter how lowly or menial, that does not require proof of capability, experience, training, character references—*something* to certify the applicant's credentials. But for parenthood—one of the most important, demanding, and complicated long-range tasks known to human society—there are no requirements whatsoever. In fact, no application is necessary. There is no "employer"—though we all pay. If a boy and a girl have reached sexual maturity, parenthood comes automatically (barring abortion or miscarriage) with conception and pregnancy.

The idea of applying newfound knowledge to improve the quality of people always brings on (and so it should) a profound sense of unease. There is probably no real controversy in terms of the desirability of turning out children who will be as healthy and happy and creative as possible; the discomfort lurks in how one goes about making it happen. Most of us are extremely wary of government intervention or coercion in personal matters. We have seen the consequences of too many such examples in our time. And most emphatically, we the authors do not advocate government licensing for parenthood. Nor would we care to see the resurgence of an ill-advised eugenics movement, or a return to anything like social Darwinism. We do advocate what we consider to be the only viable alternative: *voluntary procreative responsibility*, a consciousness raising on behalf of the future.

When a man and a woman decide to become parents, they have, by virtue of that decision, appointed themselves *trustees of the future*. The emotional well-being of your child, and to that extent the well-being of all the other people she will interact with during her life-time, is largely dependent on your capacity to steer her lovingly to her full humanity.

This book concentrates its attention mainly on tomorrow's children. But meanwhile, there is today.

Enormous numbers of preschool children, estimated in the hundreds of thousands, are right now either mentally ill or at high risk of serious lifelong emotional disorders. Tomorrow is also *these* children. And these children, all of them, are *our* children.

It is not too late to carry out a rescue mission commensurate with the task—and with the rewards.

Of the tragedies that afflict our times, one of the greatest and least publicized is the neglect, en masse, of emotionally disturbed preschool children. By the age of about six, the fine organization of the human brain and much of the personality is essentially complete—one of the major themes of this book. From birth to age six, then, is the time when psychiatric intervention (the earlier the better) offers the best hope for prevention, alleviation, or cure of emotional problems. Yet this is the period of life that gets the least professional attention. Nearly all the money and facilities, such as they are, are reserved for the care—most of it merely custodial (at a lifetime cost of upward of $300,000 per psychiatric patient)—of ills that are usually too far gone to be helped very much.

What we can no longer afford, beyond the dollar cost, is the fearful cost in personal tragedy and the increasing strain on the fabric of society. It is the nature of our time that new generations will have to deal with increasingly complex and unprecedented problems, a task that will require emotionally healthy people blessed with all the human creative resources that we, their parents, can nourish into being.

Whether or not today's not-quite-yet-human beings make it all the way to effective adulthood depends upon what we do today as doctors and communicators, as teachers and legislators, and especially as mothers and fathers.

Though each of us is directly answerable only for those girls and boys raised in our own household, what happens to all children really does concern us all. Just as we are the beneficiaries when genius is allowed to flower, so do we all suffer when a child gone wrong turns into, say, an assassin. Would an individual who became an assassin have taken the same direction had he or she received the proper love and care in the early years? Almost certainly not. Was it, then, the fault of the parents? But they, after all, were at least partially the innocent products of *their* early misfortunes. And so it goes, from one generation to the next.

In the chapters ahead, we will introduce such concepts as *vertical epidemics*, in which specific emotional troubles are passed along from generation to generation, and *psychological birth defects*, "inherited" almost as surely as if they were genetic in origin. What can be done? Where does one begin to attack the difficulties? One begins at the very beginning of life: the intention in the heart and mind of the would-be parent.

2

The Well-Wanted Child

Really, it was love of children more than anything else that made him
want a pack of his own. Even with a dozen, he wasn't fully satisfied.
Sometimes he'd look us over and say to Mother:
"Never you mind, Lillie. You did the best you could."
  —Frank B. Gilbreth, Jr., and Ernestine Gilbreth Carey,
  CHEAPER BY THE DOZEN

Is IT natural to want and to have children? In former
times, people got married and had children and that was that. Or so
it seems, perhaps oversimplified, in our retrospect.

It is certainly natural for human males and females, on attaining
biological maturity, to feel the stirrings of desire and to mate
sexually. And the natural biological result of that, frequently, is the
conception of a child. But do we equate such basic biological events
with what is natural for us as intelligent citizens of our sophisticated
twentieth-century civilization?

The more one considers the quantity and duration of nurturing
required by the human child, the more reasonable it seems that nature must have programmed parents biologically to provide that
nurture. In evolutionary terms, the rapid growth of the human
brain, and especially the cerebral cortex, seems to have taken place
during roughly the same stretch of time in which the newborns of
our species were acquiring an extended period of juvenile helplessness. These twin developments made it possible to create and to pass
along language and cultural learning from one generation to the
next. We have thus created a *cultural* evolutionary process that appears often to override our *biological* evolutionary program.

14

Nevertheless, it is hard to see how, without the provision of a built-in parental response to infant demands, our species could now be anything but extinct. As neoteny—the long period of dependency—evolved in us, so must our nurturant natures have evolved along with it. The biological program may no longer be as powerfully evident or relevant as in earlier times, nor the instinctual pressures generated by it so necessary after millennia of cultural adaptation; but any other scheme would surely have foundered in the inexorable testing grounds of evolution.

But while we are biologically programmed to be nurturant, our cultural programming in respect to the specifics of nurturing has grown increasingly ambiguous. As a result, women, who are generally assumed to be more intrinsically nurturant than men, must *learn* how to be mothers. Parenthood today is automatically natural only in the sense that anyone who has passed the age of puberty and has engaged in sexual intercourse may, biologically speaking, *have* a child. But culturally speaking, there is nothing automatically natural about becoming a *competent* parent. Particularly in a society as complex as ours, child rearing, from the first day of life, has become more a psychological than a biological process. While biology is not to be ignored, neither can it serve as our most reliable guide.

In this context, to ponder whether something is or is not natural is to ask: What is appropriate under the cultural circumstances—for this time, for this place, for these people? But also: Is there an underlying, universal scheme of development that is appropriate for all people in all times and places? Having a child is not a casual decision to be left to the dictates of our biological nature. *Wanting* a child is a matter to be even less entrusted to nature. The time is here and the place is now, and appropriate motivation for here-and-now parenthood is of primary importance in assessing our nurturant capacities.

Human motivation is often obscure, and it is always difficult to influence. All the more reason for bringing to bear upon it as intense a study as we can muster. Much of this chapter will elaborate on human motivation in terms of one question: What does it mean to want a child *well*—i.e., appropriately for our time, yet consistent with underlying universal developmental needs?

One of the critical traits we believe to be programmed into the biological nurturant nature we just spoke of is altruism.* Altruism is, in our view, an integral element of normal human character—and its absence is therefore an aberration. A woman or a man without altruism is to some degree emotionally handicapped. It requires a special brand of altruism, however, to be a successful parent, particularly as our times grow more troubled and our lives more complicated. The details of this altruistic ingredient as well as other aspects of adequate parental motivation are by no means obvious.

Erik Erikson, among others, has clearly delineated parenthood as a stage of identity growth, and E. James Anthony has observed that it can be a kind of "natural therapy" for some persons with arrested development. But it seems to us that this kind of growth and therapy ought to be achieved through some means other than parenthood. Clearly anyone whose *principal* concern is her own growth and therapy is thinking primarily of herself and not of her future child. Her motive, then, is something less than truly altruistic. Moreover, and this may be more important, it is not realistic. And successful parenthood does require a large measure of realism—in advance. There should be no self-deception about the long-term duties, and sometimes deprivations, that go with the full-time care of a child. On the other hand, the notion that parenthood is unrelieved drudgery while childlessness guarantees perpetual fun and games is another kind of self-deception.

The essence of appropriate motivation, then, is that it be child-centered rather than self-centered.

Yugoslavia recently became the first nation, to our knowledge, to write into its constitution the right of every child to be wanted. We do not necessarily advocate that all other nations write the same provision into their constitutions, but it should certainly be written into our individual consciences and into our collective awareness.

Obviously, if a set of parents, or either parent, fails to want the child—or perhaps even considers the advent of a child an unmitigated misfortune—then the necessary commitment for providing that

---

*We speak here of altruism in the everyday meaning of the term, not in the special sense in which it has been employed by the sociobiologists.

child with a high quality of care and nurture will be absent. True enough, even in the absence of such a commitment a new baby's presence can be so unexpectedly delightful that the parents are won over and are glad they had the baby after all. But then the baby *becomes* a wanted child. One can hardly count on the exceptional charm of an infant to bring about such a dramatic reversal.

"Nothing is more tragic, more fateful in its ultimate consequences," Karl Menninger has said, "than the realization by a child that he was unwanted." And nothing seems more unfair than for presumably intelligent adults to resent, and take out their resentments upon, the helpless child who was brought into the world without any collaboration on her part, but rather through a willful, or heedless, act of *theirs.*

A child who is not wanted, or who is wanted for the wrong reasons, is likely to be unloved, or at least incorrectly loved. (Yes, there are incorrect ways to love. All too many parents, for instance, err in loving their children *contingently*—that is, *if* they "behave," if they do as Daddy and Mommy wish, if they live up to parental expectations, no matter how unrealistic; in a word, if *they* gratify the parents. If they do not, they are under constant threat of seeing and feeling the parents' love withdrawn or withheld. A child must know she is loved—which does not imply the *approval* of every aspect of her behavior—by her parents without reservation or stint, without contingent conditions.) That child is also at risk of being poorly cared for; or at least of not being cared for in a fashion that *her* needs require.

Even in the Soviet Union, a nation whose government we in the Western world consider callous in many human respects, a leading marriage manual warns that "people who are brought up without parental love are often deformed people." The author of the manual, educator A. S. Makarenko, goes on to scold young Russian couples who look upon parenthood casually: "If you wish to give birth to a citizen and do without parental love, then be so kind as to warn society that you wish to play such an underhanded trick."

The unwanted child is usually thought of as one who was conceived inadvertently rather than by calculation. But the mere fact that a conception is planned—and that both parents profess, in all sincerity, to their desire for a child—is not enough to make that child "well wanted." People seldom think out—or seriously question—their motivations for parenthood. Nor do they face up to the real day-to-day frustrations and responsibilities that come with the pleasures and satisfactions of parenthood.

There are many varieties of infant temperament (as will be demonstrated in later chapters). Expectant parents should know that the new baby may turn out to be one of the difficult ones; or that she may not be as healthy, as brilliant, or as good-looking as they would have wished. They should nevertheless be determined to accept, love, and *want* the expected child regardless of characteristics they might perceive as limitations or imperfections. If they are lucky, they may get the easy, beautiful child of their dreams. But they are better off, and so, certainly, will the child be, if they keep their dreams unspecific enough to encompass almost any reasonably normal child that arrives. (Many parents have the resources to love and want even a child that is grossly abnormal or defective, by whatever standards.) If they insist on envisioning a set of explicit specifications for their forthcoming child, and then expect the child to live up to such fantasies, their "wanted" child may very soon become unwanted, resented, even abused. Thus a child may, in some instances, start out being unwanted and later be wanted, and in others start out being wanted and become unwanted. Despite such reversals, however, it is safest for the future child's welfare if she is wanted, and *well* wanted, from the very beginning—that is, before the decision is made to conceive her.

Let us look at a random assortment of reasons why you might—as in fact many people do—want to have a child. We will first just state the reasons baldly. Then, to make our points, we will comment upon them almost in the style of a newspaper-advice column. The reasons are numbered only for the convenience of being able to refer back to them:

1. Other people expect you to have children.
2. Your parents want to be grandparents.
3. You want to prove your masculinity or femininity.
4. You want to create someone in your own image.
5. You want someone to carry on the family name.

6. You believe your race, religion, or nationality should be more plentifully represented in the population.
7. You want someone to whom you can give all the things you couldn't have when you were a child.
8. You can afford children, so why not?
9. You will gain status.
10. You want somebody you are bigger than and can have control over.
11. You want a boy—or a girl—and you are going to keep trying until you get one.
12. You want to replace a previous child who died.
13. Your marriage is troubled and you want a child in order to bring you closer together again.
14. You are lonely for companionship.
15. You need someone to need you.
16. You need something to keep you busy during the day.
17. You want to keep your wife (or husband) at home more.
18. You want to fulfill yourself—to make yourself a "complete" person.

This is far from a comprehensive catalog of people's reasons for having children, but it is a fair enough sampling of the motivations that actually do impel men and women to become parents. Which of these reasons may be rated as right, and which as wrong?

All of these reasons are wrong—though some are more wrong than others. In most instances, the motivations listed are almost guaranteed to create an emotionally troubled child, thus are inimical to good parenthood. In other cases, the reasons are not so much wrong in themselves as *insufficient*; they are wrong only if they are the *main* reasons for wanting a child. What is wrong in all these cases is that the focus is primarily on the parents' needs and frustrations, or on outside pressures, rather than on the child's welfare.

Let us take a closer took at these reasons:

1. *Other people expect you to have children.* Married people are subjected to social pressures from all sides (though these pressures may be less overwhelming today than they once were). As Barbara Seaman has pointed out in *Free and Female*, a woman may even be badgered by her gynecologist: No children? Isn't it time you started a

family? Nora Ephron, writing in *New York*, said that when her gynecologist asked her, "When are you going to have a baby?" she told him she was working on a book that would take her another year and a half to finish, and she surely wouldn't consider having a baby until then. "You should have one now," he told her. To give in to such pressures suggests a basic insecurity, a strong need to be accepted, to wear a façade of normalcy. Such parents are likely to be overanxious about their child's behavior, striving excessively to see that she conforms to other people's standards, that she doesn't risk displeasing anybody. More risky is the possibility that people who really don't want to have children at all will convince themselves that they do because they want so badly to "be like everybody else." Few rationalizations can be more stultifying for a child's emotional future.

2. *Your parents want to be grandparents.* Of course they do. And it's nice if you want to please them. But that does *not* constitute an adequate reason for going ahead.

3. *You want to prove your masculinity or femininity.* There are other, better ways to prove your gender (and yourself). A child's existence will *not* prove your sex, your sexiness, or your worth—not for you, not for anyone else. All you will have accomplished is to put an enormous burden on an innocent boy or girl who is not able to carry it. If some ingredient of your nature is missing and seems important to you, maybe you should put off having children until you find it.

4. *You want to create someone in your own image.* If you're really beautiful, then it's no sin to wish the same for your child. And if you're not so beautiful, you're still entitled to your desire to re-create yourself. But either way, you have no assurance that the child will look like you, talk like you, act like you, or think like you (or like your spouse). Children are seldom anything like exact replicas of their parents. If you demand a re-creation of your image, you may very well be disappointed in your offspring. This should be among the most minor of reasons for wanting a child.

5. *You want someone to carry on the family name.* This is related to numbers 4 and 6. Wanting to perpetuate the family name is not a reprehensible desire. Even if the family name is not Churchill or Kennedy, pride in family may be a positive influence on the child.

But again, it isn't enough. Too many other factors are of incomparably greater importance.

6. *You believe your race, religion, or nationality should be more plentifully represented in the population.* If you are proud of your race, religion, or nationality, this pride—and perhaps the rich tradition that goes with it—can be a strong character-building influence. However, if perpetuating these—or striving for a more plentiful representation in the population—is your main aim, then your eye is on politics rather than on the child's welfare. Besides, your pride loses much of its luster if it results in the chauvinistic "putdown" of others—thus becoming prejudice, which a child may take on all too readily, and carry with her, and pass along to others, even if only in the form of a "superiority complex."

7. *You want someone to whom you can give all the things you couldn't have when you were a child.* (And she'd better *want* them.) Wanting the best for your child is natural and normal. If you were deprived, you don't want your child to be deprived. The problem is that your child may not want the things that you always wished for. You may work hard to put yourself into a position to give her what she can't or won't appreciate, and in that case you will probably be bitterly disappointed. You can't mold your child into the you that might have been. You will serve best by allowing her to become herself.

8. *You can afford children, so why not?* Parenthood should never be a why-not proposition. If you don't have a reason *why*, then desist. The very fact that you can afford children often means that you can also afford lots of other things. Some of the most neglected children we know are the sons and daughters of wealthy people who can't resist a perpetual temptation to travel around the world and do all the glamorous and exciting things that money so often allows, meanwhile leaving the children with a succession of quick-turnover governesses so that their primary emotional bonds are broken time after time. Certainly you should be able to afford children if you're going to have them, but just having enough money is no guarantee that you have enough of anything else. Your own personal checkout is more important than your bank account.

9. *You will gain status.* It is quite possible that you will gain status in the eyes of some people by having a child. But to do it for that

reason is to put your values in reverse order, for you are thinking first of all of what other people think (or what you think they think), secondly of your own desires, and lastly of the child and her welfare.

10. *You want somebody you are bigger than and can have control over.* You are not likely to admit this reason to anyone but yourself. But if you do admit it to yourself, you can change your mind.

11. *You want a boy—or girl—and you're going to keep trying until you get one.* There is always the danger that, try and try as you will, you'll keep having nothing but boys (or girls). You may not hate them all, but you'll like each additional disappointment a little less than the one before. Suppose you try several times, and hit the sex you want on, say, the fifth try. In that case, it's quite possible that you will spoil that fifth one rotten, and the numbers two, three, and four will feel increasingly unwanted, in that order. It's unfair to start a child off with a handicap in life because he or she didn't turn out to be of your preferred gender. Prepare to love the child as the case may be, or wait until science brings us to a point where we can predetermine the sex of our children.

12. *You want to replace a previous child who died.* This, too, is a heavy burden to place on a new child. You will be expecting her, whether consciously or not, to be just like the other child in as many ways as possible, and will consequently be disappointed in her when she turns out to be herself instead. When you decide to have a new child, you should be pleased to know in advance that it will be a new and different experience. Though we know of no definitive large-scale study of the destiny of these "replacement children," our own clinical experience shows that they have a high frequency of depression and obsessional neurosis.* They also tend to be timid, clinging, and anxious—especially about possible separation from

---

*Writing of the Hungarian dramatist Ferenc Molnar in *Cradles of Eminence*, Victor and Mildred Goertzel report:

> Although his parents never said so, he was always quite certain that he was an exceedingly poor substitute for the blond, angelic brother who died before Ferenc was born. Molnar's father, who was a physician, kept only the placid, sunny Lacika's picture on his desk. Nothing that dark, active Ferenc ever could accomplish erased his father's longing for the lost Lacika.

their parents. This probably comes from the parents' exaggerated fears that what happened to the earlier child will happen to this one too. The handicap is best overcome when there is already a strong determination to have a larger family; it is most hazardous when the family was considered to be complete before the tragedy.

13. *Your marriage is troubled and you want a child in order to bring you closer together again.* To bring a child deliberately into an emotional atmosphere known in advance to be troubled is one of the crueler and more irresponsible situations one can visit on a newborn. Studies have repeatedly and convincingly demonstrated that higher rates of juvenile delinquency, criminality, poor school performance, and almost every variety of emotional disturbance are the consistent products of severely discordant marriages. A troubled marriage should perhaps in itself be a disqualifier for parenthood. If you really think you want children, wait until you have worked out or at least substantially mitigated the major problems besetting your relationship.

14. *You are lonely for companionship.* A motive like this suggests self-pity, and would likely saddle a child with the responsibility of filling her parents' needs, rather than the other way around. A child usually does turn out to be good company, but that should not be her primary *purpose* in life. What kind of company will you be for her?

15. *You need someone to need you.* Most people need someone to need them. In the case of a child, however, the question is: Is it *her* need, or yours, that is being answered? We know of a schizophrenic mother who kept having one baby after another. She loved the experience of caring for an infant who was totally dependent upon her for its needs. But as soon as the child grew beyond infancy, she lost interest, and wanted another baby (oh, *really wanted* another, no doubt of it). The result was a family of neglected children.

At seventeen Ferenc finished high school and brought home a record so excellent that it opened the doors of every university in Europe to him, but Ferenc could see on his father's face the fleeting shadow of a thought, "Why not Lacika?" The identical look was manifest when his second son brought him clippings from the morning paper extolling the production of Ferenc's first play. To this intruder complex Molnar attributed his lifelong shyness, his exaggerated modesty and his uneasy feeling that he did not merit the rights freely given to others.

16. *You need something to keep you busy during the day.* This is not the world's worst motive, as long as a child is *the* thing you most want to keep busy with. Otherwise, you have your choice of a thousand jobs and hobbies. A child's main role should never be relief of a parent's boredom. Unless you feel some positive joy in the prospect, if you're bored without a child, you'll probably still be bored *with* one. And then you will have saddled yourself with a lot of busywork it's too late to get out of—which will be bad news for both you and the child.

17. *You want to keep your wife (or husband) at home more.* If you are a man and your wife doesn't like staying home, she probably won't like staying home with a baby either. It's possible, as suggested earlier, that the baby will overcome her with its charm, but that, again—like reasons 13, 14, 15, and 16—is too big a burden to put on an infant. If your wife resents being home with a child, that's bad for the child. And it can't be too good for the way she feels about you either, since you're the one who has put her into this trap. If you are a woman, on the other hand, a baby might or might not keep your husband home more, depending on how much it captivates him. But a baby cannot do for you what you cannot do for yourself. In a word, it's not likely to work. And now you'll still be at home without your husband—only with a baby you may soon learn to resent. The fact that the whole thing was your own dumb idea won't be much consolation for the child.

18. *You want to fulfill yourself—to make yourself a "complete" person.* Of the entire list of reasons given, this reason comes closest to being "right." Wanting to be fulfilled in parenthood is reasonable and commendable. But even this motivation, while good, is not enough.

What, then, constitutes correct motivation for parenthood?

Positive traits and attitudes toward children are of paramount importance. But why should it matter, you may ask, what my attitude is toward children in general? So I don't like other people's children. Isn't it enough just to love my own?

That isn't the point. The point is that if you dislike children in general, you may find it difficult to develop a fondness for your own. Or you may have inflated ambitions for them, expecting them to be different from, in some way superior to, other children—perhaps possess special skills or talents or qualities that particularly appeal to you. But chances are they won't be all that extraordinary. They may even be handicapped in some way. Then what? You will be terribly disappointed in the child, and the child will know it. Who could feel wanted under such circumstances?

A parent's attitudes, not only toward the child but toward the world, can exercise a profound influence on the child's future emotional development. And so we place great importance on a "positive outlook on life" as a motivating force. All of us have known people, at one time or another, whom we would rate as good human beings by any definition—sensitive, intelligent individuals— who, however, feel that people in general are inherently just no good; that the world is a vale of tears, is going to hell in a hurry; that life is a cruel and meaningless joke. (If a potential parent is not merely a pessimist, but suffers from a true chronic depression, such a state seriously threatens the emotional health of the future child. Freedom from depression, as we shall see, is an important qualification for parenthood.)

We may hear such people say that they would not want to be responsible for bringing innocent children into such a miserable world. And our tendency is to protest, to think: What a pity that they should feel that way. Aren't these thoughtful, educated men and women just the kind of people who, with all their advantages, *ought* to have children?

But their instincts are probably correct. We should accept their judgment and not try to convince them otherwise. Their view of the world *is* their emotional world, and that is the world into which they would be bringing their children. If you feel there's no point to life—then, indeed, why create it? Life should be offered as a gift, or not at all.

If we were given a choice of parents—of, on the one hand, poor and ignorant people with a zest for life and a great capacity for joy, or, on the other hand, affluent and educated parents full of despair and without hope—we would unhesitatingly choose the former. This is not to say that poor, ignorant parents aren't at least equally subject to despair (they have much better reason for it), or that we rate poverty and ignorance as anything but liabilities. We simply want to point up, as strikingly as possible, that our ordinary parental standards can be drastically modified by the parents' fixed moods and attitudes.

One attitude that too often prevails, especially among very young couples, is that parenthood means having a *baby*. Every parent does, of course, "have a baby." But babyhood doesn't last very long. Wanting a child, as we will emphasize repeatedly, should mean having an interest not just in cuddling an infant but in watching, and being present at, the unfolding of an entire life process. That is why we ask you to ask yourself whether you are a person capable of making long-term commitments.

The kind of natural, evolutionarily programmed altruism we postulated earlier is not enough to carry us through. An adult caregiver must have a large capacity for empathy, especially during the child's nonverbal years. The parent-child relationship (which we will examine in detail) is a complex and continuing series of subtle interactions. The parent must be sensitive to minor cues from the infant's sounds and movements, and be capable of reading accurately, from them, needs that the child cannot otherwise express—and of acting and reacting appropriately. Throughout the early developmental years, even after the child learns to speak her needs, the parent must be resonant to what remains unspoken as well.

How can you tell if you are sensitive to children in this way? Chances are that if you are "good with children" before you become a parent, you will do well with your own children too. Children are excellent judges of parental qualifications. If they come to you and act as if you understand them, you probably do. You can get a lot of preparenthood practice via baby-sitting, teaching or assisting in a nursery school, taking seriously your roles as aunt or uncle or older sibling or older cousin or neighbor—seriously enough, at least, to get involved with children in a manner that gives you some feedback on your ability to deal with them. If the whole idea bores you, if the thought of such unnecessary involvement with children seems an imposition on your time and energy, then perhaps you should question your motivation for having children of your own.

It is likely that, if you have a healthy supply of self-love and self-esteem, you will also have supplies of love and esteem to offer to children. Though we have not yet mentioned the early stages of separation-individuation and narcissistic development—which will be discussed in depth in Part Two of the book—it is not too early to say that a would-be parent must also ask herself how successfully she has completed her own individuation and achieved her own narcissistic maturity. To the extent that she has failed, her supply of self-love and self-esteem will be inadequate, and her child may be at risk of similar failure.

There are, on the other hand, some parents who are interested only in the future adult. The childhood stage is simply an unfortunate necessity to be gotten through somehow. The child is something to be groomed for whatever the parents might have in mind: an heir or heiress, a doctor, a ballet dancer, a show-business prodigy. There have been times in European history—as already mentioned—when children were regularly farmed out during this interim period to be raised by surrogate parents. But one doesn't have to go back in history for examples. We know of a young Briton who, wishing for a male heir, persuaded his mistress to become the mother—of a girl, as it turned out. The last we heard, the child was being left with a new nanny (the former one having beaten her) at home, where her parents were planning to spend only ten weeks out of their busy year. Look around almost any neighborhood for further illustrations.

The questions we ask would-be parents to ask themselves, here and in the next chapter, are not offered as a precise or comprehensive checklist of characteristics that will surely qualify them for superior parenthood, or without which they are doomed to failure. But they do represent the kinds of questions that will help an individual determine to what degree he or she is a "parenting" type of person. (An implicit question, of course, is whether the would-be parent, especially the prospective mother, is sufficiently motivated to take proper care of her physical person—to eat and exercise sensibly, to restrict smoking and alcoholic intake—in order to give the developing fetus the best possible chance to be born healthy. The father, too, should look to his physical condition; he will also need adequate energy for his parenting tasks.)

For those thinking of becoming adoptive parents, in competition with other couples who may want the same child, this kind of cautionary psychological self-quiz is perhaps even more important. You may feel a need for the child, but how well equipped are you to serve the child's needs?

A well-wanted child, by our definition, is a child who is positively desired for healthy reasons by parents who have looked to their own qualifications with a critical eye. Such a child, as she then develops and gets out into the world, *knows* that she was and is wanted, and this knowledge operates as a powerful support. For unwantedness is a defect not inflicted by parents alone. Society finds many ways to make a child feel unwanted, even if her parents clearly want her. Any of us may be guiltier than we know in this respect. We can create unwanted children without being parents at all. Every time we discriminate against anyone for any of the standard unreasons—race, religion, nationality, political affiliation, gender, sexual proclivities, age, education, economic status, IQ—we let that person know that we consider her company (or her participation in whatever it is we are denying her access to) as undesirable. Nor does the person so discriminated against, whatever her age, have to be paranoid to feel the negative response (which people do not always take the trouble to convey subtly). Quite apart from any individual overt acts, there is always the awareness on the part of a potential victim—an awareness absorbed from the social surroundings beginning very early in life—of whole areas and auras of bias and discrimination. If you live constantly with the possibility—even the expectation—that reminders of your unwantedness may be hurled at you without notice, at any moment, from any source, your emotional security is bound to be uneasy.

To a child who has received from strong, loving parents the gift of high self-esteem, it may not matter too much what other people think or say or do, as long as their acts are not directly harmful. But to a child not so fortunate, the esteem of others is a reflection of her own worth. Thus unwantedness may equal worthlessness in her own eyes.

So our responsibility for children is twofold. As parents, we should strive to furnish our children with the necessary self-esteem.

And as adult human beings, we should examine our acts and attitudes with a view to ridding ourselves of the impulses that will "put
down" other people's children—who may not be sufficiently sturdy
to ignore our opinions of them. This second responsibility implies a
corollary imperative: to do whatever we can to dissipate those areas
and auras of bias and discrimination that pervade our social atmosphere, that defeat rather than encourage the growth of self-esteem.

One of the more blatant and obvious examples of society's active
creation of unwantedness has traditionally been the status of illegitimacy—where innocent children have been, with their first breath,
stamped with a prominent Unwanted sign. It is neither logical nor
humane to attach a social stigma at birth. This time-honored and
widespread custom has gone into a steep decline in recent years—a
trend especially fortunate in view of the increasing number of children being born to unwed teenagers—but such children are still
usually unwanted. When teenage parents—married or not—really
do not, and let it be known that they do not, want their expected or
newborn child—and assuming they have not already opted for
abortion—they should be helped with a constructive alternative: to
offer the child for adoption.

It is not, unfortunately, an alternative altogether approved of by
our society. Some years ago, when one of the authors was living
near El Paso, Texas, a young soldier stationed at Fort Bliss and his
pregnant teenage wife let it be known that they planned to give
their expected baby away to adoptive parents, an older couple who
had been trying unsuccessfully for some time to have children of
their own. The young couple felt that they were not yet ready to
handle the responsibilities of parenthood. But there was a public
outcry and indignant editorials in the local papers about these "unnatural" parents. As a result, the couple decided to keep the baby
after all, mollifying the outraged citizenry—and probably guaranteeing the emergence of yet another troubled individual.

All traces of stigma should be removed from this sort of transaction. People who don't want children but have them anyway should
be encouraged to give them to people who do want them—though
of course the motives and capacities of the adoptive parents must be
carefully examined. There is a shortage of desirable babies for adop-

tion, and a long waiting line of eager would-be adoptive parents. One couple's accident can be another couple's prize.

It would be hard to improve on what Margaret Sanger had to say about the whole subject: "The first right of every child is to be wanted, to be desired, to be planned with an intensity of love that gives it its title to being."

Now let us turn our attention to the unwanted child in the most straightforward meaning of that term: A woman finds herself pregnant—and either she, or her husband (if she has one), or both, *know* they do not want a child.

Before we proceed further, it is essential to understand that a certain amount of temporary ambivalence toward the coming baby at some stage or other of pregnancy is quite *normal*. Hardly any expectant mother—especially if **she** is expecting for the first time—goes through the entire period of pregnancy without some occasional qualms, some feelings of awe in the face of her upcoming responsibilities and of doubt about her ability to manage the mysteries and unpredictabilities that surround the rearing of a new human being. Pregnancy is a time—both for her and for her husband—when all sorts of buried fears and anxieties may surface.

These normal, occasional qualms and doubts do not mean she does not want the child, or that she will not make a good parent. It is a rare person who experiences steady, unmitigated delight at the approach of parenthood, or who is supremely confident of her parental credentials. So a little worry is sensible (indeed, total absence of it may be a sign of foolishness). By the same token, it is not unusual or abnormal for a new mother to feel a letdown after birth, to feel she cannot yet love the new little stranger; but in a few days all is well, usually.

Parental motivation can be very complicated, and is often ambiguous or contradictory. An openly expressed, conscious desire can be at odds with unconscious wishes. You may think you want a child when you really don't, and vice versa. Sometimes the unconscious motivation can express itself psychosomatically. A woman who seems unhappy because she cannot have children may take a series of treatments for infertility, only to have her analyst discover that the "infertility" is a defense against her fear of motherhood. Another woman's unconscious rage and antipathy toward the child she is carrying can result in a spontaneous abortion. A wife and husband may have planned a baby—yet, once the prospect of parenthood becomes real, so many long-buried insecurities and immaturities may suddenly manifest themselves that the emotional conflict results in what Therese Benedek calls a "malignant pregnancy." This kind of problem, in which all the wantedness is canceled out, has often been rectified through psychoanalytic treatment.

And of course, as we have already indicated, an unwanted pregnancy does not invariably *result* in an unwanted child. Though conception may have occurred through carelessness, the "carelessness" could have been the expression of an unconscious desire for a child. Once pregnant, the expectant mother may be secretly pleased. If her husband is too, and shows his pleasure, then she can show hers too.

In some of these situations, a couple may have decided to postpone parenthood for economic reasons. But once the child is on its way, they are happy about it and begin looking forward to the baby's arrival. Or a couple who already have children may, through concern about overpopulation, feel they mustn't have any more, though they do love children. A new pregnancy, then, may be "unwanted" yet really welcome. If they can shed the unwarranted guilt they feel because they didn't "Stop At Two"—as the Zero Population Growth buttons implored—they will certainly want that new baby.

Again, as mentioned earlier, a baby can often, by her sheer presence, win over and captivate the mother or father who "didn't want" her. All of a parent's tender feelings may be aroused, and all doubts conquered; and soon we have a loved and wanted child. An infant can exercise great power and charm, evoking protective feelings in male and female alike, even in someone not her parent.

There is a memorable scene in *Anna Karenina* where Anna's husband, the rather dour and stiff-necked Karenin, is at his wife's bedside looking at the new baby—the child of his wife's lover: "For the newborn girl he felt a quite peculiar sentiment, not of pity only but of tenderness. At first sheer pity had drawn his attention to the delicate little creature, who was not his child, and who had been cast on one side during his mother's illness, and would certainly have died if he had not troubled about her; and he did not realize how fond he had become of her. Several times a day he would go to the nursery and remain there. . . ."

In order for such tenderness to be aroused, however, the human soul must be receptive. Another character in the same Tolstoy novel looks at his own newborn son: "Gazing at this pitiful little bit of humanity, Levin searched his soul in vain for some trace of paternal feeling. He could feel nothing but aversion. . . . His feelings for this little creature were not at all what he had expected. There was not an atom of pride or joy in them; on the contrary, he was oppressed by a new sense of apprehension. . . ."

As E. James Lieberman has pointed out, "The physician who assumes that childbirth will inevitably bring out the good old [parental] instinct is a superficial observer of the human condition." In most cases, a child who was unwanted at the beginning of pregnancy will still be unwanted at the end of it, perhaps even more so.

Large numbers of women undergo what Garrett Hardin has called "compulsory pregnancy"—defined by Mildred Beck, formerly with the National Institute of Mental Health, as "a particular pregnancy, incurred by chance or by plan, which for any reason whatsoever is steadfastly and unequivocally unwanted by the pregnant woman, but which she is compelled by external circumstances to carry to term."

In *Abortion and the Unwanted Child*, Beck describes the destiny of children born of such pregnancies. Far more than other infants, they become victims of every variety of child abuse, as well as abandonment in paper bags on doorsteps or in garbage cans; not invariably, of course, but with horrendous frequency. In less extreme cases, the unwanted child is often

neglected or abused in the sense that, if the child were brought to the attention of the courts, there would ensue a legal finding of neglect or abuse. Here we include children suffering from severe malnutrition although the mother does not lack knowledge of nutrition, and there is no evidence of financial need; the infant or young child who is left for days on end with some vague provision for someone to look in on him from time to time; the children left for prolonged periods in so-called well-baby wards of hospitals, or in shelters, or in emergency foster care when there is no demonstrable evidence of need or when the mother offers one excuse after another for failing to provide for the child in any way whatsoever.

Many of the mothers Beck cites were mentally retarded, emotionally disturbed, or addicted to hard drugs or alcohol, but even parents with no such aberrations, people of any class or category, can be guilty of visiting upon their children a spectrum of cruelties and deprivations.

Sally Provence tells of one of her young patients at the Yale clinic, a girl named Laurie. Laurie was full of troubles, though her parents were good, educated people whose other two children did not seem to be similarly troubled. Why did they fare so much better? "Laurie, we found out, was an unwanted child of an unwanted pregnancy—a pregnancy during which her mother felt unloved and unlovely. She endured the pregnancy," says Provence, "as a sentence to be served before she could again return to the world." Laurie's experience, then, was very different from that of her siblings: "Emotionally starved and isolated by intelligent parents in the midst of economic affluence, she is, sadly, a four-year-old shadow of a person. I fear she can be expected to be an inadequate mother to her own children twenty years from now."

An interesting study was made by Gerald Caplan at the Harvard School of Public Health, where mothers came to the guidance clinic to get help for their troubled children. Caplan noticed that most of the women who had more children than just their one troubled child seemed to be perfectly good mothers to their *other* children. In the course of interviews over a period of time, virtually every one of them admitted that the child under treatment had been unwanted, and that she had made attempts at self-induced abortion. In each case, the otherwise intelligent woman was convinced (1) that she had damaged the child, (2) that the child *knew* what she had done, or tried to do, and (3) that the child therefore hated her and was getting even with her in every mean and nasty way he or she could imagine!

So, the victim, the helpless baby, is doubly punished. There is no better demonstration of the kind of pathology that can be caused by unwantedness, even in apparently normal parents.

Abortion, now that it is legal, is an option often recommended. If abortion is not an acceptable alternative, however—whether for psychological, moral, economic, or religious reasons—a second choice is to carry the child to term with the intent of offering it for adoption. In such a case, it is the mother's obligation to take the best possible care of herself and the child who is developing into a human being by her choice. Does it seem unlikely that a woman would take good care of a fetus who will be someone else's baby? Not necessarily. Once she is freed of the responsibility of taking care of the delivered child, she may well lose much of her anxiety and the resentment of being trapped into motherhood.

Abortion and adoption are two alternatives, then.

A third is to take no action at all—that is, just have the baby, and keep it, and raise it, even though the parent wishes the whole thing had never happened. The great quantity of admittedly unwanted children who are born each year suggests that this is a popular alternative—though it often occurs only because the other preferred alternatives were not readily at hand, or would have been too abhorrent or embarrassing. This do-nothing alternative is one we deplore. We have seen enough of the consequences of unwantedness in the children we treat at the Center for Preventive Psychiatry, and have heard enough from other therapists, that we urge anyone who is unwillingly pregnant to do *something*.

Beyond the choices of abortion or adoption, we recommend a third alternative: *start wanting the child.*

This will be very difficult, perhaps impossible. It would be fatuous to pretend that, by a magical act of will, you can just decide to want instead of not want. If it were that easily done, we would recommend this course in *all* cases. But partial success is possible, especially if the husband-wife relationship is reasonably good, and the two can honestly face up to their reasons for not wanting children. Partial success could be of critical importance to the future child's welfare. Pregnancy, especially a first pregnancy, is usually a period of considerable insecurity. During this period, the wife and husband should both do their best to be sensitive to the other, to be considerate and offer the necessary reassurances. They should both especially understand—*brainwash* themselves* with the understanding—that the *child* is innocent and helpless and did not ask to be conceived. They should think as positively as possible of the joys, rather than the deprivations, of parenthood; to identify the new creature with their own loved and loving selves. If they try hard—and try hard together—they might at least arrive at a point where they could make the newborn feel less unwelcome in the world.

And this is where preventive psychiatry should be routinely applied. A couple faced with an unwanted pregnancy should get the best professional help and counseling they can find. The better they can resolve their own emotional problems, the better they might hope to weather the period of pregnancy and childbirth with minimal trauma to themselves. As for the child, the couple should know that the mere fact of their not wanting her is bound to create emotional problems for the newborn. Professional assistance should be lined up in advance, to give support and advice, and to start as early as possible in the child's life in order to minimize the damage. Under these circumstances, it is indeed possible that the child could become a wanted child after all. Unfortunately, the caliber of professional counseling required to bring this about is all too rare in most communities, and nonexistent in too many others.

There is a tightrope-walking nature to the advice we offer. On the one hand, we are urging some people to consider voting against parenthood for themselves. At the same time, we are keenly cognizant of the hazard that turning one's back on parenthood may entail: It could constitute, in some important sense, a denial of nature. If, as we surmised, we are biologically programmed to be nurturant, then failure to provide nurture in some form to some other human being may, for all we know, produce a subtle deprivation syndrome, the

---

*Such parents, perhaps in an emotionally depleted state, should also reach out for all the friendly and loving support those around them are willing to give, to shore up the bootstrap operation implied in the advice offered here.

result of a biological yearning unfulfilled. Though we cannot know this for sure, anyone who decides against parenthood is perhaps well advised to consider how to incorporate into his or her life some alternative means for fulfilling that yearning.

This might be achieved, as we suggested in our preface, through an interest in other people's children, which can be manifested in many ways, or in children at large. It might also be achieved through art, through helping the sick or the aged, through politics, through a variety of activities we are not embarrassed to call by that out-of-fashion label "good works." Members of religious orders sublimate their natural altruistic tendencies in exactly this way. For that matter, an ordinary life lived in any trade, occupation, profession, or business can be filled with nurturance toward family, friends, associates, even strangers. And nurturance toward oneself, in the sense of developing a self whose presence and activity in the world will make a felt, nurturant difference to others, is not to be disdained.

In any case, whether any of us wants or does not want a specific child of our own, we are all duty bound as citizens to make every child who is born into our world feel wanted and welcome in it. We hope, for all the reasons stated, that in cases where the probabilities seem high that the potential offspring will be emotionally handicapped, the would-be parents will abstain. The fewer such emotional handicaps in the world, the better for everyone. But once a child *is* born—whatever her condition or circumstances—society owes her, from that moment on, the finest resources it can muster, the best possible opportunity it can provide for a high-quality existence in a world that no one asked her whether or not she wanted.

3

Psychological "Birth Defects": The Vertical Epidemic

For the sins of your fathers you, though guiltless, must suffer.
                                                        —Horace,
                                                        ODES III

. . . a woman whose courage was gone through too much child-bear-ing. . . . And what made it doubly hard to bear was that she did not even love her children. It was useless pretending. Even if she had the strength she would never have nursed and played with the little girls.
                                                        —Katherine Mansfield,
                                                        "WE ARE AT THE BAY"

EDWARD is almost four, and you wouldn't have to be his grandmother to call him beautiful. He also seems gentle by nature—if nature could have its way. Yet this morning Edward stomps down the hall to class, eyes narrowed, lips compressed, his whole small forward-thrusting body a package of such theatrical fury that it would draw a smile from anyone who didn't understand how real and profound is the boy's anguish.

Inside the classroom, Lynn, a red-haired, slightly overweight five-year-old, looks the psychoanalyst straight in the eye and says, "You are an ugly, disgusting man."

Before the analyst can respond, there is a loud knocking on the door—though the door isn't locked. The door flings open, and there stands Edward, glowering in all directions with impartial menace. He slams the door shut behind him, gives it a final kick, and lets out a fierce bellow.

Lynn takes refuge behind the "ugly, disgusting" psychoanalyst.

Edward is not really planning to hurt anyone. But just at that moment Joanne, a tiny, sparrowlike three-year-old who has been clinging to the teacher's leg, darts away and puts herself directly in Edward's path, deliberately provoking him to hit her. Looking stricken, Edward clenches his fist and lifts it uncertainly.

The teacher moves swiftly to save Edward from a painful decision and Joanne from the painful consequences. Lynn cautiously comes out of hiding. The other children in the class (there are eight in all), having looked up briefly from their play, now resume it as if nothing had happened.

We are witnessing the beginning of a routine class hour at the Cornerstone Therapeutic Nursery, part of the unique children's division of the Center for Preventive Psychiatry, where Westchester County parents can bring their emotionally disturbed preschool children to be treated and taught at the same time.

In a moment Edward has been quieted, and Joanne rescued. But as Edward goes to the bathroom, Lynn follows him. She tries to get in so she can tell him—as she frequently does (though she fears him)—how ugly and disgusting boys are.

Joanne, Edward, Lynn. Three little children in very big trouble.

Joanne, who makes animal noises in place of speech, has been beaten savagely and repeatedly by her mother. She behaves as if her purpose in life were to offer herself up as victim. Such a child, if she survives into adulthood without being institutionalized, is at high risk of becoming a mother who beats her own child, or of marrying a man who will be a child beater.

In human nature, especially in troubled human nature, psychiatry has long recognized a terrible *repetition compulsion*, a complex need to act out one's own childhood.

Joanne's mother had been severely beaten by her own parents. Joanne is, in fact, in a direct line of at least four successive generations of child beaters. She is the victim of a *vertical epidemic*, passed on from one generation to the next, almost like a genetic disease—except that it is psychological rather than physical. What she has "inherited" is a very real birth defect—a handicap that may cripple her emotionally for life.

Edward, too, is the direct victim of such a vertical epidemic. His father, a drug addict who regularly beat his wife in the child's presence, abandoned the boy when he was only two—the same age at which his own violent, alcoholic father had deserted *him*. There is, connected with the repetition compulsion, a strange "anniversary phenomenon"—that is, if some catastrophic process or event has occurred at a given age in an individual's life, then that's the age at which the individual's own child runs the greatest risk.

Lynn's parents, for instance, recently underwent a bitter divorce. She is lonely for her father—who, she is constantly reminded by her mother, is an ugly, dishonest, sexually unfaithful and altogether contemptible individual. Lynn's mother and father both suffered the loss of parents, in different ways, between the ages of three and five; and now they have inflicted a similar parental abandonment on their own daughter.

Not that this kind of repetition compulsion is carried out consciously. Some of the best-intentioned people are guilty of it and would be horrified to learn that they are. In most cases, the parent is as much the victim as the child.

We were able at the Center to help Edward, Joanne, and Lynn; we probably caught them early enough. But any one clinic can treat only a small fraction of all the Edwards, Joannes, and Lynns across the land who are condemned to the continued transmission of their psychological defects.

To possess a repetition compulsion replete with possibilities for abandonment or abuse is something like carrying, unknowingly and therefore carelessly, a loaded gun with the safety catch off. The gun may go off, or it may not, but it is better simply not to carry the gun, or, if you are carrying it, at least to know that it's loaded.

Repetition compulsions are, more often than not, small in caliber and not always carried to their potentially hazardous conclusions. Sometimes this is due to sheer good luck. In other cases, there may be saving factors in the marital or family situation. It may take a certain set of precipitating circumstances, or a child of a given temperament, to bring out the worst in the "contagious" parent. One child may escape the curse, while the next suffers the full force of it; though even the escapees suffer some side effects of the family tragedy.

The child who is the victim of a repetition compulsion is not necessarily permanently damaged. If she is sensitive and intelligent, she may grow up doubly determined *not* to visit the same upon her own offspring. An opposite danger exists here, however—that she will lean to the other extreme. A battered child, when she becomes a parent herself, may find it intolerable to discipline her own child in any way whatsoever.

The biography shelves in every library offer living testimony that a child can be strong enough to survive and surmount the entire spectrum of parental shortcomings, and even achieve eminence.* But for every such child, there are hundreds of others who *might* have been similar or superior achievers but were cheated of their chances by ruined childhoods.

It is worth reemphasizing, however, that just because a psychological ailment "runs in the family" doesn't mean that all the children will necessarily be affected—any more than a given member of a family with a long history of heart disease will surely have heart trouble. But, in both cases, the child's *risk* is higher.

Apart from the danger to himself, a disturbed individual disturbs other individuals. He may be an addict, a child beater, a wife beater, a rapist, a robber, an assassin, a madman, a sadistic dictator, or just

---

*Joseph Conrad is an outstanding example of a writer who attained great literary distinction despite an extraordinarily difficult childhood. But at great cost. He was full of repetition compulsions, and vertical epidemics that could be traced at least from his father's father to his own son. In *Joseph Conrad: The Three Lives*, Frederick R. Karl writes:

> With a wife and infant son [the infant son referred to here is Conrad], and having squandered Ewa's dowry, Apollo [Conrad's father] threw himself into literary activity. With that incredible duplication which we find in history, Conrad, once married (in 1896) and with an infant son (1898), with no money and with many debts, also took up literary activity as a form of salvation.... Conrad ... was undergoing a transformational process such as his father also had undergone forty years earlier.

And again:

> Not only did he share his parents' exile, he must have shared in that daily expression of ailments and dispiritedness that marks a life no longer worth living. Psychologically, the effect was profound. Whether induced or otherwise, he entered into a life for himself that duplicated in many essentials the domestic situation of his early years—illness, dependency, morbidity, parent-son (child) relationships contingent upon a son catering to an indisposed, almost dying father.

Et cetera.

hopelessly inept. He may simply make a few people miserable, or, if he is sufficiently powerful, cunning, or charismatic, inflict his troubles on entire populations. Thus does the vertical epidemic spread horizontally in each new generation, at incalculable cost to humanity.

Knowing what we now know, had we been able to interview in advance the parents of Edward, Joanne, and Lynn, we would have predicted that the child of any of these unions would probably need psychiatric attention—and probably not get it, for most troubled children do not get the help they need. In the cases of Edward and Joanne, the forecasts would have been easy. Though many complexities came together to make their parents the individuals they turned out to be, a history of drug addiction and abuse alone are enough to mark the victims as likely possessors of repetition compulsions, and—if untreated—as transmitters of vertical epidemics.

But most psychological defects are transmitted in less blatant ways, and here we have Lynn's parents as illustration. Let us take a look at their history. (Some of the circumstances will be changed, just as the children's names were, to protect their identities.)

Almost anyone who had met Fred and Alice before the divorce might well have described them as a "nice normal young couple." Yet they came into their marriage with great parental handicaps. The product was Lynn, a bright and almost charming little girl, rather pretty though a bit plump—full of conflicts, angers, fears, confusions, anxieties, violent tantrums, and deep depressions—a girl now luckily getting help, but otherwise doomed to a lifetime of emotional havoc.

To understand Lynn's parents, we need to have a look at what *their* childhoods were like. As we do, we will see one liability after another emerge. It should be said at the very outset that even a formidable array of such liabilities in each individual parent can be overcome by a very good *relationship* between the two and by strong, well-grounded *motivation* for parenthood (as suggested in the last chapter).

In the case of Alice and Fred, neither of these countervailing forces was present.

First, Lynn's mother, Alice.

Alice's own mother married, at the age of sixteen, a man of twenty-one. There, right away, was one liability. She was too young to become a mother—as she did—during the first year of marriage.

What is "too young"? It varies, of course, with the individual. The important thing is to be essentially finished with one's own childhood and adolescence. Adolescent parents may really *want* a baby, and the child may accurately be called a love object, but often this is in much the same sense that a pet is a love object. People acquire pets not to gratify the pets, but to gratify themselves.

The average adolescent is notoriously self-absorbed in thoughts, needs, and feelings. He or she is often enthralled and preoccupied with her appearance, manners, prejudices, pleasures, and fantasies. All that is normal enough, part of a healthy narcissistic line of development at this stage of childhood. But a child should not *have* children.

An adolescent parent's behavior toward her child will probably be full of excessive and unpredictable ups and downs, bewildering extremes that are related more to her mood of the moment than to anything the child may have done to deserve either praise or censure. The gratification such a parent demands can be a terrible burden on the child.

Since we never had the opportunity to interview Alice's mother—Lynn's grandmother—in person, we can only suspect that she had many of the shortcomings of an adolescent mother, and that Alice, whom we *do* know (she delivers Lynn daily to the Cornerstone Therapeutic Nursery and undergoes weekly therapy herself), suffered some of the consequences. Alice also became a mother too young—at seventeen—and we daily observe the results in her daughter.

Another liability for Alice: Her mother, in addition to being very young, was also very ill—with chronic diabetes, an illness that tends to run in families. Though Alice has not yet shown any symptoms, she is still only in her twenties, and the risk remains.

Everyone understands that a parent who is *mentally* ill may have a hard time raising an emotionally healthy child. But a parent who is physically ill—depending on the illness and how incapacitating it might be—can be just as hard on a child's emotions. Thus an illness serious enough to render the victim a high-risk candidate for early death is, in itself, a strong liability for parenthood.

Alice's mother was that seriously ill, and her illness must have exaggerated her adolescent self-absorption and desire for self-gratification. She was frequently withdrawn and unavailable to her daughter. She died in childbirth (it would have been her second baby) when she was not yet twenty one. So at the age of four, Alice lost the mother she had hardly ever possessed. Her father, severely depressed by the event, threw himself into his work. He had a good job. Moreover, there was money in his family and his parents were generous with their financial help (the only thing they *were* generous with); so he could easily afford to hire a succession of housekeepers and nurses to take care of Alice.

Because he "wanted to give her everything," he bought her an abundance of toys and clothes and gifts. But he was practically never there in person. So Alice suffered a double abandonment. She understood neither her mother's death nor her father's absence, and she never forgave either one of them.

Alice's father remarried when she was seven, and her stepmother proved a kind, decent woman; but by then irrevocable damage had been done. Alice was frequently depressed. Her self-esteem was low. She had great conflict about her gender identity. She yearned for her lost mother, and she resented her father—though she dared not show it; that was the one thing that brought immediate reproof from her stepmother, who doted on her husband.

Alice was a child whose needs were never gratified in any of the critical early stages of development. She would later unconsciously look for these missing gratifications from her own child.

Alice grew to adolescence and met Fred. By then she was attractive, intelligent, and superficially charming. Everyone considered her a lovely girl, though a bit on the shy side, and ill-at-ease with boys. Certainly no one among her friends would have classified her as mentally ill. Yet the soundness of her emotional health, and her readiness for parenthood at seventeen, when she married Fred, were seriously impaired.

And what of Fred—Lynn's father?

Unlike his wife, he came from a large family, the sixth of seven children. His father worked hard, but his wages didn't stretch very far with that many kids. The family had a hard time getting by, and his parents bickered a great deal.

They were divorced when Fred was three.

After that, Fred's mother had an even harder time financially. She never remarried. Though his father did the best he could with support money—which he sent, in small, measured-out amounts, rather than brought in person—and his mother worked part time as a clerk (her education and experience had not qualified her for any but a routine, low-paying position), the family couldn't be classed as anything but poor.

Poverty is unfortunately another liability. Most poor parents do manage to raise healthy—in many cases wonderful—children. But all too often they live in an oppressive, even dangerous, environment. They are frequently tired and irritable and, unless they are unusual people or draw great strength from family or culture, they may rightfully feel they don't get much satisfaction out of life in return for their labors. They often lack the emotional stamina to give each other the support they need, let alone to provide the children with all the emotional necessities—as Fred learned at first hand.

The more children there are, the less will the family's resources stretch to satisfy even minimal needs. Under those circumstances, the later children (Fred was the sixth) are bound to be less wanted, hence more resented—even if not consciously. Psychiatric studies confirm that the children of poverty-stricken parents have more emotional disturbances than the rest of the population; and that the later children, those most likely to have been "accidents," suffer the most (and the most serious) disturbances of all.

So we know that Fred—like Alice—grew up with some strong liabilities: poverty, parental abandonment, and the absence of any male caregiver or auxiliary parent of either sex during the critical years of formative life.

Fred was a motherly type of boy—not effeminate, but with little opportunity to acquire any masculine identity (the older boys left home to make it on their own as soon as they were able). He wished for the capacity to lighten his mother's domestic and economic loads, but never found a sure way to comfort her, financially or otherwise.

He grew into a young man who was, on the surface at least, a kind, considerate, industrious person. Almost everyone who knew him thought he was a fine young fellow. Almost anyone who knew Fred and Alice together—as much as they were knowable—thought they made a fine young couple. So why should they not make good, loving parents?

If Alice had met and fallen in love with a different kind of man, his positive qualifications might have bolstered her strength as a potential mother. If Fred had selected a different mate, *her* strong points might have made up for his weaknesses. As it turned out, each of their individual liabilities magnified the other's. When Fred and Alice came together, it was a case of one and one adding up to much more than two.

We have Alice, sixteen, still very much in an ungratified adolescent stage, unknowingly looking for her missing mother, yet needing to be disappointed in the quest. Fred fills the bill: he has motherly qualities that attract her, but obviously he can't *be* her mother. As a bonus, however, he can—as soon as they have a child—serve as a substitute father whom she can openly resent.

Nor can Fred be what *he* longs to be—his own lost father. He can come closest to this goal if he marries someone like his father married, has children toward whom he can behave as his father did. (Much of this psychoanalytic surmise is based on weekly treatment and interviews with Lynn's parents for more than a year.)

When Alice comes along, she reminds Fred—again, not on a conscious level—of his mother. Like her, Alice seems depressed most of the time, usually under a thin surface of forced good cheer. She is insecure and lonely for a man, though she seems awkward, even a bit brusque with him—as his mother often was. Fred is now empowered to do the thing he was forbidden as a child: take his father's place by marrying this young emotional likeness of his mother.

Alice and Fred fit each other's deep, unconscious, neurotic needs, but not in a way that will help either one grow out of them. And their motivation for parenthood is all wrong—all wrong for the child, certainly. They both very much want a child—because each of them needs to play out tragic roles from his or her own incomplete childhood. Each comes into the marriage carrying a backpack of emotional burdens that are also parental liabilities. Each is basically depressed and unhappy, and both are ambiguous about their sexual identities. Each is loaded with repetition compulsions. One such compulsion, which they share, is especially risky for the child: They were *both* abandoned by parents, so they would both be compelled to abandon their own child (like parents who both carry the same bad gene); moreover, it happened to both of them around the same age, so we have the "anniversary phenomenon" doubly at work.

It did not take them long to create their "wanted" child.

Lynn had all the cards stacked against her from the beginning. *Before* the beginning. She might just as well have had a sentence passed on her, in advance, condemning her to be abandoned, one way or the other, somewhere between the ages of three and five—and to be furnished with her own personal load of emotional troubles along the way.

Just as in a genetic disease. Except that a vertical psychological epidemic is *not* genetic. Nor are people helpless to intervene.

But intervention requires a new approach to parenthood, that sense of trusteeship of the future—each child's future, and the world's. A society can only be as sane and free as the preponderance of individuals who comprise it.

Because society requires neither licensing nor credentials for parenthood, prospective parents must look to their own qualifications. Even the closest self-scrutiny cannot always unearth unconscious or subconscious motivations, or long-buried compulsions. But a real willingness to take an honest inward look can go a long way toward making a person aware of his or her shortcomings; then to take steps to overcome them, to *improve* one's qualifications, even if it means postponing parenthood for a while; or, if the disqualifiers (what we have been discussing up to now as "liabilities") seem too formidable, to consider disqualifying oneself, and not having children at all.

There is no clear-cut line of demarcation between qualification and disqualification, but almost any couple can begin to get a rough idea of where they stand if both individuals ask themselves five basic questions—carefully comparing each one's answers with the other's—then together, ask a sixth critical question.

The questions:

1. Am I old enough?

2. Am I young enough?
3. Am I wealthy enough?
4. Am I healthy enough?
5. Am I well enough motivated?
6. Is our relationship good enough?

The questions are not of equal importance—though all of them are important. Here are some guidelines in looking for the answers:

1. *Am I old enough?* The example of Lynn's mother and grandmother show the hazards of becoming a parent too young. There could be mitigating factors: a seventeen- or eighteen-year-old may be unusually mature, or be married to a strong and stable older person, or have parents nearby who may be counted on for help. In general, though, we believe that, in Western industrial societies, any age under twenty-one for a mother, and twenty-three for a father, entails some emotional risk for the offspring. Any age below eighteen can be downright dangerous.

2. *Am I young enough?* This question needn't be asked by anyone who hasn't reached the age of thirty-five or forty. Being older, and therefore more "mature," is no guarantee of good parenthood. For one thing, there is added danger of birth defects when parents begin to reach those ages. There is also more risk of illness and a decline in the energies needed to keep up with young children, especially if they're difficult.

Psychologically, people approaching middle age can often become *too* stable, almost rigid, in their characters, especially by age forty-five.

Another danger, which seems to be growing more common in our restless era, is the tendency in middle age for a man or woman to feel suddenly discontented with life, to want to strike out in some new creative or adventurous direction. Parenthood can of course *be* that, but only if it is so perceived and appreciated.

Otherwise, the discontent can take the form of a resurgent adolescence, a yearning for self-gratification rather than the giving of gratification to a new human being, a desire to shed responsibilities rather than take on new ones, a rebellion against the "trap" of marriage and parenthood. Anyone who feels this way should certainly not become a parent.

On the other hand, older people who are still in good health, in reasonably secure financial condition, are well motivated, and have a good relationship, can derive enormous satisfaction from parenthood, and may well turn out the kind of children anyone would be grateful to have in the world.

3. *Am I wealthy enough?* The case of Fred, Lynn's father, points up some of the disadvantages of being raised in a poor family. Not that affluence itself provides insurance. Alice's father had plenty of money—as his family did—but he didn't know how to give of himself.

Wealth consists of more than material goods. It includes all the riches of human resources—love, understanding, patience, compassion, a sense of humor, the capacity for joy.* Too often a person raised in poverty-stricken circumstances has an even harder time acquiring these other riches; so he may be doubly handicapped. On the other hand, men and women with inadequate finances may still be superb parents if they have the strength, stability, and motivation to surmount this disadvantage. So anyone who *is* disadvantaged by poverty should take an even more searching look at his or her other qualifications.

4. *Am I healthy enough?* Alice's childhood history helps us understand the emotional risks for a child when a parent is ill, even when the illness is only physical. The risks can be much greater if either of the parents is mentally ill. Psychiatric problems are of special importance in the medical history of a prospective parent. Any mental or emotional disturbances that have been severe enough for extended treatment should give long pause, though much depends on the specific nature of the trouble. Especially significant is a history of manic-depressive illness or schizophrenia in the parent. The risk of

---

*As Nikki Giovanni put it, in her poem "Nikki-Rosa":

and though you're poor it isn't poverty that
concerns you
. . . .

but only that everybody is together and you
and your sister have happy birthdays and very good christmasses
and I really hope no white person ever has cause to write about me
because they never understand Black love is Black wealth and they'll
probably talk about my hard childhood and never understand that
all the while I was quite happy.

transmitting schizophrenia, whether biologically or otherwise, is higher than 50 percent if both parents are afflicted.

Even without any official psychiatric diagnosis, care, or therapy, Lynn's family history makes clear how easily and unwittingly parents can pass on to children their own private vertical epidemics. A person studying her own qualifications should ask herself—and try hard to remember, or find out from others in her family—what her parents were like. Were they emotionally stable? Was childhood a happy time for her—or full of misery? Did her parents make her feel unwanted, deprived of love, badly neglected? Were they disappointed because they wanted a boy instead? Did either of them abandon her—physically or emotionally? Did either or both stay away for long periods of time?

There is no easy formula for assessing the damaging imprints of one's early history, or one's success in overcoming them. But it is vital for the emotional health of any future child to make an honest judgment of the ways in which one's own personal life experience may have rendered her the inadvertent carrier of a vertical epidemic. Anyone who needs help in answering these questions, or in rooting out suspected repetition compulsions, should not hesitate to seek professional help for that reason alone.

5. *Am I well enough motivated?* As we have pointed out, some people seem to make exceptional parents no matter what their handicaps, while others do poorly no matter what their advantages. The critical difference often lies in the quality and strength of their motivation and commitment.

The early years of a child's life, as we keep repeating, *are* the crucial years in setting the limits to what kind of human being she may become. The deprivations suffered by Fred and Alice—and, in her turn, Lynn—were much more damaging than deprivations in later years might have been.

To guide a child successfully through these years, to give her the necessary love and *continuity of attention*, requires the devoted care and presence of a familiar human being with whom the child identifies as her principal source of trust and gratification. This person is usually the child's mother—though it can be a father, grandmother, aunt, or a hired nurse, under special circumstances. We believe that a woman who is not ready to commit a large investment of her time and energy for these early years (hardly longer than it takes to get a college degree)—or who cannot get a willing, qualified, reliable substitute—should not become a mother. Wanting a child must include this kind of commitment. The same is true of the father, if he is to be the principal caregiver. The point is that at least *one* of the parents should take on this responsibility—and make the necessary commitment.

People who look upon motherhood or fatherhood as an imposition or a distasteful duty will be handicapped as parents—which means their child will be handicapped. The same is true of parents who have children out of the same distorted motivations that led Alice and Fred to have Lynn.

As we saw in the last chapter, there are right and wrong reasons for wanting and having children.

To feel confident about choosing parenthood, you should be certain in your own mind that you are a person who loves children, or at least likes them; that you have a realistic, unromanticized notion about what the task involves; that you have a positive outlook on life; that you are capable of long-term commitments; that you care about people; that you take pleasure in enhancing other people's lives; that you would take at least as much care with, and pride in, turning out a first-rate human being as, say, a professional gardener would in the painstaking development of a prizewinning flower or a self-respecting sculptor would in producing a massive and complicated work of art.

Unlike the sculptor, though, you can't look upon a child as raw material to carve into your own prior image. The work is more like what the gardener does—create the best environment for the flower to thrive in and to grow into what *it* ought to become.

6. *Is our relationship good enough?* This could be the most important question of all. Each partner in a marriage may feel qualified to be a parent—but are *they* qualified to be parents *together?* Not necessarily.

A poor relationship, bad communication, constant bickering and tension, a conflict of personalities, a competition of ambitions, a wide divergence of tastes in life-style—all augur ominously for the future child's emotional security. Even when wife and husband are each relatively free of liabilities, if they aren't comfortable with each other, the child isn't likely to be comfortable with them. If they aren't committed to each other, without children, neither can they make the commitment parenthood demands. If the marriage needs doctoring, they should see the doctor first—and the doctor they see shouldn't be an obstetrician.

On the other hand, a really good relationship can make up for a lot of individual disqualifiers. One could even take two people with the same list of disqualifiers as Fred and Alice—and, with a good relationship, see them overcome these liabilities.

Suppose Fred and Alice had actually come to us, prior to conceiving Lynn, looking for guidance. What would our advice have been? We would have suggested their waiting at least five years before having a child.

The prognosis for their marriage was anything but hopeful. Chances are it would have ended anyway before the five years were up. Just the same, Fred and Alice, *without children*, did stand a chance of working out some of their major difficulties. The presence of a child was bound to put too many pressures on them, and offer too many temptations to use the child to play out their compulsions, and to get even with their parents through each other—which they could not have done so easily had they not become parents themselves.

In their case, the decision to have a baby without delay triggered the reenactment of their own histories, ensured their breakup, and guaranteed that the child would be psychologically crippled. Five years later, with Fred twenty-six and Alice twenty-two, they would both have been more mature, and perhaps have outgrown their leftover adolescence. In fact, if the marriage had *lasted* five years, that alone would have been evidence that they had worked through some of their disqualifiers and built a more durable relationship.

While no one can issue a set of instructions on how to turn out perfect children, or even to say what perfection is in human terms, we can use existing knowledge to help reduce the *avoidable, predictable defects.*

If our consciousness-raising efforts are even partially successful, people may begin to reflect, *before* they marry, on their qualifiers and disqualifiers for parenthood, and those of the prospective spouse; and on what hazards might be multiplied by the combination. But self-inquiry even at this stage may be too late. It's very hard for people who are already in love to accept reasons for calling off the wedding.

At some future time, with a different emotional orientation, young people may consider these matters before falling in love—or perhaps even before dating seriously. The result could be a partial return to a more calculated form of marriage—not to ensure a perfect match, but rather to avoid a serious mismatch. There may even be computer banks to help us make such judgments.

But we do not have to wait for these futuristic speculations to be realized. Even now, as we hope we have demonstrated, it is possible for couples who are concerned, and willing to face themselves honestly, to assess their joint qualifications for parenthood. And, in each case where the disqualifiers predominate, to cut short the virulent continuation of at least one vertical epidemic.

4

The Parent's Biology
and the Child's Psyche

Every human life is in a way a successive shedding of some sort of skins
from beginning to end. We carry something of the past forward into
time but discard much as we go along. Simply to exist is to be in contin-
ual self-renewal, but to know this fully we also need to see ourselves
from egg to eternity, whatever our individual eternity may consist of.
—N. J. Berrill,
THE PERSON IN THE WOMB

UNTIL the latter decades of the twentieth century,
parents had no meaningful control over the physical well-being, at
birth, of the children they brought into the world. There were no
grounds even for the hope that prospective parents might exercise
some choice as to whether a child would be born sound or defective.
They could pray, they could propitiate the gods in whatever ways
their beliefs suggested, but intelligent human intervention was
never an option.

Now that some choice does exist, and to a more considerable degree than most people have yet come to realize, we tend to feel uneasy about using what seem to be godlike powers. Almost any new
freedom makes us uneasy. It means decisions can—perhaps must—
be made, and there are new responsibilities to be shouldered.

Uneasy or not in the matter of procreative choice, once we know
that we do have the freedom and the power, we are obliged to consider the possibility of exercising them. Nor can we avoid the realization
that a decision *not* to exercise them now becomes a positive action
with ethical consequences. The quality of the human future may

well depend upon these individual yea-or-nay votes of ours, which, all taken together, constitute a critical ballot. And any given day, for a given individual, may be Election Day.

In chapter 1 we spoke of our "biological smokestacks" and our "psychic oil spills" that "pollute," unbalance and disorganize our "social ecology." In former days, when a factory owner put up a smokestack or a tanker captain spilled some oil at sea, it was all in the name of healthy progress and free enterprise, and it would not have occurred to us to ask such entrepreneurs to think of the consequences. Now that we have some understanding of true ecological hazards, we have been forced—for the sake of the planetwide preservation of air and water—to place some limits on uninhibited free enterprise and to think in terms of more global, long-range ecological premises.

It is time now to begin thinking in a similar vein about our social ecology—*not*, as in the case of protecting our physical environment, by coercive or punitive measures, but rather through persuasion and consciousness raising. One cannot compare human children with smokestacks and oil spills except metaphorically. What nevertheless forces us to think in terms of voluntary procreative responsibility is that the parent who is contemplating the creation of a child with foreseeable physiological or emotional handicaps (depending on their severity) is very much in the position of the factory owner or the tanker captain who—before acting—can foresee the consequences and decide either to proceed or not to.

We can arrive at only a partial consensus on the meaning of a term like "birth defects." A seriously defective child, unless she is too incompetent mentally to comprehend human concerns, is likely to find life burdensome. That burden may be heavy to society too, even if measured by the purely monetary criteria of lifetime custodial care (often rather poor care) and the tying up of resources, facilities, and personnel that might be employed elsewhere.

The burden of a birth-defective child is, as a rule, borne most heavily by the immediate family of the afflicted individual. A loving family with mature parents may considerably mitigate the strain, and the presence of a defective or retarded child may even be looked upon as an enrichment, but in most cases such a presence constitutes a drain on all the family's resources. Other siblings, and the parents themselves, may feel deprived and resentful of the attention, energy, and finances that must be lavished on the special one. The resentment usually is partly unconscious and generates guilt feelings that add to the burden. As for the special one herself, if her sensitivity is not blunted, she understands that the attention she needs, even when it is freely and lovingly given, does constitute a burden on the others—and this knowledge adds to *her* burden.

We are told on all sides that the world is in a mess, that humankind is at a crossroads in its history and evolution, and that the next couple of generations may decide whether or not our species continues to survive in more than a brutish, retrogressive fashion. And we have to agree. It is a matter of no small urgency, then, that our new population-in-the-making contain a smaller proportion of individuals handicapped by avoidable afflictions that incapacitate them—or even render them dangerous to the rest of us—and a larger proportion of individuals who are sane and sound enough to contribute to the solutions rather than to the problems.

As soon as one begins thinking in this fashion, a warning flag must, on the instant, be hoisted: To try consciously to bring people into the world as defect-free as possible (we are not likely to run out of defects for a long time to come) for the sake of our future social ecology is not to be translated into similar thoughts and considerations in regard to our present coinhabitants of this planet. Though some people in unfortunate circumstances are "burdens" in that they require an unusual quantity of special care and attention, the burden, in each such case, is one we should be willing to accept. None of us is without imperfections of one kind or another and each member of the human species is our full-fledged and fully valued Earthmate. Each of us, someday, in some way, will be a burden to someone. Life, at its best, is not a carefree enterprise.

Morality here is clear-cut: We believe that, starting from the moment of birth (or advanced pregnancy), each individual who comes into being deserves every chance for the fullest possible life and the finest health; that all of society's resources—from economic through physical and emotional—be brought into play for a child's benefit. In practice, of course, society often does not succeed in carrying out its moral designs; but this is at least the authors'—and most people's—moral *position.*

Yet every set of parents who have been through a pregnancy where there is reason to worry about the outcome (and whenever is the outcome 100 percent free of doubt?) knows the anxiety of waiting for the delivery of a normal, healthy baby. If the newborn turns out to be obviously defective in some way, there is great dismay—and all-around agreement that this is a tragedy. And who does not want to avoid a tragedy?

Inasmuch as we do make ourselves, at least in principle, morally responsible for everyone in the world, then the other facet of our morality must be a firm resolution to keep every individual as free of defects and handicaps as possible, to make each new birth a fully considered and morally responsible act; in other words, to keep the harm from our biological smokestacks and our psychic oil spills at as low a level as possible.

There remains, of course, an understandable reluctance to exercise this kind of decision. Which of us does not know someone who is "defective" in some way—whom we are nevertheless very glad to have in our lives, and in the world?

One can sit, for example, on a porch in Larchmont, New York, with Karen Killilea—famous as the main character of her mother's books, *Karen* and *With Love from Karen*—and altogether forget that Karen, born with cerebral palsy, is wheelchair-bound and was kept alive only through a series of medical heroics. She is an attractive, intelligent, witty, articulate, and altogether charming young woman; and no one who knows her would be anything but scandalized at the suggestion of her absence from the world.

Or one can imagine an admirer of that brilliant literary critic, George Steiner, meeting him for the first time at Churchill College, Cambridge, and gradually becoming aware that one of his arms is considerably shorter than the other—a birth defect. Current prenatal diagnostic technology might have detected this problem. And if the admirer had recently been arguing that people with predictable birth defects be denied admittance to the world (should their parents so decide), he might be jolted to think that, had the policies he advocates been in effect at the time, there would be no George Steiner!

Turning from contemporary friends and acquaintances, we think back to the gnarled, gnomelike Charles Proteus Steinmetz, the wizard who made such enormous contributions to mathematics, science, technology—and to the happiness of other people. Or dwarfish figures from history like Alexander Pope or Toulouse-Lautrec. We are reminded that people who are stunted physically can be giants intellectually and creatively, with our planet much the richer for their passage. Thomas Mann has repeatedly made the point, especially in his writings on Nietzsche and Dostoevsky, that affliction often produces genius—just as we recognize (and will elaborate upon in a later chapter) that adversity in childhood may challenge the individual to unusual strengths and achievements.

For every Steinmetz or Pope or Toulouse-Lautrec, however, there are people by the hundreds of thousands who have led marginal, pain-racked existences because of congenital defects.* And for every defective genius in history, it is highly likely that thousands of potential Shakespeares and Mozarts have been warped and silenced forever. Moreover, the genius who is defective sometimes turns out to be an angry, evil genius like Adolf Hitler who—compensating for his misery by projecting it outward—visited pain, misery, and death on millions of innocent people. On balance, the world is poorer for human defectiveness.

Today a whole spectrum of opportunities exists to exercise some control in the matter, all the way from genetic counseling, prenatal diagnosis, and simple forethought to contraception and early legal abortion. For those who are still inclined to argue that it is somehow sinful to prevent potential human beings from coming into the world, let us review some relevant aspects of how people do in fact come into the world: Of the 500,000-or-so incipient eggs each woman carries in her ovaries (only about 500 of which develop and are released during her lifetime), no two are exactly alike in every detail; of the *hundreds of millions* of spermatozoa deposited with *each* male ejaculation (all of them competing in a random race to reach and fertilize the egg), no two are exactly alike. Even where the same mother

---

*"Congenital" is not the same as "genetic." Congenital means "born with"—but the defect may be either truly hereditary through a fault in the genetic instructions, or merely the result of some event or deprivation that occurred in the prenatal environment; or, in some cases, a combination of the two.

and father are involved, each combination of sperm and egg produces a unique individual who would not have resulted from any other combination.

Any other combination, of any egg and any sperm, would have produced a *different* individual. In brief, millions upon millions of potential human beings, each with his or her own unduplicatable characteristics (potential geniuses undoubtedly among them) *fail* to be created every day. Every normal man has in his loins the potential for creating a child almost any hour of any day in his postpubescent life. Every normal woman, during her period of ovulation, is in the same situation. Merely by abstaining from having intercourse, these men and women are—carrying this line of reasoning to its extreme—committing the sin of preventing the birth of potential people; the sperm and the egg are wasted. A male who remains celibate or a female who clings to her virginity wastes his/her entire lifetime supply of sperm/eggs.

If it is sinful to prevent the procreation of potential people—of whatever makeup—then one could argue as a corollary that it is everyone's moral *duty* to produce the maximum number of progeny. This would include everyone who had reached the age of biological competence, married or unmarried, mature or immature, mentally retarded, prisoners and religious votaries. Each would be obliged to have intercourse as frequently as possible—the male, preferably with an ovulating female; the ovulating female, with many *different* men in order to increase the chances of impregnating herself (for the good biological reason that a man who returns for an immediate repeat encounter has a lower viable sperm count).

Reduced to this level of absurdity, it is clear that everyone exercises procreative choice—if only by default—every time he or she refrains from engaging in any activity that might lead to pregnancy. Purposeful choice merely involves doing the same thing more intelligently.

Once we acknowledge the desirability of minimizing the baggage of troubled emotions that each individual totes into the world, and once we understand the monumental influence biology has on psychology, we also understand that preventive psychiatry may well begin with preventive biology.

Where, then, does the would-be parent begin?

One begins with a long, honest look at oneself—and should demand the same kind of frank self-appraisal from one's spouse or fiancé(e). What is his or her true medical history? Might any ailments be genetic in character? Have there been illnesses that seem to "run in the family"? Ask around. Sometimes this information is hard to get. Family members may be rather vague about what Aunt Nellie died of, or just why Cousin George was hardly ever let out of the house. Part of the difficulty in assessing possible genetic disease is simply lack of data, lack of awareness, lack of adequate family records, sometimes with the additional handicap of false shame—the antiquated but still prevalent notion that "bad blood will tell"—again, as in the case of illegitimacy, an unwarranted social stigma. A husband or wife may even fear that the spouse will blame him/her for being heir to some defect or disease, or the tendency toward it. Indeed, a person's own self-esteem may suffer for the same deep-rooted reasons. Birth defects have historically been looked upon as punishment from the gods (always somehow deserved), or as harbingers of bad news. In some times and places defective children were simply killed and their parents exiled or ostracized. A seventeenth-century mother in Scandinavia was burned as a witch for just such reason. No wonder we have leftover feelings of guilt and blame where birth defects are concerned. When fear is clothed in mystery, such irrational feelings inevitably result. Now that the reasons for birth defects are no longer so mysterious, however, we are free to shed the anachronistic emotions that still accompany them.

There is a long and growing list of ailments that are known to be genetic in origin—more than two thousand of them. Most are extremely rare, occurring in a range from one out of one hundred thousand to one in a million live births. Even the most common among them, cystic fibrosis, afflicts only one in every sixteen hundred newborns. Some genetic illnesses occur principally among certain ethnic groups. Sickle-cell anemia strikes mainly at American blacks, Tay-Sachs disease at Jews of Eastern European ancestry, Cooley's anemia (thalassemia) at Greeks, Italians, and other Mediterraneans. Very few of the specific genetic diseases affect large percentages of the population, and some are so rare that the average physician may go through a lifetime of practice without seeing a single case. Taken together, however, all these two-thousand-plus ailments do handicap a considerable number of people—and for each of the victims and her family, the statistics become an irrelevant abstraction.

Prospective parents usually pay little attention to the possibilities unless some gross defect or obviously hereditary disease has appeared repeatedly in the family, or unless they have already given birth to one defective child and are concerned about the odds on the next one. But now there is the opportunity of genetic counseling, and not just as a desperate, last-resort holler for help. Taken as a routine preventive measure, it can minimize or eliminate the chances of birth defects.

Genetic counseling has come alive as a practical medical specialty only in the last twenty to twenty-five years. In 1951 Sheldon C. Reed of the University of Minnesota, taking a census of genetic counselors in the United States, was able to find only himself and nine others! And the counseling they were equipped to give was quite limited. In the intervening years genetic knowledge has proliferated, and so have genetic counseling centers. They have sprung up by the hundreds, all over the country, in a cooperative network that few lay people, and even too few doctors, know about. The genetic counseling field is growing so fast that any figures we might set down here would have become obsolete between writing and publication. Even so, once the word gets around to all who need it that such counseling is available, the demand for it will quickly exceed the supply.

One reason genetic counseling has become the focus of renewed interest is that genetic diseases have taken on new medical importance. It isn't that the proportion of congenital defects has increased. The incidence has actually remained fairly steady—about 5 out of 100 live births—for the past seventy years. But the *relative* importance of birth defects has grown as other causes of infant mortality, especially the infectious diseases, have been successfully dealt with. In 1900 the American infant mortality rate was 150 per 1,000 live births. Congenital defects made up only 4 percent of that total. The mortality rate today has gone down to 16 per 1,000. Thus birth defects constitute an impressive 25 percent of the revised total.

This is not to imply that the importance of genetic medicine has been artificially inflated by arbitrarily playing with numbers. More than 200,000 children *are* born with congenital malformations or defects of one sort or another every year in this country alone. Only 20 percent of these are considered to be purely genetic—that is, due solely to the transmission of faulty hereditary information. Another 20 percent are thought to be purely environmental, caused by external factors at some point between conception and birth—viruses, drugs, radiation—something damaging or missing in the course of prenatal development. The remaining 60 percent are believed to be caused by the interaction of hereditary and environmental factors. Whatever the causes, once they are tracked down and understood, medical science can begin to treat, cure, predict, or prevent them.

The organization that rose most vigorously to this challenge is the same organization that spearheaded and coordinated the successful all-out assault against polio in the forties and early fifties, a time when polio was—in the United States, at least—the scariest of childhood infectious diseases. Fresh from that victory, the newly named National Foundation–March of Dimes turned its attention to birth defects. Since 1958 it has devoted many millions of its dollars to fundamental research, enabling numerous investigators to enter the new field. It has set up a network of genetic counseling centers for diagnosis and treatment—more than 100 of them—and encouraged the setting up of others; and has used every available resource to help educate both physicians and the public. Among its considerable contributions is a compendium of birth-defects information for doctors and an international directory telling doctors all over the world where they can get help. Since few counseling centers can provide overall expertise in the vast, sprawling frontiers of genetic research and treatment (most specialize in particular diseases, diagnostic techniques, or therapies), easy communication is indispensable to the steady flow of information to the people who need it. The March of Dimes, in collaboration with the Tufts University Medical Center, has just set up a computerized birth-defects center to facilitate this information flow.

What kind of advice can a genetic counselor offer? It is likely to be in the form of probabilities. If a woman is already pregnant, there are new methods for diagnosing close to one hundred genetic diseases of the fetus *in utero* with a high degree of accuracy. The most frequently used of these techniques is amniocentesis, which entails taking a sample of amniotic fluid, and then growing cells from that sample in tissue culture. It is now possible to diagnose some birth defects without going into the fetal sac, by measuring fetal proteins in the mother's blood.

Through use of the new prenatal diagnostic techniques, the prospective parents will be told that the child either does or does not have the feared defect. In the former case, their only option is to have the defective child or to abort.

Not all birth defects can be diagnosed prenatally. The genetic counselor will find out all she can about both spouses and both their families. She will take whatever physical tests (usually blood studies) she deems appropriate. Then she will finally say something like, "I'm afraid that your child, if it is a boy, has a 50 percent chance of having hemophilia. If it is a girl, she will be normal except in those rare instances when a female carrier marries a male who has the disease, but may have the capacity to pass the disease on to her sons."* Some genetic diseases are "sex-linked"—or "X-linked," meaning they are carried on the female X chromosome. In the case of hemophilia, only females carry the defective gene, but nearly all those afflicted with the disease are male.†

A number of congenital defects are due to gross chromosomal abnormalities. The most common of these is Down syndrome, previously called mongolism. Children with Down syndrome are mentally retarded—sometimes only mildly, sometimes severely. They usually have poor muscle tone, an oversized tongue, and the slanted upper eyelids from which the "mongoloid" designation originally derived. They have a high rate of heart defects, a greater-than-average susceptibility to leukemia. In the past, most died early. Four thousand babies with this syndrome are born annually in the

---

*In fact, amniocentesis reveals the sex of the fetus, so, in most cases the counselor will be able to omit some of these "ifs."

†If all the female carriers of the bad gene decided to go childless, the incidence of hemophilia would be considerably reduced in a single generation. The same is true of some other sex-linked diseases.

United States, and most have ahead of them a lifetime of expensive (though not necessarily high-quality) custodial care; many are successfully educated to become reasonably happy and productive citizens. Because the chromosomes of a dividing cell can be photographed and counted, the extra chromosome that is the villain in Down syndrome can be easily detected, and the disease thus predicted before birth.

Most genetic diseases do not reveal themselves so readily. The more typical genetic disorder is what used to be called an "inborn error of metabolism"—that is, a mistake in a single gene buried somewhere in that massive biochemical manual of genetic instructions. There are undoubtedly many such errors that have no harmful effect. But if the defective gene results in the absence or malfunction of a vital enzyme (which is what usually happens in a genetic disease), the consequences can be disastrous.

As one example, take the Lesch-Nyhan syndrome. This is a neurological disease that only males inherit. Its victims are mentally retarded, they engage in all manner of muscular contortions that they cannot control, and they keep biting their lips and fingers, often to the point of inflicting severe damage. All this because the mother carried a defective gene for a single enzyme, without which a simple biochemical conversion fails to take place in the cells. Most cells can get along without this enzyme, but cells in the basal ganglia of the brain cannot. The result of this tiny genetic abnormality is a writhing, self-mutilating, and altogether terribly handicapped individual.

Most single-gene disorders follow classical Mendelian patterns and can thus be assigned fairly accurate probability values. This is clearer if we look at a normal hereditary trait such as eye color. The brown-eyed gene is dominant; the blue-eyed gene is recessive. If one parent has brown eyes, and the other blue, then the brown predominates. Yet two brown-eyed parents can have a blue-eyed baby if *both* of them have a recessive blue gene. With two such parents, the odds are that, out of any four children, one will have two brown genes, two will have one of each—a dominant brown and a recessive blue, as the parents do themselves—and the fourth will have two blue genes, and therefore blue eyes. Thus any given child of these parents will have a one-in-four chance of being blue-eyed. (We emphasize that these are odds—statistical probabilities—though this is not the way the numbers would necessarily work out in a given family.)

It works very similarly with single-gene diseases, though sometimes the mathematics is more complicated. Normality usually dominates, and abnormalities are usually recessive, so a child needs to get a double dose before it is affected. Just knowing what the chances are does not automatically resolve the dilemma, of course. The parents have to decide whether or not they want to gamble; or, if they lose, what the risks entail. Some diseases may not be so impossibly hard to live with. Hemophilia and cystic fibrosis, for example, are much more treatable than they used to be—though still extremely troublesome and life-shortening.

The decision may be particularly difficult in an affliction like Huntington's disease—a *dominant* gene effect (so the odds are usually fifty-fifty)—where symptoms ordinarily do not appear until the victim is around thirty-five years old, or even older. As the years go by, the mental faculties falter, the arms and legs and even the body may go through wild involuntary motions; the person becomes ill-tempered, and just seems to grow old fast. Yet, are thirty-five good years of life to be disdained? The average human life span used to be not much more than that. The best-known recent victim of Huntington's disease was the versatile folk singer and composer Woody Guthrie, whose widow, Marjorie, has devoted herself to promoting research and public education in birth defects. One might ask: Would anyone want to have denied the world the lustrous presence of Woody Guthrie? No one can make these decisions for other people; one can only provide a realistic appraisal of the risks.

There remains a large and significant area of genetic disease that only a few genetic counselors have just begun to consider as legitimately within their purview. We are talking about those defects and diseases that, while not specifically designated as hereditary, do nevertheless seem to contain a large genetic component. They include some of our major diseases, and in nearly every case the extent of the hereditary involvement is controversial. Yet it is hard to deny that one can inherit a *tendency*, a statistical predisposition, to cancer, leukemia, heart disease, atherosclerosis, high blood pressure, epilepsy, diabetes, manic-depressive psychosis, and perhaps schizophrenia. And these by no means exhaust the catalog.

Thus faulty heredity may interfere with the health of a truly substantial segment of the population.

Just how such tendencies are inherited, or how they work in the body, is only now beginning to be understood. Cedric O. Carter of the Medical Research Council of London has studied many case records and family histories of ailments that seem to run in families, though they are not genetic diseases in the strict sense of the word. Among them are cleft lip and palate, pyloric stenosis (a narrowing of the aperture between the stomach and small intestine), clubfoot, spina bifida (a spinal defect where parts or all of the vertebral arches are missing and the membranes protrude), diabetes, heart disease, schizophrenia, and rheumatoid arthritis. None of these is the result of a simple, single-gene disorder, whether dominant or recessive. Rather they seem to be *polygenic*—having many genes involved. (It should not be surprising that defects are inherited in various ways, for so are our normal characteristics. The color of our eyes may be determined by a single gene; but traits like intelligence, stature, blood pressure, and fingerprint patterns require the interaction of many genes.) If these defects and diseases are polygenic, some are also, in Carter's term, "multifactorial"; that is, they come about through the influence of a number of environmental factors rather than from a single cause.

In the case of a disease that runs in the family, then, this is what appears to happen: Everybody in the family carries a certain number of "risk genes" from the family pool; if any member of the family has a *sufficient* number of them, he or she may be thought of as having crossed the "threshold of risk." That is, such people have a genetic predisposition to the disease—though their below-the-threshold brothers and sisters may not. This does not mean they will surely contract the disease. It means that if they encounter the environmental factors that precipitate it, their resistance to it will be lower. It may be that the same emotional stresses that produce schizophrenia in one child, for example, may not affect her siblings in the same manner (they are genetically tougher). A man who comes down with lung cancer after smoking two packs of cigarettes a day for twenty years may wonder why his brother, who has smoked *three* packs a day for twenty-five years, seems free of the disease. It might be because the first brother had crossed the threshold of genetic risk and the other, by lucky chance, had not.

Cancer is a particularly touchy area of genetics that, until very recently, all but a few* would approach in only a gingerly way. One of those few individuals has been Henry T. Lynch of the Creighton University School of Medicine in Omaha. (He has also been the compiler of the National Foundation's *International Directory of Genetic Services.*) Writing in *Cancer Bulletin,* Lynch says, "Lung cancer serves as an excellent example of host versus environmental interactions. Tokuhata has shown that the combined risk of smoking and familial factors in this neoplasm is multiplicative rather than additive. For example, the patient with the familial factor who does not smoke has about a four-fold lung cancer risk. However, if he is a heavy smoker, his risk will be about 14 times greater than that for individuals who do not have a first-degree relative with lung cancer."

As Lynch has pointed out, laboratory animals are deliberately bred, for experimental purposes, to be either especially *susceptible* or especially *resistant* to cancer. If there were no genetic factor involved in the causes of cancer, this would not be possible. But does the effect on laboratory animals necessarily apply to people? Not necessarily. But W. E. Heston had this to say in the *American Journal of Human Genetics* as long ago as 1952: "From genetic studies in mice one is forced to conclude that probably every type of cancer in man can be subject to genic influences so that under certain conditions the genotype of the individual may be the deciding factor in determining whether or not the individual develops a certain type of cancer. . . . One who has worked with these strains of mice, therefore, no longer asks if cancer is inherited in man. Instead he asks how is cancer inherited in man, and how important are the genetic factors in determining whether or not cancer will occur."

There are a few rare types of cancer, according to Louis Pelner of the Swedish Hospital in Brooklyn, New York, "in which dominant

---

*The National Cancer Institute, however, has been taking an increasing interest in the genetic aspects of cancer.

genes cause the cancer to develop." One of these is multiple polyposis, a condition characterized by the growth of polyps—sometimes by the hundred, or even by the thousand—in the intestine. These growths are seldom malignant, but they are often the precursors of carcinoma of the colon. Another such disease is retinoblastoma, a rare form of eye cancer that strikes at children in their first years of life, and is fatal unless caught and removed while still contained within the globe of the eye. C. V. Weller has suggested that the evidence here of hereditary effect is so clear-cut that a request for sterilization is justified for any child who has survived retinoblastoma, or for any mother who has already had a child with retinoblastoma.

Most other forms of cancer seem to fit into Carter's polygenic, multifactorial category. Among these is breast cancer, which does seem to run in families, though a viral involvement is also suspected here. *Biomedical News* reported a Bombay study that revealed that Parsi women have a 10 to 25 percent incidence of breast cancer, compared to 1 to 2 percent for Hindu and Muslim women living in the same part of Bombay. (American women have a 4 to 5 percent incidence.) Pelner, writing in the *Journal of the American Geriatric Society*, describes a number of case studies where as many as five sisters in a single family were victims of breast cancer.

Pelner reports similar studies of families with a high incidence of gastric cancer. Of unusual historical interest is the fact that the Bonaparte family had a strong predisposition to carcinoma of the stomach. "There seems no doubt," says Pelner, "that Napoleon died from an extensive carcinoma of the lesser curvature of the stomach with peritoneal and lymph gland involvement. Napoleon's father died at age 39 from cancer of the stomach, proved at autopsy; his younger sister, Caroline, died of cancer of the stomach; two other sisters, Elisa and Pauline, died at ages 43 and 44 of probable gastric carcinoma; and a brother Lucien died at age 65, probably from gastric cancer."

Well, what does it all mean? If someone in one's family has had cancer, should one refrain from having children? Not at all. It's a matter of care, concern, and good sense, of weighing and balancing all the considerations.

One must keep in mind, too, that the mere incidence of a certain condition in a given family is not positive evidence of its genetic nature. In the not too distant past, pellagra, a disease that unquestionably ran in families, was widely believed to be hereditary. But it turned out that pellagra ran in families only because all the members of the family ate the same vitamin-poor diet. It was then nutritional research, not genetic research, that supplied the missing B vitamin and stopped pellagra (with its gastrointestinal upsets, its nervous disturbances, and its skin eruptions) from running in families.

F. Clarke Fraser of McGill University in Montreal warns how easy it is to assume, mistakenly, that a set of symptoms are genetically caused. "This is particularly true," he writes in *Hospital Practice,* "with such pathological catchalls as 'mental retardation,' which, as we all know, can result from a great variety of causes." He cites the case of a woman patient who was worried about having children because a brother and two first cousins were mentally retarded. But an investigation showed that the apparently familial retardation was due to other causes—in two cases, brain damage at birth; in the other, coma and paralysis after a bad fall. (One of the boys the family considered to be retarded turned out to have an I.Q. of 108.) Thus reassured, Fraser's patient went ahead and had normal children.

Because of the complexity and multiplicity of the considerations involved in polygenic, multifactorial diseases, quantitative evidence is understandably hard to come by. What criteria can one use, then, to help decide whether an ailment really runs in the family? "As a rule of thumb," says Cecil B. Jacobson of the George Washington University Medical Center, "if more than one individual in your family has the same disease, it *may* be hereditary." In his own obstetrical practice, Jacobson asks each of his patients to compile a family tree for herself and her husband, listing all their relatives— aunts, uncles, grandparents on both sides, going all the way, if possible, to the level of second cousins (the children of first cousins). If there are four people in the patient's immediate family, this may produce a list of anywhere from fifty to one hundred close relatives. If as many as three or four of these have, say, diabetes—particularly if it is "early-onset diabetes," a type that begins before age thirty— then it can be thought of as an ailment that does run in the family.

The same kind of reasoning can be applied to histories of early heart attack within the family.*

Wherever you can, find out at what age your parents' relatives died and what they died of. What special illnesses plagued them throughout their lives? Were there lots of miscarriages and still-births among the women? Cardiovascular troubles among the men? Evidences of mental illness? Of "nervous breakdowns"? Epileptic seizures?

Insurance companies are always interested in familial diseases. Even in the absence of data that would document in any strict scientific sense the genetic nature of a suspect ailment, a strongly indicative tendency is enough to give insurers pause. It should also be enough to give pause to would-be parents.

Amid all these ambiguities, the average person is simply not equipped to thread her way through the perplexing combinations and permutations of genetic nuance. Professional guidance must be sought. In some instances, the family doctor may know enough; but in most cases she probably does not (no disgrace to her) and she will have to refer the patient to a genetic counseling center.† With a counselor's help, the individual couple must somehow arrive at the happy medium that lies somewhere between overreacting to small risks (like the woman—another patient of Fraser's in Montreal—who had an abortion because she'd been told there was a one-in-twenty chance her baby would be born with a cleft lip) and under-reacting to larger ones.

The risk does not have to be as large as, say, cancer. Take diabetes as a moderate example. No one takes a cavalier attitude, exactly, toward diabetes; but it is easy enough to shoulder-shrug it away as a so-what eventuality. Though not yet curable, and often tricky to

---

*Some specific cardiovascular diseases, such as hypercholesterolemia, are being explicitly pinpointed as genetic diseases—and these diseases do often result in early-onset heart attacks.

†For other guidance as to where to go for help and advice regarding birth defects and genetic counseling, the best place to write is the National Foundation–March of Dimes, Box 2000, White Plains, New York 10605 (or telephone 914/428-7100). Another good source is the National Genetics Foundation, a small but active organization: 257 West 57th Street, New York, New York 10019 (telephone 212/265-3166).

manage, it is no longer thought of especially as a killer disease (yet people still do die of it). Suppose, however, there is early-onset diabetes in the families of both spouses. This multiplies the chances (a genetic counselor can put numbers on the probabilities) that at least one of their children will be afflicted. Suppose you have diabetes yourself. Depending on its type and severity, you may be giving us that shoulder shrug and asking, "What's so terrible about diabetes? I live with it, don't I?" Well, you do, but how considerably does it restrict your activities? How much anxiety does it cause you during all the years of your life? Do you really want to risk passing it on to your children—and theirs? Many studies in this country and abroad corroborate the finding that the children—even though healthy themselves—of parents who are seriously or chronically ill are much more likely to get into psychiatric difficulties than other children. How much of a handicap is your diabetes? Do your physiological problems with the disease generate risks for emotional problems as well? Might this interfere with your children's emotional health, putting them in jeopardy on two counts? You're the only one who can judge. Most children, even of sick parents, do *not* wind up needing psychiatric services; you must decide what the risk is, and how well you think you'll be able to handle your parental responsibilities.

As time goes on, we may all develop the habit of starting early in life to keep a genetic profile of ourselves—a medical family tree—which we could then compare with the genetic profile of our prospective marriage partner to see what hazards would be multiplied by the combination. This is, in effect, what a genetic counselor asks us to do—usually after we are married, since it almost never occurs to anyone to consult a counselor ahead of time. If we were to seek such advice prior to marriage, the risks to our potential children might well affect our decision. As we suggested at the end of the last chapter, young people in the future may be sufficiently educated in, and concerned with, genetics to weigh these possibilities before falling in love, perhaps even before dating seriously.

As genetic research continues, new treatments and cures are being sought for genetic diseases—drugs, enzymes, enzyme inhibitors, dietary regimes, and the like. And it seems clear that someday we will have the capacity to manipulate the genetic material directly, fixing the faulty genes and ushering in the age of genetic engineering—though the prospect raises anxieties and controversies. A number of laboratory accomplishments have already offered convincing evidence that this is no mere pipe dream. For now, however, the only way to prevent a genetic disease is to refrain from transmitting it.

What are the alternatives for a couple who suspect they are at risk, genetically speaking?

They could proceed to conceive a child, then plan an abortion if prenatal diagnosis showed the presence of a defect. But this course does assume readiness to accept abortion as an option, and is probably ruled out if abortion violates the couple's moral or religious principles.

If it is the husband's genes that are worrisome, they could make use of artificial insemination via an anonymous donor. Doctors usually select a donor who resembles the husband physically, is in good health, and who already has at least one normal child of his own. Thousands of children are born this way every year, almost always with satisfactory results—though the physician should make his patients aware of any legal dilemmas before they undertake the procedure. Fraser tells of a young woman patient whose first normally conceived baby "showed an unusual combination of malformations." Though he couldn't pin down the trouble precisely, the young woman clearly suspected the genetics on her husband's side. "Subsequently," Fraser recalls, "she had a second child who, when I examined him in the hospital, turned out to be beautifully normal. On my visiting the mother to congratulate her, I became aware that she seemed wholly unsurprised at the infant's normality, and in fact had a certain complacent gleam in her eye. On impulse I asked her whether there was anything she wanted to tell me; with a laugh she replied, 'I think you already know!' I didn't, but on further conversation it appeared she had employed a procedure that might be labeled N.I.D.—Natural Insemination Donor (the usual designation for an *artificial* insemination donor is A.I.D.)—and had even chosen the donor for his physical resemblance to her husband. This is certainly one solution to some of the problems posed by genetic disease, though hardly to be recommended by even the most

sympathetic counselor or physician!" (In this age of the sexual revolution, some couples may prefer the personally known to the anonymous donor.)

If it is the wife's genes that are worrisome, or if a couple eschews
insemination-by-donor (whether "artificial" or "natural"), what
other avenues are open? Sometime soon the embryo transfer method (using donor eggs) employed in the celebrated "first test-tube
baby" birth in England (which used the parents' own egg and
sperm) may be more widely available—though it remains controversial, both biologically and ethically. One alternative is to adopt a
child. Though adoption is often difficult to achieve, nonbiological
parents are perfectly capable of loving adopted children as their
own, and being similarly loved in return.

Let's assume that two marriage partners have decided that they
are qualified genetically to be parents. That should be the prelude to
examining with great care their *psychological* qualifications for parenthood, as outlined in the last two chapters. And if they give themselves an A, or at least a passing grade, in that department, they
should still return once more to biology before they proceed, including, in addition to consideration of the biochemical contents of their
genes, a sharp-minded survey of their current physical condition,
especially the wife. Everything she does to, and with, her body may
now begin to affect her future child's physical and emotional health.
As Cecil Jacobson has put it (writing, with Judith Ramsey, in *Family
Health*), "Regardless of age, if you seek a perfect pregnancy you
should strive for perfect health. You owe it to yourself and your future child not to rush into reproduction until you've done everything possible to bring yourself into mint condition."

If the prospective mother has any chronic infections (urinary infections, for example) which she has been neglecting, she should get
them cleared up as soon as possible. If she has extra pounds to lose,
now is the time. Does she have dental problems? Or does she know
of any treatments she'll be needing that entail anesthesia, antibiot-
ics, other drugs, or extensive X rays? Get them out of the way now,
preferably sixty to ninety days before conception. If she has been on
the Pill or using an intrauterine device, "switch to a traditional
method such as a diaphragm for three months," Jacobson advises,
"or until normal, regular periods begin again before getting preg-

nant. The waiting period allows ovulatory cycles and the reproductive tract to return to normal."

What else? Vaccination against rubella is a good idea; but if this is done, pregnancy should be assiduously avoided for at least three months "because scientists are not certain whether the virus in the vaccine causes the very birth defects the vaccine is intended to prevent."

The mother who smokes should quit; or, if she can't, she should at least cut down sharply on her number of cigarettes per day. Her alcoholic intake should also be restricted to no more than an occasional drink. And she should start to think about adequate nutrition before she and her husband even start trying to conceive. (Most women don't begin to think about proper diet and the baby's needs until they learn they are pregnant—by which time the embryo is well on its way, having done the best it could with what was available in the mother's body.) She should learn as much as she can about pregnancy and fetal development—and prepare for it in advance. (Here again, the National Foundation–March of Dimes, with its emphasis on protecting the unborn and newborn, is an excellent source of advice and information.) The prospective father should not only be giving moral support to his wife in all this, but should think about getting himself prepared physically and emotionally for his wife's pregnancy and the baby's arrival. Future research on the male reproductive system may of course reveal that a husband's sperm, too, can be defective—or perhaps damaged by alcohol or tobacco—and thus may itself contribute significantly to the risk factors.

A lot of trouble? Yes, but people are always willing to go to a lot of trouble to win a prize. An athlete puts himself in strict training long before the key moment of competition, a student studies hard before the final exam. Winning a prize even in a dog show or a flower show entails elaborate preparation. In the case of expectant parents, their prize will be the best possible baby they were able to produce, and the satisfaction of knowing that they have already begun to help prevent those emotional troubles that stem from a child's physical troubles. And best of all, they will have given their child her most advantageous start on the first and most crucial journey of life.

PART TWO

Voyage of the Personaut

In man as in animals, the physical and mental structure can be deeply affected only while the processes of anatomical and physiological organization are actively going on; the biological system becomes increasingly resistant to change after it has completed its organization. These statements are valid not only for anatomical and physiological differentiation, but also for the emergence of tastes, social attitudes, and even the perception of space in interpersonal encounters. . . .

Prenatal, neonatal, and other early influences thus constitute a continuous spectrum through which the environment conditions the whole future of the developing organism.

—René Dubos,
SO HUMAN AN ANIMAL

5

Latency and Psychological Birth

From the standpoint of culture, latency is necessary for the formation of civilization. Latency provides the period of time in which children can learn the complicated skills needed in the society. . . . It is a period when the child consolidates his image of himself in relation to the world.

—Charles Sarnoff,
LATENCY

A transition is in progress when a parent makes a remark such as the one Gesell and Ilg attribute to mothers of six year old children . . . : "He is a changed child and I do not know what has gotten into him." We sense that a transition has been accomplished when we hear parents say: "We don't have a baby anymore. Glenda goes to school. She is a big girl and does not need us the way she used to." The child is changed, she is not the same anymore, and neither parent can remain the same. . . . There is regret, but pride in the child's advancement is there too.

—Judith S. Kestenberg,
CHILDREN AND PARENTS

THE word *latency* suggests to us a marking of time. We think of a latent talent, for example, as a talent for which a potential clearly exists, though it has not yet manifested itself in visible achievement. Or we speak of a latent virus, one that has already inserted its genetic material into the host cell, mingling its genetic information with the cell's own genes—though a long time may pass (perhaps the host organism's entire lifetime) before the viral genes spring into action to express themselves as the overt symptoms of a viral infection, or perhaps a tumor. In differentiating the word *latent* from its various synonyms—dormant, quiescent, potential, abeyant—the dictionary defines it as applying to a power or quality that has not yet come into sight or action, but may at any time.

Latency as used in Freudian terminology has often been a source of confusion to lay people because it seems, at quick glance, to have little relation to the word's ordinary meaning. The period called latency in child psychiatry is in fact an intensely active period physically, full of sports, horseplay and roughhousing. It is also a time of rapid learning and lively fantasizing. Latency begins at the age of five or six and lasts until the onset of puberty at the age of about eleven or twelve—usually earlier for girls than for boys. In arriving at latency, the child should have essentially negotiated the classical Freudian psychosexual obstacle course, passing through the oral, anal, phallic, and oedipal phases (see chapter 9). At latency, if all has gone well, conscious interest in sexuality diminishes considerably, the child having reached a point in his mental growth where parents and society can more fully instill those human ethical concepts and behavior standards that his culture prescribes. Sexually, the child has become latent—so much so (unless something makes him "regress" to a previous stage) that his earlier periods of sexuality are effectively suppressed. They do not surface again, this next time in their full genitality, until puberty. The adult in his later years may have so completely forgotten the intensities of his early sexuality that he will tell you with perfect honesty that there simply was no sexuality in his life prior to puberty. In fact, so we all believed until Freud taught us otherwise.

Yet we know with certainty, from observation, that these earlier phases do occur; and we know, from an enormous accumulation of studies, that the awareness of these earlier phases may be brought out by the psychoanalytic process. If the child does not get all the way through the psychosexual obstacle course, as we just referred to it, and instead becomes "fixated" at a given stage—say, the oral or anal—the effects will be lasting, influencing him more than he ever knows as an adult, and indeed limiting how effective a parent he might be to his own children.

But of course psychosexuality is far from the whole story of development in the first six years of life. Many complex physiological processes are going on simultaneously at any given time, a number of them in synchrony with processes begun before the child's official biological birth into the world. The brain and nervous system in particular are not fully formed and organized until almost the latency period. At the same time, the child is developing emotionally, intellectually, psychologically, linguistically, socially, cognitively—one could go on with the catalog of categories—in accordance with various stages set down by Freud and Piaget, by Bruner and Kagan, by Erikson and Bowlby, by Gesell and White, by Mahler and Kohut, among so many other theorists and investigators who have been responsible for the explosive growth of new understanding in the field of early childhood development.

This is the period of life we feel justified in calling the six-year pregnancy. What are the limits of this "pregnancy"? Where does it begin and end? There is no precise point of temporal demarcation at either boundary—no starting gun that signals, "Begin now," no picture frame that says, definitively, as at a movie's close, THE END. The six-year stretch is an approximation with fuzzy extremities. It may be said to begin even prior to conception, perhaps at some arbitrary point before the performance of the sexual act that makes it come to pass, back when the child exists only as a set of images in the minds of the prospective mother and father who are deciding whether they want to become parents or not.

One could, alternatively, describe the six-year pregnancy as lasting from latency to latency—one biological, the other psychobiological. Considered in this light, the description would cover even an unplanned conception. In a sense, the oocyte destined to ripen and descend the fallopian tube (thus making itself available for fertilization), and the still-unmanufactured sperm destined to be there at the critical moment of ejaculation (and win the race against its millions of competitors), already represent a latent life. The quiescent period comes to an end with the act of conception. Soon the incipient embryo embeds itself in the uterine wall and starts to grow with amazing rapidity, requiring a special set of intrauterine circumstances. The interruption called birth is followed by a far longer and even more special set of *extra*uterine circumstances. The entire gestation period closes with the achievement of psychosocial latency, the first relatively quiescent stage since the days before sperm and egg were joined.

This latter, psychosocial gestation period may quite validly be thought of as a kind of extended postpartum pregnancy. It has in fact been so recognized, at least in part. The first year of life has been referred to as the period of "final fetalization." In medical practice, too, the new discipline of perinatology recognizes that the mother and infant must receive a continuum of care that extends for an indefinite period after birth, so that the duties and functions of the obstetrician-gynecologist and the pediatrician (as well as other collaborating specialists) merge and overlap for a time.

One is reminded of the kangaroo, born before the baby is well formed, carried for a long time in the mother's external pouch, where it remains warm, sheltered, nourished. It can look out of the pouch and finally, for increasing periods of time, venture forth to explore the nearby world. In the human case the developing infant is transferred from its internal biological womb to a more precarious psychosocial pouch, consisting, if he is fortunate, of loving parents and family in a congenial environment. Arrival at latency, with all tasks accomplished, heralds for us the psychological birth of the human child. At latency the child has achieved a degree of security and autonomy that leaves him much freer to strike out on his own. His interests shift to skills and playmates. His ego structure has reached a point that permits him to adapt his behavior more comfortably to society's standards. He has already for some time been forming a reaction against the messy and destructive impulses of his anal period. This "reaction formation," as it is technically known, is manifested by a trend toward order and neatness in his personal habits as well as a new attitude of sharing and kindness in his relations with others. He can live at peace with his parents, even emulate parental goals and behavior. He can sublimate his aggressions and frustrations through lively fantasies that are often acted out in the form of energetic games. He has begun to learn the uses of symbol manipulation and to deal in abstractions. He is capable, for the first time, of full-fledged altruistic behavior, at least on a simple level, rather than looking upon others solely as gratifiers (or frustrators) of his wants and needs. Latency is the time when the individual's unique personality structure begins to take shape, when he begins to consolidate his humanhood; the child has become a latent adolescent, a latent adult.

Successful attainment of latency by no means renders the child invulnerable. He has, after all, just *become* a fully born human *child*, with a whole new set of vulnerabilities; and good parental care must continue unabated though modified—as for every new phase of life. But after the six-year pregnancy and psychological birth into latency, the child has traversed the time of his life when he is most deeply susceptible to the kinds of damage most difficult to reverse, if indeed they prove to be reversible at all.

In embryonic and fetal development *in utero*, there are critical periods when certain influences or substances—say, a viral invasion or a toxic drug—may inflict damage that, at other, safer times, they would not. In late pregnancy, for example, a rubella infection would do little if any harm to the fetus; but if the mother incurs this mild (to her) disease during the first three months of pregnancy, the fetus is at risk of later blindness, deafness, heart problems, or mental retardation, and other, lesser kinds of injury. A fortunately rare malformation, where the embryonic optic patch fails to separate— resulting in a "Cyclops eye" in the middle of the forehead—occurs only if some toxic substance or process is present during the second week in pregnancy; once past that narrow slot of time when the patch separates into two incipient eyes, that particular hazard vanishes. Most toxic substances do their damage by interfering with some rapid growth process. Thalidomide, for instance, a drug harmless to adults and, as far as we know, to older fetuses as well, is cripplingly injurious only at the time early in pregnancy when the leg and arm buds are just beginning to take form—the time they are growing most rapidly. On the other hand, the upper lip and palate do not come together until late in pregnancy; it is then that a toxic agent could interfere with their proper fusion, and the result may be a cleft palate.

In the extrauterine phase of pregnancy, along any given pathway of development, there are similar time stretches when the child is particularly at risk. For example, any infant or young child will find it extremely stressful for his principal caretaker, usually the mother, to vanish for a period of months—to go off, for instance, on a tour of another country or continent, or for an extended hospital stay. If this occurs while the child is beginning to learn to speak—say, between his twelfth and seventeenth months—his speech development may well be retarded, perhaps severely. There is a natural time for each developmental occurrence; if it is interfered with at that time, the task of making up the deficit later—when the state of natural readiness has ended and the organism has moved on to its next stage of development—may be painfully difficult.

If a human being can be said to have a central mission in life, it is perhaps to strive for personhood; to become (though always aware of his relatedness) a separate, independent, confidently functioning individual. The extent to which he achieves this mission may dictate to a significant degree how successfully he pursues his other missions—those he assigns to himself and those assigned to him by others (or even to know the difference).

If a seeker after the stars is an astronaut, then someone in quest of personhood can fairly be called a "personaut." It may be that we remain personauts all our lives, never attaining the full-blooming potential that our genetic framework would allow under ideal circumstances. But if we are fortunate, we do reach a point where we may be said to know, in some essential sense, who we are, and to achieve real autonomy—no longer slaves to our genes, to our cultures, or to whatever hidden agendas may have been laid upon us by others, living or dead. If we are really successful, then we continue our fitful journey toward ever fuller personhood until the trip is arbitrarily terminated by senescence and death.

If a human individual's lifelong central mission is personhood, the launching pad is early childhood; and the parent, who is Mission Control itself, has no more important overall responsibility than to help the aspiring personaut get off the ground. Lift-off occurs, not with a roar as in rocketry, but gradually, quietly, through the exquisitely complex developmental processes that take place during the first years of life.

Each human newborn is a dynamic organism possessing a unique genetic potential waiting to be selectively actualized through *interac-*

tion with the world. For, contrary to previous beliefs, the neonate is not a passive blob of protoplasm to be molded by parental whim and random outside events. It is not an instrument that, if unplayed, remains silent (though that could be the eventual result if no one chooses to play it). From the day of birth, the infant takes an active part in his own development. This is true despite the fact that he experiences the world, at first, as a bewilderingly amorphous mass of sensations and happenings. He cannot yet identify himself as an individual entity separate from his environs. In the beginning, it all runs together.

Through the early years of life, amid all the threads of development that proceed in concert, the child's central task is what Margaret Mahler has called "separation-individuation"—and which Jean Piaget, approaching from another viewpoint, has termed "assimilation and accommodation." The new organism must gradually learn to identify his own perceptions and proprioceptions—those inner biological signals that tell him what is going on inside himself, in his own organs and muscles and nerves—and to distinguish these from the myriad inputs from the external world. He becomes increasingly acquainted with the self inside his skin, and recognizes what is Out There, beyond his self and skin. He organizes his self in part by assimilating the signals from the outside world, and accommodating his self to that external environment. He also soon learns to distinguish some very special kinds of entities in that environment—people—and most particularly that one "significant other" in his life, his principal caretaker, to whom he forms an intense attachment—an attachment from which he only gradually, and in fluctuating fits and starts, learns to disengage.

The developing child is said to be "double-directed"—that is, he is attentive to his internal self and to the outside world. This double-directedness is both continuous and simultaneous, entailing an intricate and constant interplay between the child and his environment, lovingly mediated by his caretakers. He is organizing his internal psychological and cognitive structures while, at the same time, systematizing his relationships with the things and people around him. He is "testing reality," testing, too, the degree of control he might hope to exercise over what happens to him. He learns not so much through direct instruction as from the concrete context of his experience, from his relationships with others, from the stimulation—which must always be appropriate to his stage of development, not more than he can handle—provided by his parents, preferably against a background of play and pleasure.

Some developmental events must occur in the first months of life, others by, say, eighteen months; many important ego-structuring stages should be essentially complete by the age of three. And so it goes, in a complexly threaded, mutually intertwined set of bio-psycho-sociological feedback loops, proceeding all the way to latency. Failure to master these critical early stages of life—failure especially to separate-and-individuate successfully, and to assimilate-and-accommodate properly—may have lasting deleterious, perhaps disastrous, consequences for that individual's emotional future, including his own later capacity as a parent to guide another new being successfully to his full psychological birth. Hence our emphasis on the candid self-examination by prospective parents of their own potential qualifiers and disqualifiers. It is not our intention in this book to spell out, in exhaustive detail, each theory, each thread of development, what to expect at each step along the way. For one thing, many fat books exist that do just that. For another, a parent does not necessarily have to understand developmental psychology in so thorough a manner. It is rather our intent to point out some of the perils on the personautical journey, with some guidance as to how they might be avoided—by individual parents, and by society at large.

When a female horned toad becomes a mother, she doesn't have to teach her newborns anything, or even worry about taking care of them. They come forth from the maternal sac and, from day one, they are on their own. A mother giraffe or zebra likewise has very little to do—though not quite as little as the horned toad; within a few hours of birth, their babies can run along beside them.

But a human newborn is helpless. It doesn't know anything, and it can't do anything. For a long period of time, during infancy and early childhood, en route to becoming a civilizable individual, the neonate requires a degree of devoted attention and nurture unknown elsewhere in the animal kingdom. A human baby is totally at the mercy of its caretakers. Left on its own to cope with its environment, *any* environment, it would quickly perish.

This is somehow not a tragic situation. Rather it signifies one of the principal distinguishing features of the human species. This long period of only gradually diminishing helplessness—during which we cannot survive without parental or surrogate-parental supervision and care—gives us our special potential for developing our humanity, our unique creative opportunity to become what other species cannot.

We are much less the slaves of the preprogrammed configurations of our genetic lattices. The instructions "written" by nature and evolution into our DNA molecules leave many blank pages to be filled in by circumstance. An ant's book of life is complete; there are no empty pages. It automatically knows its place and can do its work via its built-in hereditary "instincts." A bird knows how to build a nest. But a human baby needs to *learn* almost everything.

So he comes into the world with less, in a sense; but also with much more—with those blank pages. There is little doubt that what he inherits biologically is the result of aeons of evolutionary development, the slow accretion of all the innate wisdom that organisms acquire in their historical experience. Yet what happens to him during the early postnatal period, the quality of nurture he receives, may in some ways be of much greater importance. In determining the character of the adult woman or man, these few months and years of applied human wisdom may outweigh the centuries and millennia of blind evolution. And on the negative side, applied human folly during this period of time can probably destroy much of the child's innate but all-too-fragile organic wisdom.

Nature seems to have arranged matters, then, so that—

1. we have fewer of our essential personality and social characteristics dictated by our genes than any other of nature's creatures;

2. we require a much longer period of nurture and education, and this requirement enables us to develop into the most versatile and remarkable of all organisms on Earth—truly superior in our adaptive powers. While fully aware of our animal nature and origins, we are much more than just "naked apes."

We are by *nature* social creatures. We could not otherwise survive. *Nurture* is dictated by nature.

And the quality of that nurture is of supreme importance. That is why we find it useful to think of it as an extension of prenativity. Perhaps we should, at least metaphorically, drop the notions of "prenatal" and "postnatal" except as purely physical descriptions of the baby's location at a given time. After its exit from the mother's body, the baby is, in a very real sense, still in the womb—though it becomes a psychosocial rather than physiological womb. A child's psychosocial nutrition and development are vital to his humanhood.

We worry that, inside the mother's body, the fetus may fail to develop some critical physiological organ or function. But, once the new person has left the uterus, we forget to worry that, in an inhospitable atmosphere, entire *organs of the mind* (integrated functions) may never develop, or they may develop defectively. And these deficiencies might properly be classified as birth defects too, since a child's continuing nurture is part of his psychological birth into the human world. Thus his nurture must be of a high order. The future—all our futures—depend on it.

To meet the requirements set down by nature, the human mother, just like the chimpanzee mother, has traditionally provided the basic child nurturing, while the father has gone out to hunt the food or "earn the living." Until recently, with few known exceptions, the mother has tended to be the keeper of the hearth, the father the defender of it. Out of these rather constraining partnership patterns—which are no longer biologically (or even altogether culturally) dictated—have come the institutions of marriage and the family, and all the elaborate social structures that support them.

The current reexaminations of male and female roles, with a view to making them more flexible, especially in terms of which parent should do what in caring for children, may be fruitful indeed in further setting us free of stereotyped behavior. What renders people uniquely human, after all, is the option to *depart* from genetic patterning of behavior. Moreover, in today's circumstances, many people are beginning to feel that the species as a whole, through society's institutions, through day-care centers and other means, should take a much greater early role and responsibility in childhood.

But while waiting for this to happen, if it ever does, the parent still faces the responsibility. A woman and man who choose to bring a child into most parts of the world *know* there exist no adequate social facilities for child rearing, and they must therefore be sufficiently motivated to make the *personal commitment* to provide the nurture for which nature seems to have programmed them.

For a well-motivated couple who have chosen their roles freely, parenthood can be as challenging and rewarding an experience as human beings know—and one that can last all their lives, through the adulthood of their own children, and the childhood of their children's children.

Observe two people who love each other. They unite and produce the marvel of a new life. They watch, in continuing fascination, as it develops from a bawling bundle of chaos into a highly organized thinking-and-doing apparatus. (Through what miracle does a baby learn the meaning of "round"? Or "rough" or "red"?) They know the sensory and emotional joys that go with handling and caring. They also know the intellectual wonder of playing a conscious role in human evolution—heirs to aeons of cosmic, geologic, and organic history, proud inheritors of an incredible past and creative contributors to a tomorrow that is—a child.

The desire to be a parent is, we reemphasize, a natural motivation. Though the *capacity* for parenthood is inborn, the practical know-how has to be *learned*. Nearly everyone has at least a rudimentary built-in sense of what it means to fill in the blank pages that represent the nurturing of a child through the extrauterine phase of his human prenativity. But this built-in sense does not provide much guidance for the specific content to be written into those pages.

Too many children have too many of those pages still left blank forever—or torn out; and too many other pages are filled with messages so confused as to be illegible—or, worse still, flatly incorrect. Nor is it enough to fill those pages with static information. They should be filled with lively, dramatic intimate characters, rich with felt knowledge and experience. However the pages lack these ingredients from the parents, to that extent will the child's own capacity for similar authorship be lost or impaired. These earliest chapters are where many of those critical "organs of the mind" are evoked and formed. It is not in isolation, but rather in human culture and society, that a child functions fully, partially, or not at all. Thus he is dependent upon a learned tradition, tenderly transmitted.

Again, the quality of nurture he receives is of paramount importance; if it is poor, if he is not brought whole through his own psychosocial gestation into full-fledged latency, he will be to that degree handicapped in the quality of nurture he can later provide. He may be able, through his own conscious effort and motivation, alone or with professional help, to make up these earlier deficits, to repair or rebuild his own damaged or undeveloped organs of the mind. Otherwise, his personautic mission unachieved, the child is at unusually high risk of being the inadvertent carrier of a vertical epidemic, a Typhoid Mary of the psyche.

6

The Parent-Infant Bond

This original mother-infant bond is the wellspring for all the infant's subsequent attachments and is the formative relationship in the course of which the child develops a sense of himself. Throughout his lifetime the strength and character of this attachment will influence the quality of all future bonds to other individuals.
—Marshall H. Klaus and John H. Kennell,
MATERNAL-INFANT BONDING

W E have known for a long time that the early years are important to later life. But only recently have we come to understand how critical are the first few hours, even the first few minutes, in the launching of a human life—critical to the enduring future relationships between child and parents, and thus to the child's emotional future and his ability to negotiate the road to adulthood. Surveying this new body of understanding, one is at first elated that we have acquired it; then dismayed to think that it took us so long to learn what seems so obvious (now that we know it); and, finally, a bit saddened to reflect that virtually all of us in the United States (and, no doubt, much of the rest of the world), especially those born in hospitals, have been deprived of an unknowable quantity of emotional richness in our lives because of our past failure to discover—or rediscover—a few basic truths.

As preamble, we offer a statement that may sound contradictory: From the moment a child leaves the womb, he is a person, and should be prized as such. This is not to say that, prior to birth, he may not similarly be thought of as "the person in the womb" (to borrow the title of N. J. Berrill's book on fetal development). But the child's rude expulsion into the outside world turns the postnatal portion of pregnancy into a radically different existence. The body

89

is forced to take on instant and total responsibility for its own respiration and circulation. Its protective sac gone, it is exposed for the first time to light, air, temperature variations, strange textures and sensations. Liberated (without consent) from his cozy (if all has gone well) and inaccessible space-capsule-like enclosure, complete with built-in life-support systems, the newborn is suddenly available to the world, and it to him.

The seeming contradiction lies in our previous contention that a child does not become a human person—and then only an incipient one—until latency. We do not retract that notion, which remains our major theme. But the newborn may nevertheless be perceived as a person-in-process, an organism already on the way to what it might, with our help, become. He is an individual with an explicit genetic endowment, its potential expression probably already modified by his experience *in utero*. We cannot add to that genetic endowment—not in our present state of knowledge, at any rate; though we can nourish, stimulate, and strengthen it. But we can certainly subtract from it; or at the least, by failure to nurture it, set ever narrower limits to its fulfillment.

We do not, in any case, *create* the new mind-body with its unique character and personality, its temperament and talents. Rather, we encourage it, *we allow it to unfold*. The word *allow* perhaps connotes a too-passive surveillance, an implied suggestion that the parents can just stand by and watch it all happen. In fact the parents must provide the congenial nurturant environment, and purposefully guide the active and interactive child in the direction of his natural becoming. To discern that natural direction is a complex, continuing process that requires patience, energy, sensitivity, and a willingness to refrain from imposing on the child some preconceived image of one's own. By permitting the child to develop as fully as possible within the framework of his genetic limitations, the parents confer on him the maximum options within those usually generous genetic boundaries. The creative guidance provided by the parents can be at least as full of exhilaration as of tedium.

The baby born today, if he is lucky, has had the advantage of what has been called "the new science of childbirth"—perinatology, briefly mentioned in the last chapter. Perinatology means literally, from its Greek and Latin roots, "around birth." In the perinatal context, childbirth is not an event that occurs at a single *point* in time, but rather a process that goes on over a *period* of time. "In perinatology," writes Saul Kent in *Saturday Review*, "conception-pregnancy-birth as a *functional whole* becomes the new meaning of childbirth. Obviously, this approach often implies a team effort, because neither the ordinary physician nor the extraordinary specialist knows enough to give the *continuing health care* required through the entire perinatal period—especially since, in some definitions, perinatology includes pre-conception care of parents-to-be and child care during growth and development." It also includes prenatal diagnosis of many genetic diseases and chromosomal abnormalities, especially by means of amniocentesis—the drawing of amniotic fluid from the fetal sac and the careful study of the cell cultures grown from it.

The continuum of attention perinatology entails is neither simply nor inexpensively achieved. We do not intend here to dwell on the technical medical details, but we emphasize the importance of perinatology for two reasons. One is that there is seldom any such thing as a "purely physical" birth defect; any damage to the organism—especially to the developing brain and nervous system—usually means added emotional trouble for the resultant offspring. The other is that perinatology is such a new multidiscipline that most prospective parents have not yet been made aware of its existence and possibilities.

To be aware, unfortunately, does not mean automatic availability of good perinatal care. First-rate perinatal centers have begun to be established in only a few regions of the country. In 1971 the need for perinatal health-care centers was enunciated by the American Medical Association in collaboration with the American College of Obstetricians and Gynecologists, the American Academy of Pediatrics, and the American Academy of Family Physicians. The joint efforts of these professional societies have been coordinated and spearheaded by the National Foundation–March of Dimes in its role as consumer advocate on behalf of perinatal health care as well as financial supporter of some of the original pilot projects.*

---

*For details about perinatology, including the location of perinatal health centers, write to the National Foundation–March of Dimes, Box 2000, White Plains, N.Y. 10605.

It would not be an exaggeration to call perinatology a revolution in medicine, though a quiet one. Embedded in that revolution is a smaller but no less exciting and still ongoing minirevolution in childbirth itself—childbirth by the old definition this time, the specific bringing forth of the baby from the womb on his official birthday. Two of the people principally responsible for its spread are French physicians who share the same initials: Fernand Lamaze and Frederick Leboyer.

The Lamaze method, growing in popularity, is a more carefully worked out version of the "natural childbirth" devised earlier by Grantly Dick-Read and others. Here the focus is mainly on the parents, especially the mother, as they prepare for childbirth beginning virtually on the day they learn of the pregnancy. During the event itself, the mother is fully awake, actively cooperative, and aware of all that goes on. The father is encouraged to be on hand as witness to his child's emergence, an occurrence for which he, too, has been prepared. (We have already suggested, in Part One, some ways to prepare psychologically for parenthood, and some of the emotional pitfalls of the pregnancy period.)

Leboyer's attention, however, is on the child himself, during the entire birth process. And it has come as something of a revelation. Think of how little consideration has traditionally been given to the newborn's own needs and sensitivities. In fact, he has been assumed to have none. Leboyer has a favorite delivery-room photograph: The doctor is dangling the infant upside-down in front of his mother and father. The baby is holding its head and screaming. Doctor, mother, and father are all smiling, all pleased with, and proud of, themselves, having produced a normal child—who is crying, of course, as new babies are "supposed to."

Many psychoanalysts, beginning with Freud himself, have believed to varying degrees that birth is a traumatic event that may have lasting effects on the psyche. Otto Rank carried this idea to the point where birth trauma became the underlying theme in his entire theoretical and therapeutic approach to emotional problems in later life. But, like the rest of us—reinforced by most of the world's scriptures—analysts have held that in pain and suffering we are born into the world, and such is the inevitable nature of things.

Leboyer insists otherwise.

Curiously, it was while going through his own psychoanalysis that Leboyer—an obstetrician who had by then delivered more than ten thousand babies via standard hospital techniques—was convinced that he had relived his own birth experience. Though we consider it most unlikely that this was a true memory, the revelation nevertheless led him to reexamine, and then to revise radically, his obstetrical practices.

How do we treat a newborn, Leboyer asked himself, after he has endured the crushing pressures of labor pains and the terrifying journey through the birth canal?

We sear his supersensitive eyes, which have never seen light, with a blast of floodlights. We thoughtlessly fill the air with sounds that must assault his ears like thunder. We cut the umbilical cord with unseemly haste, forcing his lungs to take in air at once—an experience Leboyer believes to be excruciatingly painful. We lift him by one foot and dangle him upside down, suddenly straightening the spine that has been curved for so long, holding him, vertiginously, over the void; then perhaps spank him to be sure he cries loudly enough to clear his lungs of fluid. We put his warm raw skin on cold metal surfaces (a scale, for instance), wrap him in abrasive fabrics. No wonder he shuts his eyes so tightly, cups his hands over his ears, and screams in pain and fright, curling up into a ball.

> And when it is no longer able to cry, it collapses.
> Sinks into sleep.
> Its only refuge.
> Its only friend.

At least such is Leboyer's reading of the baby's subjective responses.

Leboyer set out to change all that in his own practice. Once the baby's head appears (and Leboyer never permits anyone to touch that tender head), out go all the lights except for a single dim bulb. As the baby emerges, everyone is silent; anything that must be said is whispered.

On his first deliveries by this new method, some of the mothers panicked: Why is everyone so quiet? Why isn't my baby crying? Is he dead? Leboyer soon learned to prepare them better for a different scene than they had been traditionally led to expect.

As soon as the baby is out, he is ever so gently placed on his mother's abdomen—again filling the hollow he has just vacated, this time from above. The umbilical cord is still connected, still pulsating, still providing an oxygen supply so that, in Leboyer's view, the lungs can take over more gradually and much less painfully; the newborn usually utters only a single cry and then subsides quietly, his back meanwhile being stroked by the mother (or a nurse or doctor) while he listens to the familiar sounds of his mother's internal rumblings and heartbeat.

The cord is cut several minutes later, after it has stopped pulsating. Then there is a gentle, body-temperature bath.

And so on. The baby usually remains serene and surprisingly alert—and sometimes even smiles! The basic idea is to do everything at the child's pace, with a full consideration of his feelings (as nearly as we can discern them), making his transition to physiological independence as easy as possible; in a word, to have a little *patience*. All that we have so far described takes only five or ten extra minutes.

After delivering a thousand-or-so babies in this fashion, experimenting with numerous variations, Leboyer was ready to write all about it in a slender, lyrical book called *Birth Without Violence*.

Some of Leboyer's insights had already been gleaned by a few pioneering ob/gyn people in this country. But the publication of his book here, along with a personal tour to promote it, made an instant impact and stirred some controversy in American ob/gyn circles. "The publicity Dr. Leboyer received during his recent whirlwind two-week tour of the U.S. and from several lay magazines," wrote *Medical World News*, "adds to the impression that he has touched something deep in the public. Dr. T. Berry Brazelton, an associate professor at Harvard, thinks he knows what: 'It's catching the public's fancy,' he says, 'because everybody feels we have been treating childbirth as if it were a disease. It should be a happy, normal event, but it isn't.' "

American doctors were somewhat skeptical and critical of some of Leboyer's details: What evidence does he have for the infant's subjective feelings? Why doesn't he sterilize the mother's abdomen, or put a sterile sheet on to separate the infant from the possibility of infection? (Leboyer claims he has never seen an infection develop in such circumstances; but it would seem prudent to take precautions in view of known outbreaks of strep and staph infections.) In such dim light, how can he identify the subtle blue color of cyanosis in case the baby is being deprived of oxygen? Et cetera. But despite these objections, the obstetrical professionals were surprisingly sympathetic (especially those who were already leaning in this direction). And there is little doubt that Leboyer's book and personal tour resulted in a considerable acceleration of the trend toward what now appears to be more humane practice in the delivery room—and, for that matter, a trend back to having babies in the home, attended by professionally trained midwives, or by the obstetrician if he'll come.

The protests raised by Leboyer and his sympathizers do not by any means exhaust the catalog of objections to traditional obstetrical practices. Some critics have argued, for instance, that childbirth in the horizontal position, with the mother lying flat on her back, is just plain foolish. Though more convenient for doctor and nurses, who can witness the baby's emergence easily when it takes place on a well-lighted delivery table, it fails to take advantage of gravity's natural downward pull—fights it instead, rendering birth harder for mother and baby alike. Will we perhaps one day see the mother deliver in an upright or bent-over position, as occurs in some cultures, with the doctor or midwife assuming the supine position of a mechanic under an automobile?

Other aspects of hospital birth have also come in for their share of criticism—for one example, the too-ready use of drugs, perhaps unnecessarily sedating both mother and child. In the light of our dawning understanding, it may be that the most damaging of all current practices, one that may even seem barbaric in retrospect, is the complete separation of the newborn from his mother—not to mention his father.

The painstaking research of early investigators such as John Bowlby and René Spitz—whose contributions will be clearer in the next chapter—have vastly increased our understanding of how infants attach to mothers, and the deleterious effects that can follow if this attachment does not take place. But we are only lately beginning to realize how equally important is attachment in the other direction—the attachment of parent to child—and especially the "sensitive period" during which this can most properly come about. If the mother does not make the attachment during this sensitive period, it does not mean that she will fail to be attached to her child, only that it will be more difficult, and the bond may not be as strong. If the bonding does not take place at all, the mother is to that extent deprived of an opportunity for which we believe her to be biologically programmed, and the child will as a consequence be deprived of some of the devoted care and attention he might otherwise have received.

The flood of new interest in parent-infant bonding constitutes yet another minirevolution in that area where obstetrics merges with pediatrics. The breakthrough in understanding is mainly associated with the name of Marshall H. Klaus of the Case Western University Medical School in Cleveland, and is most carefully spelled out in a fascinating book, *Maternal-Infant Bonding*, which Klaus co-authored with his colleague John H. Kennell.

A major impetus for studying the nature of the maternal-infant bond was a series of chance observations of premature babies in the early 1960s. The personnel of intensive care units would work with devotion and diligence to carry the preemie through that critical touch-and-go period of maximum danger, finally pull him through and, proud of their success, send him home in perfect health. With dismaying frequency, however, the infant would shortly be back in the emergency room, the victim of battering—sometimes almost lethal battering. Or he would return as victim of the malady known officially as "failure to thrive without organic cause." Having thrived perfectly well under routine hospital care, after being sent home he would fail to grow or develop at anything like a normal pace, even in circumstances where neither poverty, conscious motivation, nor lack of education could be blamed.

True, other babies were also battered and failed to thrive without organic cause. But these misfortunes seemed to befall preemies more often, significantly so. Could there be a correlation between these unhappy events, on the one hand, and the enforced early separation of preemies from parents? Was there indeed some mysterious attachment that took place after birth between mother and child, some bond which gave the parent a greater emotional commitment to the future care of her offspring? Could parents deprived of this attachment actually love their babies less, care for them less devotedly, even be more prone to beat them physically? It took investigators some years of study and analysis to convince themselves that the answer to all these questions was Yes, and to learn something about the surprising nature of this postpartum bond.

Animal studies indicate that virtually every species, especially every species of mammal, has its own biologically programmed technique for mother-newborn bonding. A variety of animals from the domestic cat to the rhesus monkey do a great deal of licking and nuzzling immediately after parturition. In the case of the goat, the mother appears to be in her state of readiness to attach to her newborn kid for only a critical few minutes. If another dam's newborn is presented to her instead of her own at that point, she will lick and accept that alien kid, and will show the same signs of distress when it is taken away as if it were actually her own. In her instinctual mind, the bonding process in fact *made* it her own. On the other hand, if no kid, including her own, is present to be licked and accepted, the opportunity vanishes. After her biological response mechanisms (believed to be essentially hormonal in nature) have returned to their normal levels, the dam will reject her kid summarily and—even though she is heavy with milk—will take no interest in assuming any caretaking or feeding responsibilities.

The goat is an extreme case. Most animals have a longer period of heightened receptivity to their offspring before rejection occurs; rats, for instance, have a period of days rather than minutes. Every species is unique, and it is hazardous to apply knowledge gleaned from observation of one species to another even closely related species. Certainly it would be foolhardy to observe what animals do in bonding behavior and expect human parents to do likewise. But the point is that virtually every species observed does evince *some* form of quite specific bonding behavior. Klaus and Kennell felt safe in drawing some generalizations:

"Separation of a newborn or young animal from its mother . . .

significantly alters maternal behavior. The sooner after birth the separation occurs the stronger are the effects. For each species there seems to be a specific length of separation that can be endured. If separation extends beyond this sensitive period, the effects on mothering during this breeding cycle are often drastic and irreversible." And again:

"Within the sensitive period, maternal behavior quickly disappears if young are not present to elicit and maintain it. . . . Because of her physiological state after parturition, a mother is sensitized to the behavioral cues of her newborn and begins to respond to them. The infant, in turn, responds to maternal behavior and patterns of interaction quickly develop that establish the bond between the mother and her infant, preventing her from abandoning him."

After years of studies in the United States, Guatemala, Brazil, Denmark, and Greece, concomitant with reviewing the work of other investigators in the field of maternal-infant bonding, Marshall Klaus and his associates concluded that this complex interaction between mother and child repeatedly observed in animals is also a fair description of what occurs in the bonding of a human mother to her newborn. And it is not only the state of biological readiness on the mother's part that matters. There is nothing automatic about bonding, however ready the mother may be. She responds to cues from her baby, and the bonding could not be achieved were the human infant not a much more aware creature than the experts had previously believed. The newborn's consciousness may not yet be able to separate itself from its surroundings, but the infant does see, does hear, can move in response to outside events. He will turn his head toward a sound. He will follow an object with his eyes. And almost invariably his favorite object is a human face, or, failing that, some representation that resembles a human face—even if it is only an oval shape with eyes and nose roughly scrawled in the appropriate places (assuming it is held at the right distance, and directly facing him).

The infant seems to have a preprogrammed recognition that the human face is of primary importance to him, as well as a built-in knowledge that he, too, is human. Within a few days, if you stick your tongue out at the baby, he will stick his tongue out at you in return. Without ever having seen himself do this in a mirror, he can perform this pure act of imitation, somehow knowing where his tongue is located and how to control it with his unpracticed muscles.

Infants, again contrary to prior belief, have periods of quiet alertness in the midst of all that crying, feeding and somnolence. During the first hour of his life, the newborn has an especially extended period of such alertness (after which he goes into a deep sleep for three or four hours)—provided it has not been dimmed by anesthetics, the trauma of birth itself, the irritating drops of silver nitrate placed in his eyes to combat infection, and all the other distractions and assaults on his sensibilities of which Leboyer complained. During this first hour of life, eye-to-eye contact between mother and child is one of the most potent ingredients of bonding behavior. In fact, in their Cleveland hospital, Klaus and his associates do not permit the silver nitrate to be put in the newborn's eyes until after this initial contact has been made. One of the more moving sights in human experience must be the mother-infant dyad gazing raptly into each other's eyes. Something is obviously happening to both of them, especially the mother.* Klaus and Kennell also repeatedly emphasize the importance of having the father present as well, to form his own bond with the baby—which gives him, too, an enormously greater sense of attachment and commitment to the child. The term *engrossment* has been applied to the impact of infant on father—who often perceives the child as perfect and exhibits extreme pleasure on several levels, as well as a heightened self-esteem. In fact, Klaus suggests that the bonding process be extended to the entire family, that

---

*Klaus and Kennell tell of their disappointment when three of the women assisting them in a research project said they didn't particularly care for babies, found newborns particularly unappealing, and planned never to have children of their own. As they carried out their assignment, however, "each of the women had her first experience with a baby in the alert state who would follow her eyes with his own, and an amazing change occurred. Suddenly each became enthusiastic about 'her' baby, wanted to hold him, and came back later in the day and the next day to visit. At night she would tell her friends about this marvelous baby she had tested. In a few weeks all three decided they would like to have and even breastfeed a baby." This anecdote illustrates "the compelling attraction of a newborn infant moving his eyes to follow an adult's eyes, and the layer upon layer of emotional meaning that a viewer may place on this."

even the infant's siblings be on hand (though not necessarily during the first contacts) to get acquainted with the newborn in the hospital, thus satisfying some of their own curiosity while allaying the mother's concerns about their reactions. In Cleveland, Klaus has made exactly such arrangements, and now other hospitals elsewhere are similarly modifying their procedures.

Apart from the eye contact, many other subtle processes go on simultaneously between mother and child during bonding. For one thing, she speaks to her baby quite naturally in a high-pitched voice, in exactly those registers to which his ears are best attuned. And the newborn's body movements respond with exquisite specificity to her tones and language, performing a kind of dance to her music. Interestingly, the movements are different when the languages are different. The baby's body seems programmed to move to any language the human tongue can speak; thus he begins to be acculturated from his first hours of life. In a real sense he learns his language with his body before he learns it with his tongue.

Touch, too, is of extreme importance. Those women permitted to spend some time with their infants in skin-to-skin contact* soon after birth—preferably within the first hour, though later contact was also effective—developed even stronger bonds. In fact, women permitted to bond closely with their infants during the first hour of life, compared to control groups who followed the standard hospital routines, did much more gazing at and fondling and kissing of their babies later on—even two years later, according to follow-up studies. By now, researchers such as Elsie Broussard and Margaret Fries

---

*In practicing early skin-to-skin contact between mother and infant, Klaus and Kennell might be subject to the same criticism as that leveled at Leboyer—enhancing the danger of infection. But Klaus and Kennell point to an eight-year study in Guatemala, where many newborns in the Guatemala City hospital nurseries contracted staphylococcus infections whereas, in an Indian village a few miles away—where *all* births were monitored—not a single such infection was encountered in home births under poor hygienic conditions. All the hospital babies had been separated from their mothers for the first twelve hours. The Klaus-Kennell hypothesis: "that if mother and baby are kept together in the first minutes of life, the mother gives her baby her own mixture of strains of respiratory organisms, such as the *Staphylococcus*. Then these maternally provided strains grow and populate the infant's respiratory and gastrointestinal tracts. Just as a lawn planted with grass will resist the introduction of weeds after the grass has had a good start, these organisms may prevent the baby from acquiring the hospital strains of staphylococci."

have worked out a convincing set of data that go so far as to show
that the mother's perception of, and fantasies about, her infant after
the first month of life are a significant predictor of psychiatric troubles for the child many years later!

A word of reassurance, however: Though bonding during the sensitive period is important, it is not everything. Studies (if studies
were necessary) have shown beyond a reasonable doubt that parents
often begin bonding to their infants *before* they are born—just as
Mission Control goes through prelaunch preparations and count-
downs. And even those who miss the sensitive period have many
other opportunities. When either the mother or child is at risk for
one good medical reason or another, there is often no way to avoid
anesthesia at birth and separation immediately after birth. In such
cases, there is no point in feeling lost or guilty about what could not
be helped. After all, most of us living now in the United States and
many other nations of the world failed to achieve this bond—either
with our own parents or with our children; yet we did manage
somehow to have loving, caring relationships. Nevertheless, had the
bonds been formed, the loving and caring might well have been
even greater, the attachments deeper and more enduring. And there
is no reason why future parents and children should not be so ad-
vantaged. In some cases, where the feelings of parents may be borderline—their desire for children ambiguous if not downright
negative, or their marital relationships troubled—the presence or
absence of the opportunity to form a strong parent-infant bond can
make a critical difference to the child's future care.

Fortunately, more and more hospitals are taking a more humane
and (in light of current knowledge) civilized approach. Even preemies are often available in their incubators to their mothers, who
can fondle them by means of rubber-glove insertions. More and
more maternity hospitals are beginning to adopt some of the Leboyer techniques (some were already practicing them, pre-Leboyer),
and liberalizing their archaic visiting rules, especially for fathers.
What took them so long? Why all those dumb rules and procedures
in the first place?

In fact, those rules and procedures were not so dumb when they
were originally promulgated. In the early 1900s, infection was ram-

pant. One virulent disease after another swept through maternity wards. Infant mortality was high, and so was the incidence of serious illness, especially infant diarrhea and upper-respiratory ailments. Mothers, too, were at risk. Stringent aseptic and antiseptic measures were necessary, including the isolation of mother and infant from all possible sources of contagion. Hence, too, the strict regulations regarding visitors.

In the early 1940s, not only were all children separated from their parents as an automatic precaution, but visiting privileges were restricted in many hospitals to a single half-hour or hour period per *week*. In more recent years, technological advances in neonatal medicine have often incurred such concentration on the techniques of lifesaving as to permit little thought left over for the patient's more personal, nonmedical concerns—in part because there was so little understanding of them. And it all worked very well indeed: Infant mortality and morbidity have gone down dramatically.

But what made excellent sense in years past may not make such good sense now. We should not continue to enforce, out of mere habit, rules and procedures that should long since have been permitted to fade into obsolescence. The standard practice in most maternity hospitals is still a quick glimpse of the newborn at the time of birth, a brief contact for identification purposes six or eight hours later, then visits lasting twenty to thirty minutes for feedings every four hours. A survey of hospitals in 1970 showed that, even at that late date, only 30 percent permitted mothers to enter the nursery, and only 40 percent permitted mothers to touch their babies in the first days of life. Thus, as Klaus and Kennell point out, "most normal births in the United States are associated with several days of deprivation for the mother." Impatience with the slowness of hospitals to change their ways has been largely responsible for the rapid growth of sentiment among lay people for childbirth at home. The only trouble with this movement is that, in case of a high-risk birth, it is nice to have all that high technology near at hand. "Ideally," say Klaus and Kennell, "we would like to use the best of present day knowledge of high-risk obstetrics, neonatology, infant development, and mother-infant attachment, and at the same time have family and parents participate in homelike births in the hospital."

However we bring about this revolution in childbirth, with its cluster of attendant minirevolutions, it should be hurried along in the interests of the emotional health of our future population. We may not go all the way with Leboyer in his estimate of the sweeping nature of the consequences of current obstetrical practice, but we do go along with the spirit, if not the literal meaning, of his words:

> This is birth.
> The torture of the innocent.
> What futility to believe that so great a cataclysm will not leave its mark.
> Its traces are everywhere—in the skin, in the bones, in the stomach, in the back.
> In all our human folly.
> In our madness, our tortures, our prisons . . .

It is, in a word, a hell of a way for Mission Control to get the personaut off the pad.

7

The Neophase: The First Eight to Ten Months

I myself feel it is impossible to spoil an infant. The concept of spoiling [by excessive attention] does not apply to babies under the age of nine or ten months, since they are utterly dependent, completely incapable of satisfying their own needs, and absolutely unable to put off any gratification without some sense of frustration.
　　　　—Lee Salk,
　　　　　　WHAT EVERY CHILD WOULD LIKE HIS PARENTS TO KNOW

TOWARD the end of his first year, by the age of roughly eight to ten months, a baby has already reached a watershed that is at once physiological, cognitive, and emotional. A number of distinct achievements have come together to prepare him for launching into the next, more visibly active stage of babyhood, where the development of motor skills proceed alongside an awakening intellect and the first nonverbal (though not necessarily soundless!) declarations of independence.

It is hardly original to stress the developmental importance of the earliest months of life. This was clearly recognized, for instance, by Mary M. and C. Anderson Aldrich* when, back in the 1930s, they wrote their admirable book, *Babies Are Human Beings*, now unfortunately out of print. The same understanding has of course been shared by more recent writers, ranging all the way from the perennially popular Benjamin Spock to pioneering academic investigators

---

*Their son, Robert A. Aldrich, is one of the nation's outstanding pediatricians and all-around medical humanists, and was the founder and first director of the National Institute of Child Health and Human Development.

such as Arnold Gesell and his collaborators at Yale. But nowadays, partly because of exciting new insights into the period of life that *begins* at eight or ten months and lasts until about age three, there is a growing tendency to give short shrift to the period of babyhood that precedes it. Thus some parents' manuals do not begin their detailed accounts of child development until this later period.

A case in point is *The First Three Years of Life* by the distinguished and innovative Harvard investigator Burton White, a book that is (and, on the whole, deserves to be) one of the most influential manuals currently in vogue. White suggests—virtually states outright—that these early months, while of course important, will pretty well take care of themselves; that it's a time when parents can feel relatively relaxed and easy, letting nature take its course while they simply see that the essentials are provided.* This is a risky attitude to encourage. Because we feel that the importance of this first eight-to-ten-month period needs reemphasis, and because, moreover, recent research has added a substantial quantity of new data about the rich contents of this stretch of infancy, we have given it a name of its own—the neophase.

The eight-month state we referred to as a watershed does not spring up of itself, spontaneous and full-blown, as if by the automatic turn-on of some genetic switch. It is not a preset chronological moment, although the required number of months do have to pass, approximately, along with their accompanying sequence of biological developmental passages. But the watershed state is not fully achieved unless a multitude and complexity of events have taken place during the neophase.

True, much of a child's development *is* biologically programmed. Sooner or later, unless there is some severe defect or handicap, the child can, for example, be expected to sit up, to stand, to crawl, to

---

*White does in fact furnish a rather detailed and very useful description of the early months of development. But he does also say: "During these early months the baby's general progress in development is largely assured by nature. . . . If they [the parents] provide the baby with a normal amount of love, attention, and physical care, nature will pretty much take care of the rest." He does not suggest that parents can't make a mess of things. "But the fact remains that nature, almost as if it had anticipated the uncertainties that beset new parents, has done its best to make the first six to eight months as problem-free as possible."

walk—without having been specifically taught these skills (though he'll be slower if he does it on his own). His eyes learn to focus better as time goes on. His capacities tend to occur in one sequence rather than another. But most of any infant's programming is only a *potential* series of developments. To become actual, they must be actively stimulated and nurtured into existence by caring parents. There must ideally be from the very beginning a constant interaction between caregiver and child to accomplish the major tasks of the neophase: to learn to recognize and love another person; to learn "basic trust" (as Erikson put it); and to learn the beginnings of self-help and self-esteem. Before he can learn to love, even to love his own self, a child must first experience being loved, without reason or reservation. Before he can begin to move toward independence, he must first experience total dependence. Before he can learn to postpone gratification and tolerate frustration, he must experience what gratification is.* If he is to trust the world, or anyone in it, he must experience the world responding to his cries and needs. A baby absorbs this knowledge, this prelogical understanding, through his whole organism. This happens long before he can comprehend language, before he has any idea who is responding to his needs, before he knows, on any logical or symbolic level, that he even *has* needs.

Failure to lay the appropriate groundwork in the neophase can result in a very different picture at eight or ten months—an autistic baby, for instance, or one afflicted with "failure to thrive without organic cause." The consequences can, in fact, be lifelong. We have no wish to frighten parents or would-be parents unduly; only to argue that those who underrate the parental role during these early months could not be more mistaken. The mother-infant dyad, that peculiar symbiotic relationship that began, if both parties were lucky, with the first day's bonding experience; the subtly nuanced interplay between the new baby and his principal caregiver; the proper development of "object relations" (the term we use in psychoanalysis for the child's sense of himself vis-à-vis outside objects, animate or inanimate—the most crucial such object being the moth-

---

*Again, this is borne out by Jean Liedloff's observations among the Yequana Indians of Venezuela, whose babies are in arms virtually all the time during their first year of life.

er herself); this entire set of circumstances, designated by whatever name, is critical to the welfare of the potential human being just entering his stay in the postnatal womb. Scientists tend to make a fine distinction between those facets of a child's progress that require explicit parental guidance and social interaction—generally classified as points of *development*, in its technical sense—and those events that will come to pass through the child's intrinsic biological programming—or *maturation*. But we cannot be reminded too often that even these "programmed" maturational occurrences will not *inevitably* occur—certainly not fully, at any rate—without the parent's attunement to the child and a certain indispensable psychological nutrition. Without these, the baby is at risk of retarded, even suspended, psychological maturation and development, as we shall presently see. On the other hand, if these are abundantly present, if they are lovingly and reliably provided by a committed caregiver, we may expect the unfolding of another loving, caring individual who will initiate among us a new chain reaction of loving and caring.

The period of time that begins when the mother comes home from the hospital with her baby may contain elements potentially hazardous to the newborn. She is still tired, tense, and perhaps a bit worried about her new responsibilities and her ability to carry them out. She may have a case of "postpartum blues." She knows it may be several weeks before her body regains its normal health and full-functioning energies. If there is a father in the house, he is likely to be tired too, though he may feel less entitled to his fatigue. Both parents are in command of less than their normal resources. Either or both may be needier than usual for special consideration, reassurance, and attention—and each may be less capable than usual of giving what the other needs. And at this very time when they crave rest and a stretch of self-indulgence, new demands are going to be made on their capabilities and energies. Everyone will expect them to be more selfless than ever because here, undeniably, is this newly-come-forth creature. It would be well for the father, if he has the leftover energy, to baby his wife for a while so she can be free to baby the baby (though he can help with that too).

No matter what their personal concerns for themselves, however, the paramount fact remains that the parents, as adults, are not help-less to help themselves. The baby is. He is totally, absolutely depen-dent upon them for everything he needs. There is no way he can possibly comprehend their circumstances, or to comprehend any-thing else for that matter, except the sharply felt urgency of his own needs. Nor is he equipped to tolerate frustration. If this conflict of narcissistic needs and wishes—the parents' versus the newborn's—is resolved in favor of the adults, that is bad news for the baby. If the parents decide that they will first indulge and renew themselves for a good stretch of time, give themselves a long breather, and then make it up to the baby a few months later—later may be too late; the baby may already have got off to a damaged and damaging start in life.

Parents should seek and accept help from any reasonable source that might offer or provide it. The mother might learn to nap while the baby sleeps (which, at first, is most of the time), and to take brief rest periods every chance she gets. If she manages to get in tune with the baby's rhythms—his cycles of alertness, inertness, and activity—she may with surprising swiftness find herself getting more than enough pleasure to compensate for her efforts.

To forestall possible confusion over what may seem to be a recur-ring contradiction, it is worth returning to our concept of the baby as a person. We keep saying that the newborn already is a person—in the words of Jerome Kagan, "a remarkably capable organism from the moment he begins to breathe." Yet we have just now, once again, depicted this same newborn as a totally helpless and noncom-prehending creature, a raw bundle of bawling wants and needs. The contradiction is only apparent. The baby *is* both a person and a not-person at the same time. To put it another way, the baby is a per-son-to-be and also a not-yet person—which is saying the same thing from two different vantage points. As a person-to-be, he de-serves our respect and consideration. As a not-yet person, however, we cannot expect him to have any knowledge of, or sensitivity to, anyone else's problems. It is the adult who must make the conces-sions—not to follow slavishly every infant whim, but simply to keep in mind that a baby is only a baby who, without appropriate care from his caregivers, cannot thrive . . . and may not even survive.

Each baby is a unique individual, and can differ radically from others in health, temperament, abilities, behavior, and pace of development (and still fall within the range of the normal). So while certain universal principles *do* apply, it would be a mistake to treat all babies alike. Yet it is a mistake we make all too frequently. If a baby doesn't behave or develop the way he is "supposed to" (according to some baby book or the advice of some friend or relative, or one's experience with a previous baby), we start worrying and wondering: What's gone wrong? Or, more likely: What have I done wrong? Where have I failed?

"We at the Gesell Institute," says Louise Bates Ames, "have long been aware of inborn differences in babies, differences that are apparent very early in infancy.... Just as babies come in different sizes, they also have different dispositions. Some are round, soft, happy, and easy to live with. Some are muscular and solid and so active that even as little babies they exhaust those around them, while others are thin, scrawny and wiry and may look like little old men and women with all the cares of the universe.... For certain individuals, it just seems hard to be a baby."

In a series of long-range studies carried out in the 1950s and 1960s of more than one hundred children, followed from birth until past the age of ten, a group of investigators* at New York University made a number of valuable observations on temperamental differences that they believe are inborn rather than acquired. They were able to identify at least three distinct types of temperament: "easy" (about 40 percent) "slow to warm up" (15 percent), and "difficult" (10 percent). The remaining 35 percent were mixed. The "easy" children, identifiable soon after birth, were generally good-natured and adaptable, slept and ate regularly, were more adventurous about trying new foods and meeting new people. They seemed to thrive without any special fuss—and were still pretty much that way at the age of ten, though anyone might run into trouble outside his home environment (school, for example) where a different set of ex-

---

*Alexander Thomas, Stella Chess, and Herbert G. Birch, who spelled out their findings in *Temperament and Behavior Disorders in Children* (1968) and in a 1970 article in *Scientific American*.

pectations prevailed. The "slow to warm up" children required more patience and attention, were shy of new experiences, were in general less active and more negative. They were adaptable enough eventually, but had to take things at their own pace, without the kind of pressure that could make them back off again. And then there were the "difficult" children, who ate and slept erratically, were even slower to warm up than the second group in terms of new experiences or people, reacted more intensely in almost every respect, from raucous laughter to temper tantrums. To try to force such a child into standard patterns only increased his resistance and withdrawal, only made him more difficult. Obviously he required a special brand of patience and understanding from his parents—who too often thought him abnormal, and blamed themselves. In fact, some 70 percent of the children in this category were brought in for professional treatment or counseling by the age of ten.

Apart from the three main types of temperament (and those inbetweens they couldn't classify), the same team of researchers isolated no fewer than nine distinct temperamental characteristics that parents might look for to indicate different approaches to the child. And all this says nothing about the built-in differences between girls and boys, which seem to dictate that certain aspects of development proceed at different rates. Nor about the differences that depend on the parents' previous experiences and the presence or absence of other siblings in the household. The point is clear: We cannot expect all children to react or behave or learn in quite the same way. Nor can we expect all parents to parent in the same way, since they too are individuals (a point we made persistently in Part One). Parents have to get to know their baby as an individual, to tune in to his temperament. Some babies are simply a lot harder to raise than others, even those in the same genetic family. It is foolish to feel inferior or guilty because the baby next door sleeps all night while yours wakes up and cries. In rare instances, a baby may be difficult in a way that a given mother is simply constitutionally unable to cope with. For instance, a baby may be so unresponsive that an ordinary mother may simply give up, whereas another type of mother seems able to attune herself to such a child and—working almost with the skill and patience of a professional therapist—finally elicits from the child the desired responses. A mother in the first situation obviously needs some relief, to be provided perhaps by some other individual (father, relative, friend, baby-sitter) who might establish a better rapport with the infant. But she should not feel that she is a failure as a mother on this account; her other children may get perfectly capable mothering. And some other woman who is proud of her success at mothering might do no better with such a child. The use of a "relief" person will best serve its purpose if the baby's own mother carefully observes and identifies with the other person's successful rhythms of "stimulus dialogue"—which may well be, for her, a not always conscious doing-what-comes-naturally experience. One of the best ways of learning "parent effectiveness" is by collaboration and imitation, by practicing what works.

To complicate matters even further (before simplifying them again): Despite the studies just cited, the temperaments of babies are not necessarily fixed forever. In fact, some can be counted upon to change. Often a baby who is excessively irritable and hyperactive during the neophase will become *more placid* than average before the middle of the second year. Babies *do* change. They change intrinsically, as they develop, and they change as their perception of the world, and of *you*, changes. Difficult babies may become easier, and vice versa. They go through stages that can be bewildering. A given parent may thoroughly enjoy one stage—and be just as thoroughly upset by the next. One can only try to take them all in stride: if the baby is going through a phase that pleases, one should enjoy it while it lasts, but not bank on its durability—and not try to keep the baby there just because it pleases the parent.

Though babies are in general comfortable with the rhythms of a regular, predictable regimen, this does not imply a rigid schedule. One should go rather with the baby's natural schedule as nearly as possible without making life too inconvenient for oneself. Feeding should go with hunger, not with the pointers of a clock. Of vital importance to the developing infant is his incipient sense of exercising some control over what happens to him—what Martin Seligman of the University of Pennsylvania calls "a sense of synchrony between action and outcome." As Seligman asks, "How can a bottle that

comes every four hours regardless of what the child is doing produce a sense of synchrony between action and outcome?"* Not that
the parent should always wait for the baby to make overt demands.
He should be kept comfortable—warm and dryly diapered, for example—without his having to cry for attention every time.

Mother (and fathers) are also different and unique individuals,
just as their babies are; and the parents have had time to become
even more individual. While one mother may quite naturally play
and chatter animatedly with her baby for long periods of time, another's natural pace may be quieter and more leisurely. Any given
mother is wise simply to go at her own pace. It would be a mistake
to revise her own style in any drastic way, to try to simulate a forced
animation. She would be unlikely to carry it off more than sporadi-
cally, and it is most important that she interact with the baby in a
consistent, *reliable* manner, one that does not confuse him with ca-
pricious ups and downs. If things tend to happen as a rule, in a certain orderly sequence, it helps to establish what Sibylle Escalona
has called "islands of confidence." The baby begins to acquire a prelogical foundation for observing causes and effects, begins to *remember*, through repetition, that one thing usually follows another, that
life in the world is not totally made up of a bewildering bombard-
ment of random events. As in later years, knowing what to expect
helps to reduce anxiety levels. Though parental styles will differ,
some minimal amount of regular play and stimulation should take
place throughout the day, preferably several times a day. A depressed mother who has no energies to give the child will behave erratically and unpredictably, and will often simply withdraw (even
when she is physically present), thus putting the child at considerable emotional risk.† She has, in a real sense, given up, and the baby

---

*When Yukio Mishima—the Japanese novelist who met his premature death in a bi-
zarre and highly publicized suicide—was a baby, he was kept downstairs in the darkened sickroom of his tyrannical grandmother, though being nursed by his mother,
who lived upstairs. Every four hours, his mother recalls, the old lady would ring, no-
tifying her that it was feeding time. After limping upstairs with the baby, she would
keep her eye on a stopwatch: He was to nurse only so long and no longer. Though the
mother longed to continue feeding and holding her infant son, he would be imperi-
ously whisked away when time was up.
†While poverty-stricken mothers are more likely to be, and have more reason to be,
depressed, they often possess special supportive networks, or historically derived in-

gives up too—or, as Anna Freud put it, he "follows her into the depressive mood." We have, at the Center for Preventive Psychiatry, seen this tragic outcome too often to take such situations lightly.

Though these consequences are serious indeed, the average mother has no cause for panic. In fact she should not be too concerned about whether or not she is following the advice of the designated experts at every step of the way. Parental common sense has often proved superior to the wisdom of experts—who have perpetrated some pretty egregious follies in their time.* Besides, the investigation of early childhood development—though being pursued intensively in laboratories, institutions, and homes around the world—is still a very young science, and still full of controversy, flux, and paradox. There is still a great deal of disagreement over such basic matters as the baby's smile. When does a baby first smile? Why? Is it innate or learned? Is there an earlier smile that is a kind of biological reflex (there seems to be), and a somewhat later smile—when the baby is a month or so old—that is more truly social and responsive? Charles Darwin, always the patient observer and recorder, noted that his own children first smiled "true smiles, indicative of pleasure" at the ages of forty-five and forty-eight days respectively.

We tend to think of development as a smooth progression, with the baby aware of more, and capable of doing more, at each stage than in previous stages because of accumulated learning and experience. Yet we also know that life doesn't quite follow this kind of sequential logic. A child's progress may go in fits and starts. At times

---

ner resources and social traditions to draw on. "The marvelous lesson to me from these observations in Africa," writes Brazelton, "was that in a place where mothers still had enough physical energy for the kind of interaction and expectation that we saw in the Zambian mothers, infants could and did respond. The black mothers were straight, dignified and caring about themselves in a depressing set of surroundings. They were able to convey this immediately to their depleted infants, who responded with postural and motor responses with the vigor that was necessary to perpetuate the interaction."

*Joel Elkes of Johns Hopkins tells of a young woman schizophrenic who had been among his more intractable cases. The patient's mother told Elkes that, under the influence of the Watsonian behaviorist school of psychology popular at the time, she had been warned not to demonstrate affection or to pick up her baby when she cried, lest she interfere with the child's natural unfolding. At night, she would desperately wait until the baby had cried herself to sleep, then tiptoe in to touch the *blanket*, and feel guilty for doing so!

he actually does retrogress, becoming *less* capable for a while before a new spurt catches him up again, or perhaps he relearns some capacity at a new level. It is only with the recent ingenious studies of neonatal behavior that we have learned how truly strange and startling human development can be. Newborn babies possess a much broader spectrum of capabilities than most parents and authorities have ever acknowledged.* Researchers have demonstrated that newborns in the first weeks of life engage in various kinds of imitative behavior, such as sticking out the tongue on seeing an adult do so. They seem not only to see, but to coordinate the eye and ear surprisingly well, and to look at their mothers in a way different from the way they regard strange women. They reach for things—even the *sounds* of things in the dark. They seem to be trying to speak, even though only bubbles appear rather than words. Under certain circumstances, and with help, they can stand—and even walk! Then it all goes away as if it had never happened!†

"If newborns are held properly," writes Tom Bower of the University of Edinburgh, "they march along a solid surface in a most impressive manner. This capacity disappears at the age of eight weeks. The reaching of newborns disappears at about the age of four weeks. Their ability, or perhaps willingness, to imitate goes at about the same time. I have already mentioned the loss of auditory-visual co-ordination. That capacity goes in the first few months and, seemingly, does not come back. . . . " So the baby who reached toward a sound in the dark at six weeks will not do so at six months.

What can the explanation be? Do the capacities atrophy from disuse? Bower believes not. Even when you give the baby plenty of chance to practice the skill, even when you do your utmost to en-

---

*For example, Brazelton's Neonatal Behavioral Assessment Scale, whereby the investigator, armed only with apparatus like bells, balls, and rattles, can assess some twenty-seven distinct aspects of newborn behavior.
†In a sense, in many such cases, it *didn't* really happen—because no one knew it was supposed to. Newborns engage in such activities only during their periods of wide-awake alertness, which, though frequent, do not last very long—hence often go unnoticed. It takes an alert parent to recognize the baby's times of alertness; researchers are trained to recognize and take advantage of them in order to carry out their experiments and observations.

courage its continuation, it still fades away. He even reports the case of a *blind* baby who, having learned to reach for a sound in the dark, lost the ability right on schedule!

Of what use are these early capacities, then? We are tempted to hypothesize a tantalizing analogy between these phenomena and those of later childhood development. For example, after going through all the standard psychosexual phases—from oral through phallic-oedipal—there is obviously a programmed *suppression* of overt sexuality at latency; then a programmed resurgence of true— i.e., adultlike—sexuality on a new level at puberty. It is as if the organism required a condensed foretaste of the future—not a rerun but a prerun—to prepare it, or one might say rehearse it, for later realities. Moreover, as Tom Bower points out, "There is some very exciting evidence that indicates that what happens to these capacities while they are present may specify the rate and course of later development." Newborns who practice walking will later learn to walk faster. Those who use their reaching ability before the opportunity disappears will later reach more quickly and surely than those who did not. And so on.

Even the neophase, then, is itself full of subphases—and full of unknowns. We are still not certain exactly which capacities depend upon maturation (the expression through time of innate genetic or biological programming) and which upon development (the impact of environment, culture, parental guidance). Most capacities are probably a mix of both, though some seem to be more overwhelmingly under the influence of one rather than the other. Many aspects of the nature-nurture controversy have been clarified, to be sure. And further research in infant development, along with valuable inputs from other areas such as crosscultural anthropological studies, will undoubtedly provide insight into some of the remaining mysteries of infancy. But we may never know how much we will never know.

There are, however, a few important things that we *do* know right now. One is that, in the neophase, the seeds are planted for the growth of trust, love, self-esteem, openness, confidence, competence, even a sense of humor; or for hopelessness, helplessness, withdrawal, and depression. Here, as already mentioned, we also see the beginnings of the critical separation-individuation process (chapter 8), the first thrusts in the direction of a healthy narcissism (chapter 9), and the earliest opportunities to take fruitful preventive-psychiatric measures (chapter 11).

There is a classic experiment with wild rats, done by Curt Richter of Johns Hopkins, which would appear to have nothing to do with child development: If a wild rat is held firmly in the experimenter's hand so that, no matter how valiantly it struggles, it cannot escape, the rat will finally give up the fight. If that quiescent rat is then thrown into a tank of warm water, it will sink, not swim. It has "learned" that there is nothing it can do, that there is no point in struggling. Now throw another rat into the water—one that doesn't "know" that its situation is hopeless and that it (the rat) is therefore helpless. This rat will simply swim to safety.

Richter and others have experimented with many variations on this theme, using both animal and human subjects. What comes through consistently is that helplessness and hopelessness have to be *taught*. Organisms of any complexity, left to themselves with some choices, will *not* give up—normally they will keep trying; they will look for new alternatives and options. A healthy human organism must feel that there is hope for solving its life problems, that it can exercise some control over its destiny, that the world responds to its efforts and its needs. Hence our emphasis on seeing that a baby's cries are heard and, in general, responded to, that his basic needs are met, and that attention is paid to his signals. He must feel he has some control over his world. If his hollerings habitually go unheeded and his basic needs unmet, and if his most frantic efforts turn out to be exercises in futility, he will learn that his situation is hopeless, and that he is helpless. He will soon subside and withdraw, perhaps in ways that will be catastrophic for his emotional future.

A danger now is "narcissistic rage," a process set in motion by major "wounds" to the child's narcissistic functions. Such a wound may be inflicted by death of, or separation from, the parent, by damage to the child's own body, by some overwhelming humiliation. Feeling helpless to prevent or repair the situation, the child's reality testing may be impaired; he may feel a compulsion to master the injury by creating situations that replicate the wound, giving him a chance to make it come out better. But his reduced ability to test reality makes it hard to recognize that the new situation *is* new. He is doomed to keep creating situations that invite harm to himself and rejection by others.

Investigators have begun to observe another kind of outcome: the rage that the infant experiences as a result of his helplessness is transformed—in the absence of alternatives—into dull, compliant behavior until adolescence. At that time, with the advent of new physical powers, this child-with-the-strength-of-an-adult, having repressed his rage all these years, may begin to let it all out. He often becomes an implacably vengeful teenage "delinquent" who may wreak havoc, major or minor, on property, people, and society at large.

We agree, on the whole, with Lee Salk and other pediatric psychologists and analysts that it is virtually impossible to spoil an infant with excessive attention—though not *altogether* impossible.* Children do of course need to learn discipline, to postpone gratification—but that kind of learning should itself be postponed for a while. Disciplinary actions are in any case wasted on a neophase baby; he is not yet equipped, physiologically or emotionally, to draw anything but negative lessons from such misguidedly premature attempts. Yet babies are battered because parents make the mistake of attributing to their children, even infants, the perceptions and motivations of adults. This pathologic process is known as "adultomorphism." One mother told us at the Center that her seven-month-old infant kept "deliberately" embarrassing her by crying in public places like the supermarket, so she simply had no choice but

---

*It is conceivable that too much attention can "spoil" an infant by leading him into a fraudulent omnipotence, a sense that the world is totally at his command, that it exists solely for his indulgence. But this is only likely to happen when there are numerous caregivers in attendance—mother, father, doting grandparents, and older siblings—so that there is always someone to leap instantly to gratify the child's tiniest whim. It's highly improbable, though, that the mother herself would possess the energy and resources to spoil a *baby*, even if she were trying to. In any event this danger of spoiling is not great, and the necessary circumstances rarely occur; so it's better to err on the side of nurture than of denial.

to discipline him—brutally. A person who knows gratification at this early stage of life may in fact find it easier to learn, later, to postpone gratification. He won't feel that the only way to get is to grab, and that whatever isn't grabbed and gobbled right now may otherwise never be attained—which is, according to Colin Turnbull, exactly the behavior practiced among the Ik of Uganda, who, as children, go notoriously ungratified. Again, the concern we express here doesn't mean you must jump at the infant's every cry or whimper, at any time of the day or night.* It does mean that you pay no attention to those people who, when you go to pick up your baby, tell you, "Don't! You'll spoil him. Let him cry it out."

We suspect that in the infant's preverbal stages, he is gaining a store of experiential memories that will influence later experiences; that, in fact, those later experiences will be interpreted by the older child according to patterns established during the neophase. When a child's cries are reliably answered and he is comforted, the message he absorbs is: When I have a need, and let the world know it, the world hears. I can trust the world to respond. I have confidence that my needs will be met.

When he is snuggled and played with, the groundwork is laid for thoughts later verbalized as: I am loved. I must be worth loving. I must be okay. It feels good to exist.

An overall message when the baby is generally well taken care of may be: People who are helpless and dependent are taken care of by those who are not helpless and dependent. The pattern may then be set for later caretaking of others who are helpless and dependent, including the baby's own future babies.

And so on. These are not verbally conceptualized experiences. They are not consciously understood at first in any articulate or articulable form. Nevertheless, they are in some manner stored in the child's developing memory, their organization perhaps related in some way to the "pleasure centers" of the brain.

In any event, pleasurable interaction in infancy appears to be vital to positive effects in later childhood. The mother may often initiate the action; or she may simply respond to the baby's cues. "As I write

---

*Once basic love and trust have been established, the baby becomes secure enough to tolerate frustration in small doses.

this paragraph," writes Martin Seligman, in *Helplessness,* "my three-month-old son is nursing at his mother's breast. The dance of development is conspicuous. He sucks, the world responds with warm milk. He pats the breast, his mother tenderly squeezes back. He takes a break and coos, his mother coos back. He gives a happy chirp; his mother attempts to chirp back. Each step he takes is synchronized with a response from the world." It is just about at this age, too, observes British psychiatrist Donald W. Winnicott, that the pleasures of play begin to go beyond this simple exchange. The baby starts reaching up to put a finger in his mother's mouth in an attempt at *mutual* feeding, thus indicating that he has begun to be at least fuzzily aware of her otherness. The late René Spitz, too, believed that this age is when the baby begins to get his first inklings of the existence of a "non-I."

Seligman tells another instructive story, this time of his daughter, Amy, at the age of eight months. The Seligmans and a group of his students were out having pizza and beer. Amy was sitting in a high chair and, at one point, banged her hands on the metal surface of the high chair. The group had been discussing the importance of control in child development, so Amy's daddy, the professor, illustrated the point by banging his own hands on the table in response. "A bright smile lit up Amy's face and she banged again. So we all banged in response. Amy banged back, laughing heartily. We all banged back. This continued for half an hour. . . . " Seligman suggests that parents—as one way of encouraging "ego strength"—should go out of their way to play "synchrony games" of this sort with their babies. "Rather than do things your child likes when the whim strikes you, wait for him to make some voluntary response, and then act. When the child repeats and intensifies his actions, repeat and intensify yours."

When a mother knowingly permits her behavior to be manipulated in this playful manner by permitting the child to start the action, it helps him experience the joy of mastering his environment. A baby who is bored may look away from his mother. She will change what she is doing to regain his attention. She may think she is manipulating him, but it could just as easily be interpreted the other way: by turning away, he induced his mother to change her "act."

Any number of experimenters have demonstrated that toys in a baby's crib, or mobiles dangling overhead, only made a *real* impression on the child if he can *do* something to make them move or otherwise react. Lights can go on and off, objects can shake, rattle, and buzz, and he will regard them momentarily with curiosity but not with prolonged interest; all the action may in fact finally cause him some distress. But if you give him the means—and teach him how—to turn the lights on and off, to make all those things shake, rattle, and buzz (or stop them), the baby is fascinated and delighted. He has some control over his environment. The world responds to his acts. What he does counts. He feels more confident in himself, more comfortable in the world. Even retarded children sometimes show marked improvement, given this kind of challenge.

Interaction, we said earlier, is the key word. Perhaps we should change that to inter*play*, emphasizing mutual initiatives. We have known at least since the 1940s, when Piaget observed and theorized so astutely as to how children assimilate their experiences in the world, that a baby learns more readily from play than from outright teaching (as is also true of many animals). For one thing, as Jerome Bruner points out, the spirit of play takes away the pressure that comes with more overtly goal-directed activity, when some kind of achievement or result is *expected*. For another, it has been repeatedly demonstrated that children are more highly motivated by the pleasurable excitement of a good game than by material rewards or the accomplishment of goals. Even more striking, says Bruner, is the fact that children will stick to a task with much greater tenacity—will be must *less* likely to give up—when it is done as play rather than as something that "really matters."

Actual physiological and electrochemical changes may be taking place in the growing brain and nervous system when the activity within a baby's awareness is self-initiated, interesting, playful, and all-around stimulating. Just as proper nutrition is recognized as critical during the early stages of development if the child's organs and cells—and especially the brain and nervous system—are to grow and form properly, so does "stimulus nutrition" appear to be similarly important. In fact, in animal brains, stimulus nutrition has been demonstrated to be able, under certain conditions, to compensate for the deleterious effects of poor diet.

Some of the pioneering experiments in stimulus nutrition were performed by the late David Krech and his associates at the University of California at Berkeley. Among other techniques, they constructed a nursery school for young rats that was a virtual rodent Disneyland of toys, games, things to climb upon, slide down, swing on, and explore, with all manner of intriguing objects put in places that required much ingenuity to reach. Living in and moving excitedly through this rich environment for even a few days produced measurable changes in the brains of young rats. After eighty days the cortex of the brain grew considerably heavier (compared to those of rats who hadn't shared the stimulus nutrition); the number of glial cells (the auxiliary brain cells that support the neurons) increased by 15 percent; and, while the neurons themselves remained constant in number, the average cell body size increased by 15 percent; the neurons, moreover, formed more intricate and numerous connections with other networks of neurons. Brain researcher Holger Hydén at Göteborg in Sweden showed that learning experiences not only added to the rats' brain mass but also measurably changed the biochemical and molecular nature of the cell structures.

Pushing their investigations further, the Krech group studied two groups of rats—one group specially bred to be much smarter than the other. When the dumb rats were given a large dose of stimulus nutrition, they became as smart as the smart rats! When the dumb rats stayed in the usual cages while the smart rats got the stimulus nutrition—the gap in intelligence between the two actually doubled! "We can undo the effects of generations of breeding," said Krech at the time. "Heredity is not enough. All the advantages of inheriting a good brain can be lost if you don't have the right psychological environment in which to develop it."

"Even slight variations in an infant's environment can have a major impact," writes Maya Pines in *Physician's World*. As a case in point she cites the work of Stanford psychiatrist Seymour Levine, who demonstrated that when infant rats are handled—rather than left cozily with their mothers—for even a few minutes a day, they become more stable emotionally than their littermates. Moreover, they cope better as adults! The theory is that the handled rats had the experience of another environment—and of adjusting to the change from one environment to another. Thus they acquired more confidence, more willingness to explore, more curiosity, less fear.

Though animal experiments are not necessarily translatable to human experience, we believe that the human mother's presence (or that of a reliable mother substitute) during the first few months of life is essential to the infant's mental functions. She is an integral part of the baby's environment, and in his "mind" an extension of his very self. The mother-infant dyad constitutes such an intimate relationship, active and interactive, each taking cues from the other (the mother more consciously, of course, but often just as spontaneously, and intuitively rather than intellectually)—and such is the absolute dependence of the baby—that Winnicott has remarked that it is almost meaningless to describe what the baby *is* without at the same time describing his environment, which includes what goes on between him and his principal caregiver. Winnicott reassures us that "we may expect good enough mothering from the mothers of the world, and of past ages, because of something that happens to women during pregnancy, something that lasts for some weeks after the baby's birth unless a psychiatric disturbance in the mother prevents this temporary change in her nature from occurring."*

One can easily see that if a newborn in these intimate and wholly dependent circumstances were to find his acute and basic needs ignored, it would be as if one part of himself had abandoned the other—perhaps laying the groundwork for a developmental schism profound enough to evolve into a psychosis. (Lee Salk believes that a baby who is generally gratified during the neophase will never become schizophrenic.) It is during these first weeks and months of life, while the infant is immersed in so-called "oceanic" feelings,

---

*What is this something that happens during pregnancy? Part of it is undoubtedly physiological, induced by the complex play of hormones occasioned by the presence in the uterus of an incipient new life. The mother of course responds psychologically to her physiological changes. She has a sense of getting ready to perform tasks of a nutritive nature, a deep-seated awareness that nutritive processes are going on within her already. Her self-concept begins to encompass the new self that will be a nourishing, nurturing mother. Successful parenthood does not require supermothers who can by some magic create a perfect environment for the new baby. The average normal mother, given half a chance by her social circumstances, is likely to provide at least what Heinz Hartmann has called the "average expectable environment" for her baby. Winnicott's good-enough mother in Hartmann's good-enough environment is a good-enough goal to aim for.

where everything is part of everything else with himself at the center, that the orchestration of mother and child can bring special blessings. Here are formed the basic building blocks of what might be called collaborative narcissism, or constructive narcissism. Here the richness of human personality begins to take root. In this gentle, loving *pas de deux*, the mother may often improvise her choreography to fit her child's, or lead him to a different step, preferably through tactful, tactile stimulation that respects his own intrinsic rhythms. Some few babies, it should be noted, may be especially sensitive to *over*stimulation, and withdraw inward (the only choice of direction at this stage), so attunement to the individual baby is all-important. Most mothers probably do this by nature.

Through all this interplay, the baby begins to build a strong attachment to his mother. Back in the early 1950s, John Bowlby in England reported his observations and theories, based on long investigations, on "attachment and loss"—that is, just how the child becomes attached to his principal caregiver, and some of the serious emotional consequences of separation from her. Bowlby's work had an impact not only on his fellow investigators of developmental psychology but also on public policy toward children—and not only in his own country. Concurrently, René Spitz in the United States was elaborating his own theories, and carrying out his celebrated studies in childhood emotional deprivation. He did not, of course, place children in deprived circumstances in order to study them; he studied those he happened to find in such circumstances.

In the thirteenth century one such experiment of calculated deprivation *was* carried out—and it is a favorite case for citation among historians of childhood. The experimenter in that case was none other than the Holy Roman Emperor, Frederick II. "He wanted to find out what kinds of speech and what manner of speech children would have when they grew up if they spoke to no one beforehand," reported the medieval chronicler Salimbene. "So he bade foster mothers and nurses to suckle the children, to bathe and wash them, but in no way to prattle with them or speak to them, for he wanted to learn whether they would speak the Hebrew language, which was the oldest, or Greek or Latin or Arabic, or perhaps the language of their parents of whom they had been born. But he labored in vain, because the children all died. For they could not live without the petting and joyful faces and loving words of their foster mothers."

Seven centuries later the studies of Spitz and others—mainly in institutions and foundling homes—reconfirmed the importance of the "petting and joyful faces and loving words." Infants deprived of them did not necessarily die (though some did), but even when fed and kept scrupulously clean, and even when what were then assumed to be their basic needs were all taken care of—if they were not also handled, fondled, played with, talked to, or given some basic stimulation from some caring person,* they failed to thrive by almost every measure. Spitz called their malady "hospitalism" or "marasmus." Its victims sickened far more easily than would be expected among infants even in very poor families; they were more susceptible to infections of every variety; and their development was retarded, often severely. Their physical growth was stunted, their intelligence dulled, their interaction with others halting and awkward. They were burdened, as they grew older, with a disproportionate load of emotional and intellectual troubles.

Especially at risk were those babies who were old enough (five or six months) to have formed a strong attachment to their mothers before being abandoned. The abandonment sometimes could not be helped, due to death or incapacitating illness; but it was usually because the mother was leaving the baby permanently to institutional care or hoped-for adoption. These babies would scream inconsolably, refuse to eat or be comforted by anyone else, and ultimately just turn their faces to the wall and withdraw from the human world—unless the mothers returned, by some chance or change of mind, in time to save them. The victims were said to suffer from "anaclitic depression," in some cases indistinguishable from infantile autism.

Many further observations and studies were carried out by Spitz, his collaborators, and those who followed him. The studies and their reported conclusions were sometimes criticized on the grounds

---

*Institutional staffs were often too small and overworked to take the necessary time for such individual attention.

of methodology—or for Spitz's failure to take into account one consideration or another, but by and large his findings have held up and proved extremely influential in science's understanding of, and attitudes toward, early parent-child relations. Hence the authors' distress when we still run across contemporary investigators who underplay the key influence of the neophase on all of later life—if, indeed, that life has not already been cut off by some neophasic tragedy.

The attachment process that Bowlby and others have delineated is a continuation of the mother-infant bond we discussed in chapter 6. It is of course closely associated with feeding, with assuaging the discomfort of hunger. The baby experiences other kinds of discomfort too—the sensation of a full bladder, for instance, or intestines in need of emptying. These discomforts he is usually capable of relieving without outside help. (The result may be the lesser discomfort of a wet or full diaper, but this is tolerable if a diaper change is not too far off in time.) The discomfort of hunger, however, is not one of fullness but of emptiness, a tension that also involves the central nervous system's responses to biochemical shifts in blood sugar, insulin, and other temporary hormone and enzyme imbalances. Filling the empty stomach with substances that will reverse the biochemical changes is something the child can achieve only through outside intervention. He does, of course, help himself to the food once it is delivered—or he is delivered to it—by means of his own sucking efforts, whether he sucks at a breast or a bottle.

Which brings us to the question of breast-feeding versus bottle-feeding. The subject has long been, and remains, controversial. Fashions (including fashions in medical advice) have swung from one to the other. When Audrey Palm Riker was writing a Public Affairs Pamphlet on breast-feeding in 1964, bottle-feeding had come into such vogue that she complained: "When two nursing mothers get together, the kinship is comparable to Stanley finding Livingstone in Africa." By 1971, writing in *The New York Times Magazine*, pediatrician William E. Homan remarked: "It is currently 'fashionable' to breast-feed. For feminine fulfillment. For the good of the infant. For God knows what juxtaposition of stars and omens." It has

by now become even more chic to breast-feed, especially in an era
where increasing respect and popularity attend the Lamaze-Leboyer
style of natural childbirth, and where increasing emphasis is placed
on handling, fondling, physical contact, and mother-infant bonding.
We ourselves are strongly in favor of breast-feeding wherever the
mother herself is in favor of it and can manage it successfully,* and
such a mother should not give up too easily. There is a quite direct
relationship between the quantity of nursing time allowed and the
quantity of milk available; the less the infant is permitted to suck,
the less milk is produced. Subtle and fascinating indeed are the interplay of the infant's desires and responses on the one hand, and
the brain-initiated maternal hormonal responses on the other. In an
actively nursing mother, the neuroendocrinological circuits may begin to work as soon as she hears the sound—even from another
room—recognized as her baby's hunger cry. The snuggling baby
soon learns to recognize his mother by smell (this may well be true
of a bottle-fed baby as well), for at no other time of life is the sense
of smell as acute and discriminating as during these first few weeks
and months. A baby's jaw is relatively small and receding at birth, a
perfect arrangement for nursing. (Then it grows faster than any other bone on the face, so that it can accommodate the teeth when they
erupt and the baby is ready to chew.) As for the mother, her complicated milk-manufacturing apparatus did not evolve without exquisite fitness for the biological tasks. "A pair of . . . mammary glands,"
wrote Oliver Wendell Holmes, "has the advantage over the two
hemispheres of the most learned professor's brain in the art of compounding a nutritious fluid for infants."

Anyone who wants as complete a set of arguments in favor of

---

*Preliminary evidence collected by Arthur Zelman, Associate Medical Director of the
Center for Preventive Psychiatry, suggests that successfully breast-fed children are
not commonly found in groups of disturbed preschoolers. Studying a group of one
hundred such disturbed children, Zelman noted that not one had been breast-fed for
more than ninety days, and only a few had been breast-fed at all. The data is too in-
substantial at this point to draw more than speculative conclusions; but Kliman's
clinical experience leads him to predict that controlled large-scale studies will show
that it is clearly and positively good for early-childhood mental health. We predict
further that breast-feeding may serve as a major (though not the sole and sufficient)
protector against certain types of child psychiatric problems such as early-arising
child psychoses and nonspecific hyperactivity.

breast-feeding as is to be found anywhere, detailing all the joys and advantages, is advised to write the La Leche League International.* La Leche's text, called *The Womanly Art of Breast-Feeding*, has gone out to hundreds of thousands of women around the world. But let that not be the *only* thing read on the subject, especially if there is reluctance or indecision. Plenty of literature also exists detailing the disadvantages of breast-feeding, though not as easily available in so handy a packet. Naturally, these arguments will not be found in La Leche's book. If the book, and La Leche's efforts in general, have an egregious fault, it is in implying there is something unnatural or abnormal about a mother who either can't, or won't breast-feed.

While we believe that the pro arguments—further supported by new scientific studies—considerably outweigh the cons, mothers who can't or won't breast-feed have a perfect right to their choice; and they should not be intimidated into thinking that choice is in any way abnormal. A mother or father who bottle-feeds can still hold the baby very close, and engage in all the kinds of interplay the infant requires. The baby is hungry not only for food but for all manner of sights and sounds, contacts and movements—the stimulus nutrition that the mother, more than anyone else, provides, though other family members can do their share as well. Whether the baby is breast-fed or bottle-fed, the important goal for parents to achieve is to provide a postnatal womb for their infant, supplying him, in his incipient helplessness, with complete life-support systems—from sustenance to temperature regulation. Though the circulatory and respiratory systems of the organism are now functioning on their own, they would soon cease if the other support systems were withdrawn. And now there is that actively growing central nervous system, which requires special human nutrients of its own.

By the end of the neophase, that eight-to-ten-month watershed we have been referring to, the infant will have just about learned to coordinate the thumb with the other fingers so that he can take hold

---

*La Leche's headquarters are located at 9616 Minneapolis Avenue, Franklin Park, Illinois 60131.

of objects with considerably greater purpose. As a result he begins
to want to "do it himself," whatever it is, even though he can't yet
do it right. He tries to feed himself, for instance, with a persistence
equaled only by the shambles that result.

He has also, about now, begun to sit and stand and crawl. If he is
precocious, he may even have taken his first few steps.* In a word,
he is no longer stationary. Moreover, he is by now probably sleep-
ing through the night and staying awake, except for a couple of
brief naps, most of the day. In no time, it seems, he has turned into a
perpetual-motion machine with a mercurial mind of its own, a
tracking problem to test any parent's radar.

As the new motor capacities come upon him, he is challenged, excited, compelled to explore. But he is generating new hazards and
new anxieties for himself as well. With good luck and good parental sense, however, he will master the anxieties as he masters
the skills.

The baby is also at the threshold of adventures in language. He
can already understand a few words. Even when he does not comprehend the explicit meaning, he can distinguish real language from
nonsense syllables, and he has by now had a couple of months'
practice babbling with energy and enthusiasm, producing a broad
spectrum of sounds. At the same time, he is learning a great deal
more about how things are in the world outside his own skin. He is
learning, as one example, that objects have an independent existence, quite apart from his own awareness of them. He has begun to
appreciate that when something is hidden, or simply disappears
from view, it has not literally ceased to exist but is still out there
somewhere, and can return or be found again.

The baby has also finally learned—in a process that began at five
or six months of age—to distinguish accurately and reliably between one human face and another, and especially to identify his
mother (or principal caregiver) and single her out by sight from all

---

*Though walking at this age, even the first steps, is considered unusually early in our
culture, Brazelton observed—during a stay in Lusaka, Zambia—two five-month-old
infants taking several steps without support. "This 5-month walking," he said, "was
in response to their grandmothers' stimulating their walk reflexes and propelling
them forward to a reflex kind of walking."

others. He often squeals and gurgles with delight when his mother appears, and may complain mightily when she leaves. This can only occur when he identifies this unique creature as the source of the good things that have passed between them.

At just about this point in his development he is also afflicted with the behavior known as "stranger anxiety." Where formerly he may have smiled at any human face that came into view, now he clearly shows anxiety instead—sometimes so strongly that the display can be read as outright fear or hostility—when approached by anyone he does not know well. The strong one-to-one attachment, his great love, is his mother (usually) and if a strong bond has also been formed with his father, the male parent can serve as an acceptable substitute most of the time. Older brothers and sisters, or caregivers who have spent a great deal of continuous time with the infant, may have formed lesser attachments and thus also be exempted from the anxiety reactions. But occasional visitors—friends, neighbors, relatives, even grandparents, people who have begun to feel they have a special relationship with the child—may be in for a jolt.

Until now the baby may have quite happily permitted himself to be fed, bathed, diapered, or played with by, say, a doting aunt. But suddenly he refuses to put up with the aunt's ministrations. Instead of cooing and gurgling, the aunt gets kicking and screaming. She may wonder what she has done to offend the child, and may herself feel offended. The parents, too, may wonder what has come over the baby. But it is important to recognize the "eighth-month stranger anxiety" as a perfectly normal and natural phase of development that will, in all likelihood, be overcome in a few weeks or months. Its arrival may, in fact, be as much biological as psychological or emotional. Kliman has suggested the special significance of adrenal development in infancy. It is only around the eighth month that the adrenal medulla has matured sufficiently to start releasing quantities of epinephrine (adrenaline) into the baby's bloodstream, making possible the whole range of physiological events that we recognize as the overt signs of anxiety attacks. This may merely be the baby's first *opportunity* to behave anxiously—the equipment was missing until now. And this opportunity—arriving, as it does, while he is becoming so possessively enamored of his mother—is expressed in the presence of anyone but the beloved individual, even someone he has seen often enough to recognize. The biological expression of anxiety, being experienced for the first time, may itself—in its frightening novelty—intensify the anxiety. Familiarity with such experiences may later render them less worrisome.

This is in any case a paradoxical period for the baby. While he has just fallen in love with his mother, as programmed (though there is nothing automatic about the carrying out of the program), he is simultaneously being pulled away by his new mobility, accompanied by urgent inner drives to explore. He keeps leaving his mother, but also keeps checking to be sure she is around. He has already begun the long process of separation-individuation, which will be a major theme of the next chapter. It has often been said that the baby at this stage has "become a person." (Pursuing our personautic analogy, one might say that the personaut has here reached what in rocketry is called first-stage separation.) He has become aware of himself as a distinct individual and has learned to love another distinct individual. He has begun to discriminate between one person and another, and to make his first unaided physical sorties into the outer spaces of his world.

It sounds contradictory, we realize, to talk of a child recognizing his mother by smell in the first weeks of life, yet to maintain that his attachment to her doesn't really firm up until about the sixth month of life; and, further, that the true "falling in love" with the mother—the recognition of her as the distinct and separate person who belongs to him and to whom he belongs—does not take place, concurrently with the advent of stranger anxiety, until the end of the neophase. But it is a matter of degree, of varying simultaneous levels of functional sophistication and awareness. By the end of, say, eight months, the child's memories of specific objects and people are more constant, and with his new sense of cause and effect, he connects his mother with all the good things she does for him—*even while she is not doing them*. This was not the case with the attachment two months earlier—though by then the relationship had already grown sufficiently powerful to bring on anaclitic depression and

other disastrous syndromes in reaction to the mother's absence.*
Even in the earliest stages, while the child was barely beginning to
become attached, he was still full of amorphous feelings, even pas-
sions. But in those earlier stages, someone else's ministrations could
more easily serve as acceptable substitutes; without such substitu-
tion he would still be susceptible to hospitalism and marasmus
(though not to full-blown anaclitic depression, an illness that requires the stronger, more specific attachment that does not occur
until the age of five months or later).

An interesting set of experiments carried out by Tom Bower at
Edinburgh serves to illustrate the child's growing recognition of his
mother, not only as a separate person, but as a *single* separate person
who has a continuous existence whether present or absent. In the
first few months of life, the baby is shown, via a mirror trick, three
simultaneous images of his mother. He doesn't mind at all, and is
happy to relate to all three. After all, he has seen her come and go at
different times and places, wearing different clothes and different
scents. For all he knows he has a whole collection of mothers. But
by the time he is about five or six months old,† when he has come
to understand that his mother is a unique person, a confrontation
with the triple image will surprise and confound him. This is the
age, remember, after which abandonment in a foundling home puts
the baby at risk of anaclitic depression. This is also the age at which,
under normal circumstances, the baby may begin to form attachments to other people as well, especially other family members, and
most especially the father if he takes the time and expends the ener-

---

*At five months, though the baby's body does not yet produce much of the anxiety-
creating (or anxiety-*permitting*) chemical epinephrine (adrenaline), it does produce
norepinephrine, which is associated with depression; and indeed these infant syndromes do closely resemble the depressive states of adulthood.

†At around this same time, the baby begins to teethe. Erikson makes a special point
of the potential conflict that may thereby arise. When the baby's gums hurt, he
wants to bite. If he is nursing, this may provoke a sharp negative response, causing
some confusion: If the mother is willing to gratify his hunger pangs, why not his gum
pains? There may be a difficult time while it all gets sorted out.

Even before teething time, the baby's so-called "oral aggressive" or "oral sadistic"
tendencies (a normal part of his oral eroticism) induce a desire to bite as well as
suck—but not with the same strength or persistence as when his gums begin to hurt.

gy to play and socialize in happy ways. If, in fact, the mother is *merely* nurturant, answering the baby's physical needs but not providing much stimulation, the greater attachment may be to the father, or even to a close and devoted friend or relative. European mothers, in the days when it was fashionable to leave their babies in the hands of nannies and wet nurses, sometimes worried that too close a "milk tie" would be formed with these surrogate caretakers. These mothers would then make it a point to appear with sufficient frequency and animation to remain the central figures in their infants' perceptions. The same kind of concern is evidenced by mothers in Israeli kibbutzim, as well as by American working mothers whose children are cared for by others, either at home or in day-care centers. In some instances, where there is no principal caretaker—in orphanages, for instance—babies may attach most powerfully to one another. One of the most startling, and touching, examples of this lateral attachment, reported by Anna Freud and S. Dann, was the case of six concentration camp babies who—after their parents had been executed—were placed under the collective care of a group of adults who kept changing, and who had to care for them under the most stressful and deprived circumstances imaginable. Though these babies never formed a solid attachment to any adult among their constantly changing caretakers, they were kept together—and thus formed strong attachments to one another. Separation from adult caretakers failed to cause the usual reactions; the children only suffered deprivation syndromes and stranger anxiety when they were separated from one another—even though none were old enough to nurture or care for one another! The Center for Preventive Psychiatry is often confronted with foster-care agencies, social workers, and family-court judges who need help in appreciating how vital it is to keep abandoned siblings together. Their attachment to one another is even more critical in the absence of their parents. Yet such children are often "farmed out" separately because it takes more time and trouble to find a foster home willing to take on the care of more than one new child at a time.

Psychosexually speaking, the infant during the entire neophase remains in the oral phase. We have some qualms about designating this phase by its bare Freudian name. For one thing, it is not exclusively oral; other parts of the body, especially the exploring hands and fingers, are also of great importance. Speaking of this phase we will also use the term *libidinal* here—connoting a generalized sensual seeking to take in and to be cared for—rather than the word *sexual* in its more explicit meaning. We might most accurately call it the orally oriented phase.

We have already emphasized the importance of feeding in infancy. Not only are the child's lips, tongue, mouth, palate, esophagus, and associated membranes and structures vital to adequate nourishment; they also afford sheer pleasure. Perhaps equally important, as Piaget has observed, the infant's oral equipment—just as much as the eyes, ears, and hands—functions as an exploratory device. He tends to want to pop things into his mouth. He licks, sucks, bites, nibbles, tastes, and tests out shapes, temperatures, and textures.

The baby has a built-in system that enables his head and neck to move in a left-to-right, back-and-forth searching path. Called the "rooting" reflex, this system is part of the mechanism that expresses the newborn's powerful sucking drive.

The sucking drive energizes the baby's feeding, whether from breast or bottle. Most babies need more sucking than they get during feeding. They will suck on their fingers or hands—even toes, if they can reach them. Hence the frequently recommended use of rubber pacifiers. (A calf fed from a milk pail instead of its mother's teats will suck away at any opportunity—at a tail, a finger, anything that is offered or that it can find.) So important is sucking that evolution has seen to it that, when a baby is starving to the point of emaciation, the suction pads in the cheeks—essentially fatty structures—remain intact after almost all the body's other fatty areas have wasted away.

The orally oriented period is a time for generalized body exploration. As the infant becomes acquainted with himself, this self to whom he is, strangely, still a stranger, these explorations—which usually don't begin in earnest until the baby is about three months old—are of course perfectly natural; to be incurious about one's body would be unnatural. A child's own attitudes toward his body and its parts may depend on the often unconscious ways his parents act and react. It is good for the infant to take pleasure in his body, including the genital organs. In the course of his baths, for instance, the genital areas should be gently washed and wiped with the same care and attention, the same expectation of providing pleasurable sensations, as any other area of the body. A parent may tend to slight the genital areas because of long-ago programming that identifies them as dirty, or as forbidden territory. The same parent, seeing the baby reach for his genitals, as he would reach for his big toe or his belly button, may feel obliged to restrain or remove the offending hand—conveying that it's a forbidden act. A continued good feeling about his body, as part of the shared relationship with his parents, is important to the child's eventual comfort with those of his own gender and has other profound effects on his future sexuality. Thus parents become instruments of sex education even in the neophase. There has been much theorizing about the time of weaning, about insufficient gratification of the sucking response and its consequences in later life—for example, excessive smoking as partly due to unresolved orality; but these areas of knowledge are still highly debatable and speculative. Debatable though some of the specifics may be, there is no doubt in our minds that how parents carry out this little-recognized responsibility to provide adequate oral-phase gratification is a matter of great importance.

Clearly much that takes place during the neophase has lasting emotional consequences. Many of the deprivations of this period have been referred to as irreversible. We at the Center believe that very few of these consequences are absolutely irreversible; over the years, we have come to suspect that almost any kind of emotional damage is potentially reversible. Much of it is in fact reversible—for we have experienced the satisfaction of reversing it (and we of course know of others who have had similar success). But to reverse it, or to salvage it to any appreciable extent, requires long, hard, patient work.

In the vast majority of the world's children in *all* nations (including ours), this hard therapeutic work is in fact never done, so the damage might as well be considered irreversible. We don't like to call it that, however. Society is already too reluctant to put forth the necessary rescue effort to save its damaged children, and budget makers always like the excuse to say no to funding by pointing out that it won't do any good anyway. If damage is irreversible, why waste the money? Why make the effort? But such a rescue effort is worth making; must indeed by made.

Still, prevention is by far our preferred solution.

8

The Personaut en Route
to Separation-Individuation

It seems to be inherent in the human condition that not even the most normally endowed child, with the most optimally available mother, is able to weather the separation-individuation process without crisis. . . .
—Margaret S. Mahler, Fred Pine, and Anni Bergman,
THE PSYCHOLOGICAL BIRTH OF THE HUMAN INFANT

I have never seen a spoiled one-year-old, but I have seen many a spoiled two-year-old.
—Burton L. White,
THE FIRST THREE YEARS OF LIFE

A MISSILE that carries an encapsulated astronaut into orbit is usually a multiple-stage affair, each of the lower stages separating at fuel burnout, then jettisoned as it boosts the remaining stages to the necessary velocities. Similarly, as the infant-personaut is launched, enfolded in his protective psychosocial capsule with his familial life-support systems, toward his initial orbital holding pattern (latency), his parental Mission Control must also guide him through several stages of separation—though, in this case, the previous stages are never entirely jettisoned and the separations never so abrupt. In the course of the personaut's launch into life, there are no more critical, or intricately complicated, stages than the series of processes Margaret S. Mahler has called by the blanket term *separation-individuation.*

Mahler's fellow analyst, Samuel Ritvo, has called her "The Compleat Psychoanalyst." Indeed, before her retirement from the Albert Einstein Medical College and a lifetime of affiliations with other distinguished institutions, Mahler's interests covered the entire range of theoretical and clinical psychiatry. She must surely be rated the reigning queen of American child psychoanalysis. Yet she is less known to the general public than she should be, because many university-based researchers in the field of early childhood development, when they write their articles and books, tend to overlook anyone whose name is associated with psychoanalysis. It is not that they necessarily go out of their way (though some do) to derogate whatever carries Freudian overtones; they simply ignore it as being outside the mainstream of their enterprise. Too bad. They (and their readers) are the poorer for it.

As one example, they would certainly have learned much from Mahler's brilliant, pioneering work. They did their research independently, without reference to hers, and it took them much longer to discover what she already knew—though her priority is seldom acknowledged.

In a survey of four new volumes on child development, a reviewer recently concluded that "the most extraordinary omission is the work of Margaret Mahler, with her detailed observations of the gradual individuation of the human infant in the first three years of life, the accompanying separation from the mother, and the extreme sensitivity of the reciprocal system between them." Neither does Burton White mention Mahler, even in his suggested reading list.

Among child psychoanalysts themselves, there has been no dearth of appreciation for Mahler's contributions.* She looms large by any criteria.

The separation-individuation process, as elaborated by Mahler and her associates, is much more than a theoretical construct. It is based on observation of her own patients (both adults and children); on studies of other people's work; on long studies of psychotic children in both hospitals and research settings; and, perhaps most importantly, on meticulously recorded observations over a long period

---

*See, for example, *Separation-Individuation: Essays in Honor of Margaret S. Mahler*, edited by John B. McDevitt and Calvin F. Settlage.

of time, not only of volunteer mothers (average "ordinary devoted mothers") but also of their normal children as they went from infancy to toddlerhood and beyond. The research was carried out by a dedicated team of investigators working with Mahler in a carefully planned experimental nursery setup, one that allowed maximum freedom and spontaneity for the subjects, day in and day out, and minimal obtrusiveness on the part of the observers.

In order to understand what occurs in separation-individuation, which goes on until at least age three, we must retrace our steps one more time, back to the early neophase. Mahler calls the first four or five months of life the period of "symbiosis." She is of course not using the term in its true biological meaning, which describes the close relationship of two organisms of two totally different species living together interdependently.

Symbiosis is the state to which adults regress in some forms of psychosis, and a state from which some psychotic children never emerge. In a healthier sense, symbiosis—at least dimly remembered—is, as Therese Benedek has pointed out, the dependency state called upon again and again by parents throughout their lives when their children, at any age, need help. Symbiosis has also been roughly compared to being in love. Freud himself wrote, in *Civilization and Its Discontents*: "At the height of being in love the boundary between ego and object threatens to melt away. Against all the evidence of his senses, a man who is in love declares 'I' and 'you' are one, and is prepared to behave as if it were a fact."

The fetus *in utero* lives in undeniable biological dependency upon its mother. Mahler's terminology emphasizes not only the newborn's continuing dependence on the mother, but also his probable perception of himself as an integral part of his surroundings— though the surroundings have changed. The gradual unfolding, to the child, of the awareness of his own separateness as an individual is a multilayered process, rich in nuance and finely textured detail. It might be likened to a piece of music, with parent and child each participating as both composers and performers in an intricate, ongoing duet. Though the parent's participation is of course more conscious and intelligent than the baby's, a surprising lot of what a mother does is more instinctive, genetically programmed, intuitive—call it what you will—than intellectual and deliberate. To underscore the conviction that a human baby is no mere passive instrument, Mahler speaks, marveling, of the infant's "sending power"—an apparently "innate ability to evoke the kind of mothering he needs!" If the baby fails to transmit the cues, as programmed, or if the parent is receiving on the wrong frequency, then the separation-individuation process may be retarded or impaired.

At each step of the way, the budding personaut is simultaneously pulled in both directions—backward to the phase where he felt safe and comfortable, and forward as impelled by his healthy developmental urges. The organism's inertial desire is to remain where it has just barely gained a modicum of hard-won security, even to put up some resistance to the progressive stages of his developmental program. Yet the normal infant really *wants* to go, is ready to go, has already worked up an organic dissatisfaction with conditions that were formerly satisfying. Thus a conflict arises between reluctance and eagerness, and the parent, by sensing both the infant's readiness and his vacillation, must gently encourage him on to the next phase. Inasmuch as the phases are not sharply defined and do overlap in time (some vestiges of all phases probably remain with us throughout our lives), it is important—an importance that cannot be stressed too frequently—for the parent to attune her own readiness to that of the child. She should be on the alert to guide and reassure him, moving at *his* pace, permitting him to return as necessary for what Mahler's colleague, Manuel Furer, has termed "emotional refueling." The parent must also remain alert to her own emotional pitfalls. She may, as we have already warned, be impatient with a given phase—or feel inferior in the competition with some *other* mother's child who seems to be moving ahead more rapidly—and thus try to hurry her own child along, to push him before he is ready. Or she may enjoy a given phase and wish to prolong it for her own pleasure—or, alternatively, feel somehow threatened or annoyed at her child's growing independence. In any event, in such cases she is not ready when he is, and she finds excuses for holding him back.

We earlier compared the mother-infant interaction to an intricate duet. Extending the metaphor, the music resulting may range all the

way from the most tragic of dissonances to the loveliest of contra-
puntal harmonies. One could compare it also to a marathon tight-
rope walk; but the distance to the ground is not far, and an
occasional stumble is permitted—in fact bound to occur; it takes repeated falls to do any lasting injury. The essential strategy is to let
the child keep moving in his uneven progress, one step at a time, in
the direction of autonomy and independence—but encouraging each
step only when the time is right. The trick is to know when that is.
When in doubt, under normal circumstances, the child's own instincts are probably trustworthy.

There is a period lasting only a few weeks at the very beginning of
life, just before the onset of Mahler's symbiotic state, which she
calls—somewhat paralleling Piaget—"normal autism." This state
corresponds roughly to what Freud termed "primary narcissism,"
referring to the newborn being aware of nothing but his undifferentiated self. If he could think a thought, the thought would be: I am
everything, and everything is me (approximately the state fervently
sought by adult mystics). During normal autism, we suspect the
newborn has no awareness of acquiring sustenance from any source
outside himself—in a sense a continuation of the fetal state, in
which a homeostatic equilibrium was achieved with the maternal
environment. After its expulsion into a drastically revised environment, the organism has to readapt. It must achieve a new homeostatic equilibrium before it can go on to anything else; and this,
Mahler believes, is the principal purpose and task of the normal autistic period. "The human newborn," Burton White agrees, "seems
to be only partially prepared for life outside the womb, and the first
four to six weeks seem more like a transitional period between two
grossly different modes of existence than a time of growth." Most
of the time during this period, except for feedings and those brief
stretches of transitory alertness in which he demonstrates the capacities so surprising to recent investigators, the baby is either asleep
or somnolent.

In this state the newborn—though he responds to various kinds
of stimuli, as we have seen and though he may be tickled and
kitchy-kooed at by various relatives and visitors—is probably un-

able to differentiate the mother's ministrations (all designed to reduce tensions or discomforts, including hunger) from his own
bodily activities (eliminating, coughing, sneezing, burping, vomit-
ing), which themselves have the general purpose of relieving tensions or discomforts of one kind or another. His sensations are
mostly whole-body, "global" sensations, and nearly all are internalized. Even at this stage, however, he is already equipped with the
program that will direct him toward his autonomy, only it cannot be
tapped or utilized until the organism has achieved the biological
balance that the normal autistic period allows; and even then it is
brought forth only through the nurturant activities of the parent.
Nevertheless, the infant probably begins, during the autistic phase,
to sort out and classify—at least in a primordial fashion—those experiences it will consider good or bad, pleasing or displeasing. Tensions and discomforts will be unpleasant, and will evoke crying
responses or other attempts to relieve them; they are forerunners of
what will later be consciously thought of as distressing or "bad."
The relief from them—the food, the elimination, the diaper
change—will be experienced as pleasurable or "good." And, within
a month or so, with the first inchoate awareness that some of his
need satisfactions come from a vague elsewhere, he begins to associate his mother with the good things, or at least relief from bad
things.

It is this first dim sense of Something Other that marks, for Mahler, the beginning of symbiosis. Though the child may now begin to
become aware of an outside world, that world is outside both himself and the mother. He and his mother are a single, unified organism. He "behaves and functions," in Mahler's words, "as though he
and his mother were an omnipotent system—a dual unity with one
common boundary." And though his tension-relieving satisfactions
may begin to be perceived as coming from elsewhere, that elsewhere
is still *"within the orbit of the omnipotent symbiotic dual unity"* (the italics
are Mahler's).

There is also a shift in the way the body experiences itself. From
an almost exclusive preoccupation with sensations from his muscles,
tendons, joints, and internal organs—their focus all inward-directed—there is a gradual switch of attention to sensory input from the

body's periphery, from its interface with external reality. This is the start on the road to understanding that an external reality does exist, stretching beyond the self and of which the self is not a part.

The infant's incipient awareness of that outside world soon reaches a point where it starts to encompass what Spitz has called a "unified situational experience," usually a mass in motion, and the first such recognizable mass is his mother's face. This process of recognition is enhanced if the mother frequently holds the baby so they can be face-to-face, preferably with eye-to-eye contact; and it is further enhanced if she also talks to him, sings to him, and plays with him on a level that pleases him. This is when the baby begins to smile those first smiles that are not as yet associated with any particular act or person.

As these repeated interactions with his mother begin to be felt as clusters of similar events, events that are experienced dependably again and again, they become "memory islands"—familiar and, in a primitive way, recognizable as having been experienced before. This is a distinguishing mark of the onset of "secondary narcissism."

Narcissism is usually thought of as self-love, especially for one's body—and Mahler does use it, as Freud did, in that sense; but whereas the primary narcissism in the autistic phase was a total immersion in the undefined sensations that included his own body along with everything else, in symbiosis the infant moves into a secondary narcissism, an appreciative focus on his body *as itself*—separate from the rest of the world (though still not from his mother). This is an extremely important step. As Mahler puts it: "Only when the body becomes the object of the infant's secondary narcissism, via the mother's loving care, does the external object become eligible for identification." When the baby *can* identify the "eligible" object—his own body—and also begins with his peripheral sense to experience another presence, even though still perceived as another part of his larger self, he begins to appreciate that other part of himself in a different way and "gives it credit," as it were, for much of the inner pleasure and security he attains. "The result," says Mahler, "should be an optimal symbiotic state out of which smooth differentiation—*and expansion beyond the symbiotic orbit*—can take place." The infant does a lot of gurgling and giggling during this middle period of symbiosis—at the age of, usually, three or four months. According to Burton White, it is the happiest period the child will ever experience in his entire lifetime. Mahler clearly considers normal autism and normal symbiosis prerequisites to the attainment of a healthy separation-individuation.

Of critical importance throughout symbiosis is the way mothers communicate with their babies through holding and handling—a complex, subtle activity that is more than merely tactile. Mahler regards "holding behaviors" as nothing less than "the symbiotic organizers of psychological birth." Breast-feeding in itself is no guarantor of satisfactory holding behavior. Among the mothers Mahler studied, for instance, there was one who simply found breast-feeding easier than sterilizing bottles; at feeding time, she supported the baby in her lap in such a way as to allow her to keep her hands free to do other things. Another mother, because of her puritanical upbringing, could not feel at ease nursing her baby, and particularly did not like to be seen doing it; there was something not quite nice about it. In both these cases, the symbiotic relationship was less than optimal. Another mother bottle-fed her babies, but cradled, cuddled, and supported them lovingly, meanwhile doing a lot of smiling and talking. These children enjoyed a visibly more successful symbiosis.

Yet another woman's mothering patterns were curiously mechanical and distant. Though she would rock the baby in her lap, she did it in a "tense, unrelated way." Later the child would rock herself for comfort, sometimes looking in the mirror as she did so—a strangely lost little person. If a mother is afflicted with certain types of emotional disturbance, and there is no strong counteracting influence from another caregiver, the result in later childhood may be the illness known as *folie à deux*, where in a close two-person relationship one person's "craziness" is "caught" by the other. Careful study of children who were in the care of psychotically delusional mothers during critical periods provides evidence that there is nothing automatic about the carrying out of separation-individuation. Though there are children who manage to survive such deleterious exposure without lasting damage, many more are susceptible to it. Much may depend on what other sources of support are available to the child.

Children caught in such situations, according to E. James Anthony, who has studied many such cases, not only fail to differentiate with complete success, but are "of less than average intelligence, dependent, submissive, suggestible, and deeply involved with the ill parent. . . ."

"When interviewing these children," Anthony writes, "it was difficult to regard them as separate individuals since only a part of them appeared to be in contact with the interviewer. . . . We were most impressed by the absence of a sense of humor. It would seem that the acquisition of a sense of humor, like the sense of reality and the sense of identity, is part of the separation-individuation process."

Anthony's observations, along with those of many other investigators, indicate that failure to separate and individuate successfully can have serious and long-range consequences.

By about four or five months, the age that Mahler regards as the "peak of symbiosis," the baby's smile has gradually evolved from a random sort of tic, to a response to the configuration of a human face, to a controlled social act. He now begins to smile specifically and preferentially at his mother—the interaction that Bowlby counted as the telltale sign that a specific mother-infant bond had been established.

The baby is now ready to "hatch," to begin breaking out of the symbiotic membrane. The hatching process, a most imprecise occurrence, takes place somewhere around five or six months. The infant now stays awake for longer periods of time. Instead of drifting in and out of semi-sleep, he looks alert and has a more persistent attention span. And now, while his mother holds him, he is no longer content merely to snuggle against her. He strains back to stare at her face. He looks her up and down. He looks around. And he begins to explore his mother with his hands—her face, her arms, her breasts, anything he can reach—thus beginning to "learn" her through touch. He is equally curious about handling anything she wears or carries—glasses, necklace, pin, wristwatch, anything. This period of increasing exploration including the first experimental crawlings away from his mother, begins at about five and a half months and lasts until the end of the neophase (eight to ten months). It is a most enjoyable time for many a parent, who is well advised to enjoy it while she can. Things will soon change.

As early as perhaps six weeks of age, the baby already began to notice his hands and, as the weeks went by, increasingly stared at these strange objects, at rest or in motion (though only at Mahler's hatching stage, around six months, can an infant's eyes really bring his hands into sharp focus). He also learned to use his hands for reaching and grasping. It is from such simple acts as these—grasping, reaching, staring, scanning, examining repeatedly with hand and eye—that Piaget believes the child begins to move in the direction of his developing intelligence. To know, to learn, he must first look and touch. Thus, what better way to know his mother—this supreme satisfier of his needs who, until recently, was considered a part of his own self?

At seven to eight months, the child is more and more checking back with his mother visually, which suggests that he has begun to recognize her separate status—and that he knows where she is (or at least where she was when he last looked). He slides down from his mother's lap; he no longer wants to be held all the time, but he does like to know she is nearby, and he keeps crawling back, perhaps to play at her feet, or to stand shakily, holding onto her knee for support. He also begins "comparative scanning." While fascination with his mother is still paramount, he is now interested as well in comparing her with other people, to learn for sure which one she is and which not, also which objects (ring, bracelet, eyeglasses) belong to her and which not, and to ascertain as well that her objects *are* objects, separate from her person. These comparative explorations are not just a matter of visual scanning, they occupy all his senses.

As we noted in the last chapter, at the very time when the child is becoming aware of his mother as a truly separate individual, when he is, in a conscious way, more attached to her and more dependent upon her than ever—has, one might say, fallen in love with her—it is at this moment that all his innate developmental urges are pulling him away from her, toward his increasing independence. He wants to stay with her, and he wants to leave her. It is a wise parent who will let him have it both ways, who will constantly reassure him not only that he may feel free to move away, but also that he can come back anytime he pleases.

At this time when his curiosity about other people is being kindled, he is also afflicted—perhaps due to the concomitant maturation of his adrenal-hormonal apparatus—with "stranger anxiety." Mahler, like White, believes that stranger anxiety in its acute form may be overrated. Many children do react with undeniable vehemence and fear in the presence of strangers—even people they "know" only slightly. Others, however, react only mildly. Much depends on the kind of basic trust the child has developed up to this point, whether or not a parent is present, and how the "stranger" behaves. Except in extreme cases, the stranger usually evokes fear or anxiety only when actively paying attention to the child, especially if the attention is aggressive, however benevolent. As soon as the stranger averts his or her gaze, or if the stranger simply hasn't paid any attention to the child from the outset, the child becomes very interested and scans the stranger with great curiosity—the activity that Sylvia Brody has called "customs inspection." This may even happen face-to-face with a stranger if the mother is at hand to lend a sense of security. How soon the child overcomes his stranger anxiety will depend upon how severe it is in the first place, and how the parents deal with it—just as is true of all other phases of development. The manner in which the parents help, hinder, or remain indifferent to their child's passage through these treacherous transition periods will, to a large extent, dictate behavior patterns— or "scripts," as the transactional analysts like to call them—that may last a lifetime. Long-term follow-up studies of such patterns have, however, barely begun.

The exploratory behavior we have just been describing is part of what Mahler classifies as the first subphase (there are four) of separation-individuation, and which she labels "differentiation and development of body image." The subphases do not represent clean-cut breaks in time or behavior, precipitous jumps from one state to another. Rather they overlap with gradual transitions. Nor do all children pass through them on the same precise schedule. (See chart on pages 173–79.)

Though apparently combined at first, separation and individuation do proceed on different developmental tracks, as Mahler takes pains to explain. Becoming an individual is one distinct task; separating oneself from other people (initially the mother) and from the environment is another task. So while the two proceed simultaneously, they do not necessarily progress in synchrony. On the one hand, the child is evolving and structuring his cognitive faculties, his "reality testing." On the other, he is differentiating himself from the rest of the world, learning where his boundaries are, learning to place himself in time and space relative to others, to study the meaning of distance between things and people, to disengage successfully when he chooses to. And concurrent with both processes, he is experiencing a continuing series of interactions between the two (and being stimulated to puzzle out what they mean), to "ask" himself: Which sensations and occurrences are purely internal and which are instigated from the outside? What impact do I have, what influence can I hope to exercise, over other people and things? What impact do they have on me—and can I avoid what is "bad" (or at least minimize it) and enhance what is "good"? Which obstacles can I overcome and which can I not? What interferes with my wishes and needs? What risks dare I take with reasonable safety?

Mahler and her colleagues found that the best way for investigators to learn about the two tracks of separation and individuation, as well as their interactions, and to see what success children had in carrying out their programs, was to observe the complicated and detailed daily transactions that took place between mothers and their children from infancy through age three (when, if all has gone well, the job is essentially done).

The first subphase of separation-individuation is essentially over by the end of the neophase. The infant has made the differentiation between himself and his mother and has become aware, as well, of the separate nature of other people and objects in his surroundings, thus reinforcing his own body image, his sense of himself as a distinct entity. This fairly clear-cut new awareness has not been without its cost in pain and anxiety. Driven though he might have been to leave the symbiotic state, it was a mighty cozy state to inhabit, one that may well have included a vague set of ideas about a magical joint existence with his omnipotent mother. (The baby's mental processes can not yet produce such abstractions as "omnipotence.") Suddenly he is more on his own than he thought, a situation that is exciting, yet scary. He begins to understand, for example, that his love object, being a separate person, can leave him, and that he cannot necessarily control the time of her return. In the beginning, he may fear that she won't return at all (as indeed, she occasionally may not, for periods of time that to the baby must seem eternities), and thus he may suffer "separation anxiety" when she departs. Hence the increased necessity for establishing the specific bond (Bowlby's "attachment" process) with the mother. The child needs to know that the omnipotent parent will still be around, on call to rescue him and to continue to serve his needs, as he enters the second subphase—"practicing."

During the practicing period, the newly toddling child puts a great deal of energy into testing the expanding limits of his orbit of independence, an enterprise that is full of risk, both physical and emotional. In a normally developing child, this phase, despite the perils involved, also brings great elation—a joy in his new locomotive powers and exploratory adventures that at times takes over his whole being, to the point where even his interest in his mother momentarily takes on secondary importance. What he is practicing, then, is not so much the perfection of his new motor skills as the feeling of what it is like to be separating himself from total dependence on his mother, and to be functioning as an autonomous individual at some physical distance from her.

"Early practicing," as Mahler terms it, actually begins during the previous subphase, as soon as the infant can move away from his mother and put some distance between them—by crawling, paddling, or standing away from her while holding onto something for support. He keeps the distance minimal, however, and his major fascination is still her own person, though his interest now spills over to any object she may offer him—say, a rattle or a piece of cloth. He examines it with the most complete curiosity, using every sensory resource at his command. He looks it over; he feels, smells, rubs, bites, nibbles, sucks, chews it; turns it this way and that; shakes it; listens to it; may, for a time, become attached to it (the notorious "security blanket"). He will soon be extending these atten-

tions to a wider diversity of objects over an ever expanding
territory.

This early practicing provides a new set of experiences for the
mother as well, and presents new adjustment problems. In some
cases, the closeness of the earlier period may have been a little sti-
fling or uncomfortable for one or the other member of the dyad. In
that event, the ability to begin relating to each other at a distance
may actually come as a relief. Children in these circumstances may
be more relaxed, and thus able to grow even more attached, and
show it more openly. In other cases, mothers who hate to see the
end of symbiosis may try to prolong it by actively preventing the
child from moving away; or, resigned to its inevitability but not
much interested in the next phase, they may be impatient for their
children to grow up, to somehow hurry their independence, to "get
it over with." An immature mother may resent the child's new mobility, may even take personal offense at it. Her actions seem to say:
If this is what you want, okay, but don't expect any help from *me*.
This same mother may still run, at unpredictable moments, to scoop
the baby up in her arms for a session of hugging and snuggling—but
only when *she* needs it.

Often the signals a child receives from his mother are subtle.
After all, the infant has come out of the neophase as at least a slightly adapted social creature, with a developing consciousness of what
is expected of him, especially by his principal caregiver. He has a
fine-tuned sensitivity to his mother's gestures, scowls, variations of
facial expression, all her body language—even her verbalizings (at
least in their tone and pitch, since he cannot yet understand any of
the words). He can sense a lot about her perception of him as worthy or not worthy of love or esteem (which will of course affect his
own sense of self-love or self-esteem), as a disappointment or a joy,
as competent or clumsy; and he can tell whether she is pleased or
not pleased with the changing state of affairs.

Mahler tells of two children, each of whom has enjoyed a close
and mutually satisfying symbiosis with the parent. One mother dislikes the revised situation; the child at a distance feels lost and bewildered. The other mother is ready to give up the phase she has
enjoyed so much and take up the new one as an equally enjoyable

challenge; *her* child still feels close and secure, even at a distance—as long as he can look back to see her, or hear her voice.

An early-practicing infant needs to return frequently to the mother for emotional refueling. The act might even more appropriately be called a refueling *dialogue*. After touching home base the child usually perks up and is ready to go again—depending, of course, on what took place during the refueling dialogue. The interactions here are complex and rich with overtones; either they help fill the gaps in the child's developing skills and comprehension, or they act as retardants. The way in which reward alternates with punishment, or praise with criticism (and what forms they take), has a great influence on the child's progress. Parental attitudes, and the child's fantasies about them, often activate one kind of behavior over another. These attitudes, real or fancied, may, as already mentioned, turn into lifetime programs (for example, Eric Berne's "winner/loser scripts"), self-fulfilling prophecies, even codified transmissions of certain self-concepts to the next generation. A child may be viewed as a replica of the parent's own disappointment with herself, thus compounding it as now visibly reincarnated; or he may be seen as a savior, a resurrected self, born to fulfill the parent's frustrated hopes now rekindled—the potential not dead after all. The refueling dialogues are thus richly textured interpersonal events that determine how one set or another of mental mechanisms are activated, cultivated—or extinguished. What the parent achieves for the child during refueling will, one hopes, activate him in the direction of his own readiness. He needs this periodic stimulus, the reward of attention and encouragement, a confirmation of his prowess, a vote of confidence. He also needs to receive permission, as it were, to come back to rest from his new exertions, to return to earlier modes and be held, cuddled, or reassured, and to recuperate from his unaccustomed and daring sorties into new emotional frontiers. These refueling interludes are necessary just as sleep is necessary. A mother with good empathic responses, resonant to the child's needs, will carefully observe his exploratory patterns and refueling rhythms at each stage of the process. If she doesn't allow the necessary respites, the child will regress to former levels rather than move ahead; either his progress in skill development will come to a virtual halt—or at least a sharp slowdown—or he may be pushed ahead to a shallow (and, in its way, just as stunting) precociousness where he operates most uneasily.

The parent is also faced, at this stage, with locating that tenuous line between overprotection and insufficient surveillance. Often a parent does err in the direction of overprotection, of inadvertently instilling in the child a conditioned anxiety, a chronic fear of moving out into the world. Or a child may be overencouraged, as we have seen, by a too-impatient parent who wants to see him get on with the job; he may then indeed achieve a certain autonomy, in order to please her, but it is a sadly depleted autonomy that lacks confidence and substance. Curiously, a similar result may be brought about by a mother who merely seeks to avoid being overprotective. She may be reluctant to set limits that might retard the child's confident development. In order to keep him from being anxious and fearful, she may fail to follow ordinary precautions and thereby expose him to unnecessary danger. She feels free to go to the child only when he falls and cries. She may in fact be worried about his safety every inch of the way, but *he* doesn't know that. Hence he feels abandoned, even when she is right there in the same room: She doesn't respond when he needs her; she doesn't care.

There are no set formulas to guarantee optimal success. Each mother must know herself as well as her own child, and must sense what behavior is called for by their constantly evolving interactions at any given time. A central reminder for the mother is simply to keep her focus, as much as she can, on the *child's* needs. If she is a mature, sensible person, she will probably do well enough most of the time.

What Mahler terms the "practicing subphase proper," as distinguished from "early practicing," doesn't officially begin until the child can really walk on his own. He may waddle or toddle with a somewhat uncertain gait, but he no longer needs to hold on to anything for support. This new talent considerably extends the range of his adventures. Moreover, he can now get from here to there much faster. Thus it becomes a problem for his caretakers to keep track of him. Nevertheless, the mother is usually relieved and happy to see this talent emerge; she feels it is a sign that her child has "made it" in some important way. And indeed he has.

He now enters a truly exhilarating period, what psychoanalyst Phyllis Greenacre has called his "love affair with the world." "The toddler," says Mahler, "takes the greatest step in human individuation. He walks freely with upright posture. Thus, the plane of his vision changes; from an entirely new vantage point he finds unexpected and changing perspective, pleasures and frustrations.... During this precious 6 to 8 months (from the age of 10 or 12 months to 16 or 18 months), the world is the junior toddler's oyster ... the child seems intoxicated with his own faculties and with the greatness of his own world. Narcissism is at its peak!"

The child is now intent on mastering his skills, and enjoying the thrill of a newly sensed "I" moving exuberantly through a world that belongs to him. With such feelings of grandeur and near-omnipotence, he is willing to make some trade-offs: his fear (definitely still there, though subdued at this point) that his new independence will somehow result in the loss of his still most-loved object, his mother, is overcome by the fun and fascination of his new capacities and the freedom they provide. For boys and girls alike, walking represents a major step in asserting individuality and in forming a sense of identity. During this period, they rediscover their urinary apparatus, genitals, and anal regions, experiencing them in a new way in the upright position. They become fascinated with the sensations and processes of excretion. For either sex, it is a somewhat euphoric period. Substitute adults are more easily accepted; the child is good-humored about bumps, falls, and frustrations;* in play such as peekaboo games, he becomes more the instigator and less the passive participant.

The child, while all this is going on, and though still strongly bound to his mother, is paradoxically eager to avoid being reengulfed by her. He runs from her, until she chases him and picks him up for a quick, close hug before letting him go again. Though he

---

*Now that endorphins, the brain's own pain-relievers, have been discovered, one is tempted to speculate on whether nature may not have provided the child's body at this point of development with an increased production of endorphins to minimize traumatic events that might otherwise discourage him from following his developmental programming.

runs to escape again, really wanting to avoid a return to the relative imprisonment of former days, he likes the fact that she still wants to catch him. More than ever at this stage, he needs his mother's emotional support. And she should take delight in it, especially since the child will soon be riding for a fall.

Her behavior, her overt acts, and her subtle cues, will seriously affect how well the child fares in all he does. Sören Kierkegaard, the nineteenth-century Danish philosopher-theologian, understood this very well. In *Purity of Heart*, he described two different mothers with their ready-to-walk children (the italics are his):

> The loving mother teaches her child to walk alone. She is far enough from him so that she cannot actually support him, but she holds out her arms to him. She imitates his movements, and if he totters, she swiftly bends as if to seize him, so that the child might believe that he is not walking alone. And yet, she does more. Her face beckons like a reward, encouragement. Thus, the child walks alone with his eyes fixed on his mother's face *not* on the difficulties in his way. He supports himself by the arms that do not hold him and constantly strives towards the refuge in his mother's embrace, little suspecting *that in the very same moment that he is emphasizing his need of her, he is proving that he can do without her*, because he is walking alone.

But watch the other mother:

> There is no beckoning encouragement, no blessing at the end of the walk. There is the same wish to teach the child to walk alone, but not as a loving mother does it. For now there is fear that envelops the child. It weighs him down so that he cannot move forward. There is the same wish to lead him to the goal, *but the goal becomes suddenly terrifying.*

These passages from Kierkegaard are quoted in an essay about separation-individuation by E. James Anthony. Anthony himself then goes on to say:

> The fearfulness, the ambivalence, the unconscious hostility, the need to encapsulate, hinder the child from stepping off on his

own. With his delicate insightfulness, Kierkegaard crystallizes the
moments of development when the toddler feels the pull of separation from his mother and at the same time asserts his individuation. It is a mixed experience of enormous developmental
significance, the child demonstrating that he can and cannot do
without his mother, and his mother demonstrating that she can
and cannot let him walk alone. The psychotic mother fills these
moments with apprehension so that the child not only has nowhere to go, but he is afraid to get anywhere.

A child deprived of nourishing, optimistic—though careful—parental guidance through this period shows signs of his deprivation
later. Such a child, says Anthony at the close of his essay, is "less
exploratory, less curious, less daring, and more inclined to operate
within a margin of safety than other children." Moreover, he
"shows a consistently deficient sense of reality and constantly re-
sorts to fantasied solutions and comforts."

We warned, in describing the "high" state of the practicing subphase, that the child was riding for a fall. The fall may be a hard
one, and it arrives inevitably with the third subphase, "rapprochement." There is no way the developing child can remain indefinitely
in the heady realm of "practicing." A major purpose of that subphase is, after all, to enable the child to proceed at an accelerated
pace with his reality testing; and that testing soon teaches him
bluntly that reality does not coincide with his illusions of grandeur
and omnipotence. A whole set of realizations crash down upon him
simultaneously.

Impressive though his new capacities are (compared to what they
were), they will not really take him very far. He now dimly glimpses
the extent of his incomprehension of that enlarged world that he
clearly sees is Out There—a world not necessarily friendly. There is
so much he still cannot cope with, on top of which he is getting a
better idea every day of how much more there is that he cannot
manage to do. For virtually all his needs he must still turn to his
mother. He suddenly feels very small and dependent, and he resents
the sudden turnabout in his perceptions. He craves his mother's

ministrations more than ever, and may even wish for a return to symbiosis; yet all his biological programming tells him: You can't go home again.

In the symbiotic state he felt himself to be merged securely in a perpetual union with omnipotence. Now, over the period of fluctuating moods, experiences, and accumulations of understanding that have come with early separation-individuation, he has learned that he *is* a separate—and rather puny, helpless, scared—little individual, ultimately not merged with anyone but himself, a self on whom he knows he cannot count for anything like adequate succor or support. These hard facts are bound to represent a precipitous comedown after such a recent ego trip. Along with this shocker comes the further understanding that his mother, too, is a separate individual upon whom he is still terribly dependent—and who can leave him at any time. Since he is pulling away from her by design, why shouldn't *she* want to pull away from *him*? Will she still be around when he needs her? Often now she isn't. Can he count on continuing care from this separate person? On continuing love from this supreme love object all his own, to whom he has become so newly and deeply attached on a conscious personal level? He has been learning the cruel truth that his mother (or for that matter his father and other adults who now begin to come more and more into his perceptual scheme of things) is not omnipotent either. His parents often cannot fulfill specific desires, even should they wish to; nor can they protect him from danger or make his hurts vanish, as if by magic, with a word or a touch.

So, having lost his magical union with omnipotence, as well as his own vague, infantile delusions of personal omnipotence, he has in addition lost the reassurance of his loved one's constant presence and the further assurance of her *ability*, let alone her willingness, to keep satisfying his needs. In other words, he has had forced upon his attention the first inklings of what it is like to be alive and human in the real world. No wonder there is a "rapprochement crisis" for almost every child. At any time of life, a major loss calls for a period of grief and mourning; why should a child at such a tender age not grieve for his lost Camelot?

The parent, perhaps not understanding such subphasal fluctuations as a natural series of events, may wonder: What's come over the child? He was so happy and exuberant—and now, suddenly, this. What am I doing wrong? She may look upon his new anxieties and somewhat depressed mood as a sign of abnormal regression. What she may not realize is that the child must now, as in many later stages of life, go backward again before he can go forward. He must go through the difficult rapprochement subphase in order to proceed to the next and final subphase of separation-individuation.

Rapprochement doesn't occur overnight, any more than did the previous subphases. Earlier—about the middle of the second year—the child was still toddling along happily, apparently having accepted and consolidated his newfound selfhood. But now he begins to be a bit less impervious to hurts and frustrations. Whereas he had all but ignored his mother while going about his vigorous practicing investigations, he now takes a new interest in her—a concerned interest. The separation anxiety that he had experienced earlier for a brief time now returns with heightened intensity. Stranger anxiety resurfaces, too, also at a heightened level.

Soon the child is stalking his mother constantly, trying to keep track of her whereabouts. If she is not around, he wants to know where she is, and remains visibly restless until she gets back. Language now takes on new importance, as does play. One of the games he plays is to shadow his mother until she notices him, then dart away in hopes that she'll chase him. If she doesn't, he comes back and tries again. Though he does not want to go back to his former state (not really), he does need to feel closer again. Everything that happens to him, he wants his mother to see and share. Every object that is of interest to him, he brings to her for inspection, approval, play, or mutual commentary—verbal or otherwise. If the mother pays little or no attention, or is impatient because her "big boy" seems to be reverting to babyhood again, he will woo her in every way he can think of. If he can get the desired attention only by misbehaving—by breaking something, hurting himself, throwing a tantrum—he may resort to any or all of these stratagems.

This is perhaps the most delicately hazardous period of the entire separation-individuation process, and requires the most understanding and tolerance from his parents, especially the mother. Very little mention has been made so far of the father's role in all this. The omission is only partly due to the fact that most of the parents used in Mahler's research were mothers; the fathers were away at other work. Some of Mahler's colleagues, however—notably Ernest L. Abelin—have made special studies of the father's role.

Where *is* the father during symbiosis and separation-individuation? He is, of course, around and participating in his own way. More than that, Abelin believes that the proper carrying out of a whole series of essential interactions may be impossible for either mother or child, or both, *without* the father's presence. (If true, the theory could have serious implications for the future of children being raised by single parents—a topic we will come to in a later chapter.) Nevertheless, from the infant's point of view, the father is not the *central* figure, at least at the outset.* During symbiosis, the father (or a sibling) is a vague something-out-there presence on the periphery of the infant's awareness. Siblings, in fact, can make an impact sooner, perhaps because of their more relatable size.

Not long after the infant's attachment to the mother has been well established, a bond begins to be formed with the father, albeit a bond somewhat weaker and different in nature from the mother's. And as the father takes shape for the baby as a separate, significant other person in his life, the baby may also become aware that there exists a special bond between this other person and his own beloved mother. This normally causes no problem during infancy. If the growing consciousness of the father's presence happens to coincide with the onset of stranger anxiety, the child could be a bit standoffish for a while, especially if the father has previously spent very little time with him. The male parent—assuming he is not the principal caregiver—comes into his own most notably during the active practicing period. When the child begins to explore the nonmother world with such great curiosity, one of the things he

---

*There occur rare instances when—if mother and infant are somehow miscuing, not getting through to one another—the father may become the preferred figure before the child reaches six months. This may make for confusion, but it may also serve as a rescue mission. Usually the bond with the mother, though delayed, *is* eventually formed, and meanwhile the father's emotional availability has tided everyone over the critical period.

discovers out there is his father. The father, who in our culture usually plays with more physical exuberance than the mother, may himself become—particularly in the context of this exuberant subphase—the very symbol of exuberance. He becomes not a "second mother," but a different parent, another person, on whom the child can depend for additional satisfactions. The awareness of an important other, non-mother person provides, to use a surveyor's term, a basis for early mental "triangulation." The presence of two separate, recognized objects in the outer world provides a more precise way for localizing the self.

The father can be of great help in getting both mother and child through the rapprochement crisis—if he is aware of what's happening, and why. If he is unaware and insensitive, on the other hand, and if, besides, he acts in ways that emphasize his "ownership" of the child's love object (such a father may have become jealous of the child and the attention he's been getting), then his presence can aggravate and prolong the crisis. A sense of premature rivalry with the father can be an additional hazard at a time when the child is developing his own gender identity. It is the period when a girl, if she has had the opportunity to be aware of genital differences—an opportunity that, more frequently than not, has occurred by now—may acquire the psychoanalytically celebrated "penis envy." If the boy has a similar opportunity, the stage may be set for later "castration anxiety." (If she doesn't have one, might I not lose mine too?) All this is further complicated by the gradual change (though the periods overlap) from the oral to the anal phase of psychosexual development—which is nearly always a somewhat jealous and aggressive time for the child (as will be seen in chapter 9).

By about the twenty-first or twenty-second month, if nothing has occurred to upset the normal course of expectable events, the rapprochement crisis should have begun to subside. The child is getting somewhat accustomed to his ejection from Eden and is learning to cope more successfully, especially as his skills continue to develop. His more expert locomotive powers help him feel more secure; his use of symbolic play allows him to express feelings he scarcely knew he had; and the beginnings of verbalization give him a new sense of having some control over the outside world, including his parents. Apart from understanding more and more of what they communicate to him, he is beginning to say real words—and is impressed by the power a single syllable (accompanied by gestures) can command: Up! Down! Here! Eat! Light! No! Yes! By the time his second birthday approaches, so does the fourth and last subphase of separation-individuation, which Mahler calls "consolidation of individuality and the beginnings of object constancy."

The child already achieved, much earlier, what Piaget thought of as "object permanence"—the understanding that an inanimate object, any object, has an independent existence of its own, whether it is within the child's sensory field or not. He knows that he can carry a toy to another room, then leave the room, with a clear-cut comprehension that the toy is still there—unless someone has moved it again, but even then he knows the toy exists somewhere, though its momentary specific whereabouts may be unknown to him. That most personal of objects, the mother, is finally "known" in the same way, but a calm certainty of her existence takes longer to achieve because all the child's relations with this "object" are so laden with self-preservative needs and stirring emotions—often in conflict. She is such an important object that he requires repeated reassurances of her permanence—or, as Mahler prefers to call it in this regard, her "constancy." The child needs to carry in his head a strongly imaged "internal mother," a keepsake that reassures him of her constant existence. Even if she is not around at the moment, she will be back; she hasn't vanished forever. Naturally, during this period of forming object constancy, the child will be particularly vulnerable to any long separations from his mother—due, say, to vacations, business trips, extended hospitalizations—or, worst of all, her death.

A constant, objectified "inner mother" goes a long way toward providing the child with the confidence to function equally well whether the mother is physically present or not. Along with this security, and developing side by side with it, comes the strengthening of the child's ego structure, a surer sense of his individual identity. This goes on all through the child's third year of life, while he continues to develop and handle multiplying relationships with other "constant objects"—his father, brothers and sisters, if any, and assorted friends, relatives, neighbors, baby-sitters, playmates, even more occasional human objects such as the pediatrician or minister.

This fourth and final subphase is a continuation and consolidation of all the rest—often with occasional regressions to previous stages. We referred earlier to Mahler's concept of "hatching," the child's breaking out of the symbiotic membrane. But the hatching process really encompasses the entire separation-individuation period. The third year of life is where it all comes together, and this is a time when parents are well advised to create the least possible disturbance of the child's stability; severely upsetting experiences may send him back to earlier subphases, with the job of doing over again everything lost—perhaps more easily because of the previous "rehearsal," or perhaps with more difficulty because the child, once burned, is more wary and less confident the next time around. And certainly a setback at this point may interfere with concomitant developments, such as rapidly evolving ability to speak, increasing expertise in motor coordination, and a new awareness of time and timed events.

As is true in all stages, the parents will be most helpful if they remain sensitive to the child's state of readiness—his vacillations, his specific anxieties and joys—and if they gently encourage him to move ahead at the appropriate time, at his own unique pace, evaluated in the context of the family's own unique circumstances—with easy permission for temporary returns for refueling stops.

With all this tender concern we keep recommending for the child's feelings and adjustment problems through these transitions, it may seem contradictory that we also strongly recommend the beginnings of discipline. As the child leaves the neophase, he *can* begin to be "spoiled." For many good reasons, he must begin to learn tolerance of frustration—in very small doses at first, then in gradually increasing quantities. We will come back to this delicate parental task, but for now we want simply to emphasize that the development of frustration tolerance will make it a bit less difficult for the child to cope with the various transitions of separation-individuation, and especially with the multiple frustrations and sense of loss that accompany the rapprochement crisis. We have seen how the child goes from the bliss of symbiosis to the gradual emergence of separation anxiety and stranger anxiety; from the euphoric exuberance of practicing to the shock of new reality that characterizes rapprochement; all toward his gradual emergence into a new period of consolidation—which will, itself, give way to the next step in his development.

In both cases, symbiosis and practicing, there is a paradise lost for which the child must, in a sense, grieve. Whenever a human individual loses something or someone dear to him, through death or some lesser calamity, grief is normal; and so is recovery from grief. Throughout each of our lives, we undergo a continuing series of phases—periods of stability followed by periods of sometimes painful transition. If our stable periods have been identified as good, then we regret having to leave them behind; it is natural to experience the termination of a period to which we had been attached as a loss, and it is therefore appropriate to mourn it—in a subdued, adaptive way, but openly and intelligently acknowledging the loss so it can be put to rest (though our recollections of it may be both endearing and enduring), leaving us free to welcome what comes next. It would not be too great an exaggeration to say that we all go through a series of miniscale deaths and rebirths.

The separation-individuation process that is the central theme of the first three years of life presents each personaut with his first opportunity to rehearse this constantly recurring grief-and-recovery, death-and-rebirth process. This first rehearsal happens at a time when the star of the show, so to speak, is largely at the mercy of his director. How the rehearsal goes will set the pattern—a pattern revisable only with much later work—for all subsequent performances. The pattern dictates how the actor perceives himself and how his various audiences perceive him: in brief, whether he develops a healthy self-esteem, whether he is capable of loving and being loved, whether he can admire and appreciate what others achieve without undue envy, whether he can attain a sane balance between selfishness and altruism, even whether he can hope to be a successful parent himself.

George Bernard Shaw once quipped that "being in love means greatly exaggerating the differences between one woman and another." Obviously a male remark, but as applicable to women as to men. Pursuing this idea seriously, Martin S. Bergmann believes that it is precisely the symbiotic bond, in which the mother is as exaggeratedly different as it is possible for another person to be, plus a successful separation-individuation, that instills in us the deep *experience*, and thus the capability, of exaggerating the difference between one human being and another—and thus the capacity to attach to someone, later in life, in the devoted manner we describe as falling in love. As Bergmann puts it, "when the symbiotic phase gives way to further development, it leaves as a residue a longing which remains ungratified until love comes."

If there is too frequent a shift in caregivers, or if a child is constantly switched from one foster home to another, in the event of institutionalization—and, for these reasons or any other, fails to make the necessary one-to-one bond with a single central individual—he may find himself incapable of falling in love as an adult. This entire early period of life will, in most cases, be submerged so deeply in memory as never to be consciously thought of again; yet the impact on the child's future will be immeasurable. No wonder this period has been characterized as "the unrememberable and the unforgettable."

We promised to return to a topic of great concern (and often of puzzlement and frustration too) to all parents, and of primary importance to the child's developing character: discipline. We did recommend an absence of discipline during the neophase—partly because the baby is not yet equipped to understand or benefit from it, partly because a major task of the parent in those first eight to ten months is to establish basic trust. If that trust has been won from the child, then the start of discipline should be easier. Just as trust was gradually achieved by consistency, by reliability and predictability of care-giving patterns, now the trusted person can begin gradually, cautiously, to set behavioral rules and restrictions in the same consistent and predictable manner. If the baby is by now secure in his parent's love, that love will not be perceived as under threat of loss with every "No" or at any sign of displeasure.

A "spoiled" child, in the popular sense of the word, is one who knows no boundaries of behavior. He is resolved to do, and to get, whatever he wishes, and whenever he wishes it. He has no regard for parental desires or expectations, no consideration for the needs of others, no sense of how others might accept his behavior or of any reason to wonder why social standards and goals outside his own are of any importance. To spoil a child by being overpermissive, then, is to deny him an essential part of his growth and education. Such neglect may well start him on the path to unhappiness—and incidentally supply him with an enhanced capacity to make others (most directly his parents) unhappy.

It is only fair to teach a child what may be expected of him by others, which kinds of behavior will be socially acceptable and which not. He needs to know "the rules of the game"—which is not to say that he must slavishly obey them all his life. Game-playing is, in fact, a good way to begin learning rules, once children are old enough to understand that a set of rules is what defines a game, as distinct from random play. A child is in any case more secure when he lives with rules, and with parental guidance as to when he is following those rules (right) and when not (wrong). He is happier knowing that the world has an organized structure, that it operates according to laws and principles: If you do x, then y may be expected to occur. These consequences are not only physical but also social. Some actions will evoke displeasure, even anger and punitive retaliation, while others will bring rewards and pleasures, smiles and renewed approval. A child should learn gradually that, to be aware of the needs of others, including his parents, and to be considerate of those needs, is in his own self-interest. This is a good enough first step in the direction of genuine altruism.

Will all these restraints not unduly impair his freedom? Paradoxically, a child cannot experience real freedom without knowledge of restraints. Some children receive little guidance and have no boundaries set for them. They find themselves in dangerous situations and may, moreover, become fearful of their own unmonitored destructive impulses—experiencing a sense of panic at possessing no internal controls (which begin with external discipline). Such children often wind up afraid to make any moves except the most necessary, because they have no confident knowledge of what is safe. They become quite self-restricted and much *less* free than others. As adults, they are often troubled and unhappy. They have a hard time making plans or decisions, even small ones. They have little understanding of the past, can't project their imaginations into the future, and don't know how to savor the present.

Discipline, by the way, is not synonymous with punishment, though the two are often associated thus in the minds of parents. Punishment may sometimes be necessary, of course, especially if, as the child gets older, he insists on repeatedly disobeying the rules. (The rules should *not* be multiplied beyond necessity. Each rule or restriction should be set for some sensible reason; not simply to "show who's the boss.") The time to start discipline is when the child, having formed an appropriate attachment to his mother, has begun to crawl and walk, to move around on his own in an extended physical space. Now he is readier emotionally to tolerate some frustration; a good thing, too, because now he begins to court danger in his explorations.

One classic situation is the crawling baby's first encounter with an electrical outlet. Here the potential danger is too great to let him discover it through trial and error. He simply must not poke his fingers—or anything else—into those holes. It may take a lot of patience to discourage him. The parent's first "No!" (perhaps emphasized by physical restraint) may be puzzling; he isn't sure what it is he mustn't do. He may instantly do it again. Or try the fingers of his other hand, or some other object. Or he may crawl to another outlet. Such behavior should not be interpreted as sheer contrariness. Rather, as Lee Salk suggests, the child "is behaving like a well-disciplined scientist who is testing a series of hypotheses to find out what is causing your reaction." When he has finally learned, over a period of time, that the parental "No" applies to putting *anything* into those outlets, at any time, under any circumstances (until he is old enough to use them for their intended purpose), he then has, says Salk, "a great sense of satisfaction at having solved the mystery." The child will soon begin to internalize what he has learned and will practice it, even as he sits there saying "No! No!" to himself—or to a doll or toy animal—with great vehemence.

The negative aspects of discipline make up, at most, only half the process. Discipline is as much Yes as it is No. A child needs to know not only what is wrong or harmful, but also what is right, or at least meets with his parents' approval. And parents should clearly show their pleasure and approval, the best reward for a child who is "behaving." Just as clearly, they should show their annoyance and displeasure at misbehavior, and usually this will prove sufficient punishment for the child. Enough positive reinforcement of "good" behavior will make it unnecessary for a child to be "bad" just to get some attention from his parents.

As for punishment—well, it *should* fit the "crime." It is best, when in doubt, to sin on the side of too little rather than too much. Excessively severe punishment will convey to the child not that he has done wrong but rather that the parent is mean. (It may, of course, signify exactly that. Parents who repeatedly or compulsively dole out large punishments for small offenses should openly and honestly direct toward themselves some searching questions as to their possible propensity for cruelty, even child battering.) Parents should not threaten punishments they are not prepared to carry out*— though an occasional lapse is better than inflicting on the child a too-harsh punishment merely for the sake of consistency. Nor should too long a time elapse between misbehavior and punishment; otherwise the child will not connect the two, and the lesson will be worse than wasted. Most important, a parent had better be certain the child really did do whatever he is being punished for. There is

---

*Harpo Marx, in his autobiography, recalls how his father, a soft-hearted man, used to punish him for a serious offense:

Frenchie [Papa Marx's nickname] would suck in his lips like he was trying to swallow his smile, frown at me, shake his head, and say, "Boy, for what you ditt I'm going to give you. I'm going to break every bone in your botty!" Then he would march me into the hallway, so the rest of the family wouldn't have to witness the brutal scene.

There he would whip a whisk broom out of his pocket. "All right, boy," he'd say, "I'm going to *give* you!" He'd shake the whisk broom under my chin and repeat, through clenched teeth, *"I'm going to give you!"*

Frenchie, gamely as he tried, could never bring himself to go any farther than shaking the broom beneath my chin. He would sigh and walk back into the flat, brushing his hands together in a gesture of triumph, so the family should see that justice had been done.

Harpo was old enough, at that point, to be able to say in retrospect: "I couldn't have hurt more if my father had broken every bone in my body."

no surer way to arouse bewilderment and resentment, and to erode
trust, than to punish a child for something he didn't do. (See the
book *Mommie Dearest*, by Joan Crawford's daughter, Christina, for
numerous examples.)

If disciplinary measures make the child feel repressed, or even
guilty, so be it. Some kinds of repression and guilt are healthy, indeed indispensable to the attainment of proper impulse control. As a
last cautionary word: Parents would do well to remember, when behaving in the child's presence, that the child is a naturally imitative
creature. A husband and wife cannot shout at each other all the
time, then expect the child to be quiet all the time. Well, maybe
they can. Maybe they can even enforce it. But only to the child's
confusion—and his emotional and developmental detriment.

Disciplinary measures should always be taken with a due sensitivity to the stage at which the child has arrived. Toward the end of
the neophase, when discipline is just being instituted, he may be in
the throes of either separation anxiety or stranger anxiety, or both.
These feelings should not be aggravated unnecessarily. There is no
point, at such times, in scolding him because he turns away from an
aggressively affectionate relative, or in being angry with him (thus
implicitly threatening to withhold love) because he is fretting as the
parents prepare to go out for the evening. In the latter case, his protests should certainly not be allowed to keep the parents at home
(not, that is, if left with someone responsible) or to spoil their evening; but the parents should be gently sympathetic with his normal,
expectable anxieties of the moment.

During the emotionally more stable "practicing" period, the child
can take a larger dose of firmness and displeasure from his parents.
But even in this happy time, "No! No!" can all too easily become the
watchword. In setting limits for the child, we must remember that
this age also marks the beginning of the independent explorations
through which he will learn to understand, enjoy, and cope with the
world outside himself, to develop confidence as well as competence.
This critical learning will take place most effectively in his own
home. If the household is organized, as it usually is, for adult living,
without considering the child's special needs, the result will be a
rapid multiplication of prohibitions, inhibitions, and constraints:

Mustn't touch this; don't go near that; you'll break it; you'll hurt yourself. No! No! The child in such a household may be confined for long stretches of time to a high chair, playpen, or high-walled crib, even when he is awake, alert, and eager to be up and moving. The outcome will be boredom and crankiness, or a resigned acceptance—thus, in all likelihood, retarded progress.

Again the parent is faced with locating that fuzzy borderline between protection and overprotection. One thing is certain: There is no way a child's life can be lived with zero risk. The fewer areas that need to be declared off limits, the more freely he can roam without being enveloped in a cloud of no-no's, and the more confidently and buoyantly can he proceed on the basis of the unspoken: Yes. It's okay! He should not be put in confined spaces any longer, or any more frequently, than is necessary. Objects or materials that are poisonous, sharply pointed, easily breakable—dangerous or fragile for whatever reason—should, wherever possible, be put safely out of his reach. The child must of course learn to keep away from unstorable things that are either hazardous or precious, but the more of these that can be kept away from *him* at the outset, the better. He is going to be curious about everything, and touching and handling will be part of that curiosity—though he spends a large percentage of his time just looking at things, visually inspecting them with great care, using his eyes to get and store information about the world.

The free-roving child will certainly require closer surveillance and a greater expenditure of energy on the mother's part. But as Burton White and his associates learned in their early studies in the ambitious Harvard Preschool Project, one of the mother's major roles during this hectic period from, say, ten to eighteen months of age, is as a "consultant-on-the-fly." The busily wandering child will run across something that excites or frightens him, an obstacle he can't deal with, or merely an object or event that's interesting. He will immediately either holler for mama or come running to her. This will happen many times a day. As she pauses briefly to consult, the interplay will be an excuse for the mother to engage in some brief conversation, further enhancing his rapid understanding and acquisition of language. Her explanations of, or questions about, whatever brought on the consultation should at once satisfy the child's curiosity in the specific instance and increase his general curiosity as he delights, with each new scrap of information, in his growing body of knowledge. The mother may at the same moment provide related ideas that he may now be motivated to think about. She is thereby teaching him an important skill that less fortunate children are slow to acquire—how to use adults as a resource.

Any such consultation may take no more than ten to thirty seconds, and the child is off exploring again, the mother usually able to go right back to whatever she was doing. Mothers who are available in this fashion, and who suffer such frequent interruptions with patience and good humor, provide an invaluable service for their children. White calls them A mothers—in contrast to C mothers, who, though loving and nurturant, do not allow their children the same freedom to explore and to consult (perhaps because they simply don't have the energy or can't provide the circumstances). White's grading is apt, for the A children do consistently better than the C's when they get to school.

Discipline during the rapprochement crisis will again call for special delicacy. Having descended from his euphoric high to a new sense of relative impotence and a new need to reestablish closeness with his primary caregiver, the child will in some ways be easier to discipline, for he will want to please. But he will also be more vulnerable to what he might perceive as threats of love withdrawal. (Not that the mother actually threatens him; the child is simply taking no chances.) When the rapprochement crisis has subsided, and he has become a bit more bumptious again—toward the end of his second year—he will suddenly start being negative, even somewhat rebellious. He has learned that he, too, can say no, that he also has the power to withhold what the parent wishes, especially in the way of behavior. During this testing period, when the apparent way to get him to do one thing is to request the opposite, a parent's patience may be sorely tried. Discipline must continue apace, but not making it too hard on him, or demanding too much; the testing period is short-lived (as long as it isn't exaggerated by the parents) and is just another natural step along the way to autonomy.

This is a time when, because sphincter control is now virtually achieved (by eighteen months of age), parents often start toilet training. Some start even earlier—in some cultures before the baby is a year old. But, most of the time, the child is not *successfully* toilet-trained (no matter when the training started) until the third year. In fact, there is good reason for not even trying until the third year, when the child is past his own worst negativistic stage and, moreover, can communicate his urges verbally.

Many parents worry too much about toilet training, and they start worrying too early. They coax, cajole, scold, reward, and threaten. One can sit a child on the potty, but the performance is up to him. At best, the training period takes anywhere from a month to a year to accomplish, and occasional regressions can be expected, especially at times when he's upset. Putting pressure on a baby before sphincter control is complete—perhaps at a year old, perhaps not until a year and a half to two years—can cause great fears of failure, since the failures seem to threaten a loss of parental love; and the fears are altogether real since his control is, at best, highly erratic. Another hazard of starting too soon is that the baby, who has not yet made a clear-cut differentiation between self and nonself, may be very confused about just what is being dropped into, and flushed down, the toilet. (Such valuable things they must be, too, judging from the parents' excitement and happiness—even ecstasy—at their appearance!)

It can even be well past the neophase, when the child is distinguishing more successfully between what he is and what he is not—especially as he moves from the oral to the anal phase—before he begins to pay clear attention to his urinary and excremental functions, to the fullness of bladder and intestines, to urethral and anal sensations. Studies have shown that these functions, especially around the age of fifteen or sixteen months, can be a source of great anxiety. The child may be particularly vulnerable if some outside circumstance—say, a long hospitalization for his mother—already constitutes a threat to his bodily integrity (his love object is still, in some important psychological sense, an extension of himself). There may now be special concern, too, about sex organs (still not distinct in the child's mind from excretory organs)—even penis envy or castration anxiety—as evidenced by a protective clutching of the genitals. To push toilet training at this stage only adds to the potential anxieties. Since the ensuing stage includes the rapprochement crisis, and the one that immediately follows it encompasses that contrary period when, whatever the parent suggests, the child wants to do the opposite—these are obviously not the most propitious times to initiate training.

All these factors contribute to our recommendation that toilet training wait for the third year of life. The two-year-old has (normally) made it more or less successfully through the most hazardous passages of separation-individuation, and, in the third year, will be consolidating his gains. He is essentially no longer a baby, though he still wears diapers. He is more secure with his parents, has begun to relate to children his own age, has added running and climbing—and perhaps tricycle riding—to his repertoire of motor skills. He is adding rapidly to his vocabulary and is sharpening his language capacities. He is not only aware of what is happening to him; he can reflect upon it. He may start to draw, and to build more complicated structures with his blocks. All in all, it's a good time to begin. Toilet training, along with conversation, can be the kind of enriching learning experience it could not have been—even if achieved—at an earlier age.

Parents should above all be patient during the time it takes for their child to be toilet-trained. They should also be quite matter-of-fact about it, letting it be known that the child is *expected*, in time, to use the toilet and shed his diapers. They should make it clear that they are concerned, that they do care, that they are pleased as success arrives—but not to make so much of the whole business that the child feels he is conferring a great favor; such a realization often suggests that a deliberate withholding is a way to punish the parent. The child, on the whole, does want to please the parent. Ordinarily, by this stage, the child possesses a history of built-up trust; he will be happy to cooperate as part of his general adaptation to expectations—to surrender willingly his body products, understanding that they are only products, not part of himself. And the parents' pleasure should be focused on the process rather than on the product.

Such complexities make it essential that parents, for their own peace of mind as well as for the child's welfare, understand the basic, expectable steps of a child's development—keeping in mind always that each child is unique, not necessarily average, and that while the pace may vary, the sequence should not.

In this chapter, we have undergone lift-off and moved into ever widening orbits with the personaut, from the neophase to roughly age three. It should be clear, even from our less-than-exhaustive account of the journey thus far, that the relationship between the personaut and Mission Control—the primary caregiver—is of paramount importance. Clearest of all is the desirability, from the child's standpoint, of *having* a primary caregiver over this period of time, preferably without significant interruption.

In the classic situation, the mother is both caregiver and principal love object. But mere feeding, diapering, and other sustaining services do not automatically elicit Mahler's symbiosis with, or Bowlby's attachment to, the person "taking care of" the baby. The individual who gives most to the child emotionally, on a regular and reliable basis, who provides what has been called "the joyful face," is the one to whom the child usually prefers to attach. Thus a mother, even if her child is taken care of by someone else during the day, either at home or in a communal nursery—such as those provided in Israeli kibbutzim—can still be the central figure in the child's emotional life, if she makes herself maximally available the rest of the time. In some instances, if the mother is low-key and relatively unresponsive to the child, he may attach to some other family member—the father, most likely, though it can be an older sibling—who has spent a lot of time with the child in energetic interplay. Where care-giving is too fragmented for the child to form a central, emotional, one-to-one bond with anyone, he may eventually have emotional problems, not least of which will be a crippled capacity to love—himself or anyone else, including his spouse and his own future children—with a deep, abiding commitment.

When a woman and a man decide to become parents, then, built into that decision should be an agreement as to who will be the child's primary caregiver. In the vast majority of families, the mother still carries out this traditional role. However, there is no reason why the father, properly motivated, could not carry out the assignment equally well. Alternate family solutions are not as satisfactory—even a grandmother, aunt, or older sibling—and a hired surrogate mother, no matter how competent, may well take another job and leave at any time, having to look to her own welfare without worrying that the child may be in some critical phase of development at the time of her departure. As for institutions, including the best of day-care centers, there is bound to be a fair amount of turnover in personnel.

Such alternative arrangements may nevertheless be decided upon. It may be that the parents have no choice; or the mother may work full-time, and perhaps have no husband. In any event, at least one parent must make the commitment to devote a good deal of whatever time and energy are left from work obligations to the care of, and emotional involvement with, the child. So desirable is this continuum of care that White advocates a three-year spacing between children to allow each child to be the parent's major focus of attention through separation-individuation. If there is more than one child under three years old in the house, then the parents must split their energies and do the best they can for each child.

With the achievement of separation-individuation, the child will have reached a point halfway to latency and the successful termination of the six-year pregnancy.

A CHILD'S FIRST FIVE POST-UTERINE YEARS: DEVELOPMENTAL AND MATURATIONAL ASPECTS

(All chronology is approximate and will vary greatly among healthy children and parents.)

Age in Months	Physical and Physiological Landmarks	Psychosexual Phases	Ego and Superego: Precursors and Functions	Separation-Individuation Processes
0	Sucking, "rooting," bonding. Preference for human face and own hands. Reaching for sounds in dark.	The Neophase Oral Passive-receptive	Exploration by eye, ear, mouth, hands. Preference for complex visual stimuli. Not disturbed by multiple images of caregiver in mirror. Reaching for sounds in darkness.	Normal autism. Symbiosis begins.
2	Marching movements with legs, if supported. Recognition of mother by sight, sound, and smell. Nonspecific smiles to indicate pleasure.		Develops rhythms of impulse regulation. Early forms of imitation. Explores self, others, and nearby things. Almost no frustration tolerance.	Early differentiation of body image and expansion beyond the symbiotic orbit of mother and infant.
4	Biting, teething, sitting, crawling. Specific smile. Increased wakefulness.	Oral aggressive-sadistic	Babbling. Withdrawal when frustrated. Primitive turning of aggression against self. Vulnerable to anaclitic depression.	Peak of symbiosis.
6	Sharp focus on own hands.		Increasing skills for independent action. Tolerance for disengagement from parents. Scanning people. Keen awareness of many caregiver expectations. Responsiveness to limited discipline.	"Hatching." Discomfort with always being held.
8	Increasing epinephrine production. Checking on mother visually. "Customs inspection." Coordination of thumb with other fingers. Sitting, standing. Sleeping through the night. Comprehends a few words.		Stranger anxiety. Simple play and humor. Much visual checking of caregiver.	Some stability of object-image. Awareness of self, nonself, and multiplicity of nonself objects.

Narcissistic Line of Development	Object Relations	Desirable Parental Traits and Related Developmental Needs That Parents Must Fill	Age in Months
Primary narcissism.	Need fulfilling, mutual bonding. Early rhythm imitation. Relates to parts of things and parts of people rather than wholes.	Primary commitment to parenting. Warm, rapid attachment, positive fantasies and concepts about the baby. Good health. Financial security. Pleasure in giving care. Freedom from chronic or severe depression.	0
Early delusions of grandeur. Ever increasing evolution of body image as core of the self-concept.	Building basic trust. Early "triangulations" (mother-child-other person). Feels joy in being cared for.	Reciprocation of the child's symbiotic needs. Caution over separations. Reliable care, stimulus-nutrition, and tactile dialogue.	2
Beginnings of "narcissistic rage."	Primary attachment to one caregiver.	Respect for sleeping, waking, eating rhythms. Encouragement of spontaneous babbling and play.	4
Beginning loss of sense of unity with primary caregiver. Joy in motor acts, in early locomotion.	Complete separation from primary caregiver may lead to anaclitic depression. Complex imitations.	Mutual supportiveness of caregivers. Avoidance of long separations, "adultomorphism," and narcissistic rage. Joy over child's body and ministering to it.	6
Joy in signs of parental pleasure.	Primitive identifications with both loved and feared persons. Basic trust established.	Deep altruism. Capacity to give up symbiosis. Humor.	8

Age in Months	Physical and Physiological Landmarks	Psychosexual Phases	Ego and Superego: Precursors and Functions	Separation-Individuation Processes
12	Capacity for complex speech, toddling and walking. Myelinization of long tracts of spinal cord.	Anal-expulsive	Permanence of memory traces for inanimate objects. Turns passive experience into active mastery. Improved but still poor reality testing. Tends to project impulses onto external world. Impulse control dependent on presence of others.	Early "practicing." Practicing subphase proper. A vigorous love affair with the world of the nonself. "Consultation" and "refueling dialogues."
16	Running well. Sphincter control.	Anal-retentive	Stubborn, unreliable, contrary; yet enjoys pleasing caregivers.	Elation. "Rapprochement" with caregiver. Consolidation of individuality. Rapprochement crisis.
24	Climbing well. Complex language and symbolic play. Approaching adult balance of epinephrine and norepinephrine.	Urethral Phallic-intrusive	Advanced "reaction formation" against anal-stage messiness. Social skills blossom. Ready for toilet training. Early sublimations appear. Complex symbolism. Castration anxiety. Concrete self-reward and self-punishment. Beginning tolerance for major separations. Capacity to mourn if led and supported by adult example. Crystallization of superego awaits resolution of oedipal/Electra phase.	Negativism. Gradual achievement of permanent images of loved persons, even when they are absent for long periods.

Narcissistic Line of Development	Object Relations	Desirable Parental Traits and Related Developmental Needs That Parents Must Fill	Age in Months
Peak of feelings of grandeur and near-omnipotence.		Urging toward individuation. Protectiveness and reliability of social network. Viewing the child as a primary engager in life.	12
Joy in control of body functions.	Early rivalries. Complicated autoeroticism.		
Humiliations by real injuries and imagined dangers. End of omnipotence. Consolidation of self-concept.	Building whole object relations. Jealous and aggressive.	Tolerance and empathy for child's autoeroticism. Beginning of social regulation. Balancing safety enforcement with encouragement of adventurous learning. Parent as "consultant on the move."	16
Narcissistic pride in genitals. Gender-identity aspects of self-concept solidify. Feels joy in being esteemed.	Beginning of intricate play with peers. Girls have penis and scrotum envy. Both sexes have womb and breast envy. Incestuous desires. Erotic preference for opposite-sex parent.	Avoidance of excessive disgust over excretions. Adequate language for body parts and functions. Continuing caution about long separations; optimism, encouragement before any separation. Early psychological immunization.	24
Narcissistic humiliation by comparison with adult powers and bodies.	Giving up of raw oedipal and Electra desires.		

Age in Months	Physical and Physiological Landmarks	Psychosexual Phases	Ego and Superego: Precursors and Functions	Separation-Individuation Processes
36	Cortical areas of the brain continue maturing. Increased coordination of eye-hand and small muscles, with one cerebral hemisphere increasingly dominant.	Phallic-oedipal/ Electra	Intense practicing of imagined future roles and identities. Ever more complicated abstract and symbolic play. Early operations of the superego ideal. Increasingly social and socialized. Character formation well under way.	Permanent "object-constancy" is established. Separation-individuation is achieved.
48	Myelination of frontal lobes progresses.	Late oedipal/late Electra Early Latency	Early use of heroes and heroines as future fantasy role models. Abstract self-reward and self-punishment by regulation of self-esteem. Excellent reality testing, impulse control, frustration tolerance, social judgment. Accurate conflict-free perception and memory.	Complex experimentation with autonomy at concrete, abstract, and moral levels. Major autonomy of the individual, with tolerance for long separations.
60	Development of the central nervous system is essentially complete.	Latency	Complicated ethical, social, and religious standards are internalized and not dependent on presence of other people. Advanced skill building. Cognitive leaps. Fully human use of tools and technology, with sublimation. Impulses dominated by ego ideal in collaboration with superego. Synthesis of demands of authority with unique self-expectations.	Separateness, with capacity for rich intimacy.

Narcissistic Line of Development	Object Relations	Desirable Parental Traits and Related Developmental Needs That Parents Must Fill	Age in Months
Continuing dependence on auxiliary narcissistic functions of major love objects to support numerous developing ego functions.	Expanding peer relations. Increasing appreciation of nuances in behavior of others. Recognition of subtle aspects of identity in others.	Patient support of progressive development. Comfort with own gender identity. Empathy for new wave of childhood eroticism. Curbing of jealousy of child. Muting of seductiveness.	36
Further solidification, elaboration, and socialization of self-concept and self-love. Well-established autonomous regulation of self-esteem.	Feels joy in being approved. Competitive, but socializing. Loving and appreciating several others. Increasingly independent, autonomous. More quiescent erotically.	Encouragement and esteem for child's sublimations. Freedom from: major unresolved oedipal/Electra problems, compulsions about own unmet needs. Joyous participation in growing cognitive and social life. Honest communications about stressful shared events.	48
Healthy narcissism with keen joy in skill mastery and social intercourse. Stable self-esteem.	Emphatic and altruistic. Relates to community of peers, adults, and social organizations.	Evolving collaborations with community caregivers. Firm, loving inculcation of elaborate values and expectations. Full use of societal resources. Gradual emancipation of child to seek own special identity.	60

9

Self-Concept, Gender Identity, and the Oedipal Obstacle Course

In sooth, beings are dear,—not because you love beings; but beings are dear because you love the Self. In sooth, the whole world is dear,—not because you love the whole world; but the whole world is dear because you love the Self.

—Yajnavalkya, (circa 600 BC)
THE BRHADARANYAKA UPANISHAD

IN all our descriptions of the six-year pregnancy thus far, we have been moving in the direction of a major goal: the development of the child's self-concept. The overall goal, to be sure, is broader than that: the development of the whole individual human organism, a self capable of fending adequately in a complex human society, and even of making significant contributions to that society. The self-*concept*, then, is not identical with the self, though the child's concept of himself does effectively limit, as an emotional-intellectual controlling element, what that self may become. In other words, the potential of the self cannot be fully realized if the self-concept is not fully realized. And that cannot happen without intelligent or intuitively correct facilitation by the parents. Faced with the task of meeting the child's needs in this respect, parents or would-be parents should be sure of the sturdiness of their own self-concepts. Because so many of the ingredients of an adult's self-conceptual structure are related to early unremembered experience—especially the psychosexual phases of early experience—and because what is happening to a child in these areas of experience

180

does not stand out visibly from the other events and behavior in his busy, boisterous life, we are giving special emphasis to them here.

One's self, and one's individual awareness of that self, seem so obvious and, well, self-evident to most normal adults, that it may be hard to understand why it takes such a complicated, long-drawn-out process in early life to evolve the self-concept. But when one considers the ocean of signals in which each of us is constantly immersed, and the sheer quantity and diversity of stimuli that assail the human sensorium without letup, it may seem extraordinary, even a miracle, that we *can* distinguish the self from the nonself, and can keep that distinction so clear and steady. Indeed, maintaining this concept of the self, even as adults, costs us a good deal of daily maintenance work; we keep reorganizing ourselves out of chaos. At night in sleep, in dreams, we are given relief from these efforts, and we permit entropy—the dissipation of organization—to prevail for a few hours. As dreamers we regress to a state where the boundaries that separate self from nonself are once again blurred. We cannot recognize that much of our dream content, even if we remember it, is actually about our selves, our impulses, interests, worries, fears, aspirations, motives. We possess an internal theater of the self in which each of us is both audience and repertory company. Much of the dream symbolism is exceedingly infantile in character, yet at the same time very useful and sophisticated. Without the sleep-and-dream experience for rest and recuperation, it is doubtful that we could muster the nonstop daytime resources required to maintain our separate and distinct self-awareness with the consistency and clarity our daily lives demand.

Experiments in sensory deprivation carried out in various kinds of isolation chambers and environments by the military, by NASA, and by individual investigators such as the intrepid John Lilly, have clearly demonstrated how easily and quickly we are disoriented, how readily our boundaries fade and dissolve when we are cut off from our customary sources of reinforcement. We slip back, in effect, to a state resembling normal infantile autism.

We do not normally take cognizance of how dependent we are, even as mature adults, on the availability of the world to our senses. We are testing reality all the time, through all our waking hours—

via sight, sound, and other sensory clues supported by inner physiological responses. We are ceaselessly checking up on ourselves and
where we are against the background of all that is not ourselves. We
achieve this by a constant radar scan of our sensory orientation
points, carried out so routinely as to remain an unconscious act. It is
no wonder that mystics and meditators, when they seek to merge
psychically with the Other, try first to "turn off," as best they can,
the sensory link to the world—for at the same time that it reveals
ordinary reality to them, it also separates them from it and, they
seem to feel, from a larger reality as well. For entirely different purposes, totalitarian inquisitors have discovered that similar deprivations and assaults on the self-concept of prisoners can achieve the
disorientation of brainwashing very efficiently. No hallucinogenic
drugs, no tortures or threats of torture, are necessary—only the
withholding of normal sensory and psychic links with the customary world. These techniques were a prominent ingredient of the
tragedy in Jonestown, Guyana. If an adult's seemingly secure sense
of individual identity can turn out to be so fragile under the stress of
sensory deprivation, we should not wonder that a reliable sense of
self, along with a confident recognition of one's individual identity—which is only one representational aspect of that abstraction we
call the self-concept—is so hard to come by in the very beginning.

Our sense of self is reconfirmed constantly in our lives, not only
by routine comparisons of the self versus the outside world, but of
the self versus itself. Touching one's own hand, for example, is not
the same as touching an outside object, even another person's hand.
Critical to such a sure distinction is the fact that the human brain
has two hemispheres—often designated as left brain and right
brain—the study of which has generated much excitement among
neurobiologists over the past decade or two. It might have appealed
to Freud, in the days when he was particularly oriented toward neu-
robiology—constructing his first psychoanalytic theories and setting
up his Project for a Scientific Psychology—to think of our double
brain as the instrument par excellence for distinguishing between
the self and nonself.

The twin hemispheres of the brain permit fascinating relationships between two sets of comparable though not identical data

about the self. Each cortex, and those parts of the brain associated with it, contains an exquisite set of representations about the body that complement and complete the set contained in the other cortex. These are vital to the development of body ego, which is after all the original basis upon which the self-concept is built. When a stimulus is transmitted from one side of the body to the other, as, for instance, the right hand touching the left side of the body, the knowledge that both objects—the touching and the touched—are parts of the same self is doubly confirmed. This confirmation is especially rich in the case of one hand touching the other. Hardly any contact with the outside world can match in quality—and perhaps not in quantity either—the reverberations that pass back and forth between the cerebral hemispheres. What is touched and what is touching are recognized on many levels—duly noted in left and right hands, in left and right brains, and in the central consciousness. Tactile, visual, and other sensory cues operate simultaneously, along with the body's inner proprioceptive apparatus, to confirm and reconfirm in redundant and overlapping circuitries that which is being perceived. An immense store of multichanneled data, built by experience upon the genetic framework, is required to build a sure, strong self-concept; it may even provide the physiological baseline from which we transact our daily business with the world of the nonself. One can thus readily understand why, in the postnatal womb of the human family, biological and psychosocial development must progress at a stately pace, as the multifarious pieces accumulate to make up the complex and open-ended design of self-concept.

The self-representation, it should be emphasized, can also be an object that the mind can seize upon and relate to, just as it can to any external object. Thus the self—the individual person—is able to love itself or hate itself; and is, in fact, usually as ambivalent about itself as it is about most other objects. (Remember that, in psychoanalytic terminology, people are also "objects.")

We will not attempt here to recapitulate in detail (any more than we have already done in the previous two chapters) this process of self-concept development through the neophase and separation-individuation. But it does go on all through the first three years of life. And of course, it does not stop there. In the years from three to six or seven, from the end of separation-individuation to the achievement of latency, children have the task of consolidating their sense of self—including their gender identities—and of completing their successful running of the oedipal obstacle course. At a time when there is so much controversy about, and reexamination of, traditional sex roles and gender identities, we will want to take a careful new look at long-accepted notions of the child's psychosexual development. What does it take to reach the haven of latency, where the child can finally begin to relate to other human selves on the social and moral level expected of him as he goes off to school and opens the next series of episodes in his continuing personautical adventures?

The sense of self—that is, the content of what later becomes the self-concept—may well begin to be formed for us by others long before we are born. Precisely because we are the malleable creatures we are, because we come into the world—unlike most other species—with so many empty pages of the self to be written upon in collaboration with our caregivers, and with no experience of authorship, we are peculiarly susceptible to the presuppositions and expectations that others impose on us. One might go so far as to say that we are programmed to fulfill those presuppositions and expectations, insofar as we are genetically and physiologically equipped to do so. These societal messages, destined for the baby, will be interpreted through and delivered by the perceptions of the parents. Hence the all-importance to the child—to his robust self-esteem, what Heinz Kohut refers to as a "healthy narcissism"—that the parents be good and faithful messengers, that is, qualified parents. Whether the child was wanted or not, and why he was wanted, perhaps even the parents' fantasies about the not-yet-conceived child, can have a bearing on his future emotional development. A number of studies mentioned earlier, as well as an ongoing study being carried out by Kliman in association with Judyth Katz and Elissa Burian, are showing that a child's psychopathology can be rooted in the very concepts of him entertained by the parent before birth. For example, a mother who decides to have a child because she is lonely and wants *her* needs answered, or in order to keep her marriage intact, is likely to wind up disappointed when her purposes are not fulfilled by the baby. Thus she sinks into a deeper depression, while the baby may sink into childhood psychosis. This does not by any means happen invariably, but the child is certainly at greater risk under such circumstances.

A secure self-concept, apart from the physiological prerequisites referred to earlier, might be essentially defined as *information*—accumulated, absorbed, organized, and charged with psychological energy. It is, as Kohut suggests, a structure that has a psychic location and is continuous in time. Its careful construction inside the mind of a developing human organism is elicited only gradually, stage by stage, through appropriate parental nurture—through mother-infant bonding, through symbiosis and separation-individuation. Many infants somehow manage to get through the process relatively intact even under the handicap of inadequate parental responsiveness to their needs; but again, such inadequacy puts large numbers of vulnerable infants at high risk of emotional damage that often proves irreparable.

The information the self-concept is made of arrives from many sources and must be simultaneously absorbed and put together. Certain kinds of information form patterns of consistency through time; these are often referred to as "lines of development." They do not necessarily proceed in synchrony with one another, as we have seen even in two such closely related lines of development as individuation and separation. It is generally expected that virtually all of a group of children of a given age—unless something has gone radically wrong with one or another—will have arrived at roughly the same point in all their developmental lines. But any nursery-school teacher knows better. One child may be well ahead of others in verbal skills while lagging behind in motor coordination; another may be ahead in feeding himself but not in dressing himself; still another may be ahead in body independence but backward in social relations. Some of such individual differences may be due to innate constitutional capacities but many others are probably based on responses to the mother's responses—the child will tend to cultivate whatever activities bring forth the biggest payoffs in smiles, pleasure, praise, approval, and physical manifestations of affection. Few mothers can guide the child simultaneously down every developmental line at the same pace. Nor is that necessarily desirable, since the delineation of developmental stages is usually based on hypothetical "average" children.

Among the earliest investigators to perceive the importance of these separate—and, in healthy children, eventually convergent—lines of development was Anna Freud. In one example of her findings, she spelled out the prototype of a developmental line, "From Dependency to Emotional Self-Reliance and Adult Object Relationships," which progressed in eight successive stages. Then she went on to others: "From Suckling to Rational Eating" in six stages; "From Wetting and Soiling to Bladder and Bowel Control" in four; "From Irresponsibility to Responsibility in Body Management" in three; and, at the same time, four stages "From Egocentricity to Companionship" and six "From the Body to the Toy and From Play to Work." She was, of course, well aware that these did not exhaust the possibilities. Throughout the literature of child development, one finds similar stages of development spelled out: in the elder Freud and Piaget, in Spitz and Bowlby, Gesell and Erikson, Bruner and Bower, Kagan and White, Mahler and Kohut, to name a few. Kohut's "lines of narcissistic development" are among the more interesting new insights in current psychoanalysis, and we shall have more to say about these in a moment. First, however, we think it will be useful to review quickly the basic lines of development set forth by Sigmund Freud as he propounded his original psychoanalytic theories.

It has become increasingly fashionable over the past few decades to depreciate Freud's insights and contributions to developmental psychology. Certainly his concepts have been modified by those who came after him; and the authors do not go down the line in total agreement with him, particularly in the areas of gender identity. Nevertheless, the validity of his overall concepts holds up remarkably well.

In Freud's early writings, the "ego" was identical to the "self." Later, however, he considered the self merely to be represented, like the rest of the world, in the mental system called the ego. The ego, as Freud conceived it, along with its mechanisms of adaptation, defense, and discharge, was not yet present in the newborn. Only the ego's primordial precursor, the id, was manifested. The id may be conceptualized as a kind of amorphous, biologically based package of wants and needs in search of immediate discharge. It constitutes the source and home of the impulses, possessing neither a sense of morality nor even the common sense that ensures—or at least enhances the probability of—self-preservation. (To describe an adult as "id-ridden" is to suggest poor impulse control and a desire for instant gratification regardless of consequences.) The id, the first mental apparatus to develop, stays with us forever—as the storehouse of all our mental energies, though usually overruled, repressed, and transformed. The id can also be thought of as the lifelong interface between mind and body—or, perhaps, as the continuing process that synchronizes and unifies mind and body. While Freud did not assign it to any specific physical location or physiological process, had he been armed with today's knowledge of the brain's anatomy, we suspect he might have located the id in the endocrine system and in the brain's hippocampus, as well as the hypothalamus and limbic system—those tiny regions of the primitive, most anciently evolved brain that regulate the interchange between conscious and involuntary regulatory activities, and between the central nervous system and the autonomous nervous system. The id, as far as we are concerned, predominates in early life, especially as the mental state presumed to exist in Mahler's "normal autistic" phase.

The ego, according to Freud, begins to emerge with the impact of life's experiences. This is consistent with the newborn's emergence from an undifferentiated universe into a gradual understanding that he is a finite creature, separate from the world outside his personal boundaries, an individual self. If we look on the ego as including the emergent recognition of the self as a separate object, we can then look on the *superego*—a much later development in the child's mental processes, toward the approach of latency—as resulting, in part, from the further recognition that he is a self among other separate selves. Just as the ego must curb the id for its own reality-tested survival and well-being, so must the ego later be curbed by the superego, with its adaptive, social-reality-tested understanding that what

our society and culture expect of the individual requires the adjustment of his purely self-centered needs and desires.

This is, of course, a deliberately oversimplified explanation of the
ego and superego, as Freud conceived them. Nor are they to be
thought of as observable entities, but rather as designations for col-
lections of developing functions. Even in early childhood, *ego* refers
to an organized system of mental functions that includes the emerging perception of the self: the testing of reality, both external and
internal; adaptation to hunger and other biological tensions, including the channeling of drives for human contact and affection; the
testing of social reality, including the ability to perceive the behavior, and eventually the needs and desires, of other people, and to
some extent predict their behavior by foreseeing their needs and desires; the capacity to learn and remember, to store experience in order to utilize one's past to deal with the tasks and circumstances of
one's present and future; the ability to assign a hierarchy of priorities to one's energies, so that proper attention can be given to lifesaving tasks, that energies directed toward gratification will more
likely attain their goal, and that frustration, when it does arrive, can
be tolerated; the simultaneous testing of inner, outer, and social realities in the selection of one's channels of personal behavior; and
the capacity to suppress or control foolish or dangerous impulses
and to postpone gratification when necessary. One could go on adding to the catalog.

The id, ego, and superego all remain with us throughout our lives,
in constant interplay. But it takes the superego, built upon the earli-
er-appearing ego functions, to complete the human self—and then
only the *incipient* human self. The personaut's journey does not ter-
minate here. While the ego might be said to represent what is needed for the individual's basic survival, a finer honing of the mind's
mechanisms is still required for confident, high-quality survival and
coping in our ever more sophisticated civilization, and for the special ethical and moral qualities valued by our species. Among the
functions encompassed by the superego are: critical self-observa-
tion, including a search for aspects not always above the threshold
of immediate awareness; the attachment of values and judgments to
the self-concept and the behavior it generates; the cultivation of

self-esteem (including the pleasure of self-reward for "good" behavior—or for no reason at all) as well as self-punishment (often accompanied by the pain of guilt, which may be recognized or disguised); consideration for others; a willingness to conform to the expectations and wishes of significant other persons as well as society at large, without necessarily subordinating one's own desires to a degree that evokes unacceptable levels of anger, resentment or frustration; loyalty, team spirit, altruism, patriotism, and similar qualities usually rated as desirable for social organisms. Again, these are merely examples, in this case to indicate the nature of superego functions. Taken together with many other functions, they make up the child's internalized mechanisms of conscience and socialization.

Neither ego nor superego would emerge in a healthy manner, and on an appropriate schedule, without parental elicitation against the backdrop of the parents' culture, society, and personal circumstances. Both ego and superego are brought forth synchronously with the unfolding of the id in accordance with Freud's psychosexual phases of childhood development: the oral, the anal, the phallic, the oedipal, and the genital (which does not burst forth in its fullest sense until late adolescence). The psychosexual aspects of development may not be as clear and distinct as Freud deemed them to be, but they are surely of basic importance.

The oral phase,* as we saw in earlier chapters, dominates at least the first year, probably the first year and a half, of life—through the neophase and well into separation-individuation. This phase has been further subdivided into "oral-passive" (the first months of sucking and feeding) and "oral-aggressive" (probably beginning with teething and biting). Freud believed that the child *is* parent of the later adult; but he also emphasized that what is normal and appropriate for the child may be abnormal or inappropriate for the adult. Thus, no one worries about a baby who is autistic during the normal autistic phase—but a continuation of it, or a regression to it at a later time, is classified as pathological. An id-ridden adult may

---

*John Money has suggested that this should perhaps be called the "haptic" phase instead, in acknowledgment of the importance touching plays during this period—not just on the infant's mouth, but its whole body.

not be abnormal in the clinical sense, but most of us will deem his behavior inappropriate. When we refer to someone as being "fixated" in a given phase such as the oral, we do not necessarily mean that his erotic drives center on the mouth, on sucking or on eating, but rather that his general attitudes, feelings, and behavior go more appropriately with that phase of development.

"Oral love is destructive and self-terminating," Benjamin B. Wolman has explained. "The infant certainly does not care any longer for the milk he drank, and as soon as the tension stimulated by hunger is removed, the infant falls asleep. Oral love, then, is a primitive love. It is a love for a while, that terminates by itself immediately after gratification. There are some adults who have not outgrown the oral stage and who retain these destructive elements in their adult love life. They love their love objects inasmuch as they can exploit them, and love them only as long as they can exploit them."

The anal phase, as mentioned in chapter 8, overlaps with the oral phase. It lasts all through separation-individuation and on into the fourth year, and it is usually at its height from roughly eighteen months to three years. Just as the ego incorporates the id, and the superego incorporates ego as well as id, so it is with psychosexual development: The anal phase does not *displace* the oral, but incorporates it; the phallic phase does not displace either the oral or the anal, but rather assimilates both, and reorganizes them into a different hierarchical order; it puts them "in their place," as it were—at least it puts them in the place meant for them at that particular phase of development. Thus the phallic phase organizes the earlier stages into a different perspective, rendering their impulses less raw, less evident, more in keeping with the child's current enterprises.

The anal phase, like the oral, has been subdivided into "anal-expulsive" (characterized by the virtually uncontrolled elimination of feces whenever the bowels are ready) and the "anal-retentive" (where the self begins to take over some control, able to retain the feces for ever longer periods of time, eventuating in successful toilet training). The act of willful retention—when it is not done deliberately to frustrate or punish the parents but rather in the interest of controlling the time of expulsion—can mark the beginning of new attitudes toward oneself and others. In the act of retaining feces and using the toilet, the child derives a certain joy through exercising some active control over a biological process that was heretofore experienced only passively. He also takes pride in a product of his own that he can give away. It is the first opportunity to offer his mother a material gift that seems invariably to please her. These pleasant feelings will soon extend to controlling or influencing other biological processes, and even to handling property, and then dealing with people, with more care and consideration. We reemphasize the importance of timing and matter-of-factness in toilet training. The optimal time to initiate training is somewhere in the third year, probably no later than age two and a half. The task should ideally be achieved when the child can *enjoy* the mastery, but no later than three and a half; otherwise there may be some distraction from and interference with the tasks that follow.

In later life, a person fixated to the anal-expulsive phase is cruel, destructive, wasteful, messy, intemperate, and inconsiderate; while an anal-retentive type is a hoarder—stubborn and stingy. During the actual anal-expulsive stage, and even into the beginning of retention, the baby is not certain whether or not what he is expelling is part of his body, or what its source is in the body. A baby may notice the similarity between the shape of a fecal tube and the shape of a penis. For children of either sex the anal phase, as indicated earlier, is likely to be a confusing period. The child may, for instance, believe that childbirth is similar to elimination, and imagine that bowel fullness has some relationship to childbearing. The confusions begin to clarify themselves only with the acquisition of additional motor and verbal skills around the age of two or two and a half. Confusion may continue, however, in regard to gender identity, and here we come to one of the least-agreed-upon aspects of early psychosexual life.

Much has been made, in the Freudian tradition, of penis envy on the part of girls and castration anxiety on the part of boys. A generally accepted psychoanalytic idea is that a girl, when she discovers that a male is equipped with penis and testicles (she may learn this through seeing her father, a brother, or any random boy in the neighborhood or at nursery school), and knowing she has no such visible projections, is stricken with envy. She may wonder, at first, whether she once had a penis and testicles and lost them, or flushed them down the toilet. The lack makes her feel inferior. She is cross and discontented, blames her mother for failing to provide her with male genitals (or for taking them away), and may devalue her mother for not having them herself. It may be only later that the girl undergoes a series of transformations that lead her to want a baby and to value the associated female organs more than a penis and testicles.

The boy at first accepts and then is proud of his genital organs, and—unless there is active discouragement—is happy to display them, especially after he learns to stand erect to urinate. He may at first assume that everybody has a penis and testicles, just as everyone has a nose, eyes, ears, fingers, and all the other appurtenances he shares with all human individuals. His discovery that females do not have penises and testicles can often be a source of castration anxiety. He fantasizes that females may have had these organs and lost them—that they were perhaps injured, cut off, somehow taken away. At the approach of anything he regards as possibly threatening in this respect, he may clutch his genitals protectively. These developments are already well begun during the anal phase, and become more pronounced as the phallic phase comes on, and perhaps even more so, in some respect, with the advent of the oedipal phase—which is not really a separate phase at all, but rather the main feature of the "latter phallic." At that point it is clearer to speak of oedipal conflicts than of castration anxiety.

We believe that Freud overrated both penis envy and castration anxiety in the singularity of their importance as unique events governing the developmental life cycle of every child. A girl's "whole development," wrote Freud, "may be said to take place under the colours of envy for the penis." This view simply leaves out too much, and oversimplifies what occurs in the development of gender identity. It is natural for all children of either sex, at certain stages, to envy what others possess, and to be very anxious about the possible loss of body parts that they cherish. It would be surprising, considering the emotional energy and curiosity humans devote to their own bodies—and in particular to their genital organs—if a girl, discovering she lacked an organ boys possess, did not wonder *why* she didn't have one and feel cheated in some manner by its absence; or if a boy, seeing that not everybody has a penis after all, did not worry about the danger of losing his. But there is good reason for believing that the boy is equally envious of females—because, for instance, they have breasts and can bear babies. Though our culture tends to inhibit little boys from expressing open interest in breasts and female genitalia, there are grounds for believing that womb envy begins very early, long before the oedipal phase sets in. The breasts of women are at least as conspicuous to boys as the penis is to girls. Moreover boys make their acquaintance with breasts in infancy. They are just as likely to blame their parents for failure to provide them with the capacity to give milk and grow babies as girls are to blame their parents for their lack of a penis. Girls of course also note their breastlessness, and may similarly harbor anxieties that they will fail to develop breasts (they feel "breast envy" toward their mothers, just as boys do), or be unable to become mothers themselves. A girl soon learns, however, that she may one day hope to grow breasts and have babies, while the boy is reconfirmed in his deprivation.

It takes a long time for a male child to appreciate the contribution he can make to procreation via his sperm; to him, at certain times, the bounty may appear to be all on the female side. It is interesting to note that many more men than women request the radical transsexual surgery and treatment that will transform them into members of the opposite sex. In a number of primitive tribes, the males go through a ritual known among anthropologists as *couvade*: as a woman's period of pregnancy ends, the prospective father also takes to his bed and goes through all the apparent throes of labor and giving birth. Edith Jacobson has suggested that, in our culture, male psychoanalysts fail to pay proper attention to the wish for children in their male patients in order to avoid facing their own unconscious wish to bear children.

There is no doubt that Freud was culture-bound and accordingly, despite his great contribution to women's liberation, by current standards a male chauvinist. One cannot help noticing that although most of his early patients were female, his terminology tended to be masculine. It's the *phallic* phase—named for the Greek word for an erect penis—though Freud intended it to cover the female's dawning awareness of her vagina as much as the male's awareness of his penis. The term *Oedipus complex* denotes the boy's sexual desire for the mother and subdued antipathy for the father, who possesses her; but the term applies equally to the female during this stage of development (though she was later awarded a complex of her own, the *Electra complex*—which many nevertheless persist in calling the "feminine Oedipus complex"—to designate her own analogous feelings-in-reverse toward her parents). "It does little harm to a woman if she remains in her feminine Oedipus attitude," Freud commented (referring to his belief that the female is slower to resolve her oedipal conflicts and dependencies), because she would then "choose her husband for his paternal characteristics and be ready to recognize his authority." Freud's was a time of male chauvinism as nearly all ages have been; so we can forgive him his limitations.

A contemporary tendency, laudable for the most part, was born out of the consciousness-raising efforts of the various recent women's movements: to reexamine sex-role stereotypes. This has led to a searching critique of traditional child-rearing practices, and a desire to root out those which appear to foist upon our children cultural gender roles that have become anachronistic and will no longer serve in a revised social milieu.

Such reappraisals are long overdue. We have been much too rigid in our propensity to label whole complexes of thought, feeling, attitude, taste, and behavior as either masculine or feminine in nature. The current trend toward an androgyny of roles is belated recognition and acceptance of the fact that both "feminine" and "masculine" characteristics are almost universally present in individuals of both sexes.

But early childhood, and especially the phallic-oedipal period, is decidedly *not* the time to impose our recently acquired views about sex roles on our children. It is vitally important, and typifies a normal stage of individuation, for each girl and each boy to individuate further by identifying her or his own explicit gender in a clear-cut manner. This is essential if the child is to sort out the conflicts and confusions of the oedipal period and move into the safer harbor of latency. Parents are thus well advised to be wary of sexually politicizing their children at this early age.

Consider again the formidable psychic, emotional, and developmental tasks* of early life: First to form a symbiotic bond—to "fall in love"—with the mother; then to separate from that first love object and become an individual; then to master and channel a variety of biological drives, and at the same time to accommodate this intensely developing gift to *both* parents, the natural foci for all the child's most powerful drives, while at once loving and fearing them.

The newborn starts from total immersion in himself—not his "self" in the later individuated sense, but his narcissistic infant self which is undifferentiated from the entire world. He dwells in the world and the world dwells in him. Everything and everyone seems responsive to him. If the parent doesn't encourage this illusion (and of course the good parent *does* encourage it), it is quickly enough shattered. But in the normal course of events, the child's narcissism will change, broaden, and transform to include a proper consideration of other people—people who, he learns soon enough, are more powerful than he. And he learns as well to submit, at least to a degree, to *their* control. These people, from their standpoint, can of course simply be brutal about forcing quick acceptance. But for parents the trick is to bring about a willing acceptance, combined with joyous self-discovery and self-mastery, in manageable increments, as the child turns ready. The toilet-training experience, for instance, can provide a series of occasions for the child to realize that he can control his actions in a responsible way. He discovers the pleasure of actively producing and giving up something he deems valuable in order to please someone else, and he begins to develop the tender feelings that go with this kind of giving. He perceives other personalities as individuals and can value them as such, most especially his parents. This growing appreciation of and love for the mother and father becomes bittersweet with conflict as the phallic phase emerges.

---

*Though they are "tasks," they are usually achieved as if on their own in Hartmann's "average expectable environment," where parents and children are free to follow their natural programming. Any number of personal or environmental circumstances can intervene, as we have seen, to make the tasks difficult; even to guarantee failure.

The child of either sex, once he has discovered his individual self and learned that his mother, who was earlier perceived as part of himself, is also a separate self to love, feels that she is his possession. Why should she not be as immersed in him as he is in her? These perceptions present special problems if the child is a boy, for he is soon aware that there is another separate person in the house, a very large male person, who also exhibits tender feelings for the child's love object—feelings that seem, alas, to be returned. Jealousy! Rivalry! And if there are brothers and sisters in the house, who also have claims on the loved one, there arise sibling rivalries. Especially provoking to the child of either sex would be the sudden arrival of a new sibling requiring the kind of care and attention he formerly merited and would still like to receive. Anger! Resentment! Each family drama is different, complicated and ever changing.

While the mother was advised to gratify the child's desires during the neophase, she would do well, with each successive phase of development, to teach the child to live with his frustrations. She should not, of course, transform herself overnight from the maximal supplier of needs to the tough disciplinarian, but rather gradually teach him to tolerate—in such doses as he can manage at a given stage—the frustrations he will have to meet as a member of the human social species. He must learn to understand that he is only one member of his household—a well-loved member, to be sure—and that his desires can only be gratified insofar as they do not tread upon the legitimate claims of others in the family. If the child is not exposed to these small, manageable, "immunizing" doses of socialization and acculturation—is not taught to begin adapting to family habits, sleep times, and other reasonable necessities of scheduling and behavior *before* the oedipal period—then the sudden requirement that he learn frustration tolerance all at once, and in areas laden with pleasures, fears, intense emotions, and confusions, may be almost insuperably difficult. The teaching must, however, be done gently, never cruelly, never humiliating the child unnecessarily and always allowing him not only to retain his self-esteem but to build its strength as he learns where his behavioral boundaries are, and what is expected of him in relation to others. He must be allowed to regress occasionally too, as long as the general developmental movement remains forward.

All this is related to Kohut's line of narcissistic development. In its traditional Freudian sense, the term *narcissism* carries mainly negative overtones. It is equated with vanity and selfishness, a lack of consideration for others, an overwhelming preoccupation with one's own desires and needs. But to Kohut there is a healthy narcissism that needs nurturing and encouragement throughout childhood. As the child learns to consider others, to take on responsibilities, to obey willingly certain rules and restrictions, to tolerate frustrations, to control impulses, to postpone gratifications—all this should not be perceived by the child as a whittling away of his newfound self, but rather as a clearer defining of that self. As he guides it with increasing control and confidence through often complex family scenarios, his appreciation of it should increase.

A strong self-love—that is, a wholesome and vigorous narcissism—is almost a prerequisite of loving and appreciating others in any but an infantile fashion, also of respecting other similarly healthy egos, and of accommodating to the sometimes unwelcome demands of the developing superego. To bring this healthy narcissism into latency with him, the child must negotiate the always treacherous oedipal obstacle course. One can easily imagine, even without observing the results that every psychoanalyst sees routinely, the damage that can be done by parents who are rigidly puritanical, who find certain of their children's body parts and products revolting, who have never adequately resolved their own oedipal conflicts, or who have themselves remained fixated somewhere in the oral, anal, or phallic phase of their psychosexual past (in which case it is not past but present).

Freud believed, as do many contemporary clinicians, that the human individual is initially programmed for bisexuality in that he or she must form attachments to the parent of the same sex as well as to the parent of the opposite sex. Since this procreative programming is heterosexual, the task of the boy is somewhat easier: He is "in love" from the outset with a member of the opposite sex, and it is usually only later that he is called upon to form a major bond with his father. The girl must undergo a more intricate transformation. One cannot help wondering, as more and more fathers begin taking on the job of primary caregiver, whether the situation will be reversed. Will the infant male, falling in love with his father in sym-

biotic union, encounter some strange and unprecedented oedipal
transitions? These complexities may cause new problems, but they
may also enrich the male, as we believe they now more regularly enrich the texture of female life.

As matters now stand, the boy's line of development is, in some
important respects, reasonably direct and easy to follow. In the earlier part of the phallic phase—sometimes called the urethral phase,
denoting the transition from the anal to the phallic—the boy, having discovered that touching the penis gives him pleasure, is usually
content merely to fondle it. This gives him the same kind of good
feelings he still associates with his mother. The two after all have
had an intimate physical relationship from the beginning, full of
cuddling, nursing, kissing, nuzzling, and stroking. Later, as his sexual drive becomes more active and insistent, he begins to indulge in
more advanced autoerotic activity. More intense feelings may also
be directed secretly toward the mother. We say "secretly" because,
by now, the child is usually aware that their relationship has
changed, that it is somehow not quite right to have such feelings
openly toward the mother (the incest taboo is picked up early) who
is also perceived by this time as belonging with a senior priority to
his father.

The parents should recognize that these feelings are normal—and
extremely difficult for the child to deal with in isolation. The mother, while remaining her loving, admiring self, should exercise care
not to be inadvertently seductive in her behavior. The father can
help by controlling his own infantile feelings of jealousy and rivalry
toward the child—though ideally he should permit such feelings to
surface; he should become aware of them, and perhaps be amused
by them. He should also be openly admiring and encouraging of his
son's progress in all his developing skills. While the child's impulses
must be curbed if their effect is unacceptable—if, for instance, he
should begin to masturbate in front of disapproving people, as children often do, or wish to sleep with his parents when they don't
wish him to—the curbing should be done as gently and sensitively
as possible, not inculcating a burden of guilt along with each lesson,
each dose of frustration tolerance, nor imparting a sense of his having committed some nasty, unnatural act. If these aspects of his life
are handled intelligently, the child's sexuality will be a routinely

honored part of his self-concept accepted without burdening the rest of his mental life—which is now also beginning to fill with marvelous fantasy, imaginative play, wide-ranging intellectual interests, a new awareness of and fascination with other people, and the beginnings of the internalized conscience that will, one hopes, become his not-too-inflexible superego.

Though the phallic-phase boy is pleased with, and proud of, his sexual organ, he is aware how inferior it is to his father's. The comparison reminds him how powerful his father is, and how puny he is. This at a time when the boy has begun to have incestuous desires for his mother, often accompanied by wishes that his father would disappear or even die so he could have her all to himself. Guilt feelings often go hand in hand with these wishes, inasmuch as the boy has formed a close bond with his father as well. In these circumstances, his castration anxiety may suddenly appear to be well founded. He imagines that penises are cut off by angry adult males, or eaten up by female vaginas. So great is his fear, in fact, that he suppresses his sexual feelings for his mother as being too dangerous. Instead of indulging them, he begins to identify more closely with his father and to use him as a role model.

This family drama, enacted in the child's mind-theater, was considered by Freud to be universal (many anthropologists concur) and part of normal growing up. He called it the Oedipus complex after the legendary king of Thebes who unknowingly fulfilled the prophecy that he would kill his father and marry his mother. Though Oedipus seemed blameless—in that he had no way of knowing that the stranger he had killed in a fight was his father or that the queen he subsequently married was his mother—ignorance was not acceptable by the gods as an excuse; the tragedy, foreordained, had to be played out. Freud felt that the ancient Greek myth, best known through its dramatization by Sophocles, was a symbolic expression of the universal experience of every child. The child, blameless as Oedipus, is doomed to carry out the drama foreordained by nature—to wish to possess his mother and to get rid of his father—and to suffer the pangs of the resulting conflict. Unlike the Sophoclean version, however, the child's drama more often has a happy ending as the conflict is resolved.

Some examples of how it may remain unresolved: The boy may

not only suppress his desire for the mother, he may repress desire altogether, giving up masturbation and becoming inactive sexually. Also repressed, in that case, and therefore not dealt with, would be his fear and hatred of the father—and perhaps also the mother (who, in a sense, has "rejected" the boy)—leading perhaps to an automatic stance of antagonism toward all authority figures in later life. The child would still feel a real affection for his mother, even though sexual desires had been suppressed; but he might then become too attached to her, too dependent on her, and even identify with her to a greater or lesser degree. He might thus eventually choose for a mate a strong woman upon whom he could be passively dependent. Or he could, while identifying with the mother, have a passive affection for the father—the so-called negative Oedipus complex—which might dispose the child to homosexual relationships in adulthood. The same outcome is even more likely if the boy's mother happens to be an aggressive, dominating personality while the father is weak and passive. Variations on these themes (especially when one adds cultural influences), while perhaps not infinite, are nevertheless too numerous to catalog.

A girl goes through similar phases, but with notable differences, particularly in the "phallic" phase. Whether or not it is for want of a penis—and Mahler's observations seem to substantiate Freud here—the girl does seem to grow disturbed and discontented, and works up a hostility toward her mother. The fact that the girl, as an infant, fell in love with a member of the "wrong" sex is presumed to imprint her more strongly with bisexual inclinations (a partial explanation of why women in our society seem so much more comfortable displaying affection toward one another than men do). For this reason a strong *reaction* against the mother is often part of an effort to overcome earlier programming. Meanwhile the girl does attach strongly to the father as well, in most circumstances. Consequently she perceives herself and her mother as rivals for the father's attentions, which, depending upon the parents' maturity, may actually become the case.

In infancy, with the initial bond to, and love for, her mother, the girl wants to possess her love object, just as a boy does. Thus she too is jealous of the *father* at first. But later, it is the father she wants to possess, and the jealousy switches to her mother. Here we have the "feminine Oedipus" or the Electra complex, named after the Electra of Greek tragedy who encouraged her brother, Orestes, to avenge their father's death by killing their mother. As Oedipus-in-reverse, then, she wishes to possess her father and get rid of her mother. These shifts of emotion again make the girl's life a bit more richly complicated and confusing than the boy's. The girl is often less pressed by her family to resolve her conflicts. She, too, can develop a *negative* Electra complex, making homosexuality a likelier outcome. But the resolution most likely to be effective for the sake of her future emotional health is the repression of her own overt desire for the father—whom she can of course continue to love nonsexual-ly—and her identification with her mother. Using her mother as a role model, she usually wants to become a mother too—and, in the Freudian interpretation, to replace her desire to have male genitals with desire for a baby. Whatever the course of her future, the important thing now is that she establish her gender identity clearly and unequivocally—that she accept herself as a biological female.

Parents can help in this respect. The father should be a strong, supportive, affectionate parent, but never actually seductive during these critical phases. Both parents can be more influential in developing a positive body image than parents usually are. To admire a boy's body is not at all unusual. But a girl is more customarily complimented for her good *behavior*, or perhaps for her pretty *face*. Somehow we still convey to our female children more than to the males that something about the body is not quite nice. A girl's masturbatory tendencies, equally natural, are curbed more summarily. Where a boy's sex play may be regarded as expectable and harmless, a girl at the same stage may be rewarded with open expressions of disgust, and often with severe and insistent disciplinary action—as though she were some adult seductress behaving outrageously. Unprepared for her parents' "moral" standards, the girl is understandably confused. Moreover, her self-esteem is likely to plummet ("I am a terrible person doing bad things"), and her healthy narcissistic development may be seriously impaired.

We also pay too little attention to a matter that, superficially, may

seem trivial—the naming of sexual organs. The failure to be provided with nomenclature for one's own genitals can be a real narcissistic deprivation for the child; and here again the girl tends to be
discriminated against. It is Kliman's observation that, while a boy is
frequently given the designation penis, or an equivalent word, for
his genitals (though usually not separate names for the scrotum and
testes), a girl is seldom provided with a designation for the clitoris—
probably her most sensual area—and only occasionally is given a
word for the vagina. Even then, the word, more often than not, is
"pee-pee," which identifies it excretorily but not sexually. Such
omissions indoctrinate girls into intellectual timidity. They especially create a basis for cognitive problems, and encourage the submer-
gence of curiosity.

For a child of either gender, sexual curiosity is an extension of the
natural healthy curiosity about the body—and about the whole
world—that goes with healthy growing up. Many of today's parents
and would-be parents (and these include some of the most intelligent and educated) seem impatient with what they consider to be an
outdated Freudian exaggeration of sexuality in early childhood.
That is one reason we reassert its importance here. Parents, having
buried the memories of their own childhood psychosexual phases in
the universal amnesia of latency, often do not really *see* what is going on (as we said earlier, it does not necessarily stand out from the
child's other varied activities)—sometimes because they do not want
to see it, or to face it head-on. Useful questions parents can ask
themselves in this regard: Am I essentially comfortable with my
own body, my own biological products and functions, and gender?
Am I comfortable with, and free of envy of, the opposite gender?
Am I tolerant of oral, anal, and phallic interests? Can I feel natural
with the child's naturalness, even transmit admiration for his developing narcissism?

Sex play is not only normal and natural; it may even be a necessary subconscious rehearsal for adult sexual activity. John Money
speculates, based on studies of primates and primitive human cultures: "It could well be that the dysfunctional mating behavior that
is prevalent among us adults comes as an unplanned, unbargained-
for result of the imposition of the taboo on sex play in childhood."

If the parent can tolerate—or, better still, encourage—the child's healthy narcissistic development, allowing a full appreciation of specific gender identity, of the uniqueness of body and organs (as well as the pleasures they provide), and of the special procreative roles with which each sex is endowed—all this will not make a child overconscious of his body or sexuality. On the contrary, it is more likely to put sexuality in its appropriate place; after its initial aggrandizement that comes with new discovery, it will be taken for granted. That settled, the child will then be free to appreciate the other facets of his fascinating life, to understand that there is much more to destiny than anatomy. Sexual sensations and drives can have great intensity, to be sure, but an easygoing recognition of their existence by the parents will make it much easier to sublimate these drives into socially acceptable directions as the superego takes over with the onset of latency. A harsh display of negative emotions about sex and sexual organs will virtually guarantee that, driven underground, they will take on inordinate importance—and distortion—in the child's mind, perhaps to resurface at some later time and wage a kind of guerrilla warfare against his best emotional interests.

Among the child's more visible activities, hardly any ranks higher in importance than play. At least since Piaget, virtually every investigator of child development, and of child psychopathology, has recognized the centrality of play as an organizer of experience—past, present, and future. A child who does not know how to play is in deep trouble. Though we all know what play is, we have a difficult time defining it. The authors rather like Jerome L. Singer's definition of play as "what children do when they are not actively involved in direct biological need-reduction or in carrying out required tasks such as household chores or specified school work."

"For the child between two and five," says Singer, "a period when there is a simply fantastic growth in the full range of motor and cognitive skills far beyond anything that will occur later on, the major activity of the child is in play."

There are of course many kinds of play, all the way from purely physical play, which is not ever to be underrated in sensorimotor development, to games that are played with others according to sets of rules—games that can have a great socializing effect. Especially valuable is make-believe or symbolic play. Singer proposes, in fact, that "the dimension of *as-if*, the activity of pretending and the world of make-believe, is one of the greatest potentials for enriching the experience of childhood and for preparing the child for the continuing and more formal aspects of education in the years after five and six."

A child can make use of his imagination in much the same way the Pentagon employs computers to play out simulated war-or-peace scenarios. By means of his own imaginary scenarios the child can replay a past event, editing or revising as he will, perhaps trying out new endings, testing whether another set of words or behavior might generate a different outcome. He can test future possibilities, too, in his imagination—or simply fantasize experiences that he knows are never likely to occur at all. He can, through fantasies and games, modify or discharge a variety of fears, tensions, anxieties, and aggressions in relative safety.

Consider a child's puzzlement, at early stages, over the reality of objects when they are out of sight. Consider also a child who is in the throes of separation anxiety. Then consider simple games like peekaboo and hide-and-seek. In peekaboo, a face comes over a shoulder or chair, then disappears; then, as the child watches, the face reappears—not necessarily at the site of disappearance. The child squeals with delight as the game continues. He is learning that objects, including people, have continuity in time, whether he sees them or not. Objects that vanish may return, or be found again. Someone who goes away may come back. In a game like hide-and-seek, which usually comes at a somewhat more advanced stage, the lost person is hunted with increasing confidence. If it's the mother who is hiding, the child gets a small, immunizing dose of separation anxiety, but the thrill of finding the mother offers quick reassurance; anxiety is transformed into the happiness of make-believe. The child, himself hidden, knows that he has not vanished but is only waiting to be found, and he understands, by projection, that the same is true of the other player. When the mother really has to go out for a while, the child's experience of make-believe disappearance allows his anxiety to be less desperate, more manageable; it suggests that the mother will return.

One can witness play scenarios in almost any normal household. A little girl may say, "I'm hungry!" Because lunch is only recently over, the mother understands that her daughter is only pretending hunger; she wants to play. So she hands her a make-believe sandwich. "What kind of sandwich is it?" "Turkey." "But I want a peanut-butter sandwich." "Okay," says Mother agreeably, reaching back to her pretend sandwich tray to make the desired switch. "That's better," says the daughter, taking large, make-believe bites, chomping and swallowing, finally wiping her mouth with a pretend napkin. A few minutes later she is make-believe feeding her doll, playing mother to her own make-believe little girl. The variations on play themes are infinite. Parents can play them with children. Or children can play them by themselves, with other children, or with other adults.

Parents sometimes worry that imagining and fantasizing will turn a child into an impractical dreamer, unable to face or cope with reality. If that occurs, there are undoubtedly other reasons for the child's retreat into fantasy. In fact, imagining and fantasizing have great practical value and are more likely than not to help the child face and cope with reality. A child who can visualize and recall will have a better memory and be more creative. A child who can pretend to be other people is learning to project himself into other people's subjective states—whether accurately or not—and is learning both sympathy and empathy. In imaginary situations, with imaginary parents and siblings, perhaps represented by dolls, the child can do and say things he would fear to do in reality—can even kill a few people off, if the mood strikes him—thus harmlessly getting rid of built-up tensions and aggressions.

At first the parent will initiate most of the play and games. But the child, as his general behavior goes from passive to more active, quickly learns to take the initiative, especially with his favorite kinds of play; and that play is usually favored for some good reason in terms of the child's needs at that particular time. For this reason it is well for the parent to go along with repetitions of a game he may have found boring, and not insist on switching to a form of play

that may be more interesting, though the child lacks enthusiasm for
it. There is always time. The game the child finds uninteresting now
may suddenly become his favorite later. The same is true of stories
and fairy tales. It is best to stick with those that delight the child.
Others may be offered but should not be imposed.

Even before a child can read, he enjoys having stories told or read
to him. He becomes particularly voracious for invented tales as he
approaches the age of four or five. Anyone who fails to appreciate
the importance of storytelling, and especially of fairy tales, is advised to read Bruno Bettelheim's *The Uses of Enchantment*. "For a story
to hold a child's attention," says Bettelheim,

> it must entertain him and arouse his curiosity. But to enrich his
> life, it must stimulate his imagination; help him to develop his in-
> tellect and to clarify his emotions; be attuned to his anxieties and
> aspirations; give full recognition to his difficulties, while at the
> same time suggesting solutions to the problems which perturb
> him. In short, it must at one and the same time relate to all aspects
> of his personality—and this without ever belittling but, on the
> contrary, giving full credence to the seriousness of the child's pre-
> dicaments, while simultaneously promoting confidence in himself
> and in his future.

"By dealing with universal human problems," Bettelheim argues,
"particularly those which preoccupy the child's mind," fairy tales
"speak to his budding ego and encourage its development, while at
the same time relieving preconscious and unconscious pressures."
Fairy tales also provide a subtle kind of moral education by implica-
tion, reaching children in a way that abstract ethical concepts
cannot.

> Freud's prescription is that only by struggling courageously
> against what seem like overwhelming odds can man succeed in
> wringing meaning out of his existence.
> This is exactly the message that fairy tales get across to the
> child in manifold form: that a struggle against severe difficulties
> in life is unavoidable, is an intrinsic part of human existence—but
> that if one does not shy away but steadfastly meets unexpected

and often unjust hardships, one masters all obstacles and at the end emerges victorious.

The parent who does not make use of fairy tales, or of stories in general, in entertaining and educating a child is passing up a marvelously helpful and enjoyable laborsaving device. Parents can of course make up stories of their own. And so is the child likely to. And to invent games of his own. The uses of stories, fantasy, and of play in general have filled too many books to try to do more than touch on the subject here, in order to underline the critical role that play fulfills in the child's development.

One ingredient that stories contribute is role models. As Bettelheim points out, once more, in regard to fairy tales: "It is not the fact that virtue wins out at the end which promotes morality, *but that the hero is most attractive to the child*, who identifies with the hero in all his struggles."

As children go into healthy latency, they should carry in their minds strong images of heroes or heroines to identify with and to emulate. These images are conscious aspects of deeper functions called "the superego ideal." They should preferably be heroes or heroines they admire and find inspiring rather than those they might fear or by whom they might have been victimized. It is especially tragic when a parent provides the negative role model. The principal identification, for instance, could be with a parent who has beaten or exploited the child mercilessly. The child's self-esteem will thus be low, his self-concept fuzzy, his narcissistic development seriously impaired. He not only expects little of his future self but is certain that he doesn't deserve better. He may continue to play the role of victim, or his own future children will be at greater risk of being abused—either by him, or by the abusive mate selected in marriage.

Any child's image of himself, patterned on real, fictional, or composite adult models, may have a great deal to do with how his life turns out, and with the energy he can bring to his life's multiplicity of tasks.

From age three to about six or seven, while the personaut is negotiating the tricky psychosexual passages en route to latency, a great complexity of changes, physiological as well as developmental, are taking place continuously and simultaneously. While we have dwelt on psychosexuality in order to make it stand out against a busy background of activity (just as one stains a cell in order to make certain features visible under the microscope), a naïve reader might picture the child between separation-individuation and latency as mooning about the house, too paralyzed by his psychosexual conflicts to function at all. In fact, as we have already noted, the psychosexual aspects of a child's life are simply not very noticeable in the context of his almost explosive busyness. It is the time of life when a child is all over the place, into everything, wanting to know everything—in detail. He is insatiably curious, tirelessly questioning, eager to explore with senses and mind whatever comes into reach or view. He is fascinated with people, from the postman to the saleswoman; he wants to go everywhere, do everything, to touch and test in all directions. This unwearying busybody can be wearying at times even to the most loving mother and father; the parent who does not occasionally get exasperated and impatient is either a philosopher or a saint.

The normal child during this period is constantly at play, often intensely energetic play, often engaged in with playmates, if they are available. The interplay with other children not only enhances the imagination, it also helps socialize the child. He has to adjust to other children's desires and needs, and they to his. The disciplinary task begins to be taken over somewhat by the outside world—not only by other children, but by other adults as well: baby-sitters, neighbors (the parents of his friends, perhaps), nursery-school teachers, aunts and uncles, grandparents. The child, who has a much more tenuous emotional relationship with these people than with his parents, can sometimes take discipline more easily from them. They may not have the same official authority over him, but learning at first hand what other people expect probably leads him to a quicker understanding of the need to accept some rules and regulations.

If the child, in the midst of all this activity, seems reasonably well adjusted and is progressing in his physical and verbal development, it is often difficult for the parent to remain aware—especially in the absence of an inclination to do so—of the child's continuing psychosexual conflicts and adjustments. These are often made more difficult by the very fact that so many other changes are taking place simultaneously in the child's life. Not only do the parents leave the child in the care of others more frequently, but the child begins to spend time away from home—perhaps to be left with friends or relatives, perhaps to go to camp or nursery school (at first only for hours, then for days or weeks), and finally to kindergarten and public school. During these passages there will be many opportunities for anxieties—particularly separation anxiety—left over from earlier phases to resurface with renewed intensity. Parents should be tolerant of these anxieties, and expect occasional regressions. Even when the child enters first grade, he may still be far from having solved his oedipal conflicts; both parents and teachers should understand this and make allowances for it.

Any help the parent can provide with each new separation situation will make the transition easier for the child. If the parent can get acquainted with camp, school, or teacher ahead of time, so much the better. If the child can visit the camp or classroom in advance, so much the better. The younger the child, the frailer his self-concept is likely to be, and the harder it will be to separate. Time spent away at camp or in nursery school can be a continuing stress if the sending-off is done cavalierly or carelessly. If the child is reluctant to be left, the parent will do well to stay for a while. Or the parent might go away for a while and come back shortly, just to reassure the child that there is nothing final about the separation. The child should always know, if possible, when the parent is leaving. To depart when the child isn't looking, or while someone else is holding him or occupying his attention, may result in a feeling of abandonment.

Even by the time the child enters first grade, perhaps with previous experience at nursery school and kindergarten (and especially if he has not had such previous experience), he may still burst into tears on opening day and want to go home. In such cases, patience and tolerance are called for. It doesn't help matters to make him feel he is being a baby. Unless the school is a poor one, he will soon enough begin to feel at home; and if he has enjoyed learning through play at home, he will probably enjoy learning at school.

There are many variations on these separation themes. The child, for instance, may have no problem whatsoever on opening day. He may be so eager to start school that he will scarcely bother to say good-bye to his mother—who may, as a result, be disappointed, even angry, thinking: He doesn't even care, he won't even miss me. (Parents, too, must be ready for the separation!) On the other hand, the child may *seem* quite well adjusted. He "just loves" school. But after a few exciting days he may suddenly fear the separation as a potential loss of parental love, as a subtle forfeiture of his place at home. He will in that case need reassurance. It is normal for him to want to be "Mama's baby" again now and then—especially if there is a younger sibling in the house. In fact, the presence of a new baby may, at any vulnerable stage of childhood, induce a fear in the child that he is in danger of being displaced—and thus bring on, or aggravate, separation anxieties.

The extra patience and understanding of caring adults can make all the difference in the successful resolution of oedipal conflicts and the consolidation of a fully operating superego. With these achievements, the basic foundations of a whole human personality will have been created, marking the end of the six-year pregnancy and the entry into latency (see chapter 5)—which is, of course, only the beginning of new adventures in personautics. The child can now begin to become a functioning member of a community. He will probably be safe from childhood psychosis, having arrived basically intact at this point; but seldom will he be entirely free of neurotic problems.

The underlying organization of the personality is never perfect. A lack of neurotic reactions under today's circumstances carries no guarantee for tomorrow. There remains in all of us, at all times, a neurotic potential as we react to experience. The specific form a neurotic reaction takes will be governed in part by the external events and pressures that deprive us, stimulate us, or overload our coping capacities at a given, vulnerable moment. But it will also be largely determined by the unique patterns of personality organization that become rather firmly set in place at the end of the oedipal phase. This organization has many unconscious features, characteristic for each child, and many levels of equilibrium between the child's drives and his defenses against them. He has developed by now a characteristic style—or, rather, a complex of styles—for dealing with the world: styles of behavior and of relating to other people, styles of dream and fantasy, styles of problem solving, styles of balancing activity and passivity, styles of avoidance and engagement. In a word, his character has been formed.

This character will now influence the child's entire future. It will resist alteration, though it will seek to alter the child's surroundings and relationships in ways that suit his nature and needs. The character will be modifiable, of course, and will indeed modify itself as it interacts with the world. But any drastic change in its essential nature will be difficult to produce except in the special conditions of the state analysts call "transference." In this state the phallic-oedipal organization is rearoused, as it were, and the fundamental organizing forces and structures of the personality become once more accessible to massive revision. This can come about in intense personal relationships—say, between an exceptional teacher and a susceptible pupil, between an employer and employee in certain circumstances, between a therapist and patient, and of course between lovers. It can also come about as the result of a religious revelation or a political conversion.

We have thus far been describing the six-year pregnancy, its developmental phases and its booby traps, with little attention to what happens when things go wrong. It is a rare and lucky family where no stressful events or crises occur to disturb the smooth comfort of domesticity for a period as long as six or seven years. What if the child is physically ill in any serious way for a long period of time? What if a parent has a long illness—or dies? What if the primary caregiver is mentally ill—schizophrenic or depressive? Or is brutal, or is a drug addict? What if the child lives in a dangerous neighborhood, or in times of war, revolution, famine, or other disaster—not in some faraway land, but right there at home? The catalog of possible mishaps is endless, and certainly the vulnerable child is at risk of every variety of mental disturbance, the more serious ones entailing long-range consequences.

Can the child be psychologically "immunized," at least to an appreciable extent, against crises and disasters? Is there anything parents, or the community, can do to prevent mental illness and provide emotional insurance against hazardous pressures? The answer to both questions is a qualified but emphatic yes, as we shall see in Part Three.

Meanwhile, before leaving Part Two, let us look at the kinds of mental illness and emotional disturbances children are most vulnerable to—and at the phenomenon of apparent "invulnerability," which suggests that many children may be able to survive, and even thrive, under the most adverse circumstances.

10

Psychosis, Neurosis, and "Invulnerability"

Henrietta screamed and Samuel scolded: Henny daily revealed the hypocrisy of Sam, and Sam found it his painful duty to say that Henny was a born liar. Each of them struggled to keep the children, not to deliver them into the hands of the enemy: but the children were not taking it in at all. Their real feelings were made up of the sensations received in the respective sing-songs and treasure hunts. . . .

The children tried to make head or tail of these fatal significant sentences, formed in the crucible of the dead past, and now come down on their heads, heavy, cold, dull. Why were these texts hurled at them from their parents' Olympus: Louie tried to piece the thing together; Ernie concluded that adults were irrational.

—Christina Stead,
THE MAN WHO LOVED CHILDREN

THE Pollit children, in Christina Stead's novel, seem to possess some special, built-in protective mechanisms that keep the external emotional storms of their parents from being translated into internalized emotional storms. Some children seem better equipped by nature than others to maintain their balance in the face of adversity—as is indeed evidenced by the varying accommodations of the Pollit children as that remarkable novel reaches its climax.

To take a nonfictional instance: When Lee Harvey Oswald, the man generally believed to have shot President John F. Kennedy, was a little boy, he and his older brother, Robert, were put in a boarding school. "Lee wanted a normal family life," Robert was to write. "So did I, but I think I had already accepted the fact that our family was

213

not like other families. . . . When parents of the boys at Chamber-
lain-Hunt [the school] came to visit, I could see that their relationship with their sons was not at all like the relationship we had with
our mother. Maybe because she had to worry about supporting us
she never had time to enjoy us. Other parents, it seemed to me, enjoyed their children. I just knew that we learned, very early, that we
were a burden to her." Both boys were faced with the same unhappy set of family circumstances; but one brother, Robert, was older at
the time some of the stresses (such as the loss of two fathers) occurred; he learned to accept reality, to do the best he could with
what he had, and he went on to reasonable success and happiness,
while the other brother, Lee, remained more vulnerable.* Like so
many assassins and would-be assassins, Lee's self-esteem was low,
his healthy narcissistic development arrested, his desperate need to
"be somebody" and to be noticed leading finally to tragedy, not
only for himself but for a nation.

A number of investigators have lately taken a special interest in a
group of children they call "the invulnerables"—those children
who, by all expectations, should have been overwhelmed by the
misfortunes of their early upbringing, yet who managed to overcome adversity and to flourish. For example, E. James Anthony and
his colleagues at Washington University in St. Louis, in a large
study of the children of psychotic parents, were amazed to discover
that some 40 percent of such children were able to prevail over their
handicapping circumstances and grow up normal—with some even
displaying unusual gifts. Anthony describes the case of a child—one
of three brothers—who did beautifully despite being "part of one of
the most disorganized, chaotic, relentlessly pressuring situations I've
ever seen." The boy's father was a chronic alcoholic who regularly
beat up the mother and destroyed furniture in the children's presence; the apparently masochistic—or perhaps merely resigned—
mother "accepted all this as part of life." The two younger boys suc-

---

*His disturbance could have been detected at least by age two, had he lived in a com-
munity with good psychiatric resources. His mother complained that he was a veritable Houdini in his ability to get out into the street, breaking locked windows and
doors to do so. She was often unable to work because no baby-sitter was able or willing to manage the difficult boy.

cumbed completely to mental illness, but the oldest "seemed to go from strength to strength," turning out to be a good student, and later a poised and competent adult. How does one explain such cases?

We will come back for a more searching look at the phenomenon of apparent invulnerability, but first we would like to concentrate on the vulnerable children, those who are at special emotional risk; and these are of course the ones we know best from firsthand experience. (People who are invulnerable emotionally, if they exist, have no need of psychiatrists.)

We stressed the importance, in chapter 8, of bringing our personaut successfully through the separation-individuation process to roughly age three. Now we must examine some of the deleterious emotional consequences of an aborted mission—when age three is reached in chronology only, leaving the aspirant-personaut stranded on the launchpad, destined never to get off the ground. This is another way of describing childhood psychosis, a state of infancy without end.

There are autistic children who simply never leave their early-infantile state. They remain withdrawn from an outside world whose existence they have never acknowledged; they have indeed failed to develop the minimal equipment required for such acknowledgment. Others remain forever in the symbiotic state—or regress quickly to it—never arriving at any understanding or acceptance of their separateness from their caregivers, or from anyone else. In either case the child, even when grown eventually into an adult-size body, remains bizarrely dependent on his caregiver. Most of the preschool psychotic children we have seen and tried, with varying success, to help at the Center for Preventive Psychiatry suffer from a mixed form of psychosis, possessing features of both the autistic and symbiotic phases of development, as well as some of the characteristics of schizophrenia.

Such a child tends to avoid outside human contacts. He resists any attempt one makes to communicate with him, verbally or otherwise, or to form any kind of emotional relationship. He will turn away from people, avoiding eye contact whenever possible. He may be fascinated, however, by inanimate objects. He may spend long periods of time absorbed in play, sometimes vigorous play, with a bit of string, or intently watching the spinning of a phonograph turntable. Useful language is usually quite limited. Often such pronouns as *you* and *I* are employed with their meanings reversed or apparently at random in terms of subject and object, indicative of his failure to separate his "I" conceptually from all the "you's" and "theys" of the world. All social and intellectual skills are of course severely disordered, and people are often treated as things; the human "object" becomes an object in the ordinary sense of the term.

At times the psychotic child will try to use another person's hand to pick up a toy, as if he could not distinguish the hand from his own, or as if he considered it to be a mechanical tool, unconnected to its owner. Closed off from linguistic communication, the child may nevertheless invent a private language of his own, often full of nonsense syllables and, as a rule, totally incomprehensible to anyone else. Or he may echo the words of another person in a seemingly empty, uncomprehending fashion, as if a tape recorder had been turned on in the middle of the speaker's sentence, then played back as soon as the sentence was completed. The behavior is, on the whole, a disorganized welter of robotlike, thing-oriented, people-shunning actions, nonhuman to the point where such afflicted children seem almost to belong to an alien species.

There is one aspect of the child's behavior, however, that demonstrates his profound attachment to at least one human being—his principal caregiver, usually his mother. This aspect is what we call "symbiotic panic," a state of great distress whenever the child is taken from the company of his caregiver, or when she departs. The severity of the distress is evidenced by violent tantrums, self-attack (biting his own flesh, for instance, or banging his head against a wall or floor with dangerous persistence and intensity), and implacably destructive attacks on anything within his reach, including people. These acts are clear signs of the most vehement protest at what the child perceives as a catastrophic event—separation from his caregiver.

The caregiver of such a child is afflicted with a double burden that calls for the utmost love and patience, at times perhaps more than anyone should expect from a human parent: The child is at the same time totally withdrawn yet relentlessly attached. The heart-break of these parents can scarcely be imagined or appreciated by people who have children with only ordinary problems.

There are uncounted numbers of psychotic children in the United States—and, undoubtedly, the world over. Though childhood psychosis is a highly malignant disorder, and not by any means a rare one, we are unable to find authoritative estimates of its frequency. Standard textbooks of child psychiatry do not tackle the question at all. So we are reduced to guesswork: At our Center, we treat about twenty-five psychotic preschool children in any given year, some very severely afflicted, and beginning very early in life indeed—though this kind of psychosis is rarely diagnosed before the age of two. Perhaps another twenty-five victims are treated by other agencies in our community, and we estimate, conservatively, that another fifty are undetected or unreported. Extrapolating from this number, we estimate that there are roughly one hundred psychotic children of preschool age in the community we serve—about one case per six hundred preschoolers—or, if this admittedly speculative number were valid nationwide, about twenty thousand cases in the United States.

Whatever the total number, it is beyond question that each case is an unmitigated tragedy. The long-term effects erode, distort, and retard every one of the victim's major lines of development. The parents know little hope, and they experience much despair as they stand by helplessly, watching society's almost invariably futile efforts (those efforts are nevertheless large—and costly too) to help them.

Because, in the previous chapters, we drove home the possibly serious consequences of failure of a child to attach to, and separate from, his principal caregiver, we now feel it necessary to emphasize that there is no simple cause-and-effect relationship here. The appearance of a childhood psychosis is not necessarily anyone's *fault*. Its origins remain a mystery. The majority of investigators looking for clues to the causes of childhood psychosis are pursuing biochemical, neurological, and genetic (rather than psychological or behavioral) factors, but so far without much definitive discovery. Tantalizing clues do offer good reason to hope that biochemical abnormalities and genetic predispositions may eventually explain—at least in part—the nature of childhood psychosis. A careful Danish-American collaborative study carried out under the auspices of the National Institute of Mental Health is an instructive case in point. It centered on a group of 150 children who were adopted in infancy and raised by normal parents. Many of these adopted children were the offspring of schizophrenic parents. These children—raised from infancy, remember, in normal surroundings—had a dramatically higher incidence of schizophrenia than the children of mentally healthy parents. Other studies—some of them carried out by the same group—showed that among identical twins, where one had schizophrenia, so did the other in more than 40 percent of the cases, and another 40 percent had "borderline" symptoms. Such findings strongly suggest that a genetic factor is at work in this all too common ailment. A series of family studies carried out by Fini Schulsinger, a Danish psychiatrist, in collaboration with the American psychologist Sarnoff Mednick suggests that in many childhood psychoses the central nervous system may be functioning abnormally. In some instances the child's neurophysiological responses may be overactive, so that he is in a constant state of exhausting biochemical stress; in other cases the child's nervous system may be *under*-responsive so that he simply is never sufficiently organized, neurologically speaking, to attach or relate to anyone. In neither eventuality could the ordinary parent do much to change the physiological abnormality that holds up the child's developmental progress.

No more successful in the way of clear-cut answers have been psychological, including psychoanalytic, explorations. Nevertheless, we feel that some physiologically oriented researchers have gone overboard—perhaps to save parents from unnecessary guilt and self-blame—claiming flatly that psychological factors, including the nature of parental nurturance, have *nothing* to do with the occurrence of childhood psychosis. Such extreme statements do a disservice to parents and children alike.

Many longitudinal studies—those that keep track of the same group of subjects over long periods of time—demonstrate quite convincingly that there is often a direct correlation between what happens in early childhood, including what parents do, and the later emotional outcome. We have, in fact, only recently begun to develop some intriguing leads in this direction.

Our clinical experience at the Center for Preventive Psychiatry has itself raised some cautious hopes that at least one of the causal factors of childhood psychosis lies precisely in the area of parent-infant relationships. We say "hopes" because if there do exist such causal links, then we can discover them, study them, understand them, and use our knowledge preventively (as we have already tried to do, through certain pragmatic applications in Part One). True enough, our results thus far are preliminary and our methods relatively crude; yet there is a certain public-health importance in alerting parents—being careful not to place *blame*—to the possibility that they can play a part in the early detection of indicators that might help them prevent the living nightmare of an endless psychological pregnancy.

Suppose a team of psychiatric investigators were to pose a simple question: Does handling by the mother in the first weeks of infancy really have much effect on the child's future emotional life? How could one prove it one way or the other? What critical experiment might be proposed? To compare any one group of children in a given set of circumstances to the most similar group one could possibly select by the most careful imaginable means would still leave too many questions unresolved. What of the genetic differences in the individual children, for instance; and what of the variations in the styles and temperaments of the mothers—or even of the same mother at different times of her life?

There is a piece of research one might suggest to get around these experimental shortcomings: Take a pair of identical twins, born of the same fertilized egg, hence possessing the same genetic endowment, also born of the same mother at the same time of her life. Tell her to give one of the twins a great deal of loving, cuddling attention, but forbid her to handle the other twin at all—letting someone else take care of its basic minimal needs for a period of, say, sixty days; thereafter both twins would be treated normally and in time it would be determined whether the difference in early handling made any difference in the adult outcome. Now of course no one would seriously propose this experiment. And even if someone did, and even if mothers would agree to such conditions, no ethics committee in any research center would approve it. However, such bizarre experiments sometimes come about without planning. As luck would have it, just such a situation occurred, and Kliman learned of it almost by accident. In the course of treating a middle-aged man who suffered from severe depressions, it was revealed that the patient had a schizophrenic daughter, Paula. More interesting, Paula had an identical twin, Jennifer, who was quite normal in every way. Vocationally, socially, intellectually, physiologically, she functioned with superb success. Paula, on the other hand, had gradually entered a regressed state in late childhood. Then, at about twenty, she had dropped out of college, ceased all efforts to support herself, and gradually entered a hermitlike existence in one darkened room of the house from which she seldom emerged. When she did come out, she was terrified of being seen; she harbored the delusion that cancer was reducing her to a shrunken and shriveled state, rendering her repellent to others. She kept to herself as much as possible and increasingly sought the hallucinatory retreats of her inner world, her lightless self-made womb, fed and cared for by her parents as if through a psychosocial umbilicus. Meanwhile, intensive psychotherapy, including a variety of medications, was bringing about a gradual improvement in her condition.

How could it happen that identical twin girls with the same genetic inheritance, with a depressive father and, incidentally, grandparents with a history of mental illness, should turn out so differently—one afflicted and the other not? The twins were born prematurely, which is not unusual. Each girl weighed about four pounds. The now psychotic girl, Paula, being the firstborn, was actually a bit heavier, which would ordinarily bestow an advantage. But this firstborn twin developed a severe bronchitis almost immediately. As a result, she was kept in isolation, fed only by impersonal and frequently shifting people on the hospital staff. The mother was not permitted to touch Paula for two months. The other twin, Jennifer, was in an incubator too, but the mother was free to take her out frequently to hold, cuddle, and fondle in the usual maternal manner.

When the two months were over, and Paula's infection cleared up, the mother was able to take over and treat her—or try to—just like Jennifer. But Paula was hard to please from the very beginning, and also hard to relate to. Though she ate enough to maintain a slight weight advantage over Jennifer, she did not seem to enjoy her food with anything like Jennifer's zest. As a preschooler, Paula was more withdrawn, as a latency child more antisocial, as an adolescent more obstinate and more immersed in her own private world and, physically, in her own private room; and, as a young adult, she developed an overt schizophrenia.

Though the mental illness (or group of illnesses) we call schizophrenia does seem to have a strong genetic component, we can see from cases like Paula's that genetics alone does not dictate the outcome—otherwise Jennifer too would have become schizophrenic. It seems probable that both twins were genetically vulnerable, inasmuch as they came from the same fertilized egg, but in Paula's case, later events somehow pushed her over the risk threshold, whereas Jennifer was able to come through without succumbing to the hazards. A single instance cannot be cited as sure proof, but it is our guess that the deprivation of maternal handling in that first critical month made the tragic difference for Paula.

If we are right in this surmise, then it is not unreasonable to suppose that Paula's illness might have taken a much milder form, or even been altogether prevented, by the simple expedient of allowing the mother to give her, as a newborn, as much care and cuddling as would have been consistent with the child's (and the mother's) health during that month of hospitalization. One could indeed have made the suggestion that she do so with some insistence. Perhaps all that Paula needed to protect her from her presumed genetic susceptibility to schizophrenia was the same kind of loving attention that apparently enabled Jennifer to thrive psychologically. It surely makes sense, in view of what we now know about early development, that Paula, given the existing circumstances, must have had a more difficult time forming the necessary symbiotic attachment to her mother, and also a more difficult time separating-and-individuating as well as making her way over the psychosexual hurdles to latency.

What "makes sense" does not, of course, constitute scientific evi-

dence. But the case of Paula and Jennifer is bolstered by studies
made by the National Institute of Mental Health in which other sets
of identical twins turned out to be quite different from each other
emotionally. In many of the instances where one twin became
schizophrenic there had been damaging events similar to Paula's in
early life—for example, "a life-threatening cyanosis" during the
first month of life, or a severe case of Rocky Mountain spotted fever. The researchers noted that not only was the infant's physiology
changed, but also the parents' *concepts* of the victims. This observation raises a fascinating question, equally applicable in the case of
Paula: Is it possible that the different way the parents perceived the
ailing newborns subtly influenced their handling of the children?
Did Paula's mother, seeing how hard to handle Paula was compared
to Jennifer, make a quick and early judgment: This is a difficult
child and I am going to have trouble with her? And did her expectations affect the outcome, as a self-fulfilling prophecy?

These considerations bring us to a striking series of long-range
studies carried out by psychoanalyst Elsie Broussard of Pittsburgh
with 318 normal, full-term, firstborn children. She started her studies on the day they were born and followed the children for many
years. Broussard developed an ingenious "neonatal perception inventory" that enabled her to compare a mother's perception of her
newborn child with the same mother's perception of the "average"
infant. In each case she took an inventory of traits attributed by the
mother to her own child, then another inventory of traits attributed
by the mother to the average child, however she might conceive that
abstraction. Looking at the discrepancy between the two inventories, Broussard could rate the infant in question as either above
average or below average in the mother's eyes. We emphasize again
that this entire population of infants was within the normal range of
health and included neither preemies nor babies with serious physical defects.

What Broussard wanted to test was the effect, if any, of a mother's attitude toward her normal child on that child's psychological
and emotional future. If a mother considered her child to be below
average, would that perception serve as a self-fulfilling prophecy?
Would she, *because* of her perception, entertain a different set of ex-

pectations than if she had given him a higher rating? Would those expectations lead her to treat the child differently? And would the child's responses to her, and all the other complexities of their relationship, be thus influenced and the child's development thereby altered?

The first real predictive test came when Broussard's study subjects reached the age of four and a half. At that point she arranged for 120 of the children—those whose inventories departed significantly from the "average"—to be evaluated fully and carefully by child psychiatrists who had no knowledge of the mothers' original ratings. The children they deemed superior turned out to be largely the ones initially rated by their mothers as "above average." The children they diagnosed as behind in their psychological development, or as having emotional problems, were largely those whose mothers had perceived them as "below average."

Again at age ten the children were evaluated by yet another set of psychiatrists who knew nothing about either the Broussard neonatal inventory or the previous evaluations. They were simply asked to evaluate this group of children. And what they found was that those ten-year-olds who had been rated above average at the start still maintained a clear and significant advantage.

Results such as these are indicative rather than conclusive. Nevertheless they were impressive enough to win for Broussard the prestigious Hofheimer research award. Based on her work, it would appear that what a parent *thinks* about a child at birth can give us some reliable clues as to the probable psychological outcome. A conceivable preventive measure for a psychiatrist, in that case, would be to take a neonatal perception inventory and, if the mother seems to be underrating her perfectly normal child, to persuade her somehow that her child is at least average—perhaps above average in some ways. It is conceivable, for instance, that in Paula's case, if her mother had been convinced that the initial difficulty was simply the expectable result of the child's rough first sixty days and that, after a period of adjustment, she would catch up with Jennifer—why, then perhaps that's what would have happened. We don't really know, of course. In either case one must be impressed by the long-lasting emotional correlates of parental attitudes and handling.

Consider now a quite different type of long-term study—Robert Skeels's thirty-year follow-ups of infants born in an institution for retarded mothers. Such abandoned children are, as a rule, left to the impersonal care of the institution, with minimal interaction between the child and any one adult. And, as a rule, the children usually develop poorly. Many of them are soon perceived to be definitely retarded, and they remain institutionalized for life. But Skeels arranged for a number of these abandoned infants to be "adopted"—each by a retarded adolescent girl, also institutionalized. As adoptive mothers, the girls—with some help and instruction at the start—took personal responsibility for "their" babies, forming close bonds with them that seemed to benefit both parties of the dyad. Nearly all the children thus raised grew to have normal intelligence and, as young adults, were able to live on their own in the world outside the institution. They were even able to thrive intellectually, although the genetic odds seemed to be stacked against them and their adoptive mothers had been retarded! Early love, attachment, and a continuity of individualized care apparently made the crucial difference.

It has been more than twenty years since Kliman had the opportunity to treat his first profoundly psychotic child patient, an institutionalized six-year-old boy we'll call Herb. The first time the nurse tried to introduce the doctor to his unconsulted patient-to-be, Herb darted away, easily eluding the nurse's attempts to catch him as he skipped with grace and agility down the hospital corridor. The mad, elfin creature looked at no one, stopping in his mindless flight only to examine, momentarily, a piece of dirty kite string he carried with him constantly. In the first phase of treatment, in fact, Herb never looked directly at the therapist nor spoke a word—except now and then when he seemed to be addressing the kite string.

After a few patient weeks, Kliman learned, with the nurses' help, that there was one form of human contact Herb could tolerate: being carried around. He would put up with it for as long as a half hour at a time. Kliman carried Herb around and around whenever the opportunity arose—and always noted the pain that was clearly readable on the boy's face, a grimace of agony that remained there most of the time he was being either embraced or carried. During these moments of relative intimacy, Herb would speak only in short, nonsensical echoings of whatever the therapist said. If Kliman said, "Herb, we're going to get you some ice cream in the cafeteria," Herb would reply, "In the cafeteria." After another few weeks, the echoings began to take on more meaning; Herb would include the key word *ice cream*, for example. But the pronouns *you* and *I* were randomly distributed, suggesting that Herb had no way of recognizing which word referred to whom. Moreover, he used the therapist's hands as if they were his own, trying to pick up small objects or turn on water faucets by holding the other's hand on them.

Soon a gradual recognition of pronouns and people did take place. Herb not only showed a growing and visible interest in Kliman's daily visits but began for the first time to look at him directly; and *you* and *I* were being used correctly more often than not. Herb also started making certain demands. "Rub!" he would say, bringing the therapist's hand to his belly; or, switching it to his back, "Scratch!" If Kliman obliged for any length of time, there would be a striking change: "*You* rub!" "*You* scratch!" Small but important victories. As the therapist stimulated the outer boundaries of Herb's physical self, he became, increasingly, the instrument of a new process of organizing the boy's inner self-representation. Herb was beginning to sort out one set of ideas as applied to himself and another as identifying another separate self. The two beings were no longer amorphous and undifferentiated in his mind. Each was acquiring its own distinct existence.

Much encouraged by this progress, Kliman conveyed his feelings to Herb's parents, whom he had gradually come to know in the course of therapy. They were intellectually concerned people who came to visit Herb every weekend and usually stayed for several hours. Occasionally they took him out on pass for part of a day. But they impressed Kliman as being rather like the mothers and fathers whom Leo Kanner, in his first observations on the families of autistic children, had described as "icebox" parents—competent but cool, even cold, certainly not malicious or abusive, but somehow subtly inhibited from forming any loving attachment to their child.

Soon something strange began to happen, a phenomenon that, we learned only later, has been all too commonly observed: As the therapist's relationship with the child improved, his relationship with the parents deteriorated. Herb's improvement was somehow not applauded by his father and mother. They learned of his progress principally through the nurses. Only a few weeks after they had been made aware of Herb's growing alertness and appropriate use of language, the parents accepted—against the outspoken wishes of the therapist—an administratively dictated transfer of the boy to another institution. Herb's new home would be an institution of the large, state-run variety that would certainly be unable to supply him with the intensive personal interaction he would need to continue his progress—or even to keep him from rapidly regressing to his former state of isolation. Kliman was deeply grieved at the boy's fate—and impressed with the power of the hospital administration and parents to consign him to it. It even crossed his mind, in a nagging way, that perhaps the parents' own psychological needs required that Herb remain in his state of psychotic withdrawal rather than get better—a prospect that might in some mysterious manner have posed a threat to their security. There was not much in the literature to support such a suspicion; even Kanner's "icebox" parents still lacked confirmation by other investigators.

Years later, the cumulative impact of experience at the Center for Preventive Psychiatry, along with trickles of converging data from other sources, began to convince us that early life experience *had* to be involved in early childhood psychosis—and that an important ingredient of this early experience had to be the attitude and behavior of parents. Mind you, we are carefully *not* saying that childhood psychosis is the fault of the parents, or that it is ever *solely* caused by parental behavior; only that, if a child happens to be particularly vulnerable to mental disturbances of this nature, then what his parents think and do can be a critical factor in the outcome: whether he does or does not succumb. (Succumb to what? The stresses of his environment—which the child's family, of course, helps create.)

The late William Goldfarb was an eminent child psychiatrist who, while agreeing that childhood psychosis may have multiple causes, described the parents in such cases as "characterized to an unusual degree by passivity, lack of spontaneity, lack of empathy in response to the child's needs for gratification, and an unusual failure of direction and relative discipline. The family environment seemed ambiguous and undefined, with little investment in the enhancement of the child's perceptions and discriminations." In a series of studies carried out by Goldfarb and others, there were marked differences in all these respects between the families of psychotic children and those of normal comparison groups.

What exactly do these parental differences mean, present as they so often are in juxtaposition with psychotic offspring? Do such "missing ingredients" in parental character doom a child to psychosis? Of course not. The children of such parents may not get the full emotional sustenance they might have received from more energetically caring parents, but they do often make their way successfully in the world. Few of them become psychotic, and those who do, many investigators are convinced, are probably *born* with special vulnerabilities, perhaps some genetic or organic incapacity to respond as readily to the world as most infants do, or to organize their experiences into meaningful entities without a special brand of parental care and attention. Even when a psychosis occurs, however, one cannot say that the parents have *caused* the illness; only, at worst, that they have not been able to supply the compensatory organizing experiences, the impulse regulation and the stimulus nutrition needed by such a child in quantities more copious than usual.

If a child with higher-than-average needs, then, comes into a household with a lower-than-average capacity to supply them, the combination appears to create a special risk of psychotic outcome. The same child with different parents might not have succumbed. The same parents with a less vulnerable child might not have known there was a problem. But in such specifically vulnerable children, the quality of the parent-child interaction *can* make the critical difference. Still, blame is not in order—especially since, paradoxically, a vulnerable child often does not *show* his neediness through crying or crankiness. He may rather be, on the surface, an undemanding baby who appears content. Even at later stages in life, especially in adolescence, the frequently observed "paranoid breaks" usually occur in a child who was always considered to be an easy child, causing no trouble, making no demands. It is important for parents to understand that a child's needs are not necessarily proportional to the amount of noise he makes. A baby who is not vocally demanding is as likely as not to be one of the more vulnerable ones. A child needs love just as he needs food. If a baby never cried for food, would we not feed him?

Staff members at our Center have become convinced that parental characteristics and behavior have a bearing on childhood psychosis, specifically on that causal chain we have identified as the "vertical epidemic" (chapter 3). Our first inklings in this direction grew out of our treatment of children in the Center's Cornerstone Therapeutic Nursery. There, from time to time, we would get a child who was profoundly ill, who met all the criteria of symbiotic psychosis—a tragically retarded, withdrawn, panic-filled child who nevertheless possessed surprising islands of intelligence and skill but who was catastrophically attached to a single caregiver, usually the mother. We tried in every way we could think of to help these children (often classified by others as hopeless), and we always made it a point to involve the parents intensively in our experimental therapies. We thus came to know that the parents were often people whom one would ordinarily consider thoroughly competent, people who carried out complicated and arduous domestic and career responsibilities. Yet there was about them a quality we could only think of as a sort of emptiness. The therapists felt they were dealing, in each case, with someone who was not quite present emotionally—a well-functioning but drained-out shell of a person. Such parents were not really cold, in Kanner's sense; rather they seemed to be depressed and emotionally needy. At first our reaction was: Well, who wouldn't feel depressed and drained, having such a child to deal with constantly? But the consistency of these patterns motivated us to pursue our observations further.

Acting on Kliman's suggestion, Judyth Katz, a graduate student working at the Center, undertook a comparative study of sixteen case histories of our most severely psychotic children, on the one hand, and, on the other, sixteen children who were clearly neurotic but *not* psychotic. She was to search for revealing differences, if any, in parental personalities, attitudes, methods, and histories. Among the questions asked were the reasons parents gave for having conceived the child, and the degree and type of any depressions they may have suffered—as well as the timing of any such depressions in relation to the conception, pregnancy, and early months of the child's life. Some striking distinctions emerged:

The parents of the psychotic children not only experienced a greater number of depressions, but their depressions were more severe and more enduring. Some of the depressions were chronic—present prior to conception and present almost without letup throughout pregnancy and the earliest months of the patients-to-be. The parents of the merely neurotic children were not always entirely free of depressions, but the depressive episodes, when they occurred, *were* only episodes; they were transitory, infrequent, and not very intense, and they tended to occur later in the child's life. These parents usually had child-centered reasons for wanting the child, whereas the parents of the psychotic children gave self-centered and depression-related reasons for their parental desires (along the lines of the motives examined in chapter 2). Such reasons suggested an immature narcissism among the prospective parents. These woman (it usually still is the mother upon whom the child must depend as principal caregiver) were thus psychologically handicapped from the outset.

Inasmuch as depression is usually associated with low self-esteem as well as with low levels of energy, a depressed expectant mother would lack the capacity to feel good about herself during the pregnancy and thus perhaps lack both the will and the energy to take proper care of herself and of the child within her. This could mean poor nutrition, excessive inactivity, and a general low state of health—though still above the threshold of diagnosable illness; in any case, the opposite of the exuberant bloom we tend to associate intuitively with a robustly healthy mother carrying a properly developing fetus. The early months of life, as nearly as could be gleaned from these case histories, were dreary for both mother and child. Missing was the stimulus of maternal joy, the vivacious dialogue between the two parties of the dyad. In most cases the father was busy, hardworking, or downright uninterested in either mother or child—or at least insufficiently interested to take time out to lavish much attention on the baby. And the baby, in need of gratification, was surely unable to give the disappointed mother the attention *she* craved.

These initial studies, limited as they were, could only suggest to us the special importance of taking complete family histories in dealing with psychotic children. During the following years, we paid much closer attention, and made it a point to develop family profiles for every psychotic child. Meanwhile, Elissa Burian of our staff began to work out a new method for the simultaneous treatment of symbiotic children and their parents. In the course of this endeavor she came into possession of large quantities of intimate information about the children's parents, as well as the parents' parents. Building upon the Kliman and Katz observations, she and Kliman developed a three-generational family profile of each case. We were all astonished at the patterns of consistency that appeared, patterns that led us to formulate our hypothesis of "the three-generation psychosis-making machine." The pattern begins with a certain type of withdrawn, depressive grandparent—most often the mother's mother. (It probably is not accurate to say that such a process "begins with" the grandparent; where, after all, did *her* depression come from? But that is as far back as we have carried our investigations thus far.) In any event, the psychotic child—whom we generally refer to as the "index patient"—did not, as a rule, have psychotic parents or grandparents. Nevertheless their emotional problems did seem to culminate in this full-blown psychosis in the third generation.

Not every case is exactly like every other case, naturally. But we have now reached a point where we can, with a modicum of confidence, offer a composite impressionistic profile, drawn from a carefully detailed study of thirty-five such families.

At least one grandmother—usually the mother's mother—was the victim of a serious depression, accompanied by emotional withdrawal, including withdrawal from her children. Her condition was perhaps exacerbated by the fact that her husband (the index patient's grandfather) was also moderately depressed. He tended to be the kind of man who was also emotionally unavailable, in that his major social interests were outside the family and he was immersed in his work or career, leaving him little time or inclination for intense family involvements. In a number of such cases, the man actually moved out of the house. In a few instances the man died—and, in those instances, he may have been a normally attentive husband whose death precipitated his widow's depression. Whatever the initial cause of the depression, it tended to be long-lasting, becoming a virtually permanent feature of a personality that, while not outright psychotic, contained schizoid as well as depressive ingredients.

The onset of this depression and withdrawal usually occurred when the grandmother's own daughter (the index patient's mother) was in her early or middle childhood. The daughter was suddenly given substantial adult-type responsibilities, often including the total daily care of one or more siblings—and with little emotional or practical assistance from her mother. In addition, one member of the family was periodically placed in isolation, or subjected to some form of ostracism, by the troubled mother, who then ordered all the other children not to speak to, or have anything to do with, the selected victim.

The daughter thus put-upon did not herself become psychotic. In fact, she did reasonably well in school, and even socially. By adolescence or soon after, however, she usually developed a somewhat depressive personality. Moreover, the same would probably be true of the young man she was destined to select as her husband—the future father of the index patient. It was as if she was foredoomed to pick a man who would withdraw from her psychologically in extreme ways*—even to separate from her physically; a perverse yet powerful compulsion. He was usually a man, like her own father, who tended to be preoccupied with the world outside his home—his friends, his career, his business—to the exclusion of any deep domestic concerns.

This is the typical situation into which the index patient was born—conceived because the mother-to-be wanted to alleviate the emotional emptiness in her life, to draw her husband closer to her, or for some similar motive that focused not at all on the future

---

*The pattern is somewhat similar to that described in the case of Lynn (chapter 3). That case, while a prime example of a "vertical epidemic," was not a "psychosis-making machine," inasmuch as Lynn—while very troubled—was not psychotic.

child's welfare. The baby, when he came, was usually undemanding and tranquil, and his mother, full of her own problems and possessing little energy in any case, assumed that he was content. Developmental lags became evident only in the middle of the second year, when the toddler experienced great difficulty in achieving even the early stages of separation-individuation. He felt panic rather than joy at any sign of autonomy or separation from the mother. He could not use language correctly, especially personal pronouns. By the age of two and a half or three, his development was unignorably arrested in a full-fledged state of symbiotic psychosis. The panic on separation now became desperate and violent; the language deficit grew more profound; he not only asked no questions, he showed no interest in any play or social activities with either peers or grown-ups. The resulting syndrome was all too tragically familiar, a bizarre mixture of autistic symptoms: attention primarily to inanimate objects; a fondness for whirling and twirling; avoidance of eye contact with other human beings; the meaningless echoing of words said by others; the persistent repetition of—and absorption in—the same action, again and again, without apparent reason; and a general developmental standstill.

The pattern sketchily described here is not invariant in its details, but it is consistent in its overall outlines. Such children, when they come to us, can be helped—and then not always—only through long-drawn-out intensive therapy, especially by a method called "therapeutic incubation"* which requires the full and willing participation of the mother as well. As we treat more and more of these children, we have become aware—as Goldfarb and others also found—that the parents tend to be perplexed, doubt-filled and indecisive people. They have trouble arriving at a course of action, then worry about whether or not it was the right action to take. They change their minds a lot—or sometimes just let matters drift rather than come to a decision. These qualities are no doubt amplified and exaggerated by the presence of a child whose troubles the parents can neither help nor fathom. But we also suspect that these

---

*A variant of Mahler's methods developed by Kliman along with Elissa Burian and M. A. Frazier.

qualities did not originate with the child; that the disorganized and disorganizing experience of being raised in an atmosphere of ambiguity and perplexity contributes heavily to the psychotic result. The child is in special need of firm support, and that support is missing. Ill-equipped to decide what his boundaries are, he is supplied with no decisions. This child whose inner world is already a blur gets further blurring instead of clearer definition.

A surprising additional factor has emerged only in recent phases of our studies. Many of these parents finally confide that they are really violent people under bland exteriors. The violence is mainly between the parents, and usually perpetrated by the father upon the mother. Even stranger, this violence—rarely enough to result in any severe injury—seems to be acted out as a form of intimacy.* We suspect it is part of the mutual depression. It is as if, to arouse themselves from their apathy, husband and wife have to become angry enough to lash out at each other, to externalize some of the inward-directed aggression that appears to be an inherent ingredient of the depressive process. Such is the fate (not inexorable, of course) of the middle generation of the three-generation psychosis-making machine.

We have the impression, incidentally, that the children of overtly schizophrenic mothers fare better, by and large, than the children of depressive mothers. In a schizophrenic atmosphere, the child is at least stimulated to activity, his senses are engaged, he does get a more energetic brand of attention, sporadic and erratic though it may be. The vulnerable child is still at risk here too, of course; but the point is that these "crazy" circumstances—as Manfred Bleuler has observed—are still preferable to the empty pall of enduring depression.

Childhood psychosis of the primordial type we have been describing is a particular hazard of the first three years of life. In the ensuing three years, emotional troubles are more likely to take the form of neuroses or behavioral disorders. These are not to be taken light-

---

*This is not put forth in any sense as a general explanation of the "battered wife" syndrome; we are talking here only of the parents of psychotic children.

ly. They create their own kinds of disturbance and heartache. But they are much less drastic in nature, and more surmountable than the disaster of psychosis. This does not mean that the personaut's mere arrival at age three, free of psychosis and successfully separated-individuated, offers any guarantee that he will be evermore beyond the threat of psychosis. At critical periods during the years from four to six, he may *regress* to an earlier stage so that, psychologically speaking, he is back in the first three years once more, vulnerable to all its dangers, including psychosis.* This now and then comes about through a single catastrophic event, but more often as the result of a basic change in family circumstances that erodes the hard-won earlier progress. In the first case, the child is catapulted backward in psychological time. We know, for instance, of a pair of parents who had been trying without success to adopt a second child, their first child being a natural offspring. One day, with no advance warning, they were suddenly given their opportunity. They eagerly accepted. But their first child—who up to this point had been developing normally—was altogether unprepared for the overnight appearance in the household of a new rival. Unable to accept the situation emotionally, he went into a delusional state and regressed into the kind of psychosis one usually associates with the stages prior to separation-individuation.

In another case, because of problems with the father, the mother grew more and more depressed. Consequently, her child's previously dependable source of emotional support dwindled. He grew increasingly discontented, more demanding and clinging, less interested in seeking autonomous adventures. Gradually he lost the ground he had earlier gained in the direction of independence, and when the withdrawal of care-giving was virtually complete, he finally regressed into a symbiotic-psychotic state.

Fortunately such occurrences are relatively rare. The child who gets through the first three years in good emotional health, though not immune from regressions, will usually make his way into laten-

---

*Regression may in fact occur at almost any time of life (the most hazard-fraught period perhaps being adolescence, when all vulnerabilities are reactivated), depending on the sturdiness of the individual psyche and the severity of the stresses operating upon it.

cy free of psychosis (and of course a regression in itself does not necessarily result in a psychosis). The problems encountered in the years from four to six or seven can nevertheless be troublesome enough to tax the patience, the energy, and the frustration tolerance of any parent. A child who is hyperactive, for instance, can be hard to keep up with even if no other complicating factors are present. He may find it difficult, if not impossible, to regulate his impulses. He may seem to be randomly antisocial or aggressive. He may even engage in overtly destructive acts such as setting fires or breaking windows. Children who reach this point are in need of professional help. Far short of such difficulties, however, the four-to-six child may still be expected, at one time or another, to experience anxieties, to develop phobias, sleep disturbances, speech difficulties, or learning inhibitions. He may be given to excessive brooding, or develop special rituals, compulsions, or obsessions. He may become a hypochondriac, or in fact develop real—even if psychosomatic—symptoms, ranging from asthma, cramps, and headache to bed-wetting or daytime incontinence. A child may undergo gender-identity conflicts—or simply behave in ways (such as wanting to wear the clothes of the opposite sex) that, while they cause no conflict in the child, may well cause concern in the parents.

The variety of possible childhood attitudes and behaviors is virtually limitless, and it is often difficult to say what constitutes a problem and what does not. A child who is merely departing from some cultural stereotype—the "tomboy" girl, or the boy who enjoys doll play—may not represent a problem at all. If there is something that the child perceives as a problem, something that causes chronic fear or anxiety, something that leads him to restrict the development of his interests and activities, then that something *is* a problem. If the parent perceives something as a problem, even though the child may not, that too is likely to become a real problem for both. If neither parent nor child is personally concerned about some specific attitude or activity, but society at large, or any influential third parties—friends, relatives, neighbors, community officers, or authorities—consider it unacceptable, that will also turn into a problem for the family.

This whole area of neurosis is one we explore gingerly, with little confidence as to what is known for sure about causes or cures. We advise a general attitude of nonpanic toward the simpler neuroses of childhood. Neurosis may be the price of living in the advanced evolutionary state our species has attained. It is a rare human being who does not run into neurotic problems of one kind or another at one time or another. And there seems to be no clear correlation between the kind of neurosis one has in childhood and the kind one has as an adult. There is even less correlation between childhood neurosis and adult psychosis. In fact, some forms of childhood neurosis seem almost to be *protective* against certain later-occurring psychoses, such as paranoid schizophrenia.

We do not fully understand the lack of correlation between childhood and adult neuroses. True, many of the emotional and behavioral problems that occur between the ages of four to six are self-limiting in nature. A child may experience a period of night terrors, or sleepwalking, or stuttering, or a compulsion to practice some inexplicable ritual. Any one of these could result from the impingement of a particular event or worry at an especially vulnerable moment in development; and the behavior may well go away by itself in short order if not too much fuss is made over it. If there is a multiplicity of problems, or if one persists for more than a few weeks, then some real concern is warranted. More often than not, childhood neuroses are fairly uncomplicated. Perhaps they occur because the various facets of development are not proceeding in precise synchrony; or because the personality structures—the id, ego, and superego we spoke of in the last chapter—have not yet been sufficiently integrated. Such neuroses, too, tend to be self-correcting.

There is a set of childhood behavioral developments, however, that we consider more worrisome, though they may be less obvious in their overt symptoms. These are the narcissistic problems, those that stem from a poorly developing self-concept, from narcissistic injury or deprivation, about which Kohut has written so astutely. Often the problem here is not so much a deficiency of self-esteem as a deficiency of *self-esteem regulation*.

A securely developing self-concept incorporates two requisites: on the one hand, a sufficiently high sense of self-esteem to engage the world with enough confidence to risk vulnerability, rejection, or failure; and, on the other, a balancing awareness of other people's similar need for confidence and self-esteem. A child needs to know that he is important enough to have his needs answered; but also that other people—including his parents and siblings—have their importance, their needs and desires, which cannot always be put aside instantaneously in order to gratify any high-priority whim that may occur to him. To the child thus "spoiled," the tyrannized, overly gratifying and subservient mother may never become a fully realized outside "object," but instead remain a kind of self-object who exists for the gratification of that self. In this strange manner the child may never truly break away from the perception of their relationship as still symbiotic in nature. The end result may well be an unhealthy narcissism, in its former meaning as synonymous with being totally self-centered.

Unlike the simpler and often more visible neuroses, these narcissistic disabilities are really *character* disorders—more basic, more insidious, and more likely to last beyond childhood to cripple the future adult's ability to function in the world. Such disorders encompass a diversity of behavior traits; and, in terms of their emotional effects, they may be rated as slight, severe, or borderline-psychotic. The narcissistically immature individual has trouble forming satisfying relationships with other people. He tends to maintain them at a shallow, superficial level, unable or unwilling to give of himself (or to accept what is given) and to commit himself deeply; he is wary of rendering himself vulnerable. This cautionary behavior is commonly seen in foster children, particularly when they have been passed from one home to another. They have been hurt too often through broken attachments, and they will no longer permit themselves to attach to anyone. Attachments come to be defined emotionally as short-lived and unreliable, therefore potentially hurtful, hence threatening. Similar tendencies can appear in children whose families have moved too frequently from one home to another, or from one city to another, or even from one country to another. They made friends, formed close ties with people, places, and atmospheres, then were forced to pull up roots and leave all that behind; and they simply found it too hard to take. A child who has been through this routine once too often (and, for some vulnerable children, even once may be too often) begins to protect himself; he simply won't *care*; he mustn't let anything or anyone *matter* that much.

This outcome is of course not inevitable, and is probably avoided most of the time. The children of highly mobile families—where the parents may be in the military or diplomatic services, or may work for companies that require frequent transfer as the price of promotion—can thrive if ties *within* the family are strong, stable, and secure; in that case the child, each time he moves, is encapsulated in his "life-support systems" wherever he goes. But, failing that, he is at risk of a typical narcissistic disorder. Sometimes in adulthood he may be so intent on protecting himself from narcissistic injury that he either keeps a number of shallow, nonintimate relationships going simultaneously, or isolates himself socially, priding himself on his self-sufficiency, rather than run any risks.

Neuroses, neurotic episodes, even psychotic regressions, may be triggered by any number of childhood events and experiences—all the normal hazards of personautics. There may be family troubles, extended illness of the child or a parent, economic dislocations, separations, divorces, deaths, accidents, injuries, fires and floods, wars and insurrections, the whole catalog of life's vagaries. Kliman delineated many of these and their observed and possible effects in *Psychological Emergencies of Childhood*—some of which will be drawn upon in Part Three—and tried to sort out the diversity of pathogenic experiences into some rough-cut classifications. One can, for instance, differentiate between experiences of overstimulation, on the one hand, and of deprivation or deficiency on the other. The latter can come about through parental apathy or neglect, and the amount of emotional damage depends at least partly on the nature and timing of the deprivation and whether it was intermittent or chronic. Overstimulation, too, can take many forms. A child may be overstimulated sexually, perhaps through the conscious or unconscious seductiveness of a parent or some other adult. He may undergo, or merely witness, severe physical beatings or overt emotional cruelties, perpetrated perhaps on a sibling, or by one parent on the other. He may be crammed with too much learning too soon, overstimulation that applies in particular to child prodigies. The most celebrated of these was probably John Stuart Mill, whose father, James, spent many hours each day force-feeding the youngster with incredible quantities of abstruse knowledge from his first year forward. As Bruce Mazlish comments in his psychobiographical study of the Mills, "John Stuart Mill never was a child, and yet in large part remained one, although in a twisted fashion, all his life." Such cases combine deprivation with overstimulation.

There are also fear, anxiety, or conflict experiences of many varieties. There are interference experiences, where the interference with certain developmental activities may be unconscious or deliberate on the parent's part, or accidental, through a child's illness or physical defect. On and on goes the list of categories. Fortunately, some of these childhood hazards, or at least their effects, can be prevented or minimized through wise and well-informed parental guidance. One important such means is "psychological immunization," a process you will hear more about in Part Three.

When one considers the sheer multitude of hazards that can lead the child into psychosis or neurosis, one wonders that any child survives childhood in decent emotional health. We have, of course, been directing our attention to emotional vulnerability rather than emotional sturdiness. Happily, as the saying has it, "Kids are tougher than you think." Most kids, at any rate. So let us now turn our attention to the more robust and resilient aspects of child psychology, and to the controversies that have lately generated around them.

Most children do succeed in life despite early disadvantages and adversity, including parenting that would be rated as poor by almost anyone's standards. Because this fact has been too little appreciated in many quarters, a trend has been growing among child psychologists that suggests, even argues, that the way children are raised by their parents, and whether their homes are happy or not, has little to do with the way they turn out as adults. It is further suggested, contrary to all we have been saying until now, that the experiences of infancy and early childhood have little or no real impact on later life; that these experiences, rather than being repressed, may simply vanish and be forgotten.

This trend has become so current among at least a handful of esti-
mable, impeccably credentialed authorities on child development as
to constitute a virtual movement. It is not an official movement, in
that it does not represent a group of consciously participating members who have formally organized themselves into a "school of
thought." Nevertheless, their agreement and vocal advocacy on key
issues, the importance of these issues, and the thrust they have already generated, gives us license to identify them as a movement—
and we now do so. If we had to give the movement a name, it would
be some oversimplified designation such as the Childhood-Doesn't-
Matter Movement. Let us emphasize at the outset that the movement's general position contains a number of valuable and liberating
ingredients. There is always the danger, for instance, that in dwell-
ing on the hazards and vulnerabilities of childhood, one may imply
that there is a *necessary* connection between a disadvantaged childhood and a troubled adulthood; this isn't so, and we need to be reminded, every now and then, that it isn't so. Inadequate parenting
does not condemn a child to failure or unhappiness. In a word, *complete* "parental determinism," as it has been called, does not exist.

As a corollary of this point, it is undoubtedly true that parents,
and especially mothers, have taken too much of the blame when
children are perceived to have turned out badly (by whatever definition), and they have therefore had too great a burden of guilt laid
upon them. As is too often the case with poverty-stricken and otherwise socially handicapped parents, they are faulted for consequences more rightly attributable to the failings of the community
at large. Most important, perhaps, is the point made by Orville G.
Brim, Jr., that damage of various sorts in childhood has been looked
upon as "irreversible"; and that labeling it as such does not encourage the therapist to try to turn matters around. Yet we know from
our own experience at the Center that such efforts are not wasted,
that much of what is done to children *can* be undone—as has been
shown in cases where the necessary energy and imagination have
been applied. University of Chicago psychologist Bertram Cohler,
one of the movement's spokesmen, is perfectly right when he points
out that people do keep refashioning their lives all their lives, and
many succeed in refashioning theirs for the better even without pro-

fessional help. The movement seeks, admirably, to accentuate the positive, to offer hope, to lessen guilt.

What is it, then, that we find objectionable in the movement? Our concern is perhaps more related to its style than to its substance—though the two are not always easy to separate. Its statements tend to be too extreme, too unqualified. Cohler, for instance, has said publicly that all the longitudinal studies—those studies that follow the same people from childhood into their later years—show that what happens in early childhood has *no* demonstrable impact on adult life; that people who had unhappy childhoods do just as well later on, and are just as *happy*, as those who had happy childhoods. He has further insisted that the way parents raise their children—and how troubled the parents might themselves be—really doesn't matter very much, because what happens to them later, including what they do for themselves, pretty well compensates for earlier disadvantages in upbringing. As for the current emphasis on "parenting," and on training young people for parenthood, Cohler scoffs at such programs as a waste of time, money, and energy. (Incidentally, Cohler's own studies into the consequences of being raised by a depressive mother confirm our own results. Children up to age ten—which is as far as he has carried his longitudinal studies—still show the ill effects of depressive parenting. Despite these findings, Cohler is convinced that, by adulthood, the children in his study group will be just as happy, just as successful, just as productively functional, on the average, as any other group of people raised under more congenial circumstances.)

Perhaps the most influential figure in the movement is no less an authority than Harvard's Jerome Kagan. It is rather disconcerting to hear Kagan refer to convictions to which we strongly adhere—along with most other investigators and therapists of our acquaintance—in the past tense, as though they had already acquired a quaintly anachronistic flavor. As Kagan writes, in the magazine *Human Nature*:

> Western scientists used to believe ... that infantile autism, a form of childhood psychosis, could develop simply because a mother rejected her baby. . . .

Many still believe that most of an infant's experiences have effects that reach many years into the future.

Accordingly, we have awarded certain early experiences a mysterious power. . . . As a result, middle-class parents worry about providing sufficient stimulation to their month-old infant or wonder whether failure to unite the newborn with its mother immediately after birth might have harmful consequences.

. . . parents were supposed, through proper nurture, to prepare their children to be psychologically healthy adults.

In the article from which these remarks were taken, Kagan concludes that new discoveries about the human infant—which he details from a number of sources, including his own cross-cultural studies—"imply that [the infant's] first experiences may be permanently lost. . . . I suspect that it is not until a child is five or six years old . . . that we get a more reliable preview of the future. The infant's mind may be more like a sandy beach on a windy day than a reel of recording tape."

We acknowledge Kagan to be indisputably one of the world's leading experts in child development. Nevertheless, we obviously consider him to be dead wrong in these surmises (otherwise we would not be writing this book). We were perturbed, too, by an article that appeared shortly after Kagan's, this one by Arlene Skolnick. It appeared in *Psychology Today* and was titled "The Myth of the Vulnerable Child" (the author disclaims the title). We clearly believe that the vulnerability of the child is not a myth, but a fact. This is perhaps the key to our disquiet over the movement. Its "members" of course acknowledge that serious emotional problems do afflict people both as children and as adults, but that the two sets of problems are essentially unconnected. The underlying theme is that what happens after childhood constantly modifies the individual's life program so that childhood problems disappear and adult problems arise in response to new events closer in time; and these problems can be just as severe for people whose childhoods were relatively untroubled as for those whose childhoods were very troubled indeed. This theme contains much truth, and we surely agree that lives are modified by later events, including the individual's own efforts. We are convinced that, if the movement's more extreme statements are taken seriously, they can all too easily let parents (and the community, too, in all its social and governmental manifestations) off the hook. If what happens in childhood doesn't matter, if children are going to come out the way they are going to come out, if poor parenting (whatever that can mean under the newly defined circumstances) is of no great consequence, then what's all the fuss about? Why orate about "child advocacy"? Why practice "child psychiatry"? Why give child-rearing advice at all?

Yet look at what is happening in our world. The statistics on child abuse have become obscene. Family life is perceived to be increasingly fragmented. The landscape abounds with children in anguish, even while parents increasingly seem irked with the responsibilities of parenthood. Will the movement not give us all license to care even less about children than we in our "child-centered society" do now? In a word, the movement appears to us, in certain respects, to represent a big step backward. And at whose expense? The children's.

To characterize the dedicated people who make up this movement as being antichild would be most unfair. They spend their lives thinking about children and children's welfare. Just the same, the net effect of their pronouncements could turn out to be the inadvertent encouragement of antichild behavior. (Truly loving parents, of course, find it sufficiently rewarding to treat children well so they'll feel good *now*, regardless of later outcome.) If they were making their statements based upon a firm body of substantial evidence, we would simply have to swallow hard and accept the consequences. But such studies and evidence on which they base their challenge to the earlier positions is, it seems to us, fairly tenuous at this point— much more so, in our opinion, than the case for the special vulnerability of early childhood, and of the profound ill effects of certain kinds of defective parenting. Thus they perform a disservice by the premature publicizing of what must be looked upon, at best, as tentative conclusions.

The careful investigations of mother-infant bonding (see chapter 6) carried out by Klaus and Kennell offer impressive—and only recently accepted—evidence that parent-child interaction even in the first hours of life can affect later emotional life. Apart from the intuitive conviction that one acquires from observing one's own and one's friends' children, the formidable accumulation of psychiatric and psychoanalytic case histories offers quantities of evidence (mostly retrospective, to be sure) of the connection between early childhood and adult troubles. Many studies of varieties of criminals and delinquents bolster this view. Moreover, many longitudinal studies of the very kind cited by Cohler, studies made by respected investigators such as René Spitz, Ian Gregory, Margaret Fries (some of whose subjects have been followed for forty-five years), Marie Crissey, Sylvia Brody and Sidney Axelrad, Stella Chess and Alexander Thomas, those of Elsie Broussard and Robert Skeels we have already mentioned, and many more, all point to the fact that what happens to children in their early, vulnerable years is strongly influential on their later emotional lives. All this, and more, adds up to too strong a body of already established evidence to brush aside so cavalierly. Those in the movement have every right to challenge any prevalent assumption they believe to be challengeable. But one would wish they could frame their challenges less sweepingly, especially considering the possible consequences if it turns out they are wrong—as we so far believe them to be. We have unequivocal long-term evidence that babies who fail to get an adequate diet of "stimulus nutrition" from a reliable caregiver are at great risk of developing later emotional problems, and that troubled children are often under the compulsion, as adults, to repeat their early experiences—that is, to visit similar experiences upon their own children. We also have equally clear evidence that some severe early life problems can be reversed, even when due in part to pathological treatment by parents. But such reversal is achieved at great cost, and only with great effort. Prevention is so much better.

We in our culture are finding it increasingly difficult to bear the pain of our children. We no longer have the excuse we used to have when people had large families and could say they were too busy to give each child a lot of individual attention. So we must rationalize our collective neglect of children by denying that the neglect does them any harm. Just as each of us has individually repressed all the painful memories of those earliest, most vulnerable years, we would like to be able to say of children in general: Early experience doesn't matter. It all just goes away and is forgotten.

It may not be remembered, but it doesn't go away.

These considerations bring us back to that fascinating group of children who have been identified—and defined—as "the invulnerables." The investigator most responsible for the upsurge of interest in the invulnerable child is Norman Garmezy. Along with his colleagues at the University of Minnesota, Garmezy has made exhaustive studies of everyone else's studies as they bear on children who, despite disadvantages of every description, managed to achieve emotional health and high competence. E. James Anthony, as already mentioned, is among those who have given special attention to the children of psychotic parents, especially those who somehow escape the consequences that often overtake their siblings, and even become "supernormal" through having their talents and capacities sharpened by coping with adversity. The work in this area has been admirably summarized by Julius Segal and Herbert Yahraes in a chapter ("Children Who Will Not Break") of their book, *A Child's Journey*. "Instead of an image of despair, degradation, and deficit," they write, "he [Garmezy] invites us to focus on children who, despite their membership in the lowest social and economic classes, not only remain unscarred but function at a remarkably high level." People like Garmezy and Anthony emphasize the positive side of the risk statistics, and indeed these new studies are exciting and hold out great hope. We need to know what it is that makes children prevail as well as what makes them succumb.

We do not consider Garmezy, Anthony, Segal, and the other investigators of childhood invulnerability as in any way part of "the movement" that we have just been discussing—though their reports have been pointed to as further evidence against the idea of childhood vulnerability. If so many children succeed as adults despite being born into the most inauspicious circumstances, the argument goes, then childhood adversity cannot be as deleterious as advertised; in some cases, it may even be an advantage, as with Anthony's "supernormals." Manfred Bleuler, as the result of a long study of schizophrenics, was "left with the impression that pain and suffering can have a steeling—a hardening—effect on some children, rendering them capable of mastering life with all its obstacles. . . . " In *Cradles of Eminence*, a study of the childhood of more than four hundred famous twentieth-century woman and men, Victor and Mildred Goertzel found that fully three-fourths of them were stressed as children—"by poverty; by a broken home; by rejecting, over-possessive, estranged, or dominating parents; by financial ups and downs; by physical handicaps; or by parental dissatisfaction over the children's school failures or vocational choices." And further: "Handicaps such as blindness; deafness; being crippled, sickly, homely, undersized or overweight; or having a speech defect occur in the childhoods of over one-fourth of the sample. In many of these individuals, the need to compensate for such handicaps is seen by them as a determining factor in their drive for achievement."

Even if one questions whether parental dissatisfaction over school failures or vocational choices is enough to label a childhood as troubled; even if one questions whether being considered ugly, say, is a "physical handicap"; even so, the numbers of problem children who became high achievers are impressive. As we poke around at random in our own explorations into the lives of such diverse figures as Winston Churchill, Eleanor Roosevelt, Albert Einstein, James Cagney, Samuel Johnson, and Thomas Edison, we find childhoods that were most unsatisfactory from almost any point of view. It would have been all too easy to declare these children as most unpromising candidates for later distinction. (Such predictive errors were indeed one of the major surprises that came out of the longitudinal studies carried out by Berkeley's Institute of Human Development.)

Frustration, deprivation, and illness have often been looked upon as spurs to creativity. George Pickering, in *Creative Malady*, makes a case for the role of ill health in shaping the lives of Charles Darwin, Sigmund Freud, Marcel Proust, Florence Nightingale, Mary Baker Eddy, and Elizabeth Barrett Browning. Martin Grotjahn, discussing Emily Dickinson, writes: "Hostile maternal neglect disturbed Dickinson to the point of collapse; it severely damaged her as a person and kept her from developing a normal female sexual identity. It also motivated her to seek relief from pain in her poetry. Without the great pain of her childhood, Emily Dickinson might never have been more than a mildly interesting sentimental and conventional poet—if indeed she had written at all."

It all is enough to make one wonder if we are not perhaps being subversive in our attempts to reduce emotional troubles in childhood. Should we not, for society's sake, encourage parents to mistreat or neglect their children in order to challenge them to their best efforts? By helping make childhood happier, will we be guilty of reducing the sum total of creative achievement to dangerously low levels? It would, of course, be perverse to answer such questions positively. Yet there are many children who, despite poor nourishment and physical beatings, are so well endowed that they grow up healthy anyway; and others who, always sickly in childhood, turn themselves into superhealthy, superathletic adults, veritable models of fitness. In the area of psychological development, the phenomenon of invulnerability leaves much to be explained, many confusions and apparent contradictions to be sorted out.

To return for a moment to physiology, we know of many diseases which, while not strictly genetic in the sense of being attributable to a single gene defect (as in, say, sickle-cell anemia, Tay-Sachs disease, or cystic fibrosis), do have a genetic component. These are known as multifactorial polygenic diseases, and we have already discussed a number of them as "biological birth defects" in chapter 4. But in a given family, different siblings may have inherited varying degrees of susceptibility to such diseases, including some below the "risk threshold," thereby leaving those children *immune*. In terms of general psychological development, we believe that such babies are constitutionally sturdier and, as children, possessed of an innate thrust toward healthy ego development and self-esteem so strong that it can overcome almost any amount of adversity.

Tying behavioral traits to genes is, of course, highly speculative at this stage of our knowledge. Sociobiologists have been attacked—sometimes deservedly, sometimes not—for attributing too much of human behavior to genetics. Nevertheless, we are at least tentatively persuaded that genes do affect human behavior in significant ways. Recent studies of the "interest styles" of children adopted early in their lives by 870 Minnesota families, for example, suggested to the investigators that these interest styles—so different in most cases from those of their adoptive parents—were in part inherited and only in part shaped by the environment. We do not pretend that these answers—or our speculations in regard to "invulnerable" children—are definitive. They are more in the nature of first guesses.

Apart from the possibly inherited constitutional factors at work, many disadvantaged children may thrive because of factors unknown to the investigators—factors perhaps not included in their questionnaires. There is often a significant, loving person in the life of a child who has been neglected by his parents—perhaps an aunt, or a grandfather, or a close neighbor—someone who "adopted" him, who cared about him enough to spend the time, energy, and affection to inculcate the necessary self-esteem.* Studies of success despite adversity show that, in many a poor and disadvantaged family, one person—usually the mother—fought valiantly to instill in the child a desire to learn and to achieve, and to maintain in the home at least a minimal atmosphere that could allow it to happen. In other cases there was a strong mentor who was able to "turn on" the child.

Often success is achieved at some emotional cost, so that the invulnerable child may at times grow to be almost indistinguishable from the person with a narcissistic character disorder. The child of a psychotic parent, for instance, may have survived by learning, perhaps after much anguish, to keep himself at a safe psychological distance. "Invulnerables," says Segal, "seem to develop an objective, dispassionate, and remote relationship to people, thus allowing them to maintain their own integrity and to fend off disturbing influences." And one must be careful how one defines success. For instance, the Goertzels, in their study, remark that "an overpossessive parent of a peer-rejected child (especially a mother who dislikes her husband) is the most likely to rear a dictator or a military hero who enjoys the carnage of battle." Such dictators and military heroes are among those eminent people cited as prime examples of success despite adversity. What did such "success" cost the rest of us?

Such questions are raised simply to indicate the complexity of the investigative task. On the whole, we agree with Segal that the study

---

*Writing of his grandmother, whom he had never seen until she came to help when his father was dying, Maxim Gorky said in *My Childhood*: "Until she came into my life I seemed to have been asleep, and hidden away in obscurity; but when she appeared she woke me and led me to the light of day. Connecting all my impressions by a single thread, she wove into them a pattern of many colors, thus making herself my friend for life, the being nearest my heart, the dearest and best known of all; while her disinterested love for all creation enriched me, and built up the strength needful for a hard life."

of so-called invulnerability may be among the most important research projects under way in child development today. If we can discover what the factors are (other than genetic) that make the difference between prevailing over and succumbing to adversity, we can hope to learn how to impart these capacities to the children who need them.

Meanwhile, our conviction remains firm that the preferred way to ensure the best outcome for *all* children is preventively, by good parenting throughout the vicissitudes of the six-year pregnancy. This should not only protect the vulnerable children, but would probably offer the invulnerables the opportunity to be happy and successful without having to work so hard for it, at so much emotional cost. A happy childhood does not, of course, mean a childhood free of challenge. Whatever it is that makes the small percentage of "supernormals" rise to greater heights, we can surely find some way to incorporate those ingredients—whatever they turn out to be—into childhood. That has to be a better solution than to advocate adversity as a positive virtue.

PART THREE

Emotional Life–Support Systems: The Social Network

On the whole, babies and young children in the 13th and 14th centuries appear to have been left to survive or die without great concern in the first five or six years. What psychological effect this may have had on character, and possibly on history, can only be conjectured. Possibly the relative emotional blankness of a medieval infancy may account for the casual attitude toward life and suffering of the medieval man.

—Barbara W. Tuchman,
A DISTANT MIRROR

Like most parents from time to time I have experienced very angry if not violent thoughts about my children, and on one occasion when I was furious at my then ten-year-old son I took a favorite trophy of his and threw it on the floor. Of course it was irreplaceable and broke to bits. I was not only ashamed and sorry, I knew I had wanted to do it. It never occurred to me that I was experiencing the same feelings of rage, frustration, inability to cope, hopelessness, and helplessness that causes many parents to harm their children, sometimes severely. I do know now that like most mothers I could have used a lot of help when my children were little because, despite my B.A. and my M.A. and even my teaching experience, I knew nothing about caring for a child. Unfortunately, many if not most young mothers today—rich, poor, black, white—don't know anything either.

—Naomi Feigelson Chase,
A CHILD IS BEING BEATEN

11

Parents as Preventive Psychiatrists

There was so much to worry about, when worrying about children, and Garp worried so much about everything: at times, especially in these throes of insomnia, Garp thought himself to be psychologically unfit for parenthood. Then he worried about that, too, and felt all the more anxious for his children. What if their most dangerous enemy turned out to be him?

—John Irving,
THE WORLD ACCORDING TO GARP

. . . practically every effort aimed at improved child rearing, increasing effective communication, building inner control and self-esteem, reducing stress and pollution, etc., in short, everything aimed at improving the human condition, at making life more fulfilling and meaningful, may be considered to be part of primary prevention of mental and emotional disturbance.

—Marc Kessler and George W. Albee,
ANNUAL REVIEW OF PSYCHOLOGY, 1975

No one raises much objection to the idea that parents or guardians have the duty to safeguard the physical health of children—to see that they are properly fed and nourished, clothed and sheltered, protected from harm and provided with necessary medical care. We recognize, at the same time, that parents cannot always keep children perfectly healthy, cannot protect them from all harm or injury, and we acknowledge that there are limits to what parents can do for any child physically. We can't turn a boy who is destined to have the physique of a jockey into a professional basketball center, or make eyes blue or hazel when the genes dictate brown. We know too that some children are more vulnerable, weaker constitutionally than others. Some have allergies we can (so far) do little about. Some have poor eyesight and need glasses. In many cases, economic and other deprivations may simply make it impossible for the parents to provide adequate nutrition, clothing, health care, or shelter. Nevertheless, allowing for all these well-recognized limitations, we almost universally agree, as a matter of principle, that in some basic, inescapable fashion, parents are responsible for the physical health of their children.

In this same spirit, then, with a similar regard and respect for the limits of what is possible, we believe parents are responsible for their children's mental health. A child exists in an emotional environment largely created, modulated, and modified by the parents. That environment, especially in the critical earliest phases of life, can be said to consist essentially of a set of dialogues, mostly non-verbal at the start, that take place ad lib between child and parents, without a consciously prepared script, but heavily weighted by the programming built into the parents by their own psychological histories.

The mental processes of a child are in part—often in large part—the product of the way she is perceived by her caregivers. Indeed, Elsie Broussard's fascinating studies (cited in chapter 10) with her "neonatal perception inventory" suggest strongly that the way mothers perceive their newborns can exercise a powerful influence on the child's later development—a classic instance of the self-fulfilling prophecy. Such parental perceptions were themselves influenced by the caregivers' own self-concepts—which were in turn partially shaped by the way *their* parents viewed themselves and their children. We talked earlier about "vertical epidemics" and "psychological birth defects" as metaphorical concepts. We could also think of the parental self-concept, again only metaphorically, as somewhat akin to a set of chromosomes, in that it contains patterns of codified and influential information capable of being transmitted from one generation to the next. The information thus transmitted affects the capabilities and failings, the life-styles and behavior patterns, of each individual offspring.

Preventive psychiatry, then, begins with the parents.

One might argue that it is meaningless to talk about the prevention of mental illnesses or serious emotional disorders when our understanding of their nature is still so fuzzy, and our knowledge of how they are caused and how they develop is so sparse and imprecise. Once more we turn to biological analogies to demonstrate that the success of preventive measures is not necessarily dependent on a detailed knowledge of the chain of cause and development:

For centuries it was known that draining swamps cut down the incidence of malaria in their vicinity. Yet no one knew that the disease was caused by a mosquito-borne microorganism or even had the tools at hand to formulate such a concept. Nevertheless, the preventive measure worked. Similarly, typhoid was prevented by cleaning up contaminated water supplies long before anyone knew about the existence of the typhoid bacillus. And Semmelweis discovered that the childbed fever that killed so many new mothers could be prevented if doctors would only wash their hands (fresh from surgery or corpse dissection) before attending the childbirth. (Unfortunately, most of the doctors in his hospital laughed at him and refused to wash, and the victims kept dying at the same rate for a long time before the truth of his advice finally penetrated.) Even today we use a variety of drugs and medications, from aspirin to insulin, with a far from precise understanding of their therapeutic mechanisms.

Preventive psychiatry—which we know from long experience does work—must for now still be based on a not very thorough grasp of the chains of causation and complex force fields at work within the minds, bodies, and interpersonal social networks of the victims. We can note that certain correlations do seem to exist—like swamps and malaria, like contaminated water and typhoid, like dirty hands and childbed fever—and take advantage of the preventive opportunities thus offered. We have earlier cited many examples of such success—such as Robert Skeels's ingenious demonstration (see chapter 10) that the incidence of mental deficiency in abandoned infants could be dramatically reduced, even eliminated, by permitting retarded young women in the institution to "adopt" and mother the infants on an individual basis. We know, too, that the "anaclitic depression," "marasmus," and "hospitalism" (see chapter 7) noted by René Spitz as high-risk occurrences during the neophase in institutionalized infants has been prevented or considerably diminished by changes in institutional staff care and procedures.

In our fourteen years of experiences with troubled children and their parents at the Center for Preventive Psychiatry, we have seen many correlations between certain sets of family circumstances, or certain clusters of parental attitudes and characteristics, and certain undesirable results in the child. It is, in fact, on such correlations that we have based most of the advice and recommendations in regard to parental qualifications and motivation advanced in Part One. We do not have to understand all the details in the causal chain to see that the correlations are important, and prevention possible.

Our descriptions in Part Two of the child's intricate, multistaged developmental progress through the six-year pregnancy pointed up the recurring opportunities for judicious parental intervention, with measures for enhancing normal progress and thus future mental health. Implied along the way were similar "opportunities" for hampering development. By avoiding such negative opportunities, the parent helps prevent mental illness. This kind of prevention is achieved principally by the parents' awareness of the potential pitfalls by caring, by commitment, by a fine attunement with their unique and individual child, by a well-balanced understanding of the child's changing needs, by love and good sense—common and uncommon.

We have said very little, however, about the impact of events that might upset the normal or average course of a child's development—events usually outside the parents' control, events that range all the way from the highly disturbing to the catastrophic, events that cause psychological emergencies: The child becomes seriously ill and perhaps requires hospitalization, surgery, or some potentially frightening form of therapy.

The child who suffers severe or painful injury may require long-term rehabilitation or even experience permanent crippling.

A parent becomes seriously ill (mentally or physically), perhaps needing periodic or long-term hospitalization. A parent is separated from the child, for whatever reason, for an extended period of time. A sibling or a parent dies. A close friend falls ill, has a serious accident, or dies. The house burns down. The child is subjected to violence or sexual molestation. The child sees a parent injured or molested. The family moves to another city, or even to another house. A new baby suddenly appears in the house, getting large amounts of the parents' attention. The parents are divorced—or are seriously considering a divorce. The family is caught in a tornado, a hurricane, a flood, an earthquake, a famine, a war. One can hardly list all such potentially disorienting events. A very unlucky child may experience several of them.

The effects of most such crises are best handled with professional help. (They are dealt with at some length in Kliman's *Psychological Emergencies of Childhood*.) Many communities now provide a "situational crisis-intervention service," of the type pioneered by our Center, but unfortunately most communities still have no such services to offer. What can individual parents do to cope, to help children through such critical times? Obviously, most of the kinds of occurrences we have listed cannot be prevented by parental actions. But there is something parents can do to *prepare* a child for potentially disastrous happenings, and thereby prevent the more devastating long-term psychological and emotional consequences. We call it "psychological immunization." And here, one final time, we draw on biomedical analogy:

There can of course be no vaccine against mental illness (though there are biochemical treatments for some forms of mental illness), yet a certain degree of immunity may be deliberately developed against specific kinds of psychologically damaging experiences.

A baby, as we know, is born with several months' worth of immunological protection left over from her stay in the uterus, including circulating antibodies. If she is breast-fed, she gets even more protection via her mother's milk. But soon her own immunologic apparatus must begin to function. To do so, it must be properly challenged. It is the paradox of immunology that, unless the child is exposed to the kind of bacteria that could make her ill (though not in large enough quantities actually to bring on the disease), she will not grow strong enough immunologically to stay healthy! In the normal course of her daily life, the average baby will be exposed to plenty of bacteria in a considerable variety of species. She will acquire these microorganisms from the surrounding air, from her bedclothes, from her food, from the objects she touches, from people—especially from her mother, who is most frequently in contact with her—no matter how "clean" these objects of contact are. The mother alone will inadvertently be bringing small quantities of pathogenic microorganisms into the baby's orbit, thus affording her small body the opportunity to begin building up immunity against them. Mind you, the doses must themselves be small and safe, not massive enough to be threatening. Apart from all these naturally occurring immunities, we have learned how to impart, artificially and deliberately, an effective immunity against various infectious diseases that were once rampant and frequently fatal. Our technique is vaccination.

We are now suggesting that a child may be similarly immunized psychologically. Parents who protect their child too assiduously from outside experiences on the grounds that the exposure might be hazardous are perhaps depriving the child of the necessary challenge provided by new objects, new people, new situations—and of the stimulation required by the child's mental mechanisms to begin adapting to a complex, changing, and at times potentially hostile world. A cozy, consistent, unchanging environment may be momentarily safer and more comforting, but it may also be deficient in such challenge and stimulation. As the infant grows into a toddler, she requires wider and wider exposure—permitted to occur in as controlled and careful a manner as possible, never more than she can handle at a particular stage of development—to small doses of potentially hazardous or disturbing experiences.

If we go back to reconsider the stages of separation-individuation (chapter 8), we see that the toddler must learn to absorb inner as well as outer hurts, to feel her sense of grandiosity slipping away and yet tolerate its loss, to be fortified rather than crushed by the revelation that she is only human, and only one separate, finite, lone human being, whose caregivers are not omnipotent, as she had believed them to be. Throughout this period she is learning to accept parental separation in small doses. She learns, as well, sometimes to her pain and chagrin, that the physical and emotional resources of her caregivers are not unlimited, that she must adapt to their rhythms and irritabilities, and that a rebuff has no finality but is usually followed by a happy reconciliation. As her verbal capacity grows, anxieties can be expressed and explored more effectively, and the preventive dialogues can be enhanced. But in complex and cumulative ways, the child has begun to develop frustration tolerance, which, like immunologic tolerance, is partially dependent on the degree, the quality, and the efficacy of the exposure.

The neophase of infancy was too early to begin any attempts at inculcating frustration tolerance. But from late infancy on, immunizing doses of frustration can and are safely given by most parents. And by the middle of the third year, with the child well advanced toward separation-individuation, she is probably ready for the acquisition of immunity against the specific kinds of stressful events we listed earlier.

If there is another child on the way, for instance, wise parents will begin—early and in small doses—to prepare the present child for the potential stresses inherent in the scheduled new arrival. The mother's physical enlargement during pregnancy and the visible preparations in the household to receive a new resident offer many little opportunities for anticipatory dialogues. These will help immunize the child against perplexity, against the brief separation from her mother during hospitalization, against powerful feelings of jealousy, against the narcissistic downfall that accompanies displacement from her unique status in the parents' eyes. Successful immunization does not mean these stressful feelings and challenges will be totally absent; simply that they will be tolerable, manageable.

The arrival of a new baby is an expectable and relatively benign event. But what of the shocking tragedy that strikes without warning? What of that most massively stressful event, the death of a child's sibling or parent?

We at the Center have come to believe that any child who is old enough to speak in sentences is old enough to be exposed to some simple concepts about death. True, premature death is much rarer than it used to be. Nevertheless, any child still may, at any time and without warning, face the loss of a parent, a sibling, or a close friend—who may be killed, for example, in a car accident. Considerate parents will try to ensure the gradual buildup of immunity against this hazard. No child should have to deal with the overwhelming experience of bereavement without prior exposure to small doses of ideas and feelings about death.

A family can begin this process by providing cautious encouragement to the preschool child's natural curiosity about the death of insects, plants, and animals. If a pet dies—whether it be a goldfish or a turtle, a cat or a dog—the child is not protected, or her interests well served, by deception. The parent may well take what appears to be the easy way out: flush the goldfish down the toilet or throw the turtle down the incinerator and pretend he or she has no idea how it could have disappeared so mysteriously. Or attempt to replace the pet with a new lookalike and insist the pet didn't die at all. The child will probably see through the deception and wind up doubly baffled by the pet's death and the parent's unacknowledged duplicity. It is better to share the truth, to face the child's questions, to allow the appropriate anxiety and grief to surface, especially if the dead animal was a beloved pet. The family should talk openly about the pet, to remember its good and bad habits, the happy, endearing, and worrisome events that occurred during its life, even to provide a funerary occasion if it feels appropriate.

Similarly, if someone in the neighborhood, or a distant relative, dies, such a tragedy could provide a safe, not enormously threatening, opportunity to talk about death in the child's presence—or in direct dialogue with the child, answering her questions as freely and frankly as her understanding allows. Such discussions may sadden the child or make her somewhat apprehensive for a brief moment, but these experiences—in a low emotional key—will serve as minimournings that can help build up her psychological immunity against the possible death of someone closer to her.

We have found, at our Center, that many childhood mental illnesses have their origin in psychological emergencies or "situational crises"—of which a death in the family is one of the most common. Such an early-childhood stress is statistically associated with a higher than expectable incidence of later learning disabilities, school failures, juvenile delinquency, and adult-life hospitalization for depressive illness. The most serious risk, statistically, is for girls under age four whose mothers die.

Often a child does not *show* by any overt behavior just how stressed she is, or what is disturbing her, or how her perceptions may have distorted the real event in her own mind. Suppose the mother of a two-and-a-half-year-old child has been killed, for example. Someone may finally break the news to her in some euphemistic fashion. They may tell the child that Mommy has gone on a long trip, or gone to heaven, and the child may shrug and accept the explanation. Adults around her may change the topic of conversation in her presence, may smile and be cheerful, fearing to show their grief lest the child be upset. And on the day of the funeral they pack the child off to some neighbor's or relative's house so that she won't be exposed to the tears and turmoil. It may seem to them all that the child is fine and surely doesn't need any psychiatric help. But do they know what's really going on in the child's mind?

To begin with, the child may believe—through the process psychologists call "magical thinking"—that she is somehow responsible for her mother's death because of something she has done or failed to do. Or she may feel that her mother has gone away and abandoned her, that Mommy doesn't and never did love her. Seeing that the others smile and do not grieve, she may think: Nobody cares that Mommy has died. And then, being sent away from home just at a time when she is most bewildered, she may feel as if she is being banished from the family—thus inflicting a double loss on her.

The specific problems and reactions will of course depend on the specific details that pertain to the specific family. Obviously such a child, who is seemingly placid and untroubled, is very badly in need of some professional help, preferably in the company of her father and siblings, so they can all think and feel and experience and work their way through the grief of their situational crisis together. That is real insurance, real preventive psychiatry.

This is why we try hard at the Center to get people to bring in their children with the least possible delay when psychological emergencies occur. We have educated parents, clergymen, physicians, nursery-school teachers, anybody associated regularly with young children, to be on the alert for incipient though persistent troubles that can be dealt with on a short-range basis, preventively, rather than waiting until severe mental illness has set in. We treat the children, and we treat and counsel their young parents—often with the grandparents. We encourage every agency in our community to be aware of, and alert for, the troubles of young children, and to alert *us* when they think we might help. We try to get adults or teenagers to act, on a long-term basis, as special friends to our young, troubled children, providing someone else who cares about and who will spend significant amounts of time with them. We have sought, wherever possible, and with heartwarming success, to enlist the support of all sorts of people—newspaper editors, beauty-parlor operators, policemen—to act collectively as an at-the-ready network committed to whatever prompt assistance may be needed by troubled youngsters and their hard-pressed young parents and families.

Many of our experiences at the Center illustrate the kind of qualities parents should possess in order to take advantage of immunizing opportunities. Let's take an actual case—one of Kliman's—which did involve the supreme stress of parental death. The mother had a brain tumor that not only caused a great deal of pain, but also periods of confusion and an occasional grand mal convulsion. She had just learned that the tumor was inoperable, and was thus forced to recognize herself as terminal, or at least potentially so. When she and her husband, the parents of two daughters aged three and four, first described their situation, their overall attitude was most impressive. They had already given some thought to the problems they would be facing, and clearly possessed the traits most desirable for parents of children perhaps already under stress. This woman and her husband were frank and courageous, and they understood that the best way to help themselves and their children would be to work in unison toward the conscious goal of preparing as intelligently as they could for her probable death. (The opposite of these desirable traits—evasiveness, dishonesty, divisiveness, hostility, lack of direction or purpose—would certainly have militated against the family's chances of successfully adapting to their tragic circumstances.)

The couple's fears turned out to be well founded—the mother did die. But she was able to survive for two years before she lapsed into her terminal coma. By that time her two daughters, then five and six, had received the benefit of a lengthy immunizing process. As one example, the mother had dictated a long, taped archive for the children, in which she encouraged them to participate. She answered numerous questions about their own earlier childhood, especially those parts about which they remembered little or nothing. Apart from providing them with an extensive education in their family's history—the kind children seldom get under any circumstances—the mother was demonstrating a cardinal human function: the capacity to give help and support to others when one is under severe stress. Again, the opposite of this trait—drawing heavily upon the *children's* resources when they are under stress ("role reversal")—is a damaging practice too often indulged in by parents who are less narcissistically mature and secure than these particular parents.

Another valuable aspect of their parental behavior was a good sense of balance. Though they gave careful attention to the immunizing process, they did not focus on the tragedy too intensively. They continued to perform their ordinary parental guiding functions in terms of the children's development. They both took a keen interest in the girls' cognitive progress, giving narcissistic assistance by virtue of the esteem in which they obviously held the children's efforts. (When this is not done, children often undergo learning disabilities—sometimes severe—following bereavement.) Moreover the mother, despite her own unremitting distress, had the altruistic capacity to let them know that she cared about their social activities. Though she was not able to accompany them physically, her attitude permitted the girls to feel free (even to know that they were *expected*) to be happy, to have a good time, rather than to feel guilty because they could enjoy their social experiences. Throughout her last months of life, their mother taught them that she fully expected their progress along all their lines of development to continue, and, gently, that they must separate themselves in their thinking from her own increasingly limited but still loving self. In a word, she was encouraging a special form of separation-individuation.

Because the immunizing process worked, there was a true sharing of anticipatory mourning—including the mother's own mourning for her consciously anticipated death. Thus the most important person, the central figure in the tragedy, the one who felt her life to be strictly limited in future time, was able to give permission—and to serve as an example—for facing this otherwise often unapproachable cluster of dreads.

The father's task grew even more difficult and sensitive after his wife's death. It takes a high degree of altruism, in the midst of one's own newly painful mourning, to sustain a constant availability to one's children, to see that the basic needs of these still incomplete human beings are taken care of without serious interruption. The quality perhaps most difficult for a parent to preserve under such circumstances is real empathy, the kind of tolerant insight that allows him to understand how appropriate it is that young children cannot sustain sadness for more than a few moments at a time. A parent lacking such empathy could easily get angry at children who seem perfectly cheerful at a time when he is devastated by the depression of his mourning.

Though the mother's death in this case was difficult and lingering, there was every reason to expect a good outcome for the remaining family; the two children were basically healthy, and the two parents well qualified. So far, five years after the mother's death, the surviving members of the family are doing well. It is worth underlining that the most essential reason for optimism in this case was the advanced state of narcissistic health of the parents, which permitted the children's own lines of narcissistic development to proceed unimpaired. The father was able to make up somewhat for the loss of the mother by serving as a narcissistic auxiliary and supplier; and the mother herself, before her death, had helped nourish the children's concepts of themselves as competent to get along without her.

This case that we have dwelled on at some length is not typical, however. It is in fact relatively uncommon for a young parent to have the opportunity to prepare her children for her death. More usually, death comes suddenly—in an automobile accident, a murder, a suicide, a heart attack.

In such events it is the surviving parent who, coping with the task

without the help of the other partner, must possess additional qualifications. The abruptly bereaved parent has to deal with a rupture in
his own narcissistic lifeline, a total and unexpected cutoff of his
supplies. The same problems are simultaneously besetting his children, and he is the main one to whom they now turn desperately
for help.

Among the most valuable assets he could have at this time is an
already established network of helping family and friends in the immediate vicinity. Obviously this would have had to be acquired pri-
or to the event over a period of time. If the suddenly bereaved
parent is fortunate enough to have such a network at hand, these
people can help answer the children's basic needs more ably than
he, in his state of shock. The complexities of the parental task at
such a moment can be overwhelming.

We recall, for example, the dilemma of a chemical engineer of our
acquaintance who had just tried unsuccessfully to save his wife and
his brother from a fire. He had succeeded in rescuing his two sons,
aged two and a half and four; but he could not forgive himself for
failing to save his wife and brother as well—a feat that would have
required superhuman capacities. His grief was thus even more complicated and stress-wracked than in a more usual kind of death. It
took him some forty-eight hours to reach a point where he could
make even the most minimal and basic life-support arrangements
for his two little boys. Worse still, it took the father another full day
before he could honestly discuss with them the reality that their
mother and uncle were dead—perhaps because of his own reluctance to accept the reality. The boys were already aware of the true
facts, though only partially and confusedly. The father's delay cost
him loss of the boys' confidence in his truthfulness, not to mention
his general parenting ability. At the same time they felt he had no
confidence in their own abilities to deal with facts and realities.

We can see from this example that there are times when a parent,
under extreme pressure, may be called upon to exercise a degree of
calmness, competence, clarity of judgment, and ability to communicate honestly and sensitively that may be beyond ordinary capacity—just as it was beyond the physical capacity of the distraught
father to rescue every member of his family. So we cannot fault this

father for his initial omissions. What could still be done (and was done), however, was for the three remaining members of the family to begin sharing the burdens of the disaster—gradually, and at a bearable pace. The father was able to pull himself together and, without professional help in this instance, to bring his two boys to an understanding that, as a bereaved trio, they could all help one another do what Freud called "the work of mourning."

In a case like this, the essential qualification for a parent—and a most difficult one for this particular parent—is *freedom from excesses of guilt and ambivalence* in relation to the deceased. Until the father could overcome his self-blame and guilt over his inability to save his wife and brother, he could not fully help his children face the reality of their losses. Fortunately, it took him only a few extra days to shake off his crippling feelings of shock and begin the work of mourning.

Such work entails a lot of remembering—remembering thousands of bits of experience with and surrounding the dead person, a remembrance that may be painful at times but also healing. If the memories are to convey the required healing effect, however, they must carry a proper weight of reevoked emotion. And the emotions must run the gamut: tender, loving, passionate, nostalgic, poignant, resentful, angry, hateful, and bitter. We are all ambivalent about our major love objects. It is a matter of degree. To the extent that the mourner is ambivalent, to that extent will his mourning work be handicapped. Fortunately in this case, the stricken father was able to conquer his original attitudes and recognize them as unreasonable. He was thus able to make the boys understand why he had reacted as he had in the immediate wake of the tragedy, and to help them remember their mother—and, to a lesser extent, their uncle—and to remember them easily and thoroughly over a period of many months and even years. He served as their guide and collaborator, with a wise and gentle mixture that was loving in nature, but also now and then mildly critical of the dead individuals, when honesty required it, as they worked over the nature of the lost relationships.

Strange to tell, death may not be the most difficult of crises in which parents must act as preventive psychiatrists. It turns out to be harder to help most young children deal with separation and divorce than with the death of even a mother or father. Studies of thousands of children by clinicians Ian Gregory (in Minnesota) and Judith Wallerstein (in California) in the sixties and seventies show fairly convincingly that the loss of a parent by divorce usually causes a child more emotional problems than the loss of a parent by death. How does one measure such problems? By criteria such as failure of one or more grades in school, dropping out of high school, being arrested four or more times. The difference between the effects of divorce as compared with parental death, according to Gregory's large-scale studies in Minnesota schoolchildren whom he followed for many years, were striking: in terms of the dimensions of stress-related troubles, the children of divorce were about 300 percent worse off than those whose mother or father had died.

If we examine the qualities and qualifications needed by parents to help their children weather the stresses of a divorce, we can understand some of the reasons why the outcome is so unsuccessful so much of the time. The necessary parental traits would be, for example, reasonable freedom from hostility, reasonable honesty, and a reasonable lack of ambivalence. Such qualities are frequently missing because, first of all, the marriage was probably marked by conflicts that promoted and exacerbated the very opposite—an emotion of parental hostility with which the child might identify only to his own detriment. Moreover, the relationship between the parents was probably contaminated by long periods of severe ambivalence, a process in which fluctuating or simultaneous feelings of love and hate served to weaken all members of the family in their adaptation to the resultant strains. Finally, when the state of separation and then divorce became a reality, often the parents—without any ill intent—were simply handicapped in their abilities to be honest. Their own feelings were too bruised, and too much had gone on, was perhaps still going on, which the parents felt could not be entrusted to the discretion of children, partly through fear of gossip. (The children, in most cases, were quite aware of what was going on.)

One extreme case of Kliman's that produced a psychosis in a young child occurred in a family where the father had been a concentration-camp survivor. He seemed compulsively attached to a sadistic wife who tormented him with tales of her infidelities, and who used their boy as an ear for her contemptuous tirades about the father's sexual inadequacies and his generally spineless character. By age four the boy had lapsed into hallucinatory and delusional episodes in which he saw his mother dressed as a man and possessing a large set of male genitals. The boy also feared that his pet canary, loved and trusted in the daytime, would peck his eyes out in the middle of the night; he often went sleepless, constantly checking to see that the bird could not get loose to maim him. A vertical epidemic of sadomasochism had reached across time and space from the mad milieu of Buchenwald to invade American suburbia. Ironically, as in Nazi Germany, the courts were almost helpless to protect this victim; the parents managed to sustain both their vestigial relationship and the abuse of their child despite several efforts of family court judges to stop the process.

Before we leave this admittedly out-of-the-ordinary case, let's see what lessons we can learn from it in terms of a saner management of divorce as it affects children. We can see, for one thing, that certain indispensable parental abilities were altogether absent. At age four, when a child is moving cautiously in the direction of his gender identity and oedipal conflicts, he would certainly require in a separation/divorce crisis that the parent in whose custody he remained be sensitive to his needs. He would need help in mourning his substantial loss, directly proportionate to the amount of time and attention he had previously received on a daily basis from the now partly absent parent. Such help was obviously not forthcoming in this case; the boy's custodian was instead intent on using him as a pawn and weapon in the service of parental compulsion.

In order to reduce any tendency or temptation to use the child as a pawn or weapon in interparental struggles, what is principally needed is a high degree of intelligent, collaborative altruism in the child's best interests. These collaborative efforts must include the working out of arrangements designed to cause the least possible disruption in the child's relationship with the parent who has moved out of the house.

At least half the divorcing couples referred to Kliman privately or to the Center for Preventive Psychiatry in recent years have been sufficiently endowed with the necessary traits to support a recommendation for joint custody. Kliman frequently uses a form of custody consultation in which he establishes a set of ground rules.

Everyone involved must understand and accept that (1) the child whose custody is in dispute is the primary patient; (2) the adults who are disputing the custody are *not* the primary patients and will not be granted any "privileged communications" or "confidential" status if the dispute reaches court (they can of course have their own separate therapists who will safeguard their confidentiality, but this does not apply to the custody consultation); and (3) whatever any of the parties in the dispute reveals to the psychiatrist (or psychologist, social worker, clinician) may be used at the professional's discretion to aid in the custody recommendation to be reached—and may, further, be communicated to other family members, also at the professional's discretion.

These ground rules, and one more—payment in advance—make it difficult for any parent or attorney to manipulate the consultative procedure. Even the party paying the bill has little power to prejudice the process, because the payment is made before there is any inkling of what the recommendation will be. These rules are important in safeguarding children who are at their most vulnerable. The child, already the victim of a discordant marriage, and perhaps also the victim—if not the living arena—of an often bloodthirsty custody dispute, is at extreme risk of emotional damage, as confirmed by Wallerstein's systematic studies.

Surprisingly, there is seldom much opposition to the ground rules. More often, in fact, parents as well as attorneys are relieved to be treated with such firmness. Once the rules have been accepted, we begin—through interviews, psychological tests, and home visits—to determine a number of crucial variables: To whom is the child attached as the main *psychological* parent (a different question from who is now in physical custody of the child)? Is the main psychological parent fit to raise the child in physical and psychological safety? What outcome can be predicted if either parent raises the child? If the two parents are of equal psychological importance, are they capable of collaborating in a joint custody agreement that will be adequate for the child's continuing development? If they cannot collaborate, then which of the two is most likely to contribute to the child's healthy development, or least likely to retard that development?

Such are the Solomonic questions that nowadays are occasionally handed over to clinicians to help resolve. Kliman has been able to persuade several families to settle bitter custody disputes out of court. He regards this outcome as infinitely more likely to result in better mental health for all parties than will the adversary procedures carried out by attorneys whose interest in a child's development (where sensitivity to and knowledge of such development exist) is necessarily subordinated to an aggressive interest in satisfying their clients' demands.

Essentially, Kliman's procedure says to the family's adults: You are at this time not qualified to make collaborative decisions about the welfare of your child. If you are willing to suspend your responsibilities for a while, and transfer parental decisions about custody to someone designated by society as an expert, then you are showing a commendable recognition of your own temporary incapacity to make these decisions. In return for your transfer of responsibility, which will entail the payment of a fee to the designated expert (or team of experts), that expert will do his best to see that your child's future is arranged according to the child's best interests. This means that the situation is now so serious that the child's interests and rights will take priority over the adults' interests and rights. Your recognition of this must be complete and immediate, or the clinical procedure cannot take place.

Such a procedure in effect declares the parents to be in partial bankruptcy as a team. Their parental liabilities at the moment so outweigh their assets that, as in a business bankruptcy proceeding, the court must appoint a manager to handle certain vital transactions.

So far we have discussed only those devastating, long-term losses that come with those ultimate separations, death and divorce. But there is a spectrum of other crises that occur in the life of a family that test and illuminate the assets and liabilities of parents. When does a somewhat troubling experience become a "crisis"? What makes the difference between a transitory episode and an event that leaves lasting psychological scars? This frequently depends on those very assets and liabilities, the sensibility and sensitivity with which parents handle a given situation. Let's look at an experience that is shockingly common—the sexual molestation of a child by a baby-sitter. We'll take a case out of our own records.

A trusted baby-sitter, whom we'll call Monroe, a boy in his middle teens, has been taking care of three-and-a-half-year-old Laura for a period of nearly a year. He has been her friend, companion, and responsible baby-sitter since she was barely able to speak sentences. But now Laura has become a pretty and seductive little girl who is in the midst of her Electra feelings toward her father. Monroe is also changing. He is now almost a year older than when he began his baby-sitting job (he still needs the money). At fifteen he is now sexually active, and often feels compelled to masturbate—not necessarily at the most convenient times.

On this particular night Monroe is in a sexual turmoil because he has just spent the afternoon with two friends watching a provocative movie, and has been especially preoccupied with a scene in which an attractive nude woman comes out of a large birthday cake. Since he does not have a girl friend with whom he can even partially discharge his sexual tensions, Monroe at such times is inclined to retire to a bathroom to masturbate. After ejaculation, he can then relax and concentrate on whatever he is supposed to be doing— homework, social life, errands, baby-sitting. Tonight, however, he is careless. He has put Laura to bed and, he believes, to sleep. He goes into her parents' bathroom, and though he does so with the intention of masturbating, he forgets to lock the door.

Laura is not asleep. Hearing strange noises, she tiptoes to the bathroom, quietly opens the door, and watches, fascinated but also frightened. She is transfixed by associations with recent efforts she has made to catch views of her nude father in the bathroom. Soon Monroe realizes he is being watched—but the realization does not take place until he has reached a high pitch of excitement, a state in which his frustration tolerance is low and when his consequently altered mental functioning impairs his social judgment and general reality testing. In this poorly adapted condition, he invites the little girl to open the door wider so she can watch him better, cautioning her meanwhile not to tell her parents because they will surely be angry at her for peeking into the bathroom.

As a next step in this ill-fated encounter, he invites the little girl, now highly excited, to do whatever she wants, suggesting that maybe she would like to "pet" his penis—at which she is still staring with a mixture of fascination, excitement, and a distinct sense of being "bad." Up to this point she has had no clear idea what she would like to do, but now she decides that she'd better run to her bedroom and lock the door. Before she can carry out her intention, however, Monroe, behaving in a highly uncharacteristic manner, becomes frightened and grabs her. He spanks her for being a naughty peeker, and, somewhat to his own surprise, begins demanding that she pet his penis to make him feel better. Laura complies. Monroe ejaculates, an event that again both fascinates and frightens Laura, whose own excitement is now being deliberately heightened by Monroe—who is, in fact, manipulating her genitals. After a few more minutes, Monroe recovers his composure and calmly tells Laura that she should take a quick bath and go to bed before it gets so late that he will have to tell her parents how late she stayed up. In fact, if she does this fast enough, he won't tell her parents about any of the naughty things she did.

Neither Monroe nor Laura mentioned the occurrence to anyone that night or the next day. But when, on the weekend, Laura's parents made plans to go out to an evening ballet performance, with Monroe scheduled to be her sitter, Laura began a circumlocutory unfolding of the story. Here her parents' qualifications were critical to whether or not the outcome of the episode would become a harmful sexual crisis in Laura's life. First, they had to be patient in listening to the garbled story the child told, recognizing that it was partially falsified and full of ambiguities. Surmising the true nature of what occurred, they had to exercise empathy, or at least tolerance, for Laura's developmentally appropriate curiosity and sexual excitement—and for the legitimacy of her desire to observe for herself. At the same time they had to understand that Laura had experienced a dose of excitement and overstimulation that went beyond her developmental capacities to handle; it certainly helped explain her recent agitation, her guilty-looking responses to minor infractions of household rules, and some difficulty in going to sleep.

Once they grasped the general story line as it really occurred, the parents had a number of options. They could call the police to deal with this terrible young man. They could inform Monroe's parents about it and let *them* deal with it. They could speak to Monroe directly or in joint confrontation with Laura. Or they could pursue a

combination of these possibilities. What they chose to do was to respect the relationship they had established with Monroe over the
past year and give him a chance to tell them the story himself, in
private, without at first involving Laura or anyone else. By taking
that option, which demonstrated some empathy and compassion for
the older child's dilemma, they set an example for Laura in that their
response was free from extremes of punitiveness. Monroe did in fact
admit, in turmoil and tears, what had happened and begged forgive-
ness from Laura's parents. They in turn shared this outcome with
Laura—and later with Monroe's parents.

Monroe was permanently banned from baby-sitting, by agreement with his own parents, and was given a brief stretch of psychotherapy, which helped him resume a normal adolescent social life.
Laura needed no special psychotherapy, as her parents had the capacity to let her debrief her memories of the experience; they answered numerous questions about the functions of the wet white
stuff that came out of Monroe, and allowed Laura to settle into a
sexual quiescence helped by the assurance that someday she would
be old enough to have a man sex friend who could be close to her
own age and not a lonely big boy who got mixed up and wanted a
little girl for his sex friend. Subsequently, the parents' healthy attitude toward their own sexuality—and their mutual enjoyment of
each other sexually, evident without being blatantly on display—
helped Laura realize that their words were sincere, not just a grown-
up be-a-good-girl story.

More than eight years later there was no sign that Laura had been
harmed, permanently excited sexually in any way, or overly inhibited in her early adolescent development. Had the parents lapsed into
agitation, horror, severe condemnation—and especially had they
condemned the girl for her role in the episode—we would have expected to see a number of pathological consequences by adolescence: a shift toward inhibition of intellectual curiosity; a mild,
anxiety-induced difficulty in paying attention to any educational or
social process that was emotionally charged in some way; and ultimately a fixation on the entire stage of development at which the
child's overstimulating experience with her baby-sitter had taken
place.

We have in this chapter listed a number of crises that can occur in the life of a child. Now it is time to spell out a few general guidelines that, taken together, might serve as a kind of rough-cut technology of crisis management.

1. *Awareness of the child's present developmental stage.* This is critical to the way he will react to a situational crisis. There is nothing the parents can do to change this factor, but merely by giving thought to it, and by possessing the necessary *empathy* (a quality we have emphasized before as a parental qualification), the developmental needs of the child are more likely to be met regardless of the crisis atmosphere.

2. *Patience regarding the next developmental stage.* A child may be right at the entry border of his next phase of development at the time a crisis occurs. The empathic parent will recognize that this is not the time to insist that the child move on abruptly to that next phase. If the child is really ready to, say, give up his bottle without undue complaint, fine; but if the child is reluctant, the parents should understand that, though the child is "old enough" to take the next developmental step—and might have been easily able to do so had the crisis not occurred—he is better served if permitted to remain for a while in a "holding pattern." Harsh or merely immature parents may be especially poorly qualified at a time of crisis—which may bring out the worst in them. The parents may feel the need for being parented themselves—a need that is of course not recognized. The child's relative helplessness and need for parenting, on the other hand, is legitimate and beyond dispute. The only way the parents can express their unconscious envy is by making cruel demands on the child for performance at a time when he is least equipped to carry them out.

3. *Enhancement of the child's trust in the parents.* A vital factor in the outcome of a situational crisis will be the nature of the child's relationship with his parents. A time of crisis, met in the proper spirit of challenge, could become a time for the deepening of ties between parents and child—but this can only happen if the ties have been well forged beforehand. A time of crisis is *not* a time to build a relationship from scratch. Especially important is the child's trust in the honesty of what the parents communicate to him, and his confidence in the reliability of their caregiving.

4. *Building on the child's prior immunizing experiences.* A time of real familial crisis allows the parents to take advantage of those small doses of immunizing experience that have perhaps given him a greater intellectual and emotional readiness to meet the specific crisis at hand. Again, this is something that must have taken place prior to the current crisis; if it was not done, then there is no immunity, and the crisis will be consequently more difficult to handle.

5. *Continuing immunization.* Even when no advance immunization has been provided—prior to a child's sudden admission to the hospital, say—there is still time to prepare him for what is to come: how and why an injection may be given, when it will happen, who will be taking care of him (it will help to introduce him to doctor and nurses by name). Doctor-and-nurse games in which a doll is the patient may also serve as immunizers for preschoolers and even many older children, especially if the child can actively participate, using a doll as the patient, in the kind of procedures he will himself be undergoing more passively. As always, the empathy, creativity, and ingenuity that parents can bring to the situation will make it easier for the child to get through the experience emotionally whole.

6. *Including the child in what is happening.* At a time of crisis the child, whether he expresses concern or not, is likely to be confused about the new turmoil of events that has entered his life. The parents should, from the outset, let him in on what is going on, and why. They should let him know what is being done, and how they and other grown-ups feel about it.

7. *Activation of social network forces.* The social network called upon may include not only friends and relatives, but community agencies as well. Here, too, it helps to know in advance what community facilities are available and what kinds of help they offer. For example, if the house catches fire and the family has to move out—even though everyone is safe, it is foolhardy for the parents to try to take care of all the resulting problems themselves. There *is* a social network of some kind out there, even in places without highly sophisticated professional agencies, and this network should be called on to the extent possible, and always as early in the crisis as possible.

8. *Protection through preparation.* Not all crises are unforeseeable. A car crash, a fire, a sudden illness or death must be dealt with as it arises. But there are *scheduled* events that are almost certain to pre-

cipitate crises; they can be mild crises, however, if the child is properly prepared. For instance, if a child is going to nursery school for the first time, visiting the school in advance—even just walking around it to take away the total strangeness of it—can be of help. It is even better, of course, if he can go inside to meet the teacher and perhaps some of the other children once or twice before school starts. In first-rate nursery schools the mother can remain in school for a while to provide reassurance for the separation-sensitive child.

Similar preparations and specific immunizations apply to the child's first camp experience. No prelatent child should go away to camp without having met the director and counselor. He should, if possible, have seen accurate pictures of the camp and talked at some length about the details of what he may expect to find when he arrives. There should be definite plans for visiting and writing, and permission to take along transitional objects such as favorite toys, photographs, or items of clothing that have special emotional importance (a favorite baseball cap, for instance). If there are special supplies or items to be purchased for the camping season, it is a good idea to have the child along on the shopping expeditions.

9. *Avoidance of role reversal.* Parents hard hit by a crisis themselves are often in danger of forgetting their responsibilities to the point of expecting a child to act as parent to them, or to other siblings. A child is still a child, no matter what is going on, and maintenance of his appropriate role is essential. He should not be expected to be the caregiver when his own needs have suddenly increased. Though a child should be made to feel that he is part of the events, and not isolated, so that he is aware—to an extent that makes sense for his stage of development—of what is happening, a very young child should not be allowed to have a vote or any powers of decision unless he has already reached the appropriate stage *prior* to the crisis.

10. *Continuation of reliable care.* Most important for a preschool child who has been separated from his home because of a crisis—perhaps through his own hospitalization, for example—is the maintenance of uninterrupted contact with his family. This means long, regular visits—every day, if possible—by one of his primary caregivers. With this kind of support, the child's confidence is bolstered; he may feel confident that his future will be as reliable as his past, that

the crisis represents only a temporary interruption of his life. Here again, a wider social network can be called upon for help—perhaps to baby-sit for siblings who must be cared for while the parent is with the sick child, or when the parent cannot leave work. Friends and neighbors can offer relief from household chores and feed the other children, thus enabling the parents to give more attention to the momentarily most needy child.

11. *Avoidance of overstimulating experiences.* What constitutes a proper level of stimulation is always dependent on the child's stage of development. It is probably unwise, for instance, to permit a preschool child to watch his own surgery; it could be horrifyingly overstimulating. Yet many latency children, adolescents, and adults benefit from watching the surgeon at work and cooperating in the procedure, on the alert for instructions—to change position, or even to hold an instrument. If a child is too young or for any reason not permitted to watch, the parents should be sure he isn't kept ignorant of what is going to happen. A void of information is almost certain to be filled by morbid fantasies.

12. *Helping other young siblings.* When tragedy strikes one small child in the family while there are still other young children to be cared for, parents are especially called upon to exercise their best qualities. Ideally, immunization should have already been practiced—literally, mini-rehearsals for events in which extra burdens will fall on everyone. If, let us say, a life-threatening disease like leukemia strikes a two-year-old girl, and she has a healthy five-year-old sister, then that older sibling will be fortunate if she is already familiar with concepts of sickness, even fatal sickness, and is also used to being called upon to carry out some housekeeping chores. When the illness of her younger sister occurs, she can rise to the challenge and at the same time reduce what psychoanalysts call "guilt of survivorship" by doing extra work, being extra helpful—not being given full responsibility, mind you, but helping enough to reduce measurably the load the grown-ups will have to carry. If she has never been familiarized with serious illness or the threat of death, and never been trained to be helpful, this is a bad time to start a crash program. Only in small doses can the knowledge of what is happening, and extra tasks, be given her. In either case, her

own nurturant needs will be great. Even in the newly hectic atmosphere she must be given her share of loving attention and the assurance that the disease has a rational rather than a magical cause (for which she might otherwise consider herself somehow responsible—for example, her darker wishes made her sister sick).

Parents must have empathic qualities at multiple levels to handle these situations—at the very moment when they are being devastated by the potential loss of a child as well as new and enormous physical and emotional burdens. (It is no coincidence that divorce rates among parents of leukemic and other severely ill children are much greater than in the general population.) When potential mothers and fathers are deciding whether or not they want to be parents, and especially whether they want to be parents of more than one child, such contingencies should be kept in mind. The couple should ask themselves if they are really up to handling such a multi-level task of self-management while remaining narcissistically nourishing, supportive, empathic—and technically competent—to do what the best interests of their children may require.

We see, then, that responsible parenting requires more than the capacity to get from one normal day to the next, to see the child from one developmental stage to the next, with the expectation of a smooth and seamless life. True, situational crises are not likely to arise with great frequency in the course of most lives; but they *do* occur in most lives at one time or another. Yet the management of situational crises involving children gets little attention in most parenting manuals. Each situational crisis calls on all the parents' capacities to be loving and caring; but it also calls for special technical abilities. The tasks will be easier to the extent that the child has successfully achieved, through a stepwise development, a reasonable state of self-esteem and a trust in his own and his parents' ability to cope with life in general. Even when that is the case, however, the new emergency retests the parents in the eyes of the child.

A child who has just established toilet control but is now faced with going to the hospital for major surgery may wonder, though he probably will not ask: Will my parents allow me to regress without humiliating me? Will my parents *listen* to my questions, fears, and worries? Will they allow me to pour out my memories of an experience after it has just devastated me? Will they let me keep pouring out my worries until I've gotten them manageable? (These questions are of course phrased in more adult language than will occur to the stressed child.)

The parent who can allow a child immediate and continuing emotional catharsis or "debriefing" is practicing excellent psychological first aid, a technology only recently acquired in the most advanced clinics that treat children's emotional problems. Similarly, the parent does well to provide an adult intellectual perspective while at the same time supporting the child emotionally. This dual awareness, carried out in practice, can allow even the most perplexing and distressing events to be integrated into the child's experience. Such understanding can make all the difference in the child's continued normal growth, or lack of it.

Parental capacity to see a child through emotionally troubling times may entail a sensitivity not only to events within the family but also to events outside—especially those that, because they are heavily covered by the mass media, television in particular, may make a profound impact on the child's awareness. The assassinations of John F. Kennedy, Robert Kennedy, and Martin Luther King serve as good examples. A more recent one is the incredible mass tragedy at Jonestown, Guyana.

The way in which adult caregivers react to such fast-breaking news events can have great influence on the behavior, the character, and the mental health of children. Following the 1963 assassination of President Kennedy, Kliman made a systematic study of the behavior of both adults and children in a metropolitan school system. He acted quickly to obtain data on behavior from twenty-five teachers with a total of six hundred pupils. The information thus gained has implications for parents, caregivers, and adults generally as to their responsibility for the emotional climate in which children receive their exposure to unsettling world events.

On the East Coast, the news that the President had been shot reached radio and TV audiences after two o'clock on Friday afternoon, November 22, 1963. Millions of schoolchildren were still in class, and thus tens of thousands of teachers, principals, and school superintendents had to make decisions that were fateful examples for their pupils. From questionnaires and interviews, we learned that some superintendents and principals, as well as many teachers, made a deliberate decision to withhold any communication about the event, leaving it to the children themselves and their families to handle the shocking tragedy—after the children got home, or perchance on the way home. These children were much more disturbed in their behavior—that day as well as later on—than the children whose teachers had elected to share the news with them immediately in the classroom. The best outcomes were in classes where the teachers clearly displayed their own shock and grief, but were also able to maintain scholastic activities—especially when they shifted the orientation of those activities to a discussion of the assassination itself. In such classes children as young as five were able to talk about such matters as presidential succession, police activities in trying to catch the assassin, and what steps might be taken to protect leaders from assassins. The correlation between adult behavior and pupil behavior was strikingly close. The more emotionally expressive and constructively active the teacher, so it was with the children.

From a preventive-psychiatric viewpoint, this suggests that a family—as well as a school—should communicate openly and verbally with children about even the most distressing events, especially those that the children are going to know about anyway. (Many of the most troubled children in the wake of the Kennedy assassination were those who heard the news from other children, or from portable radios listened to in washrooms, with the news transmitted in a fragmented and disorderly tumult.) Communications in crisis should be structured and deliberate, but should contain the appropriate emotions—not hiding the adults' own distress or even their confusions—and the fullest possible discussion should be shared on whatever level the children are able to use at their particular stages of development.

It is surprising how much bad news, in terms of other people's stressful experience, comes to a child's attention. Adults tend to picture the lives of preschool children—at least, American middle-class preschool children—as idyllically protected. But back in 1968 Kliman carried out another study, this one in a class of sixteen nursery-school children. Over a period of only two weeks, here are some of the things that happened: one girl had a tonsillectomy; others experienced the injury of a relative in a car crash, the sudden hospitalization of a sister in the middle of the night, a brother's surgery, the death of a grandmother, a prolonged parental absence, the revelation to the family that an uncle had died the previous month, the death of a cat, the death of a turtle.

Usually such an experience comes to the attention—and immediately goes. But for positive effect it can be called to the attention, held in the attention for a longer span, and used as an immunizing opportunity. Teachers and parents trained to utilize the vicarious experiences of others in order to build the child's psychological strength have learned the importance of remaining aware, at every step of the way, of the developmental stage of that particular child. Because the preschool child is inclined to worry that any untoward event may threaten to cut him off from safety or from the basic sources that satisfy his needs, discussion of the tragic event should take place in a setting that is both safe and reassuring. The child should be reminded in some concrete way that his own life continues as before—even as he sees his caregiver express genuine distress. The reassurance that accompanies the distress offers the child a model to identify with: He learns that one can experience emotionally, face, and discuss honestly events that are stressful—and still continue to function.

A warning note, however: We are *not* advising parents to seek out stressful experiences for the child. Enough will occur in the normal course of any childhood. Our recommendation is simply that parents remain sensitive to stressful events as opportunities for safe, psychologically immunizing experiences. At such times—in fact, especially at such times—the child, though not *over*protected, *does need protection*. He needs the security of knowing he is cared for. The family and home should serve as what Winnicott has called a "holding" environment—that is, the child feels held, cuddled, in a safe haven from which he can view and deal with the troublesome circumstances under discussion. During the six-year pregnancy, remember, the parents' major function is to provide the postnatal, psychosocial womb in which the child continues his personaut's journey to the shores of latency.

In this book, we have fallen into the trap that ensnares virtually everyone who writes about children and parents: The parent written about almost invariably turns out to be the mother. The father remains a shadowy figure somewhere out on the periphery of family life. Obviously, this is at least partly because of stereotyped tradition, in which the father is assumed to be the absent parent, most of the time, while the mother is always at hand. But it is also partly due to the fact that fathers simply have not been very much studied by researchers. Could a Margaret Mahler have induced a large group of *fathers* to accompany their children to a research nursery school day after day so she could study their interaction with the children? Even those investigators who do their observations in the home are usually observing mothers. We simply do not know nearly as much as we should about fathers, though we do know that the father's role is undergoing rapid and fascinating conceptual changes. (Perhaps the best single volume encompassing the existing studies is *The Role of the Father in Child Development*, edited by Michael E. Lamb. A shorter and somewhat more up-to-date survey is contained in the chapter, "Fathers: The Hidden Force," in *A Child's Journey* by Julius Segal and Herbert Yahraes.)

When a child is away from home, or abandoned to an orphanage, it is customary to say that he suffers from *maternal* deprivation. People as wise and sophisticated as John Bowlby and Margaret Mead have airily underrated the role of the father. Nevertheless, all the studies that have been made, in many cultures on all continents, imperfect as they are, suggest that the father is—or can be—extremely important to the child from earliest infancy on. "There is convincing evidence," say Julius Segal and Herbert Yahraes emphatically, "that the father's inadequacy or absence can erode the child's emotional well-being and that his wholesome, committed presence can help promote the mental health of his children."

There have been numerous studies of children whose fathers have been absent for years at a time—as prisoners of war, for example—and in every such study the children do less well by almost every measurement and have a higher incidence of emotional problems than children who have both parents. In homes where the fathers themselves are emotionally disturbed, the situation can be worse for the child than having a mentally ill mother, because the disturbed father is usually the official authority in the house. So the mere presence of a father is not enough in itself to answer a child's paternal needs. Sometimes the father is so completely absorbed in his work or outside activities, or travels so much, or simply has so little interest in his children, that he might almost as well not be there. If he is harsh or authoritarian, or if, on the other hand, he is weak, indecisive, and totally dominated by his wife, it can be difficult for a boy to become comfortable about his own gender identity. Though boys who are fatherless have been more studied, and are thus somewhat better understood, it is clear that girls too are affected negatively by the lack of a father. In some cases, they may be chronically suspicious of men, or anxious in their presence; in others, they may form a highly idealized and unreal picture of what men are like.

On the whole, it seems safe to say that scientific observation confirms what common sense already tells us—that a child of either sex is much better off with two caregivers than one. There is no adequate substitute for a good care-giving team, when their relationship is good and when they jointly care for, and care about, their children. Though we usually think of the care-giving team as wife and husband many homosexual couples are also capable of the enduring teamwork involved in child care, and a growing number are trying it. Many variations are possible even among heterosexuals.

Teamwork should be fostered even in the common situation of the father being away working all day while the mother remains at home with the children. Men have been increasingly influenced over recent years by the sensible persuasion of the women's movements, which have succeeded in liberating men as well (those who wish to be liberated) from their restrictive, stereotypical sex roles. Men feel increasingly free to be "maternal," to show their emotions, to help with household chores and with child care, and a growing number of them find open joy in their expanded paternal roles. Indeed it is no longer the greatest of rarities to see the father take over the primary responsibility for a child's care while the mother goes off to work.* The earlier in the child's life the father's involvement

---

*Some behavioral scientists, such as Alice Rossi of Amherst, offer cautionary advice here: Inasmuch as males are probably *less* programmed by their own natures and cultures to be nurturant, they may require some compensatory training in order to do the job adequately and with confidence.

begins, the better—starting with attendance at the birth, and bonding with the newborn soon after (see chapter 6). <u>The presence of multiple caregivers surely gives a child greater security</u>, even if the central parent-infant dyad remains with one parent.

But what about the case of the single parent? We may all generally agree that it's best to have two parents, but in a society where the divorce rate is high, where parents sometimes die prematurely, where desertion is not uncommon, the ideal situation of a loving-caring, mother-father team is simply not available to a great many children. Indeed, millions of families are now headed by a single parent. It has even become common, in some quarters, for women to decide, on purpose, to have children without marrying, thus taking on alone the double burden of earning a living for the children as well as caring for them at the same time.

There is no doubt that single parents can do, and have done, admirably well in raising children who are both productive and happy. But it is hard enough, as we have seen, for two good and well-meaning parents to give a child what she needs and to guide her to her own fulfilled development. Even a mother-father team often needs help—which, most of the time, the community cannot provide. Much more often, then, will single parents and those otherwise burdened by social prejudices or disapproval need help.

Such help should be routinely built into the structure of a society that thinks of itself as civilized and humane, a society that professes its concern for the welfare of children and, indeed, an interest in its own future. We in our society do think of ourselves in these ways; yet the built-in, helping network that would support our expressed desires is lamentably absent.

12

Society as an Extended Family

*In this century we have come into knowledge about childhood and the
constitution of personality that can be fairly placed among the greatest
scientific discoveries in history. But the children themselves are not yet
the beneficiaries of our science. Our juvenile laws are chained to archaic
principles, and the social policies which govern the welfare of children
are shaped by the needs of the moment, or the budgetary crisis of the
year. They are blind to the psychological needs of the child and his
family.*

—Selma Fraiberg,
EVERY CHILD'S BIRTHRIGHT

*The devotion that individual parents now feel to their own children
would be broadened to include everyone's children. The next generation's strength and well-being would become everyone's responsibility.*
—Kenneth Keniston,
ALL OUR CHILDREN

W E have been describing, throughout much of
this book, what a child needs in order to be delivered whole and
healthy into latency at the end of his six-year gestation. We have
particularly dwelt on what a child needs from his parents. We know
beyond doubt that many parents possess important disqualifiers,
that many are downright unqualified to be "good enough" parents,
to provide a home that will serve as an adequate psychosocial womb
for the child's extrauterine development.

Beyond parental disqualifiers, however, are larger issues. Incalculable numbers of parents *could* be, are equipped to be, good enough
parents, but their social—including economic—circumstances make
it difficult, at times impossible, to carry out their task. There is only

so much a parent can do, or that even an "invulnerable" child can do for himself, in the face of overwhelming adversity.

Though we know of no other nation whose practices and policies we would want to adopt in their entirety, there are lessons we can learn about a proper concern for children from many other cultures—not only from Western capitalist nations, but from the Russians, the Chinese, and the Cubans; and from such "primitive" tribal groups as the Ik of Uganda, the ancient Mayans, the Sanema and Yequana of Venezuela, and many others. We will be examining some of these examples later in this chapter.

Our own society does in fact play an official surrogate role in parenting, but it does so in a scattered, usually impersonal, and frequently unintelligent manner, so far as the best interests of children are concerned. We are guided by a fragmented chaos of stitched-together laws, regulations, and court precedents, often erratically applied in individual cases by state and municipal authorities. Children may be torn unwillingly from foster parents with whom they have formed strong attachments, to be returned to the home of a parent where they will predictably be at great risk of serious emotional troubles. Or they may be given back to parents who have severely and repeatedly beaten them, with every reason to expect that the beatings will continue and the child be injured, perhaps permanently maimed, or even killed. On the other hand, children may be snatched away on someone's arbitrary judgment or misjudgment, or through adherence to the letter of some rigid regulation, from parents who are doing a quite creditable job.

Americans tend to worry, politically, about the human rights of oppressed and disadvantaged people in foreign nations, people who are inaccessible to our ministrations and at the mercy of governments whose chiefs we can only hope to persuade on their behalf. But what of the human rights of those incipient beings who, though living in our midst, are quite cut off from the rest of us in those isolated enclaves we call families? These children have no voice and no vote, and are at the total mercy of their "heads of government." Abuse and neglect of all mental and physical varieties are unbelievably commonplace. Society must do much more than it is doing to protect these hostages of misfortune (always remembering that the line between protecting children and meddling in family affairs is perilously slender).

Over the past few years a spate of books—some (such as Kenneth Keniston's *All Our Children* and Nathan Talbot's *Raising Children in Modern America*) based on large collaborative studies, others (for example, Selma Fraiberg's *Every Child's Birthright*, Julius Segal's and Herbert Yahraes's *A Child's Journey*) based on individual investigations—have put forth long lists of recommendations on behalf of children. Lee Salk is one among several who have argued for a national child advocate with full Cabinet rank—a Secretary for Children. Most of the criticisms of current practice, and most of the suggested solutions, are in surprising agreement—in principle, if not in detail. Clearly, if we continue our present policies—or lack of them—we are on a course that risks mass psychological disaster. Right now there are millions of children getting mental-health services—seldom adequate—and uncounted others who should get those services earlier. Troubles in the preschool years, as we noted earlier, go especially unattended. While admissions to mental institutions have been going down in all other age groups (due largely, perhaps, to psychochemical medications), the admission of children has been rising steadily; the rate more than doubled between 1962 and 1975.

One-third of the mothers of preschool children are in the labor force. Most of them have to work. Many are the sole supports of their families. Six and a half million children under the age of six are in need of someone to care for them while their mothers work; and there are nowhere near enough substitute mothers, either at home or in day-care centers, to go around—even for those who can afford to pay for the service. Though a small percentage of existing day-care centers may be rated as excellent, staffed by well-trained people who are aware of the needs of children at different developmental stages, most of them are below standard—a great many far below. Some are just places to keep children "in storage," as Selma Fraiberg puts it. Others are guilty of downright neglect and abuse. Fraiberg estimates that about two million additional well-trained "substitute mothers" are required to meet the current need for day care. Many children get no supervision at all. These are the legion of "latchkey" children, left to shift for themselves as best they can.

About a sixth of American families are still below the official poverty level, and the children of these families are multiply disadvantaged. They are hungry as well as malnourished (the two are not the same). Their parents are often harassed and distressed, and have good reason to be. Their health is poor, their energy levels often as low as their self-esteem. They live in fear and anxiety amid muggers, junkies, and prostitutes, and are themselves at risk of succumbing to the temptation of crime, addiction, or prostitution. Their families are fragmented, their clothing and shelter are inadequate, and they are less likely than other children to do well in school. They are also considerably more likely to store up despair, anger, and outright hostility, which will be acted out in adolescence with a consequent price to society in vandalism, arson, rape, muggings, and other varieties of destructiveness.

One of the problems with current children's programs is that they have no unifying focus, no central theme or purpose. We rather like Fraiberg's suggestion: "The unifying principle is found in the primacy of human attachments." Throughout this book we have seen the central importance of parent-child attachments during the first years of life. Obviously millions of our young undergo serious interruptions and disturbances of their separation-individuation processes, if indeed they ever experience a loving symbiotic relationship with a caring parent who can commit the time necessary for the task, or can provide a suitable substitute. We would enlarge Fraiberg's idea by substituting for it *the primacy of the child's healthy narcissistic development* (in the sense that we, borrowing mainly from Mahler and Kohut, have used it previously). Such a principle incorporates within it the primacy of human attachments, since healthy narcissistic development cannot proceed without them. With such a central theme in mind, one can see that the ambiguous principles by which we have been administering foster-care and aid-to-dependent-children programs are interfering with, rather than enhancing, the child's development. It soon becomes obvious that we are spending vast sums of money creating and perpetuating the vertical epidemics of psychological defects that we should be stretching our ingenuity to combat. Even under current systems, by hewing to this

central guiding principle of healthy narcissistic development, judges
and caseworkers would make many fewer mistakes in the placement
of children.

"Every social program in medicine, law, education, and public
welfare," says Fraiberg, "must commit itself to the protection of the
human rights of children, the rights of enduring human partner-
ships, the right to be cherished by family and community, the right
to fully realize their human potentials." She emphasizes the psychological as well as the physical well-being of children, and suggests a
built-in "moral accountability to the public."

But *do* we really care? Or are those cynics who poke fun at our so-
called child-centered society hitting uncomfortably close to the
mark? One does not have to look far for evidence indicating the
need for a vigorous consciousness-raising effort to shore up our positive feelings toward children.

A lot of people who are now middle-aged can remember when
much of our society was more like a tribal village in its embrace of
children. Even if they lived in some big-city neighborhood rather
than a small town or rural village, they can remember how they as
children were more interactive with adults beyond their parents.
They were perhaps aware of many of the occupations by which
adults earned their living, observing people at work in their stores,
workshops, and wagons. Almost any passing adult felt free to take
joy in children's achievements—to stop to pat a child on the head, to
say a word of approval, to pay a compliment—or to reprimand a
misbehaving child, assuming the role of surrogate parent when no
parent was around, even if that adult had never seen the child before. Nowadays, a strange adult—especially a male—who stopped
to speak pleasantly to a child would be suspected of intent to mo-
lest. And the man who says "Don't do that!" to a child not his own
may be risking a punch in the nose from the parent—or at least an
invitation from the child to mind his own business. Nor do children
get much chance to see adults at meaningful work, a situation de-
plored by Urie Bronfenbrenner, the outstanding Cornell authority
on child development, who depicts row upon row of similar houses
from which fathers depart each morning, briefcase in hand, to catch
trains and disappear for the rest of the day at their mysterious busi-
nesses, reappearing at dinner time, and often having to work

through the evening as well. Many young men with very young children, just at the stage when the children could most use the presence of a father and the wives could most use a bit of help, are precisely at that stage of their careers when they must impress their employers, demonstrate that they care about their work, stay extra hours at the office or take clients to dinner, and travel a great deal. Such upwardly mobile men and women are more frequently transferred to other cities on short notice, too, with a consequent uprooting of their young families.

Behavioral scientists like Bronfenbrenner wish that the corporate world were more sensitive to the needs of children, making it possible for young parents to get home nights without being penalized, giving them more options in terms of travel and transfers, perhaps providing opportunities for children to come visiting, to see where Daddy or Mommy works, to dispel some of the mystery of what the parent does in all those hours of absence, even to feel a sense of vicarious participation in the enterprise. The navy, for instance, has a program that permits wives and children to come aboard vessels when they are in home port. (In Sweden, a father can quite respectably get a leave of absence to stay home for a while with his wife after a baby is born.) Bronfenbrenner decries the fact that in America children are raised less and less by their parents, and more and more by their peers—and by the television set. "The socialization of children," as University of Pennsylvania sociologist George Gerbner puts it, "has largely been transferred from the home and school to TV programmers who are unelected, unnamed and unknown, and who are not subject to collective—not to mention democratic—review." This surrogate role of television operates on children in families of all economic classes, from the wealthiest suburbanites to the poorest urban ghetto dwellers.

The impact of television on children has belatedly become a major concern, thanks largely to angry grass-roots movements led by organizations like Action for Children's Television (ACT), soon joined by others such as the national Parent-Teacher Association (PTA). A *Newsweek* cover story on the subject begins:

His first polysyllabic utterance was "Bradybrunch." He learned to spell Sugar Smacks before his own name. He has seen Monte

Carlo, witnessed a cocaine bust in Harlem, and already has full-color fantasies involving Farrah Fawcett-Majors. Recently, he tried to karate-chop his younger sister after she broke his Six Million Dollar Man bionic transport station. (She retaliated by bashing him with her Cher doll.) His nursery-school teacher reports that he is passive, noncreative, unresponsive to instruction, bored during play periods and possessed of an almost nonexistent attention span—in short, very much like his classmates. Next fall, he will officially reach the age of reason and begin his formal education: His parents are beginning to discuss their apprehensions—when they are not too busy watching television.

Experts are increasingly disturbed by their findings in regard to TV's influence on developing psyches. Children under five are conservatively estimated to watch an average of about thirty hours of television programs every week. Wide agreement now exists that all this viewing increases a child's aggressions, anxieties, and fears, and instills a distorted picture of the outside world (while subtly changing the world in the direction of TV's imaginings).

The subject of violence on television has remained controversial. Does witnessing violence make the viewer more violent? Or does it serve as a catharsis for violent instincts, as some have argued? Shouldn't a child—in keeping with our advice about being "immunized" to the real world—*see* acts of violence at a safe remove as a way of preparing him for what he may in fact experience, or at least witness, at firsthand?

The evidence is in fact overwhelming that children who witness violence will *be* more violent, according to Kathryn Moody of the Media Action Research Center (MARC). Though she has not personally carried out research on the topic, she has extensively reviewed all the existing studies. She recognizes that the "immunization" argument may possess some validity. "But it makes for a strange, self-defeating cycle—doesn't it?—when we insist that children must see violence because it's out there in the world, and, in so doing, we make the world still more violent. And then, I suppose, we'll insist that children must see even more violence in order to keep up? Where does it end?" Moody's major objection is TV's penchant for serving up violence as *entertainment* for children. For that she sees no justification whatsoever.

Of special concern, too, are the commercials directed at children. Advertisers use this unparalleled opportunity to sell products that may at times be harmful—excessive sweets, for example, or dangerous toys—to a totally vulnerable and defenseless audience. It's possible to teach children to be skeptical of TV commercials; in fact, experiments have shown this can be done. "But is that a satisfying solution?" asks Moody. "Do we really want our children to become cynics, to be trained *not* to believe anything they read or hear?"

Unlike the print media and radio, which force readers and listeners to exercise their imaginations and their visualizing powers, TV bombards the passive nervous system with a totality of stimuli that requires little collaboration from the viewer.

Of course much has been made, and deservedly, of the effect of TV on children's reading habits. But reading is only one facet of a child's life affected by the medium. "The time spent, immobilized, in front of the TV set," says Kathryn Moody, "means a great deal of time lost from experiencing the world as *participants*. This has an immeasurable, though undoubtedly large, negative effect on children's perceptions of that outside world—not to mention their physical play habits, their social interactions, and virtually all their other developmental activities."

The influence of television is felt not only in its images of the adult world, but in those of children themselves. One symbol of current trends is the family scene as depicted day by day on television's afternoon soap operas, among the more enduring staples on the American entertainment menu. The soap opera, as Cornell sociologist Rose K. Goldsen points out, has become an important part of the shared social experience of two generations of Americans, going back to the days of radio. As a self-imposed study project, Goldsen watched—through the 1974–75 season—fourteen serialized soap operas, the self-labeled "family dramas" that take up nearly forty hours of broadcast time each week.

"Everyone knows by now," she reports in *Human Behavior*, "that soap opera people live in a world of fly-apart marriages: throwaway husbands, throwaway wives and—recently—throwaway lovers. Quite plausibly, the disposable marriage is a source of disposable

children. Indeed, I think the most effective way the soaps do violence to images of family commitment is by their visual code denying that children are important in family living. For example, as the
episodes spin out their daily show-and-tell, the country is scarcely
permitted to see any children at all."

On those rare occasions when a baby is successfully born on soap
opera (always after much travail), the odds are that the baby will
turn out sickly. "The few children the soap operas show are a sorry
lot," says Goldsen, "riddled with genetic malformations, subject to
exotic diseases, accidentprone." In this and other ways, the soap opera formula presents the child as both threat and victim—themes
that students of propaganda claim will undermine anyone's image.
Goldsen continues:

> Soap opera people create a social world for children that's stuck
> together with spit and Scotch tape. Every one of the children in
> the country's daily dosage of daytime serials—every one—goes to
> bed unsure whether the woman called "mother" or the man called
> "father" will still be around for breakfast. Has one or the other
> taken off, checked out?
>
> And saddest of all: in the daily show-and-tell of soap operas,
> nobody cares. Nobody really cares. Oh, sure—there are lots of pi-
> ous expressions of concern: but they fool nobody. . . .
>
> And so it goes—flushaway fetuses succeeded by defective chil-
> dren victimized by their own parents, betrayed by the very people
> children have to place their trust in. Adults responsible for chil-
> dren in soap operas get up and walk away from them or just pass
> them on from hand to hand as if they were Easter chicks.

But surely the soap opera dramas are not meant to reflect American life? Surely people don't take these silly stories seriously? The
soaps may represent an exaggerated version of trends and attitudes
in contemporary family life, but millions of people do watch them
faithfully every day and do identify closely with the lives of the
characters—who are, by the way, *not* poverty-stricken economically,
only emotionally. There are bound to be some subtle shaping influences at work here. Rose Goldsen believes that "every child in the

country is affected by the soaps" and that "no child can escape the cultural environment we make and share with each other."

"Television," sociologist George Gerbner agrees, "has profoundly affected the way in which members of the human race learn to become human beings."

The way in which members of the human race learn to become human beings: that is the crux of the matter. Children have traditionally learned it, in all cultures, from other human beings. From the expectations conveyed and from the examples displayed. From the love, support, and individual attention they receive from adults, singly and collectively. From the circumstances in which their lives are embedded.

Among the Ik of the Ugandan highlands, whose shattered society has been evoked with such discomforting vividness in Colin Turnbull's *The Mountain People*, the adults, including parents, are so exaggeratedly selfish, individualistic, loveless, and abandoning that it is hard to see how a child living in such a context could become anything but loveless and abandoning in turn. Another way of saying it—and as Turnbull does say it—is that a child learns to be not human but inhuman. By contrast, the Yequana Indian children described by Jean Liedloff in *The Continuum Concept* are in almost constant physical contact with their mothers during the first year of life. The security engendered leaves them free to enjoy the stimulation of going through a variety of jostlings (they constantly adjust their own otherwise serenely relaxed bodies to their mother's busy activities) and changes of scene and weather without feeling threatened. They are handed off now and then to other tribespeople of all ages, and even a child of three or four has already had a lot of experience handling babies. Teenage boys, at the end of a day's chores, will look for a baby to play with and toss around, to the baby's howls of glee.

Feelings are freely expressed at any age. Liedloff remembers doctoring a ten-year-old who hollered mightily because he really hurt (an American ten-year-old might have felt obliged to "be brave"—that is, quiet, stiff-upper-lipped, nonsissy); he didn't feel it was any disgrace, even in front of his peers, to let his honest feelings out. The same was true of a grown man, having a wound tended; he wept quietly, his head nestled in the lap of his available but unperturbed wife.

Yequana children, once the "in arms" phase is over, are trusted with surprising autonomy. They often play without supervision, and no area is off limits. They are clearly expected to take care of themselves (though help is always there when solicited). They observe all around them the confident and joyous attitudes and deportment of happy adults. They of course turn out to be an altogether different breed of human being from the Ik.

Children who see adults enjoying their work and their pleasures alike, in a milieu where adulthood is perceived as valuable and rewarding, are more likely to look forward to the satisfaction of growing up. Nor does one have to search exclusively in the jungle to find this. One still sees it in some geographical and social regions of the United States. And Martha Wolfenstein's studies in France led her to observe that French children, too, seem to enjoy this kind of anticipation.

In Israeli kibbutzim, children are in many cases cared for by surrogate parents, and the care is both stable and able. The children also maintain close contacts with their own parents. The system works something like this: Soon after the mother's return from the hospital, the newborn is placed in the "infants' house." There the child is cared for, educated, and socialized by designated nurses and teachers. That is where the mother goes to feed the baby, and where the father goes to see or play with the baby after working hours. The child is often six months old before she is taken to her parents' room, which is located in another building. As time goes on, the child sees more of her parents; eventually she is free to go see them whenever school and work hours permit, though she is expected back in the children's house by bedtime. Various adults are responsible for the child's welfare at any given time; in fact, kibbutz children are supported by a community network of other adults of both sexes who care about all their children—individually and collectively. Nevertheless, says anthropologist Melford Spiro, parents "are of crucial importance in the *psychological* development of the child. They serve as objects of his most important identifications, and they provide him with a certain security and love that he obtains from no one else. If anything, the attachment of the young children to their parents is greater than it is in our own society." Under these conditions, children seem to thrive in a special way. (One interesting, inadvertent test of the kibbutz as a psychologically fortifying climate is the improved emotional outcome in the case of children of Holocaust victims who were raised in kibbutzim as compared with those reared in more conventional Israeli family circumstances or in the United States.)

American visitors to China express surprise and guarded admiration at the uniformly good behavior—and good cheer—of children everywhere, even very young children in nursery schools. When the visitors question the Chinese teachers as to what methods they use to solve misbehavior problems, the teachers really do not seem to understand the question. They are not aware of having solved any problems, or even that such problems exist. They are simply taking care of children, who behave the way they are supposed to behave.

In late 1973, for example, a group of thirteen distinguished American child-development authorities under the chairmanship of Yale's William Kessen went on a tour of China. Though they were there for only three weeks, "we saw thousands of young children, in schools, in their neighborhoods, in parks, on city streets. Almost never did we see any antisocial behavior," they wrote in their collaborative report, *Childhood in China.*

They were astonished at the "general absence of aggression, shoving, pushing, grabbing of property, and rough-and-tumble play" among kindergarten children. "Rarely did we see any anxiety or fear, and crying and whining were virtually absent. There were no instances or rage, anger or temper tantrums. . . ." They were especially impressed with the way kindergarten children could "sit calmly for long periods of time—waiting in turn to play with a ball, waiting for a turn to sing, listening to a story told by a teacher or classmate, or just being a spectator. They do not nervously poke their neighbors, shuffle their feet, pick at their faces, or shift their trunks." The children were able to concentrate remarkably well and learned complicated tasks quickly and easily.

On the single occasion when a child in class required disciplining in their presence, the teacher simply "removed the child from the setting ... with a quiet accompanying remark." When asked what teachers did when a pupil was naughty, she explained, "We persuade him." The only time the group witnessed an act of physical aggression was in a play area during recess, when one boy shoved another to the ground. "Quickly the teacher came over, sent the aggressor off, and comforted the crying child. In a moment the aggressor returned, apparently on the cue of another teacher, and helped brush the dust off the victim's clothes."

The Americans kept looking for the "trade-offs" of such tight self-control—in nervous behavior, anxiety, aloofness. But they found the Chinese children to be warm and friendly, not at all timid, and full of spontaneous laughter when the occasion called for it. The group noted a lack of the "traditional Western marks of tension. None of us observed sustained thumb-sucking, nail-biting, tics, masturbation, or other tension-reducing behaviors in kindergarten children." They concluded that "the careful control exerted on interpersonal aggression is not accompanied by any sign of tension or anxiety that experienced Western observers can readily detect."

They kept wondering how the Chinese brought it off, and remarked constantly on "the almost serene certainty of the teachers that the children would, of course, do as they were taught."

Americans have now and then expressed some envy of these results. Although we retain reservations as to their validity and the social costs of achieving them, nevertheless we surely have as much to learn from the Chinese child-raising experience as we have from any other cultures. One recalls Jean Liedloff's reaction on her first encounter with the Yequana Indians: "In that utterly foreign land I failed to notice that much of the unreal quality of its people was accounted for by an absence of unhappiness."

In our own society, it is all too easy to spot the negative results of the signals children pick up from their surroundings. We do have an unfortunate penchant for labeling people, starting early—as retarded, dumb, low-I.Q., clumsy, cross-eyed, short, fat, hyperactive, lazy, whiny—so that transient characteristics (which may be correctible or even self-correcting) are viewed as if they were permanent character traits. We act toward these children as if the labels were factual descriptions—and therefore predictors of their future states. If a child believes his label, he may well accommodate us and live down to our expectations. Perceptions revise reality. Most minority groups, and at least one majority group—females—learn at an early age the downgraded manner in which they are perceived by the rest of society. Indeed, most of the adults in these very groups have probably also absorbed the prevailing social values and perceptions and may be the first to convey them. The children are thus made aware of limitations implicit in what is expected of them, and in opportunities henceforth open to them. Self-esteem, and the determination to achieve success and to enjoy satisfaction with assurance and an absence of guilt, are thus hard earned by these socially and narcissistically disadvantaged children.

Males are also considerably restricted in their possibilities by the social roles they are expected to play, even though the limitations are different and the opportunities "better" in many respects. In *macho*-oriented societies, both Western and Westernized Oriental males have been burdened with a culturally encouraged phallic obsessiveness that forces them into overcompetitive pursuits that deny their innate tenderness, arrests them at a halfway point en route to their humanity, and contributes to their premature deaths from heart attacks and other stress-induced deteriorative ailments. Images of violence and sadism, *models* of violence and sadism, have tended to dominate male self-perception, while kind, gentle, and tender feelings have been disdained and ridiculed as sissifying, feminizing.

Kliman's study of an earlier civilization, the Mayans of the Yucatan peninsula in Mexico, led him to conclude that emotional hyperspecialization in the masculine direction (masculine, that is, in the restricted *machismo* sense) precipitated the downfall of that civilization, including the suicide of large segments of its population. While they achieved prodigious feats of mathematics and astronomy, the Mayans ultimately used their knowledge for power and destruction rather than for life enhancement and survival. Originally a matriarchal society, the Mayans methodically removed not only female leadership from all political and religious arenas, but all traces of femaleness itself from their canon of honored traits. Over a period of centuries almost all their female gods of fertility and agriculture were replaced by forbidding male deities. Meanwhile, as Mayan society grew more violent, both the phallus and death itself began to be worshiped. Ritual suicide, decapitation, and mass sacrifices became common "religious" rites.

Instead of turning their technical talents to the solution of their increasing agricultural problems, to the improvement of their harvests, to the devising of soil-fertilization and land-reclamation techniques; instead of turning their attention to the better nurture of their children; instead of directing their considerable ingenuity and analytic powers to internal improvements of their society—instead of all that, they developed ever more clever means of making war and of exploiting their neighboring tribes in the cruelest fashions imaginable. Ultimately this "civilization" collapsed, in large part as a result of what Kliman terms *hypermachismo*. Mayan sporting events and religious rituals seemed almost designed to acknowledge and at the same time overcome the combined influences of castration anxiety and death anxiety. Mayan men actually vied for the honor of being decapitated, an outcome one is tempted to interpret as an upward displacement of castration. So strong was the urge to master the threat to the integrity of the masculine body that the Mayans employed psychological defense by reversal—that is, turning the threat into an honor. Eventually, as the society evolved (or retrogressed), the honor of being decapitated was strictly reserved for noblemen who defeated other noblemen in long games of skill and endurance. Women, of course, were not permitted such honors.

The formerly feminine gods of agriculture and fertility meanwhile were less and less able to support the growing Mayan population (some forty million by the fifteenth century); the familiar crisis of too little food for too many people. It is not surprising—bizarre as the results might be—that the male priests, representing male gods, adopted their by-now-familiar psychological defense-by-reversal: conquering the threat of a passive death by seizing control themselves. Taking life and death increasingly into their own hands, they finally chose to abandon their cities en masse in an abrupt, phallic, and systematic ritual suicide, leaving not a trace of their once teeming populations in the empty cities. The exodus victims died by the millions in the surrounding jungles. All of this, Kliman believes, was part of a last mad effort to be "hypermasculinely" in charge of the earth's agricultural bounty, the realm most closely associated traditionally with the female functions of life-giving and feeding.

This cautionary historical speculation has reverberations for our own time, in which we have seen similarly tragic dramas play themselves out—in Nazi Germany and Fascist Italy, for example, where brute strength was deified and tenderness equated with weakness. Our own present-day civilization could, with its emphasis on macho military ambitions and excessively phallic technological adventures, eventually go the way of the Mayans. Or of the Iks, or some other way, some as yet unidentified mass pathology distinctly our own. Forestalling such a calamity, the recognition and honoring of our best selves, including our innate tenderness and nurturing capacities, would not only allow the development of our children to their fuller potential, but would go a long way toward preserving our very future.

Well-loved children are much rarer than one would guess. Most people in our society unfortunately do not really know how to love other people well. And as we have argued throughout this book, those children who *are* well loved will mostly grow up to be loving adults. *Their* repetition compulsion will be to love their children well, and to teach their children to love others well.

Right now, in contrast to the calmly cheerful children reported by visitors to Chinese classrooms, we are afflicted with what appears to be a nationwide outbreak of disruptive "hyperactivity." Hundreds of thousands of our schoolchildren have been diagnosed (more often misdiagnosed, in our opinion) as suffering from one kind or another of "minimal brain damage." With consent of parents and teachers, these children are put on "happy pills" (Ritalin or Dexedrine, for instance) whose long-range side effects no one can yet assess. Caregivers and caretakers who follow such practice are apparently content to keep the children more quiet, more manageable.

We consider this "therapeutic" trend to be both a tragedy and an outrage. Even if the prescribed medications turn out to have no visibly harmful long-range effects, the pharmaceutical solution to an essentially psychosocial malady represents a shameful cop-out. We remain—along with many others—extremely skeptical of the brain-damage diagnosis. It is more likely that, because of our failures at home and in society at large, we have been seeing an epidemic of *depression* among children—a depression compensated for by wild, manic-seeming activity in a frantic search for unfindable satisfactions. Family psychotherapy for parents and child would be a more appropriate, and a more realistic, approach than instant resort to a questionable "upper."

The major thrust of our efforts at the Center for Preventive Psychiatry is the rescue of children. Ordinarily, very young children do not get any psychiatric attention unless they are severely disturbed or have developed a full-blown psychosis. Often no one pays adequate attention to a troubled child until she arrives at school age; then, if she doesn't do well, a teacher or a school psychologist may suggest psychiatric evaluation. Often, by then, much damage has already been done—damage that could have been prevented or at least considerably alleviated by early detection and treatment of the problem.

As matters now stand, an emotionally disturbed child under five has very little chance of getting treatment almost anywhere in this country (and less in most other countries). There are probably a half-million such children. To meet the need, each of the nation's more than twenty thousand psychiatrists would have to be treating twenty preschoolers—extremely unlikely, since few psychiatrists work with children and those specializing in early childhood are rare indeed. As for fully trained child psychoanalysts, who do the deepest work, they are scarcest of all. There are probably no more than six hundred in the whole world.

In 1968 three separate surveys were made of the Center's "catchment" area—that is, the geographical boundaries within which we offer our services. Each of the surveys—one made by the Center, the others by the local Mental Health Association and the child psychiatric society—came up with similar findings: Of more than 64,000 preschool-age children living in the area, over 3,000 were in a moderate or severe state of mental illness. Apart from those we had already begun to treat at the Center, only 40 of those 3,000 were getting any treatment at all. Only 1 of them was being given the kind of intensive treatment (being seen more than once a week, for instance) usually needed in such cases. This neglect was close to scandalous, considering that our catchment area was located just north of New York City and had over 200 psychiatrists in private practice, as well as more than 20 community mental health agencies treating thousands of patients. What was wrong with the psychosocial womb for these young beings still undergoing their six-year gestation?

Fortunately, once the situation was exposed, the community rallied to remedy its neglect of preschoolers. The Center now has what may be the nation's largest outpatient treatment service for disturbed preschool children, treating over 330 each year—more than half from impoverished families. Moreover, a handful of other community agencies and private practitioners in the area, following our lead, began turning their attention to children of these ages. Today some 600 or more disturbed preschoolers are in therapy compared with 40 in 1968, a fifteen-fold improvement. We have had our share of failures, but some of our children who were diagnosed as severely retarded ten to fourteen years ago are now brilliant teenagers. In some cases, I.Q. scores have gone up 50 to 80 points. Some who were sent to us as psychotic preschoolers are clearly no longer psychotic, and some who are can nevertheless function very well in community and school.

Other preventive psychiatry programs have sprung up in many places over the past few years. While most clinics do not yet offer a full range of preventive psychiatric services, this spread of preventive psychiatry is most encouraging. Even so, too many communities still remain untouched.*

Part of our difficulties at the Center in initially educating the community to our novel premises was traditional human reluctance to present oneself for psychiatric attention unless one was . . . well . . . crazy—a reluctance compounded in the case of a child. In the

---

*Though federally funded mental health centers are required by regulation to provide children's and preventive services, on the average less than 5 to 10 percent of such centers' budgets are used for these purposes.

popular mind getting treatment often meant the patient was psychotic, or had had a "nervous breakdown," or had been behaving so bizarrely as to alarm his family and friends, or was experiencing neurotic or emotional difficulties so disturbing as to render him virtually nonfunctional. For physical ailments, any person accepts that he will probably become a patient at one time or another. He goes to see the doctor when he isn't feeling well. If he, or one of his children, falls hard on his head, he is likely to check it out to see if a fracture has occurred. If his tooth aches, he goes to see a dentist. Our aim was to induce our local citizenry to come in to see us as readily and as quickly as they would go see any other doctor. The idea has finally caught on, and today the Center can barely handle its patient load. Over one thousand patients are now served per year, including not only three hundred preschoolers but also hundreds of persons of all ages in situational crises such as a death in the family. (The Center's Situational Crisis Service is headed by Ann Kliman, who described this phase of the Center's work in her book *Crisis: Psychological First Aid for Recovery and Growth*.) Children are referred to us by physicians, teachers, nursery-school administrators, clergymen, social workers—and, more and more, by simple word of mouth from others who have heard or read about the Center, or have themselves by now made use of its services.

We urge other communities to encourage the establishment of such clinics and programs. There is no need to wait for a chronic mental illness before children are given the help they need. The earlier in the six-year pregnancy difficulties are spotted, the easier it is to head off emotional troubles before they become entrenched. Rescue efforts later are arduous, expensive, and sometimes must end in futility. Often the untreated child will remain an afflicted adult. Some will spend lifetimes in and out of (mostly in) institutions. What a terrible waste of human resources. What a chain of avoidable human tragedies. And how preposterous a set of priorities. Surely it is just as important to save a three-year-old child from, say, seventy more years of mental illness, as it is to give extended therapy to a fifty-year-old psychotic (not that we advocate his neglect either!).

One reason preschool children have tended to get short shrift psychiatrically is, as we have indicated, that so few psychiatrists specialize in this area—and those who do often shift to other specialties as they grow older. These earliest years of a child's life, with their raw, undisguised, and messy emotions, are difficult for most adults to deal with. There is a strong propensity for the child psychiatrist to begin treating older children, then adolescents, then adults. By the time he is past fifty there are few, if any, preschool children left in his practice. A standard joke in the profession is the definition of a child psychiatrist as "someone who used to treat little children." People over fifty are perhaps reluctant to get into the intimacies and untidiness of play therapy. They begin to feel more out of touch with their own infantile selves—and become less inclined to be reminded of them. There is something in the rapid rhythms, high-pitched speech, and sheer physical vitality of young children with which many older people become increasingly out of tune—or can remain in tune with for ever briefer periods of time.

The notable exceptions to this pattern are nearly all women. In our society, women, for whatever reason, seem better equipped or better trained to be the long-distance runners of child psychotherapy. Another class of people—also mostly women—who seem to have the capacity to continue working with very young children throughout their professional lives are nursery-school educators. In fact many of the best and most durable child therapists are those who began as nursery-school teachers, then went on to acquire analytic training and become well-qualified therapists. It may be no coincidence that Anna Freud, the pioneer of child analysis, spent some of her own early professional experience in nurseries. People who seek out work in nurseries or nursery schools may already have made a deep and abiding commitment to children of these early age groups and thus find it no hardship to remain in the field. They do not become narcissistically depleted as easily as the rest of us.

The fact that even trained professionals (indoctrinated by their education with a presumably thorough understanding of the developmental processes of infancy and early childhood) so often lack the long-range tolerance for dealing with the drains and demands that go with the developmental phases of the six-year pregnancy suggests that those not similarly trained will run into even greater difficulties. All the more reason for prospective parents to understand in advance, as clearly as possible, the realities and responsibilities of care-giving during these first, formative years. A parent confronted with a troubled young child often finds—just as therapists do—her tolerance and her capacity to give succor stretched beyond her limits. Parents in these circumstances especially need the community network of caregivers. They need to know that somebody *else* cares about them and their children, and to be aware that they are part of a larger family. Though there is often initial resistance because of pride, guilt, and fear of censure for "failure"—even when truly empathic assistance is offered—our experience demonstrates that they eventually respond with growth.

Dealing with children during the six-year pregnancy, especially when something has happened to delay or retard or interfere with the expectable course of developmental progress, requires all the ingenuity that therapists can muster. Dealing with them also gives us an ever renewed conviction of the importance of the *preventive possibilities in appropriate parenting* during these critical years.

More important to us than the validation or acceptance of any specific recommendation offered in this book is to see our society—local, state, national, and global—acknowledge itself to be the willing extended family of all of its children. While this does mean official governmental support and attention on a large scale, that will be at best a palliative measure unless a critical mass of citizens in communities everywhere takes it upon itself personally to care about children—and their parents as well.

America's newfound interest in teenage parents may well serve as a model for the expansion of our interest to all parents. We recognize that the adolescent requires special attention, and we know that the adolescent—if the burdens of parenthood do not take too destructive a toll in her state of unreadiness—is still capable of growth. In fact, we know that parenthood itself can be a route to growth (though we do not recommend that as a sufficient reason to become a parent). By mustering our resources to help teenagers attain that growth and maturity, we help them reach a point where they are sufficiently rich in their own native resources to have leftover nar-

cissistic supplies for their children. Our society has been consistently critical of parents who abandon their children; yet society has
itself abandoned those children by abandoning their parents to cope
as best they can under often intractable circumstances. In the case of
the unwed adolescent, our past behavior was doubly abandoning;
we condemned the girl, banishing her from our sight, making it virtually impossible for her to develop her parental skills or provide
the child with its minimal necessities, and we stigmatized the child
for life. So it is hopeful indeed to see that we have finally, in response to the crisis of the teenage-pregnancy epidemic, changed our
ways. It suggests we are capable of changing our ways on a broader
scale.

To possess a sincere *intention* to care about children is already to
have arrived halfway toward active support and help. None of us
knows all that we need to know about what is good for children,
but we do know there are certain basic types of sustenance universally needed by children from their caregivers during the first years
of life, and we are delinquent in our duty to the extent that we fail
to speed whatever measure will bring to all children their major
birthrights: to be loved, esteemed, well wanted, and to be reared by
people who love, esteem, and want them well.

We can hardly imagine what a society would be like in which every child could be brought through the six-year pregnancy with all
developmental needs supplied, all the way. Most would run into
later troubles that might diminish or undo the earlier good done by
the work-play of appropriate parenting, but we would wager that
when this generation of children grew to adulthood, they could
bring about vast and wonderful changes in the world. And *their* children, growing up in that new world—! With that generation, we
could certainly rest easier in our concerns about the future of this
still-marvelous species on a planet that remains full of surprises, and
will serve as our launchpad into the larger universe.

References
and Further Readings

Index

References and Further Readings

Ackerman, Nathan W. *The Psychodynamics of Family Life.* New York: Basic Books, 1958.

Ainsworth, Mary D. Salter. "Social Development in the First Year of Life: Maternal Influences on Infant-Mother Attachment." In *Developments in Psychiatric Research Viewpoints in Review* (Essays Based on the Sir Geoffrey Vickers Lectures of the Mental Health Trust and Research Fund), J. M. Tanner, ed. London: Hodder, 1977.

———. "Object Relations, Dependency, and Attachment. A Theoretical Review of the Infant-Mother Relationship." *Child Development,* Vol. 40, Sept. 1969.

———, et al. "Individual Differences in the Development of Some Attachment Behaviors." *Merrill-Palmer Quarterly of Behavior and Development,* Vol. 18, No. 2, 1972.

———, et al. *Deprivation of Maternal Care: A Reassessment of Its Effects.* New York: Schocken Books, 1966.

Ainsworth, Mary D. Salter, and Silvia M. Bell. "Attachment, Exploration, and Separation: Illustrated by the Behavior of One-year-olds in a Strange Situation." *Child Development,* Vol. 41, No. 1, March 1970.

Akmakjian, Hiag. *The Natural Way to Raise a Healthy Child.* New York: Praeger, 1975.

Albee, George W. "The Protestant Ethic, Sex, and Psychotherapy." *American Psychologist,* Feb. 1977.

Albee, George W., and Justin M. Joffe, eds. *Primary Prevention of Psychopathology,* Vol. 1: The Issues, University Press of New England, for the University of Vermont, Hanover, N.H., 1977.

Aldrich, Robert A. "The Role of Government in Strengthening the Family Unit." Address to Second Annual Family Living Seminar, North Carolina State University, Raleigh, N.C., June 9, 1977.

———. "Children, Families, Inhuman Cities, and a Basic Optimism." An interview. *The Mayo Alumnus,* April 1977.

———. "Introduction to Pediatrics: A Change from Pediatrics to Child Health and Human Development." *Brennemann-Kelley Practice of Pediatrics,* Vol. 1. Hagerstown, Md.: Hoeber Medical Division, Harper & Row, 1967.

———. "Mobilization and Application of Resources for an Effective Approach to the Management of Human Congenital Defects." Unpublished essay.

———. "The Future of Pediatrics." *Pediatrics*, Vol. 38, Sept. 1966.

———. "Recreating the Child's World: Where Do We Start?" Presented at the Annual Meeting of the American Academy of Pediatrics, Chicago, Oct. 23, 1973.

———. "Are Cities Destroying Our Children and Youth?" Presented Before the Annual Meeting of American Public Health Association, Philadelphia, Nov. 11, 1969.

———. "Recent Developments in the Science of Child Care and Implications for a Children's Medical Center." Presented at the Philadelphia Children's Hospital, Sept. 22, 1962.

———, and Ralph J. Wedgwood. "Examination of the Changes in the United States Which Affect the Health of Children and Youth." *American Journal of Public Health* Supplement, Part 2, April 1970.

Ames, Louise Bates. *Child Care and Development*. New York/Philadelphia: J. B. Lippincott, 1970.

———. "Why Good Mothers Have 'Bad' Babies." *Family Circle*, Oct. 1971.

Anthony, E. James. "Primary Prevention with School Children." *Progress in Community Mental Health*, H. H. Barten and L. Bellak, eds. Vol. 2. New York: Grune & Stratton, 1972.

Anthony, E. James, and T. Benedek, eds. *Psychology and Psychopathology of Parenthood*. Boston: Little, Brown, 1968.

Anthony, E. James, and Cyrille Koupernik, eds. *The Child In His Family: Children at Psychiatric Risk*, Vol. 4. New York: John Wiley & Sons, 1978.

———. *The Child In His Family: Vulnerable Children*, Vol. 4. New York: John Wiley & Sons, 1978.

———. *The Child In His Family: Children and Their Parents in a Changing World*, Vol. 5. New York: John Wiley & Sons, 1978.

Apgar, Virginia, and Joan Beck. *Is My Baby All Right?* New York: Trident Press, 1972.

Ariès, Philippe. *Centuries of Childhood*. New York: Alfred A. Knopf, 1962.

Arnstein, Helene S. *The Roots of Love*. Indianapolis/New York: Bobbs-Merrill, 1975.

Arzoumanian, Alexander. *Love and Mankind's Future*, New York: Persepolis Press, 1976.

Auerbach, Aline B., and Helene S. Arnstein. *Pregnancy and You*. Public Affairs Pamphlet 482. New York: Public Affairs Committee, 1972.

Babcock, Dorothy E., and Terry D. Keepers. *Raising Kids O.K.: The Only Complete Parents Guide to Transactional Analysis*. New York: Grove Press, 1976.

Bach, Sheldon. "On the Narcissistic State of Consciousness." *International Journal of Psycho-Analysis*, Vol. 58, Part 2, 1977.

Back, Kurt W., and James T. Fawcett. "Population Policy and the Person: Congruence or Conflict?" *The Journal of Social Issues*, Vol. 30, No. 4, 1974.

Bane, Mary Jo. *Here to Stay: American Families in the Twentieth Century.* New York: Basic Books, 1976.

Barman, Alicerose. *Helping Children Face Crises.* Public Affairs Pamphlet 541. New York: Public Affairs Committee, 1976.

———. *Motivation and Your Child.* Public Affairs Pamphlet 523. New York: Public Affairs Committee, 1975.

———. *Your First Months With Your First Baby.* Public Affairs Pamphlet 478. New York: Public Affairs Committee, 1972.

Baum, Charlotte. "The Best of Both Parents." *New York Times Magazine,* Oct. 31, 1976.

Bayley, Nancy. "Some Increasing Parent-Child Similarities During the Growth of Children." *Journal of Educational Psychology*, Vol. 45, 1954.

———. "Consistency and Variability in the Growth of Intelligence from Birth to Eighteen Years." *Journal of Genetic Psychology*, Vol. 75, 1949.

———. "Mental Growth During the First Three Years." *Genetic Psychology Monograph*, Vol. 14, No. 1, 1933.

———. "Development of Mental Abilities." In *Carmichael's Manual of Child Psychology*, P. N. Mussen, ed. 1st ed. New York: John Wiley & Sons, 1970.

Beck, Aaron T., E. B. Sethi, and R. W. Tuthill. "Childhood Bereavement and Adult Depression." *Archives of General Psychiatry*, Vol. 9, 1963.

Benedek, Therese. "Parenthood As a Developmental Phase: A Contribution to the Libido Theory." *Journal of the American Psychoanalytic Association*, 1959.

Bergman, Jerry. "Licensing Parents: A New Age of Child-Rearing?" *The Futurist*, Dec. 1978.

Berrill, N. J. *The Person in the Womb.* New York: Dodd, Mead, 1968.

Bettelheim, Bruno. *The Uses of Enchantment.* New York: Alfred A. Knopf, 1976.

———. *The Children of the Dream.* New York: The Macmillan Company, 1969.

———. *The Empty Fortress.* Glencoe, N.Y.: Free Press, 1967.

Bleuler, Manfred. *Die schizophrenen Geistesstörungen im Lichte langjähriger Kranken und Familiengeschichten.* Stuttgart: Thieme, 1972.

Block, Jack, in collaboration with Norma Haan. *Lives Through Time.* Berkeley, Calif.: Bancroft, 1971.

Bloom, Benjamin S. *Stability and Change in Human Characteristics.* New York: John Wiley & Sons, 1964.

Bower, Thomas G. R. "The Object in the World of the Infant," *Scientific American*, October 1971.

———. "Competent Newborn." In *Child Alive!*, Roger Lewin, ed. Garden City, N.Y.: Anchor Press, 1975.

———. *A Primer of Infant Development.* San Francisco: W. H. Freeman, 1977.

Bowlby, John. *Maternal Care and Mental Health.* Monograph 2. Geneva: World Health Organization, 1951.

———. *Forty-Four Juvenile Thieves.* London: Bailliere, Tindall and Cox, 1946.

———. "Grief and Mourning in Infancy and Early Childhood." *The Psychoanalytic Study of the Child,* Vol. 15, New York: International Universities Press, 1960.

———. "Separation Anxiety." *International Journal of Psycho-Analysis,* Vol. 41, 1960.

———. "The Nature of the Child's Tie to the Mother." *International Journal of Psycho-Analysis,* Vol. 39, 1958.

Bowlby, John, J. Robertson, and D. Rosenbluth. "A Two-Year-Old Goes to the Hospital." *The Psychoanalytic Study of the Child,* Vol. 7. New York: International Universities Press, 1952.

Brazelton, Thomas Berry. *The Neonatal Behavioral Assessment Scale.* Philadelphia: J. B. Lippincott, 1973.

———. "Mother-Infant Reciprocity." In *Maternal Attachment and Mothering Disorders: A Round Table,* M. H. Klaus, T. Leger, and M. A. Trause, eds. New Brunswick, N.J.: Johnson and Johnson, 1975.

———. "Does the Neonate Shape His Environment?" In *The Infant at Risk,* D. Bergsma, ed. Birth Defects: Original Articles Series. White Plains, N.Y.: National Foundation–March of Dimes, 1974.

Brenton, Myron. *Playmates: The Importance of Childhood Friendships.* Public Affairs Pamphlet 525. New York: Public Affairs Committee, 1975.

Briggs, Dorothy Corkille. *Your Child's Self-Esteem: The Key to His Life.* Garden City/New York: Doubleday, 1970.

Brim, Orville G., Jr. *Education for Child Rearing.* New York: Free Press, 1975.

———. "Macro-Structural Influences on Child Development and the Need for Childhood Social Indicators." *American Journal of Orthopsychiatry,* Vol. 45, No. 3, 1975.

Brody, Sylvia. *Patterns of Mothering: Maternal Influence During Infancy.* New York: International Universities Press, 1956.

Brody, Sylvia, Sidney Axelrad, and Marsha Moroh. "Early Phases in the Development of Object Relations," *International Review of Psychoanalysis,* Vol. 3, No. 1, 1976.

Bronfenbrenner, Urie. *Two Worlds of Childhood: U.S. and U.S.S.R.* New York: Russell Sage Foundation, 1970.

———. "The Disturbing Changes in the American Family." State University of New York. *Search,* Vol. 2, No. 1, Fall 1976.

———. "The Changing American Child: A Speculative Analysis." *Journal of Social Issues,* Vol. 17, 1961.

———. "Socialization and Social Class Through Time and Space." In *Readings in Social Psychology,* E. E. Maccoby et al., eds. 3rd ed. New York: Holt, Rinehart and Winston, 1958.

Broussard, Elsie R. "The Neonatal Prediction and Outcome at 10 and 11 Years." *Child Psychiatry and Human Development*, Vol. 7, No. 2, Winter 1976.

————. "Evaluation of Anticipatory Guidance Counseling to Primiparae Using the Medium of Television." Paper presented at the American Public Health Association meeting, San Francisco, 1966.

Broussard, Elsie R., and M. S. S. Hartner. "Further Considerations Regarding Maternal Perception of the First Born." In *Exceptional Infant, Vol. 2: Studies in Abnormalities*, J. Hellmuth, ed. New York: Brunner/Mazel, 1971.

————. "Maternal Perception of the Neonate as Related to Development." *Child Psychiatry and Human Development*, Vol. 1, 1970.

Bruck, Connie. "Battle Lines in the Ritalin War." *Human Behavior*, August 1976.

Bruner, Jerome S. *On Knowing: Essays for the Left Hand*. Cambridge, Mass.: Harvard University Press, 1962.

————. *Processes of Cognitive Growth: Infancy*. Heinz Werner Lecture Series, No. 3. Worcester, Mass.: Clark University Press with Barre Publishers, 1968.

Bruner, Jerome S., A. Jolly, and K. Silva, eds. *Play: Its Role in Development and Evolution*. New York: Basic Books, 1976.

Calder, Nigel. *The Human Conspiracy: The New Science of Social Behavior*. New York: The Viking Press, 1976.

Caldwell, Bettye M., et al. "Infant Day Care and Attachment." *American Journal of Orthopsychiatry*, Vol. 40, No. 3, April 1970.

Callahan, Daniel. *Abortion*. New York: Macmillan, 1970.

Callahan, Sidney C. *Parenting: Principles and Politics of Parenthood*. Garden City, N.Y.: Doubleday, 1973.

Cantor, Pamela, ed. *Understanding a Child's World*. New York: McGraw-Hill, 1977.

Carson, Ruth. *Nine Months To Get Ready*. Public Affairs Pamphlet 376. New York: Public Affairs Committee, 1965.

————. *Your New Baby*. Public Affairs Pamphlet 353. New York: Public Affairs Committee, 1963.

Carter, C. O. "Multifactorial Genetic Disease." *Hospital Practice*, May 1970.

————. "Genetics of Common Disorders." *British Medical Bulletin*, Vol. 25, No. 1, 1969.

Chase, Naomi Feigelson. *A Child Is Being Beaten*. New York: Holt, Rinehart and Winston, 1975.

Cherry, Sheldon H. *Understanding Pregnancy and Childbirth*. Indianapolis/New York: Bobbs-Merrill, 1973.

Child Study Association of America. *What to Tell Your Children About Sex*. New York: Permabooks, 1959.

Church, Joseph. *Understanding Your Child from Birth to Three.* New York: Random House, 1973.

Cohen, Theodore B., chairman. "The Child At Risk: Child Abuse." Interdisciplinary Seminar No. 2, American Psychoanalytic Association, Quebec City, Canada, April 30, 1977.

Cohler, Bertram J. "The Effects of Maternal Depression on Offspring." Paper presented at Council for the Advancement of Science Writing, New York City, Nov. 16, 1977.

———, et al. "Social Relations, Stress, and Psychiatric Hospitalization Among Mothers of Young Children." *Social Psychiatry*, Vol. 9, No. 1, 1974.

Condon, William S., and Louis W. Sander. "Neonate Movement Is Synchronized with Adult Speech: Interactional Participation and Language Acquisition." *Science*, Jan. 11, 1974.

Cooper, David. *The Death of the Family.* New York: Pantheon Books, 1971.

Cutright, Phillips. "Illegitimacy: Myths, Causes and Cures." *Family Planning Perspectives*, Vol. 3, No. 1, Jan. 1971.

Davis, Glenn. *Childhood and History in America.* New York: Psychohistory Press, 1976.

Defense Documentation Center. *Environmental Effects on Behavior: A report Bibliography.* Alexandria, Va.: Defense Documentation Center, 1970.

Demany, Laurent, Beryl McKenzie, and Eliane Vurpillot. "Rhythm Perception in Early Infancy." *Nature*, April 21, 1977.

deMause, Lloyd. *The History of Childhood.* New York. Psychohistory Press, 1974.

———. "The Evolution of Childhood." *History of Childhood Quarterly*, Vol. 1, 1973.

Derdeyn, Andre P. "Child Abuse and Neglect: The Rights of Parents and the Needs of Their Children." *American Journal of Orthopsychiatry*, Vol. 47, No. 3, July 1977.

Dodson, Fitzhugh. *How to Parent.* Los Angeles: Nash Publishing, 1970.

Dodwell, P. C., D. Muir, and D. DiFranco. "Responses of Infants to Visually Presented Objects." *Science*, Oct. 8, 1976.

Dohrwend, Barbara S., and Bruce P. Dohrwend. "Stress Situations, Birth Order and Psychological Symptoms." *Journal of Abnormal Psychology*, Vol. 71, No. 2, 1966.

Dunn, Judy. *Distress and Comfort.* The Developing Child series, Jerome Bruner, Michael Cole, and Barbara Lloyd, eds. Cambridge, Mass.: Harvard University Press, 1977.

Duvall, Evelyn M. *Family Development.* New York: J. B. Lippincott, 1971.

Eastman, Nicholson J., and Keith P. Russell. *Expectant Motherhood.* Boston: Little, Brown, 1970.

Edelson, Edward. "Improving on Heredity." *Family Health*, Dec. 1970.

———. "It's the Parent Who Needs Help." *Family Health*, July 1970.

Elkes, Joel. Personal communications.

Endler, Norman S., Lawrence R. Boulter, and Harry Osser. *Contemporary Issues in Developmental Psychology.* 2nd ed. New York: Holt, Rinehart and Winston, 1976.

Engelmann, Siegfried, and Therese Engelmann. *Give Your Child a Superior Mind.* New York: Simon & Schuster, 1966.

Erikson, Erik H. *Identity: Youth and Crisis.* New York: W. W. Norton, 1968.

———. *Children and Society.* 2nd ed. New York: W. W. Norton, 1963.

———. *Identity and the Life Cycle,* New York: International Universities Press, 1959.

Escalona, Sibylle K. *The Roots of Individuality.* Chicago: Aldine Publishing Company, 1968.

Escalona, Sibylle K., and Harvey H. Corman. "Early Life Experience and the Development of Competence." *International Review of Psycho-Analysis,* Vol. 2, 1974.

Escalona, Sibylle K., and G. M. Heider. *Prediction and Outcome.* New York: Basic Books, 1959.

Farson, Richard. *Birthrights: A Bill of Rights for Children.* New York: Macmillan, 1974.

Fass, Jerome S. *A Primer for Parents.* New York: Trident Press, 1968.

Flaste, Richard. "The 'Invulnerable Children' Who Thrive Against All Odds." *New York Times,* July 22, 1977.

Flescher, Joachim. *Childhood and Destiny: The Triadic Principle in Genetic Education.* New York: International Universities Press, 1970.

Folstein, Susan, and Michael Rutter. "Genetic Influences and Infantile Autism." *Nature,* Feb. 24, 1977.

Fraiberg, Selma. *Every Child's Birthright: In Defense of Mothering.* New York: Basic Books, 1977.

———. *The Magic Years.* New York: Scribner, 1959.

———. "Libidinal Object Constancy and Mental Representation." *The Psychoanalytic Study of the Child,* Vol. 24, 1969.

———. "The Origins of Human Bonds." *Commentary,* June 1967.

———. "On the Sleep Disturbances of Early Childhood." *Psychoanalytic Study of the Child,* Vol. 5, 1950.

Fraser, F. Clarke. "Genetic Counseling." *Hospital Practice,* Jan. 1971.

———. "Genetic Counseling and the Physician." *Canadian Medical Association Journal,* Vol. 99, 1968.

Freud, Anna. *Normality and Pathology in Childhood: Assessments of Development.* New York: International Universities Press, 1965.

———. "Obsessional Neurosis: A Summary of Psychoanalytic Views as Presented at the Congress." *International Journal of Psycho-Analysis,* Vol. 47, 1966.

———. "The Concept of Developmental Lines." In *The Writings of Anna Freud,* Vol. 6. New York: International Universities Press, 1965.

――. "Some Remarks on Infant Observation." *The Psychoanalytic Study of the Child*, Vol. 8, 1953.

――. "The Role of Bodily Illness in the Mental Life of Children." *Psychoanalytic Study of the Child*, Vol. 7, 1952.

――. "The Mutual Influences in the Development of Ego and Id: Introduction to the Discussion." *The Psychoanalytic Study of the Child*, Vol. 7, 1952.

Freud, Anna, and S. Danne. "An Experiment in Group Upbringing." *The Psychoanalytic Study of the Child*, Vol. 6, 1951.

Freud, Sigmund. *The Standard Edition of the Complete Psychological Works of Sigmund Freud*, 24 vols., translated and edited by James Strachey. London: Hogarth Press and the Institute of Psycho-Analysis, 1953–66.

――. "Three Essays on Sexuality." *Standard Edition*, Vol. 7, 1905.

――. "Sexual Enlightenment of Children." *Standard Edition*, Vol. 9, 1907.

――. "On the Sexual Theories of Children." *Standard Edition*, Vol. 9, 1908.

――. "Analysis of a Phobia in a Five-Year-Old Boy." *Standard Edition*, Vol. 10, 1909.

――. "On Narcissism: An Introduction." *Standard Edition*, Vol. 14, 1914.

――. "Observations on Transference Love." *Standard Edition*, Vol. 12, 1915.

――. "Instincts and Their Vicissitudes." *Standard Edition*, Vol. 14, 1915.

――. "The Unconscious." *Standard Edition*, Vol. 14, 1915.

――. "Mourning and Melancholia." *Standard Edition*, Vol. 14, 1917.

――. "A Child Is Being Beaten." *Standard Edition*, Vol. 17, 1919.

――. "Beyond the Pleasure Principle." *Standard Edition*, Vol. 18, 1920.

――. "The Ego and the Id." *Standard Edition*, Vol. 19, 1923.

――. "The Infantile Genital Organization: An Interpolation into the Theory of Sexuality." *Standard Edition*, Vol. 19, 1923.

――. "The Dissolution of the Oedipus Complex." *Standard Edition*, Vol. 19, 1924.

――. "Neurosis and Psychosis." *Standard Edition*, Vol. 19, 1924.

―― "Some Psychological Consequences of the Anatomical Distinction Between Sexes." *Standard Edition*, Vol. 19, 1925.

――. "Civilization and Its Discontents." *Standard Edition*, Vol. 21, 1930.

――. "Female Sexuality." *Standard Edition*, Vol. 21, 1931.

――. "Why War?" *Standard Edition*, Vol. 22, 1933.

Friedmann, Theodore. "Prenatal Diagnosis of Genetic Disease." *Scientific American*, Nov. 1971.

Fries, Margaret E. "Longitudinal Study: Prenatal Period to Parenthood." *Journal of American Psychoanalytic Association*, Vol. 25, No. 1, 1975.

――. "Psychosomatic Relationships between Mother and Infant." *Psychosomatic Medicine*, Vol. 6, 1944.

Fries, Margaret E. and P. J. Woolf. "Some Hypotheses on the Role of the

Congenital Activity Type in Personality Development." *The Psychoanalytic Study of the Child*, Vol. 8, 1953.

Frommer, Eva A., and Gillian O'Shea. "Antenatal Identification of Women Liable to Have Problems in Managing their Infants." *British Journal of Psychiatry*, Vol. 123, 1973.

Galinsky, Ellen, and William H. Hooks. *The New Extended Family: Day Care That Works.* Boston: Houghton Mifflin Company, 1977.

Gardiner, Muriel. *The Deadly Innocents.* New York: Basic Books, 1976.

Gardner, Richard A. *The Boys' and Girls' Book about Divorce.* New York: Science House, 1970.

Garmezy, Norman. "Children at Risk: The Search for Antecedents of Schizophrenia, Part II. Ongoing Research Programs, Issues, and Intervention." *Schizophrenia Bulletin*, Vol. 9, 1974.

Garmezy, Norman, et al. "Invulnerable Children: The Fact and Fiction of Competence and Disadvantage." *American Journal of Orthopsychiatry*, 1972.

Garvey, Catherine. *Play.* The Developing Child series, Jerome Bruner, Michael Cole, and Barbara Lloyd, eds. Cambridge, Mass.: Harvard University Press, 1977.

Gaylin, Willard. *Caring.* New York: Alfred A. Knopf, 1976.

Gesell, Arnold. *Infant Behavior: Its Genesis and Growth.* New York: McGraw-Hill, 1934.

———. *The Mental Growth of the Pre-School Child.* New York: Macmillan, 1925.

———, et al. *The Child From Five to Ten.* New York: Harper & Row, 1977.

———, et al. *The First Five Years of Life: A Guide to the Study of the Preschool Child.* New York: Harper & Bros., 1940.

Gesell, Arnold, and Catherine S. Amatruda. *Developmental Diagnosis.* New York: B. Hoeber, 1941.

Gesell, Arnold, and F. L. Ilg. *Infant and Child in the Culture of Today: The Guidance of Development.* New York: Harper & Bros., 1943.

Gilbert, Sara D. *What's a Father For?* New York: Warner Books, 1975.

Glueck, Sheldon, and Eleanor Glueck. *Predicting Delinquency and Crime.* Cambridge, Mass.: Harvard University Press, 1959.

Goertzel, Victor, and Mildred G. Goertzel. *Cradles of Eminence.* Boston: Little, Brown, 1962.

Goldberg, S., and M. Lewis. "Play Behaviour in the Year-Old Infant: Early Sex Differences." *Child Development*, Vol. 40, 1969.

Goldfarb, William. *Childhood Schizophrenia.* Cambridge, Mass.: Harvard University Press, 1961.

———. "Childhood Psychosis." In *Carmichael's Manual of Child Psychology*, P. N. Mussen, ed. 3d ed. New York: John Wiley & Sons, 1970.

———, et al. "Parental Perplexity and Childhood Confusion." In *New Fron-*

tiers in Child Guidance, A. H. Esman, ed. New York: International Universities Press, 1958.

Gordon, Thomas. *Parent Effectiveness Training.* New York: David McKay, 1970.

Gottesman, Irving I. *Schizophrenia and Genetics.* New York: Academic Press, 1974.

————. "Personality and Natural Selection." in *Methods and Goals in Human Behavior Genetics.* New York: Academic Press, 1965.

Gottesman, Irving I., and M. Fischer. "A Long Term Follow-up of Children Born to Two Danish Psychiatric Inpatients." The Benevolent Foundation of Scottish Rite Freemasonry, Northern Jurisdiction, U.S.A., 1974.

Gottesman, Irving I., J. Shields, and L. L. Heston. "Characteristics of the Twins of Schizophrenics as Fallible Indicators of Schizoidia." *Acta Geneticae Medicae et Gemellologiae*, in press.

Gould, Robert E. "The Wrong Reasons to Have Children." *New York Times Magazine*, May 3, 1970.

Gould, Stephen Jay. "The Child as Man's Real Father." *Natural History*, May 1975.

————. "Human Babies as Embryos." *Natural History*, Feb. 1976.

Granger, Richard H. *Your Child From One to Six.* U.S. Dept. of Health, Education and Welfare Publication (OHDS) 77–30026, rev. 1978.

Gray, Jane D., et al. "Prediction and Prevention of Child Abuse and Neglect." *International Journal of Child Abuse.* Oxford, England: Pergamon Press.

Greenacre, Phyllis. "Considerations Regarding the Parent-Infant Relationship." *International Journal of Psycho-Analysis*, Vol. 41, 1960.

————. "Early Physical Determinants in the Development of the Sense of Identity." *Journal of the American Psychoanalytic Association*, Vol. 6, 1958.

————. "The Childhood of the Artist: Libidinal Phase Development and Giftedness." *The Psychoanalytic Study of the Child*, Vol. 12, 1957.

Greenblatt, Augusta. *Heredity and You: How You Can Protect Your Family's Future.* New York: Coward, McCann & Geoghegan, 1974.

Gregory, Ian. "Anterospective Data Following Childhood Loss of a Parent. Part II. Pathology, Performance and Potential Among College Students." *Archives of General Psychiatry*, Vol. 13, 1965.

Grotberg, Edith H., ed. *200 Years of Children.* Washington, D.C.: Office of Child Development, U.S. Dept. of Health, Education and Welfare, 1976.

Group for the Advancement of Psychiatry. *The Joys and Sorrows of Parenthood.* Vol. 8, Report 84. New York: Group for the Advancement of Psychiatry, 1973.

Gruber, Howard E., and J. Jacques Vonèche, eds. *The Essential Piaget.* New York: Basic Books, 1977.

Gulhati, Kaval. "Compulsory Sterilization: The Change in India's Population Policy." *Science*, March 25, 1977.

Guttmacher, Alan F. *Pregnancy, Birth, and Family Planning.* New York: The Viking Press, 1973.

———. *Pregnancy and Birth.* New York: Signet Books, 1962.

Hall, Warren G. "Weaning and Growth of Artificially Reared Rats." *Science,* Dec. 26, 1975.

Haller, Alex, Jr., et al., eds. *The Hospitalized Child and His Family.* Baltimore: Johns Hopkins University Press, 1967.

Hardin, Garrett. "The Evil of Mandatory Motherhood." *Psychology Today,* Nov. 1974.

Hartmann, Heinz. *Essays on Ego Psychology: Selected Problems in Psychoanalytic Theory.* New York: International Universities Press, 1964.

Heilman, Joan Rattner. "We're Not Having Children." *Family Circle,* June 1974.

Hendin, David, and Joan Marks. *The Genetic Connection: How to Protect Your Family Against Hereditary Disease.* New York: William Morrow, 1978.

Henry, Jules. *Pathways to Madness.* New York: Random House, 1971.

Hinde, Robert A., and Lynda M. Davies. "Changes in Mother-Infant Relationship After Separation in Rhesus Monkeys." *Nature,* Sept. 1, 1972.

———. "Removing Infant Rhesus from Mother for 13 Days Compared with Removing Mother from Infant." *Journal of Child Psychology & Psychiatry,* Vol. 13, 1972.

Hinde, Robert A., and Yvette Spencer-Booth. "Effects of Brief Separation from Mother on Rhesus Monkeys." *Science,* July 9, 1971.

Homan, William E. *Child Sense: A Pediatrician's Guide for Today's Families.* New York: Basic Books, 1969.

———. "Mother's Milk or Other Milk?" *New York Times Magazine,* June 6, 1971.

Hoover, Eleanor Links. "A New Psychological Parameter: Invulnerables." *Human Behavior,* April 1976.

Howard, Jane. *Families.* New York: Simon & Schuster, 1978.

Howells, John G. "Fallacies in Child Care: That Children Are Brought Up By Parents." *Acta Paedopsychiatrica,* 1970.

Ilg, Frances L., and Louise Bates Ames. *The Gesell Institute's Child Behavior.* New York: Dell, 1955.

Irwin, Theodore. *To Combat Child Abuse and Neglect.* Public Affairs Pamphlet 508. New York: Public Affairs Committee, 1974.

Jacobson, Cecil B., with Judith Ramsey. "How to Have a Better Baby." *Family Health,* April 1970.

Jacobson, Edith. *The Self and the Object World.* New York: International Universities Press, 1964.

———. "On Normal and Pathological Moods: Their Nature and Functions." *The Psychoanalytic Study of the Child,* Vol. 12, 1957.

—— "The Self and the Object World: Vicissitudes of Their Infantile Cathexes and Their Influence on Ideational and Affective Development." *The Psychoanalytic Study of the Child*, Vol. 9, 1954.

——. "The Development of the Wish for a Child in Boys." *The Psychoanalytic Study of the Child*, Vol. 5, 1950.

Jacobson, Gary, and Robert G. Ryder. "Parental Loss and Some Characteristics of the Early Marriage Relationship." *American Journal of Orthopsychiatry*, Vol. 36, No. 1, Oct. 1969.

Jansky, Jeanette, and Katerina DeHirsch. *Preventing Reading Failure: Prediction, Diagnosis, Intervention.* New York: Harper & Row, 1972.

Jersild, Arthur T., Charles W. Telford, and James M. Sawrey. *Child Psychology.* 7th ed. Englewood Cliffs, N.J.: Prentice-Hall, 1975.

Jonas, David, and Doris Klein. *A Study of the Infantilization of Man.* New York: McGraw-Hill Book Company, 1970.

Josephson, Martin M., and Robert T. Porter, eds. *Clinician's Handbook of Childhood Psychopathology.* New York: Jason Aronson, Inc., 1979.

Journal of the American Medical Association. "Change of Home Can Help Psychosocial Dwarfs." June 2, 1975.

——. "Teaching Ex-addicts to Become Adequate Parents Is a Tough Job." May 12, 1975.

——. " 'Clinical Genetics' Gain Notice." Sept. 28, 1970.

Kagan, Jerome. "The Baby's Elastic Mind." *Human Nature*, Jan. 1978.

——. "The Emergence of Sex Differences." *Scholastic Review*, Vol. 80, 1972.

——. "Parental Correlates of Child's IQ and Height: A Cross-Validation of the Berkeley Growth Study Results." *Child Development*, Vol. 30, 1959.

——, et al. *Change and Continuity in Infancy.* New York: John Wiley & Sons, 1971.

——, et al. "The Child's Differential Perception of Parental Attributes." *Journal of Abnormal and Social Psychology*, Vol. 61, 1960.

Kagan, Jerome, and Ernest Havemann. *Psychology: An Introduction.* 2nd ed. New York: Harcourt Brace Jovanovich, 1972.

Kagan, Jerome, Richard B. Kearsley, and Philip R. Zelazo. *Infancy: Its Place in Human Development.* Cambridge, Mass.: Harvard University Press, 1978.

Kagan, Jerome, and Robert E. Klein. "Cross-Cultural Perspectives on Early Development." *American Psychologist*, Nov. 1973.

Kagan, Jerome, and M. Lewis. "Studies of Attention in the Human Infant." *Behavioral Development*, Vol. 11, 1965.

Kanner, Leo. "Problems of Nosology and Psychodynamics of Early Infantile Autism." *American Journal of Orthopsychiatry*, Vol. 19, no. 3, 1949.

——. "Early Infantile Autism." *Journal of Pediatrics*, Vol. 25, 1944.

——. "Autistic Disturbances of Affective Contact." *Nervous Child*, Vol. 2, 1942.

Kanner, Leo, and Leon Eisenberg. "Notes on the Follow-up Studies of Autistic Children." In *Psychopathology of Childhood*, P. H. Hoch and L. Zubin, eds. New York: Grune & Stratton, 1955.

Kastenbaum, Robert. "The Kingdom Where Nobody Dies." *Saturday Review*, Dec. 23, 1972.

Keniston, Kenneth. "The 11-Year-Olds of Today Are the Computer Terminals of Tomorrow." *New York Times*, Feb. 19, 1976.

———. "The Emptying Family." *New York Times*, Feb. 18, 1976.

———. "Do Americans Really Like Children?" *Childhood Education*, Vol. 52, 1975.

———. *The Uncommitted: Alienated Youth in American Society.* New York: Harcourt, Brace & World, 1960.

Keniston, Kenneth, and the Carnegie Council on Children. *All Our Children.* New York: Harcourt Brace Jovanovich, 1978.

Kent, Saul. "Perinatology: The New Science of Childbirth." *Saturday Review*, July 13, 1974.

Kernberg, Otto. *Borderline Conditions and Pathological Narcissism.* New York: Jason Aronson, 1975.

Kessen, William, ed. *Childhood in China.* New Haven: Yale University Press, 1975.

Kestenberg, Judith S. *Children and Parents: Psychoanalytic Studies in Development.* New York: Jason Aronson, 1975.

Kety, Seymour, et al. "Mental Illness in the Biological and Adoptive Families of Adopted Schizophrenics." *American Journal of Psychiatry*, Vol. 128, 1971.

Kirsten, Grace, and Richard C. Robertiello. *Big You, Little You.* New York: Dial Press, 1977.

Klaus, Marshall H., and John H. Kennell. *Maternal-Infant Bonding.* St. Louis: C. V. Mosby Company, 1976.

Klaus, Marshall H., Mary Anne Trause, and John H. Kennell. "Does Human Maternal Behaviour After Delivery Show a Characteristic Pattern?" *Parent-Infant Interaction*, Ciba Foundation Symposium 33, 1975.

———. "Evidence for a Sensitive Period in the Human Mother." *Parent-Infant Interaction*, Ciba Foundation Symposium 33, 1975.

Klaus, Marshall H., et al. "Mothers Separated from Their Newborn Infants." *Pediatric Clinics of North America*, Vol. 17, 1972.

Klein, Carole. *The Single Parent Experience.* New York: Avon Books, 1973.

Klein, Ted. *The Father's Book.* New York: William Morrow, 1968.

Klemer, Richard H. *Marriage and Family Relationships.* New York: Harper & Row, 1970.

Klemesrud, Judy. "Adoption Costs Soar as Births Decline." *New York Times*, Feb. 20, 1973.

Kliman, Ann S. *Crisis: Psychological First Aid for Recovery and Growth.* New York: Holt, Rinehart and Winston, 1978.

———. Personal communications.

Kliman, Gilbert W. *Psychological Emergencies of Childhood.* New York: Grune & Stratton, 1968.

———. "Results of a Psychoanalytically Based Pilot Project Interacting with a Foster Care System." Westchester Psychiatric Society, Purchase, N.Y., 1979.

———. "Facilitation of Mourning During Childhood." In *Medical Management of Bereavement*, David Peretz, ed. New York: Arno Press, 1979.

———. "Psychoanalytic Approaches to Prevention of Mental Illness in Vulnerable Young Children." Presented at the American Psychoanalytic Association Workshop on the Vulnerable Child, New York, 1978.

———. "Special Problems of the Single Parent Child." Jason Aronson Psychotherapy Tape Library, New York, 1978.

———. "Psychoanalytic Approaches to Prevention of Mental Illness in Childhood." Presented at the Westchester Psychoanalytic Society Scientific Meeting, White Plains, N.Y., 1978.

———. "Psychoanalytically Based Approaches to the Problems of Foster Care: A Pilot Project." Presented at American Psychoanalytic Interdisciplinary Seminar, Psychoanalytic Observations of Foster Care, 1978.

———. "Psychoanalytic Approaches to Prevention of Mental Illness." Jason Aronson Psychotherapy Tape Library, New York, 1977.

———. "Analyst in the Nursery: Experimental Application of Analytic Techniques in a Therapeutic Nursery—The Cornerstone Method." *Psychoanalytic Study of the Child*, Vol. 30, 1975.

———. "Children in National Disasters." Presented at Eighth International Congress on Child Psychiatry, Philadelphia, 1974.

———. "Death in the Family—Its Impact on Children." Terry Friedman Klein Memorial Lecture Series, Behavioral Sciences Tape Library, Leonia, N.J., 1974.

———. "Death of a Parent Occurring During a Child's Analysis." In *Trauma*, Monograph V of the Monograph Series of the Kris Study Group, New York Psychoanalytic Institute. New York: International Universities Press, 1974.

———. "The Case of a Dying Child." In *Trauma*, Monograph V of the Monograph Series of the Kris Study Group, New York Psychoanalytic Institute. New York: International Universities Press, 1974.

———. "Preventive Approaches to Preschool Psychiatric Disorders: Some Assessments." Presented at Academy of Child Psychiatry, Washington, D.C., 1973.

———. "Children's Reactions to National Events: The 1968 Federal Elections." Presented at the American Orthopsychiatric Convention, Washington, D.C., 1969.

————. "Adrenal Medullary Function." In *Yearbook of Endocrinology*, G. Gordon, ed. Chicago: Yearbook Publishers, 1955.

Kliman, Gilbert W., and Elissa Burian. "The Three-Generation Psychosis-Making Machine: Successive Narcissistic Depletion as a Clue to the Etiology of Early Arising Childhood Psychosis." Unpublished.

Kliman, Gilbert W., Elissa Burian, and Martha A. Frazier. "Therapeutic Incubation: A Variation of Mahler's Tripartite Technique for Treatment of Symbiotic Psychosis." Unpublished.

Kliman, Gilbert W., and Judyth Katz. "Maternal Depression as an Antecedent to Early Childhood Psychosis." White Plains, N.Y.: Center for Psychiatry Reprint, 1973.

Kohler, Elaine E., and Thomas A. Good. "The Infant Who Fails to Thrive." *Hospital Practice*, July 1969.

Kohut, Heinz. *The Analysis of the Self.* Psychoanalytic Studies, Monograph 4. New York: International Universities Press, 1971.

————. "Forms and Transformations of Narcissism." *Journal of the American Psychoanalytic Association*, Vol. 14, 1966.

Lamb, Michael E., ed. *The Role of the Father in Child Development.* New York: John Wiley & Sons, 1976.

The Lancet. "The Handicapped Family." Aug. 30, 1975.

Langer, William L. "Infanticide: A Historical Survey." In *The New Psychohistory*, Lloyd deMause, ed. New York: Psychohistory Press, 1975.

Lappé, Marc. "The Moral Claims of the Wanted Fetus." *Hastings Center Report*, April 1975.

Leach, Penelope. *Babyhood.* New York: Alfred A. Knopf, 1976.

Leboyer, Frederick. *Birth Without Violence.* New York: Alfred A. Knopf, 1975.

Leiderman, Peter. "Mother-Infant Separation: Delayed Consequences." In *Maternal Attachment and Mothering Disorders: A Round Table*, M. H. Klaus, T. Leger, and M. A. Trause, eds. New Brunswick, N.J.: Johnson and Johnson, 1975.

LeShan, Eda. *How to Survive Parenthood.* New York: Warner Books, 1973.

Levine, James A. *Who Will Raise the Children?* Philadelphia: J. B. Lippincott, 1976.

Lewin, Roger, ed. *Child Alive!* Garden City, N.Y.: Anchor Press, 1975.

Lichtenberg, Philip, and Dolores G. Norton. *Cognitive and Mental Development in the First Five Years of Life: A Review of Recent Research.* Chevy Chase: National Institute of Mental Health, 1970.

Liedloff, Jean. *The Continuum Concept.* New York: Alfred A. Knopf, 1977.

Liley, H. M. I., with Beth Day. *Modern Motherhood.* New York: Random House, 1966.

Loebl, Suzanne. *Conception, Contraception: A New Look.* New York: McGraw-Hill, 1974.

Loehlin, John C., and Robert C. Nichols. *Heredity, Environment, and Personality.* Austin: University of Texas Press, 1976.

Logan, Ben, ed. *Television Awareness Training.* Rev. ed. New York: Media Action Research Center, 1979.

Lopez, Thomas. Personal Communications.

Lopez, Thomas, and Gilbert W. Kliman. "Mourning, Memory and Reconstruction in the Analysis of a Four Year Old Bereaved at Age Sixteen Months." *Psychoanalytic Study of the Child,* Vol. 34, 1979.

――――. "Treatment of an Impoverished Intellectually Retarded Ghetto Child by the Cornerstone Method." Unpublished. 1979.

Lynch, Henry T. "Cancer and Heredity: Implications for Early Cancer Detection." *GP,* Dec. 1968.

――――, et al, eds. *International Directory of Genetic Services.* 5th ed. White Plains, N.Y.: The National Foundation–March of Dimes, 1977.

Lynch, Margaret A. "Ill-Health and Child Abuse." *The Lancet,* Aug. 16, 1975.

Lynn, David. *The Father: His Role in Child Development.* Belmont, Calif.: Wadsworth Publishing Co., 1974.

Macfarlane, Aidan. *The Psychology of Childbirth.* The Developing Child series, Jerome Bruner, Michael Cole, and Barbara Lloyd, eds. Cambridge, Mass.: Harvard University Press, 1977.

Mahler, Margaret S. "Rapprochement Subphase of the Separation-Individuation Process." *Psychoanalytic Quarterly,* Vol. 41, No. 4, 1972.

――――. "On the First Three Sub-Phases of the Separation-Individuation Process." *International Journal of Psycho-Analysis,* Vol. 53, 1972.

――――. "On the Significance of the Normal Separation-Individuation Phase: With Reference to Research in Symbiotic Child Psychosis." In *Drives, Affects, Behavior,* M. Schur, ed. Vol. 2. New York: International Universities Press, 1965.

――――. "On Early Infantile Psychosis: The Symbiotic and Autistic Syndromes." *Journal of the American Academy of Child Psychiatry,* Vol. 4, 1965.

――――. "Thoughts about Development and Individuation." *The Psychoanalytic Study of the Child,* Vol. 18, 1963.

――――. "On Sadness and Grief in Infancy and Childhood: Loss and Restoration of the Symbiotic Love Object." *The Psychoanalytic Study of the Child,* Vol. 16, 1961.

――――. "Autism and Symbiosis: Two Extreme Disturbances of Identity." *International Journal of Psycho-Analysis,* Vol. 39, 1958.

――――. "On Two Crucial Phases of Integration of the Sense of Identity: Separation-Individuation and Bisexual Identity." Abstract in Panel on Problems of Identity, reprinted in *Journal of the American Psychoanalytic Association,* Vol. 6, 1958.

———. "Autism and Symbiosis: Two Extreme Disturbances of Identity" *International Journal of Psycho-Analysis*, Vol. 36, 1958.

———. "On Normal and Pathological Symbiosis: A Contribution to the Understanding of Psychoses in Children." Presented at the Baltimore Psychoanalytic Society, 1954.

———. "On Child Psychosis and Schizophrenia: Autistic and Symbiotic Infantile Psychoses." *The Psychoanalytic Study of the Child*, Vol. 7, 1952.

Mahler, Margaret S., and Manuel Furer. "Observations on Research regarding the 'Symbiotic Syndrome' of Infantile Psychosis." *Psychoanalytic Quarterly* Vol. 29, 1960.

Mahler, Margaret S., Manuel Furer, and Calvin F. Settlage. "Severe Emotional Disturbances in Childhood: Psychosis." In *American Handbook of Psychiatry*, Silvano Arieti, ed. Vol. 1. New York: Basic Books, 1959.

Mahler, Margaret S., Fred Pine, and Anni Bergman. *The Psychological Birth of the Human Infant: Symbiosis and Individuation.* New York: Basic Books, 1975.

Mahler, Margaret S., J. Ross, and Z. DeFries. "Clinical Studies in Benign and Malignant Cases of Childhood Psychosis." *American Journal of Orthopsychiatry*, Vol. 19, No. 2, 1949.

Makarenko, A. S. *The Collective Family: A Handbook for Russian Parents.* New York: Anchor Books, 1967.

Malone, Charles A. "Safety First: Comments on the Influence of External Danger in the Lives of Children of Disorganized Families." *American Journal of Orthopsychiatry*, Vol. 36, No. 1, 1966.

Marano, Hara. "Breast-Feeding: New Evidence It's Far More Than Nutrition." *Medical World News*, Feb. 5, 1979.

Maternity Center Association. *Guide for Expectant Parents.* New York: Grosset & Dunlap, 1971.

Maurer, Daphne M., and Charles E. "Newborn Babies See Better Than You Think." *Psychology Today*, Oct. 1976.

Maynard, Joyce. "Rearing Children of 1970's Worries Children of 1950's." *New York Times*, Dec. 24, 1976.

Mazlish, Bruce. *James and John Stuart Mill: Father and Son in the Nineteenth Century.* New York: Basic Books, 1975.

McCleary, Elliott H. *New Miracles of Childbirth.* New York: David McKay, 1974.

McDermott, John F., Jr. "Divorce and its Psychiatric Sequelae in Children." *Archives of General Psychiatry*, Vol. 23, 1970.

McDevitt, John B., and Calvin F. Settlage eds. *Separation-Individuation: Essays in Honor of Margaret S. Mahler.* New York: International Universities Press, 1971.

McDonald, Thomas F. "Teenage Pregnancy." *Journal of the American Medical Association*, Aug. 9, 1976.

McGrath, Nancy and Chip. "Why Have a Baby?" *New York Times Magazine,* May 25, 1975.

Mead, Margaret. *Culture and Commitment: A Study of the Generation Gap.* New York: Doubleday, 1970.

———. *Male and Female.* New York: William Morrow, 1949.

———. *Sex and Temperament in Three Primitive Societies.* New York: McGraw-Hill, 1935.

Mead, Margaret, and Martha Wolfenstein, eds. *Childhood in Contemporary Cultures.* Chicago: University of Chicago Press, 1965.

Medical World News. "California: Furor Over Home Births." April 4, 1977.

———. "Taking the 'Violence' Out of Birth." May 19, 1975.

———. "Where Babies Get a Running Start." May 11, 1973.

———. "Tracing a Touchy Time for Mothers." June 27, 1969.

Meltzoff, Andrew N., and M. Keith Moore. "Imitation of Facial and Manual Gestures by Human Neonates." *Science,* Oct. 7, 1977.

Menken, Jane. "The Health and Social Consequences of Teenage Childbearing." *Family Planning Perspectives,* July 1972.

Menninger, Robert G. "Fragmentation of the Family." *Menninger Perspective,* Vol. 8, No. 2, Summer, 1977.

Milunsky, Aubrey. *Know Your Genes.* Boston: Houghton Mifflin, 1977.

Missildine, W. Hugh. *Your Inner Child of the Past.* New York: Simon & Schuster, 1963.

Mitchell, Robert McNair, with Ted Klein. *Nine Months To Go.* New York: Ace Publishing, 1969.

Mohr, James C. *Abortion in America: The Origins and Evolution of National Policy, 1800–1900.* New York: Oxford University Press, 1978.

Money, John. "Childhood: The Last Frontier in Sex Research." *The Sciences,* Nov.–Dec. 1976.

———. Personal communications.

Money, John, and Anke Ehrhardt. *Man and Woman, Boy and Girl: The Differentiation and Dimorphism of Gender Identity from Conception to Maturity.* Baltimore: Johns Hopkins University Press, 1972.

Money, John, and Patricia Tucker. *Sexual Signatures: On Being a Man or a Woman.* Boston: Little, Brown, 1975.

Montessori, Maria. *Childhood Education.* Chicago: Henry Regnery Company, 1974.

Moody, Kathryn. Personal communications.

Motulsky, Arno G., and Frederick Hecht. "Genetic Prognosis and Counseling." *American Journal of Obstetrics and Gynecology,* Vol. 90, No. 7, Part 2, Dec. 1964.

Murphy, Edmond A. "The Rationale of Genetic Counseling." *The Journal of Pediatrics,* Jan. 1968.

Murphy, Jane M. "Psychiatric Labeling in Cross-Cultural Perspective." *Science,* March 12, 1976.

Murphy, Louis B. "The Problem of Defense and the Concept of Coping." In *The Child in His Family*, E. James Anthony and Cyrille Koupernik, eds. New York: John Wiley & Sons, 1970.

———. "Effects of Child-rearing Patterns on Mental Health." *Children*, Vol. 3, No. 6, 1956.

Naismith, Grace. "Teen-Age Sexuality: Too Many Pregnancies, Too Early." *Reader's Digest*, Nov. 1977.

Nathan, John. *Mishima.* Boston: Little, Brown, 1974.

National Academy of Sciences. *Toward a National Policy for Children and Families.* Washington, D.C., 1976.

The National Foundation–March of Dimes. *Be Good to Your Baby Before It Is Born.* White Plains, N.Y., 1977.

———. "Maternal and Infant Health." Annual Report. White Plains, N.Y., 1972.

———. "Intrauterine Diagnosis." *Birth Defects: Original Article Series*, Vol. 7, No. 5, April 1971.

National Institute of Mental Health. "Q's & A's on Child Mental Health." Interview with Burton L. White. U.S. Dept. of Health, Education and Welfare Publication (ADM) 77-413, 1977.

Neisser, Edith G. *Your Child's Sense of Responsibility.* Public Affairs Pamphlet 254. New York: Public Affairs Committee, 1957.

Nemy, Enid. "They Chose to be Childless: 'As a Couple, We Felt Complete.' " *New York Times*, March 23, 1970.

Neubauer, Peter, ed. *The Process of Child Development.* New York: Jason Aronson, 1976.

Newsweek. "The Parent Gap." Sept. 22, 1975.

Newton, Michael. "New Baby! Why So Sad?" *Family Health/Today's Health*, May 1976.

New York World-Telegram and Sun. "Littlest Kidnapers Go Free." July 1, 1958.

Nuckolls, Katherine B. "Psychosocial Assets, Life Crisis and the Prognosis of Pregnancy." *American Journal of Epidemiology*, May 1972.

Nyhan, William L., and Edward Edelson. *The Heredity Factor: Genes, Chromosomes, and You.* New York: Grosset & Dunlap, 1976.

Ogg, Elizabeth. One-Parent Families. Public Affairs Pamphlet 543. New York: Public Affairs Committee, 1976.

———. *Unmarried Teenagers and Their Children.* Public Affairs Pamphlet 537. New York: Public Affairs Committee, 1976.

Olshaker, Bennett. *The Child as a Work of Art.* Pleasantville, N.Y.: Reader's Digest Press, 1975.

Oswald, Robert. *Lee: A Portrait of Lee Harvey Oswald by His Brother.* New York: Coward-McCann, 1967.

Parke, Ross D., and Douglas B. Sawin. "Fathering: It's a Major Role." *Psychology Today*, Nov. 1977.

Pearce, Jane, and Saul Newton. *The Conditions of Human Growth*. New York: Citadel Press, 1963.

Peck, Ellen. *The Baby Trap*. New York: Bernard Geis Associates, 1971.

Peck, Ellen, and William Granzig. *The Parent Test*. New York: G. P. Putnam's Sons, 1978.

Pelner, Louis. "The Hereditary Aspects of Cancer." *Journal of the American Geriatric Society*, Vol. 10, 1962.

Pepper, William E. *The Self-Managed Child: Paths to Cultural Rebirth*. New York: Harper & Row, 1973.

Phillips, Celeste R., and Joseph T. Anzalone. *Fathering: Participation in Labor and Birth*. St. Louis: C. V. Mosby Company, 1978.

Piaget, Jean. *The Grasp of Consciousness: Action and Concept in the Young Child*. Cambridge, Mass.: Harvard University Press, 1976.

———. *Les mécanismes perceptifs*. Paris: Presses Universitaires de France, 1961.

———. *Logique et perception*. Paris: Presses Universitaires de France, 1958.

———. *The Origins of Intelligence in Children*. New York: International Universities Press, 1952.

———. *The Language and Thought of the Child*. New York: Humanities Press, 1952.

———. *Play, Dreams, and Imitation in Childhood*. New York: W. W. Norton, 1951.

———. *The Moral Judgment of the Child*. 1932. Reprint. Glencoe: Free Press, 1948.

———. *Judgment and Reasoning in the Child*. New York: Harcourt, Brace, 1928.

———. "Piaget's Theory." In *Carmichael's Manual of Child Psychology*, P. H. Mussen, ed., 1st ed. New York: John Wiley & Sons, 1970.

———. "Les Trois Structures Fondamentales de la Vie Psychique: Rhythme, Regulation et Groupement." *Revue Suisse de Psychologie*, Vol. 1, 1942.

Piaget, Jean, and B. Inhelder. *L'image mental chez l'enfant*. Paris: Presses Universitaires de France, 1966.

Pickering, George. *Creative Malady*. New York: Oxford University Press, 1974.

Piers, Maria W. *Infanticide: Past and Present*. New York: W. W. Norton, 1978.

Pilpel, Harriet F., Ruth Jane Zuckerman, and Elizabeth Ogg. *Abortion: Public Issue, Private Decision*. Public Affairs Pamphlet 527. New York: Public Affairs Committee, 1975.

Pines, Maya. *Revolution in Learning: The Years from Birth to Six*. New York: Harper & Row, 1967.

———. "Shaping the Infant Brain." *Physician's World*, Dec. 1973.

Population Bulletin. "Adolescent Pregnancy and Childbearing—Growing Concerns for Americans." Population Reference Bureau, Washington, D.C., Sept. 1976.

Provence, Sally, and R. C. Lipton. *Infants in Institutions*. New York: International Universities Press, 1962.

Provence, Sally, and Samuel Ritvo. "Effects of Deprivation on Institutionalized Infants." *The Psychoanalytic Study of the Child*, Vol. 16, 1961.

Psychology Today. "Close to a Mother's Heart: The Functional Value of Baby Holding." Oct. 1973.

Rahe, R. H. "Social Stress and Illness Onset." *Journal of Psychosocial Research*, Vol. 8, 1964.

Rainer, John D. "Genetics of Neurosis and Personality Disorder." In *Psychiatry and Genetics—Psychosocial, Ethical and Legal Considerations*, Michael A. Sperber and Lissy F. Jarvik, eds. New York: Basic Books, 1976.

Ramey, James. "Multi-Adult Household: Living Group of the Future?" *The Futurist*, April 1976.

Ramos, Suzanne. *Teaching Your Child to Cope with Crisis*. New York: David McKay, 1975.

Rank, Otto. *The Myth of the Birth of the Hero*. New York: The Journal of Nervous and Mental Disease Publishing Co., 1914.

———. *The Trauma of Birth*. New York: Robert Brunner, 1952.

Rapoport, Rhona, Robert Rapoport, and Ziona Strelitz. *Fathers, Mothers and Society*. New York: Basic Books, 1977.

Read, Grantly Dick. *Childbirth Without Fear*. New York: Harper & Bros., 1944, 1953.

Reiterman, Carl, ed. *Abortion and the Unwanted Child*. San Francisco: Springer Publishing Co., 1971.

Report to the President: White House Conference on Children. U.S. Superintendent of Documents, Washington, D.C., 1971.

Rexford, Eveoleen N., Louis W. Sander, and Theodore Shapiro, eds. *Infant Psychiatry: A New Synthesis*. New Haven: Yale University Press, 1976.

Ribble, Margaret. *Rights of Infants*. New York: Columbia University Press, 1943.

Rice, Gunther, Joseph G. Kepecs, and Itamar Yahalom. "Differences in Communicative Impact Between Mothers of Psychotic and Nonpsychotic Children." *American Journal of Orthopsychiatry*, April 1966.

Richards, Celia. "The Nursing Experience." *Voices*, Spring 1966.

Riker, Audrey Palm. *Breastfeeding*. Public Affairs Pamphlet 353S. New York: Public Affairs Committee, 1964.

Ringler, Norma M., et al. "Mother-to-Child Speech at 2 Years—Effects of Early Postnatal Contact." *Behavioral Pediatrics*, Jan. 1975.

Robertiello, Richard C. *Hold Them Very Close, Then Let Them Go*. New York: Dial Press, 1975.

Rodgers, Joann. "Don't Stall Whiz Kids, Urges Hopkins Psychologist." *Baltimore News-American*, Feb. 22, 1976.

———. "Recipe for Stirring Up Bright Kids." *Baltimore News-American*, Feb. 19, 1976.

Roesch, Roberts. "Should You Have Another Baby?" *Reader's Digest*, May 1971.

Roiphe, Ann Richardson. "The Family Is Out of Fashion." *New York Times Magazine*, Aug. 15, 1971.

Rollin, Betty. "Motherhood: Who Needs It?" *Look*, Sept. 22, 1970.

Rosenfeld, Albert. *The Second Genesis: The Coming Control of Life*, Part Two. Englewood Cliffs, N.J.: Prentice-Hall, 1969.

———. "The 'Elastic Mind' Movement: Rationalizing Child Neglect?" *Saturday Review*, April 1, 1978.

———. "Who Says We're a Child-Centered Society?" *Saturday Review*, Aug. 7, 1976.

———. "And Now, Preventive Psychiatry." *Saturday Review*, Feb. 21, 1976.

———. "Starve the Child, Famish the Future." *Saturday Review/World*, March 23, 1974.

———. "What Is the Right Number of Children?" *Life*, Dec. 17, 1971.

———. "Heading Off Emotional Trouble Before It Starts." *Family Health*, May 1970.

Rosenthal, Jack. "Fertility Level in Nation Close to Zero Growth." *New York Times*, Sept. 24, 1972.

Rossi, Alice S. "A Biosocial Perspective on Parenting." *Daedalus*, Spring 1977.

———. "Family Development in a Changing World." *American Journal of Psychiatry*, March 1972.

Rubinstein, Eli A., and George V. Coelho, eds. *Behavioral Science and Mental Health*. National Institute of Mental Health, Dept. of Health, Education and Welfare, 1970.

Rutherford, Robert N. "The Prevention of Viral Diseases." *Sandoz Panorama*, Jan.–Feb. 1969.

Rutter, Michael. *Children of Sick Parents: An Environmental and Psychiatric Study*. Maudsley Monographs No. 16. London: Oxford University Press, 1966.

———. "Maternal Deprivation 1972–1977: New Findings, New Concepts, New Approaches." Presented to the Society for Research in Child Development, New Orleans, 1977.

Salisbury, Arthur S. Personal communications.

Salk, Lee. *What Every Child Would Like Parents to Know About Divorce*. New York: Harper & Row, 1978.

———. *Preparing for Parenthood*. New York: David McKay, 1974.

———. *What Every Child Would Like His Parents to Know*. New York: David McKay, 1972.

———. "The Role of the Heartbeat in the Relations between Mother and Infant." *Scientific American*, March 1973.

Salk, Lee, and Rita Kramer. *How to Raise a Human Being*. New York: Random House, 1969.

Sandler, Anne-Marie. "Beyond Eight-Month Anxiety." *International Journal of Psycho-Analysis*, Vol. 58, Part 2, 1977.

Sarnoff, Charles. *Latency.* New York: Jason Aronson, 1976.

Scarf, Maggie. "Which Child Gets Scarred?" *New York Times*, Dec. 3, 1972.

Schaeffer, H. Rudolph, and Peggy E. Emerson. "The Development of Social Attachments in Infancy." *Monographs of the Society for Research in Child Development*, Vol. 29, No. 2, 1964.

Schaffer, H. Rudolph. *Mothering.* The Developing Child series, Jerome Bruner, Michael Cole, and Barbara Lloyd, eds. Cambridge, Mass.: Harvard University Press, 1977.

Schmeck, Jr., Harold M. "Nation Found Near Point of No Unwanted Births." *New York Times*, Jan. 3, 1976.

Schorr, Alvin L., ed. *Children and Decent People.* New York: Basic Books, 1974.

Schwartz, Richard A. "The Role of Family Planning in the Primary Prevention of Mental Illness." *American Journal of Psychiatry*, Vol. 125, 1969.

Scofield, Nanette E. "When Mother Goes Back to Work." *New York Times Magazine*, December 15, 1968.

Seaman, Barbara. "Do Gynecologists Exploit Their Patients?" *New York*, Aug. 14, 1972.

Segal, Julius, and Herbert Yahraes. *A Child's Journey: Forces That Shape the Lives of Our Young.* New York: McGraw-Hill, 1978.

Seligman, Martin E. P. *Helplessness: On Depression, Development and Death.* San Francisco: W. H. Freeman, 1975.

Settlage, Calvin F. "Psychoanalytic Theory in Relation to the Nosology of Childhood Psychic Disorders." *Journal of the American Psychoanalytic Association*, Vol. 12, 1964.

Sheehy, Gail. "Childless by Choice." *New York*, Jan. 20, 1969.

Sherman, Nan, ed. "Perinatal Health Promotion." Special issue of *Family and Community Health*, Nov. 1978.

Shneour, Elie. *The Malnourished Mind.* Garden City, N.Y.: Anchor Press/ Doubleday, 1974.

Singer, Jerome L. "Imagination and Make-Believe Play in Early Childhood: Some Educational Implications." *Journal of Mental Imagery*, Vol. 1, No. 1, 1977.

Skeels, Robert. "Headstart on Headstart: 30 Year Evaluation." *5th Annual Distinguished Lectures in Special Education: Summer Session, 1966.* Los Angeles: University of Southern California School of Education, 1967.

————. "Adult Status of Children with Contrasting Early Life Experiences." *Monographs of the Society for Research on Child Development*, Vol. 31, 1966.

————. "Effect of Adoption of Children from Institutions." *Children*, Vol. 12, 1965.

Sklar, June, and Beth Berkov. "The American Birth Rate: Evidences of a Coming Rise." *Science*, Aug. 29, 1975.

Skodak, M. and H. M. Skeels. "A Final Follow-up Study of 100 Adopted Children." *Journal of General Psychology*, Vol. 75, 1949.

Skolnick, Arlene. "The Myth of the Vulnerable Child." *Psychology Today,* Feb. 1978.

Smith R. C. "Society Pushes 'Monsters' Like This Into a Corner ... Now Experts Are Trying to Draw Out These Battering Parents." *Today's Health,* Jan. 1973.

Solnit, Albert J. "Mourning and the Birth of a Defective Child." *Psychoanalytic Study of the Child,* Vol. 16, 1961.

Sonne, John C. "Feticide As Acting Out." *Voices,* Spring 1966.

Spitz, René A. *The First Year of Life: A Psychoanalytic Study of Normal and Deviant Development of Object Relations.* New York: International Universities Press, 1965.

———. *A Genetic Field Theory of Ego Formation.* New York: International Universities Press, 1959.

———. *No and Yes: On the Genesis of Human Communication.* New York: International Universities Press, 1957.

———. "Metapsychology and Direct Infant Observation." In *Psychoanalysis—A General Psychology,* R. M. Loewenstein et al., eds. New York: International Universities Press, 1966.

———. "The Psychogenic Diseases in Infancy: An Attempt at Their Etiologic Classification." *Psychoanalytic Study of the Child,* Vol. 6, 1951.

———. "Hospitalism: A Follow-up Report." *Psychoanalytic Study of the Child,* Vol. 2, 1946.

———. "Relevancy of Direct Infant Observation." *Psychoanalytic Study of the Child,* Vol. 5, 1950.

———. "Anaclitic Depression." *The Psychoanalytic Study of the Child,* Vol. 2, 1946.

———. "Hospitalism: An Inquiry into the Genesis of Psychiatric Conditions in Early Childhood." *Psychoanalytic Study of the Child,* Vol. 1, 1945.

———. "Diacritic and Coenesthetic Organizations: The Psychiatric Significance of a Functional Division of the Nervous System into a Sensory and Emotive Part." *Psychoanalytic Review,* Vol. 32, 1945.

Spitz, René A., and K. M. Wolf. "Auto-erotism: Some Empirical Findings and Hypotheses on Three of Its Manifestations in the First Year of Life." *Psychoanalytic Study of the Child,* Vol. 3, 1949.

———. "Anaclitic Depression: An Inquiry into the Genesis of Psychiatric Conditions in Early Childhood." *Psychoanalytic Study of the Child,* Vol. 2, 1946.

———. "The Smiling Response." *Genetic Psychology Monograph,* Vol. 34, 1946.

Spock, Benjamin. *Baby & Child Care.* New York: Pocket Books, 1968.

———. "The Striving for Autonomy and Regressive Object Relationships." *The Psychoanalytic Study of the Child,* Vol. 18, 1963.

Steele, Brandt. "Child Abuse and Neglect: Working with Abusive Parents from a Psychiatric Point of View." U.S. Dept. of Health, Education and Welfare, Publication (OHD) 75-70, Washington, D.C., 1975.

Steele, Brandt, and Charles B. Pollock. "A Psychiatric Study of Parents Who Abuse Infants and Small Children." In *The Battered Child*, E. Heffer and C. H. Kempe, eds. Chicago: University of Chicago Press, 1968.

Steinfels, Margaret O. *Who's Minding the Children: The History and Politics of Day Care in America*. New York: Simon & Schuster, 1973.

Stickle, Gabriel. Personal Communications.

Stickle, Gabriel, and Paul Ma. "Some Social and Medical Correlates of Pregnancy Outcome." *American Journal of Obstetrics and Gynecology*, Vol. 127, No. 2, Jan. 15, 1977.

———. "Pregnancy in Adolescents: Scope of the Problem." *Contemporary Ob/Gyn*, June 1975.

Stimeling, Gary. "Will Common Delivery Techniques Soon Become Malpractice?" *Journal of Legal Medicine*, May 1975.

Stock, Robert W. "Will the Baby Be Normal?" *New York Times Magazine*, March 23, 1969.

Stone, Lawrence. *The Family, Sex and Marriage in England, 1500–1800*. New York: Harper & Row, 1977.

Stuart, Irving R., and Lawrence E. Abt. *Children of Separation and Divorce*. New York: Grossman Publishers, 1972.

Sugarman, Muriel. "Paranatal Influences on Maternal-Infant Attachment." *American Journal of Orthopsychiatry*, July 1977.

Sussman, Marvin B. "The Family and Hyperactivity of Children: Considerations for Diagnosis, Treatment and Research." Presented at the Annual Meeting of the American Association for the Advancement of Science, Boston, Feb. 20, 1976.

Switzer, Ellen. "Questions Every Pregnant Woman Should Have the Answers To." *Glamour*, July 1977.

Talbot, Nathan B. *Raising Children in Modern America*. Boston: Little, Brown, 1976.

Thomas, Alexander, and Stella Chess. "Development in Middle Childhood." In *The Process of Child Development*, Peter Neubauer, ed. New York: Jason Aronson, 1976.

Thomas, Alexander, Stella Chess, and Herbert G. Birch. *Temperament and Behavior Disorders in Children*. New York: New York University Press, 1968.

———. "The Origin of Personality." *Scientific American*, Aug. 1970.

Time. "Looking to the ZPGeneration." Feb. 28, 1977.

———. "The American Family: Future Uncertain." Dec. 28, 1970.

Tsaltas, Margaret Owen. "Children of Home Dialysis Patients." *Journal of the American Medical Association*, Dec. 13, 1976.

Tsukahara, Theodore, Jr. "Baby Making and the Public Interest." *Hastings Center Report*, Aug. 1976.

Turnbull, Colin M. *The Mountain People.* New York: Simon & Schuster, 1972.

Vernick, Joel, and Myron Karon. "Who's Afraid of Death on a Leukemia Ward?" *American Journal of the Disturbed Child*, Vol. 109, 1965.

Visotsky, Harold M. "The Joint Commission on Mental Health of Children: Progress Report." *Psychiatric Annals*, Vol. 5, 1975.

Wald, Karen. Children of Che: Childcare and Education in Cuba. Palo Alto, Calif.: Ramparts Press, 1978.

Wallerstein, Judith S., et al. "The Effects of Parental Divorce: Experiences of the Preschool Child." *Journal of Child Psychiatry*, Vol. 14, No. 4, 1975.

Watson, J. B. "Experimental Studies on the Growth of the Emotions." *Pedagogical Seminary*, Vol. 32, 1925.

Westoff, Leslie Aldridge. "Kids with Kids." *New York Times Magazine*, Feb. 22, 1976.

Whelan, Elizabeth M. *A Baby . . . Maybe?* New York: Bobbs-Merrill, 1975.

White, Barry. "Ulster's Deepest Troubles May Be in the Hearts of the Children." *New York Times*, April 10, 1977.

White, Burton L. *The First Three Years of Life.* Englewood Cliffs, N.J.: Prentice-Hall, 1975.

Winnicott, Donald W. *The Maturational Processes and the Facilitating Environment.* New York: International Universities Press, 1965.

——. "The Theory of the Parent-Infant Relationship." *International Journal of Psycho-Analysis*, Vol. 41, 1960.

——. "Primary Maternal Preoccupation." In *Collected Papers*. New York: Basic Books, 1958.

——. "Psychoses and Child Care." *British Journal of Medical Psychology*, Vol. 26, 1953.

——. "Transitional Objects and Transitional Phenomena: A Study of the First Not-Me Possession." *International Journal of Psycho-Analysis*, Vol. 34, 1953.

Wolf, Anna W. M. *Your Child's Emotional Health.* Public Affairs Pamphlet 264. New York: Public Affairs Committee, 1958.

Wolfe, Linda. "The Coming Baby Boom." *New York*, Jan. 10, 1977.

Wolfenstein, Martha, and Gilbert W. Kliman. *Children and the Death of a President.* New York: Doubleday, 1965.

Wolff, Peter H. "Current Concepts: Mother-Infant Interactions in the First Year." *New England Journal of Medicine*, Oct. 28, 1976.

Wolman, Benjamin B., ed. *Handbook of Child Psychoanalysis.* New York: Van Nostrand Reinhold, 1972.

Wren, Christopher S. "Illicit Foster Homes Here Victimize Mental Patients." *New York Times*, June 10, 1973.

Wylie, Evan McLeod. *The Nine Months.* New York: Grosset & Dunlap, 1971.

Yaeger, Deborah Sue. "Out of Wedlock: Women Who Choose Unwed Motherhood Face Unusual Problems." *Wall Street Journal*, Sept. 12, 1977.

Zelman, Arthur. Personal Communications.

Index

About the Authors

Dr. Gilbert W. Kliman founded the Center for Preventive Psychiatry (White Plains, New York) and was Medical Director for many years. He is now the principal research psychiatrist for its federally funded preventive-intervention project. Both a psychoanalyst and a psychiatrist, he is a Diplomate of the American Board of Child Psychiatry and the American Board of Adult Psychiatry. Currently Editor-in-Chief of *The Journal of Preventive Psychiatry*, his other publications include *Psychological Emergencies of Childhood* and *Analyst in the Nursery*.

Albert Rosenfeld is an outstanding science journalist and editor, formerly Science Editor of *Life* and *Saturday Review*. He is Consultant on Future Programs for the March of Dimes Birth Defects Foundation, and is adjunct professor in the Division of Human Genetics at the University of Texas Medical Branch, Galveston. Currently a contributing editor for *Prime Time* and *Science Digest*, he is also the author of *The Second Genesis* and *Prolongevity*. He is the recipient of the Lasker Award with special citation for "leadership in medical journalism."